Information Systems Engineering:
From Data Analysis to Process Networks

Paul Johannesson
The Royal Institute of Technology, Sweden

Eva Söderström
University of Skövde, Sweden

IGI PUBLISHING

Hershey · New York

Acquisition Editor:	Kristin Klinger
Senior Managing Editor:	Jennifer Neidig
Managing Editor:	Jamie Snavely
Development Editor:	Kristin Roth
Cover Design:	Lisa Tosheff
Printed at:	Yurchak Printing Inc.

Published in the United States of America by
IGI Publishing (an imprint of IGI Global)
701 E. Chocolate Avenue
Hershey PA 17033
Tel: 717-533-8845
Fax: 717-533-8661
E-mail: cust@igi-global.com, url:
Web site: http://www.igi-global.com

and in the United Kingdom by
IGI Publishing (an imprint of IGI Global)
3 Henrietta Street
Covent Garden
London WC2E 8LU
Tel: 44 20 7240 0856
Fax: 44 20 7379 0609
Web site: http://www.eurospanonline.com

Library of Congress Cataloging-in-Publication Data

Information systems engineering : from data analysis to process networks / Paul Johannesson and Eva Soderstrom, editors.
  p. cm.
  Summary: "This book presents the most current research on existing and emergent trends on conceptual modeling and information systems engineering, bridging the gap between research and practice by providing a much-needed reference point on the design of software systems that evolve seamlessly to adapt to rapidly changing business and organizational practices"--Provided by publisher.
  Includes bibliographical references and index.
  ISBN-13: 978-1-59904-567-2 (hardcover)
  ISBN-13: 978-1-59904-569-6 (ebook)
1. Information technology. 2. Database management. 3. Computer networks. I. Johannesson, Paul, 1959- II. Soderstrom, Eva.
  T58.5.I5285 2008
  658'.05--dc22

British Cataloguing in Publication Data
A Cataloguing in Publication record for this book is available from the British Library.

All work contributed to this book is original material. The views expressed in this book are those of the authors, but not necessarily of the publisher.

Information Systems Engineering: From Data Analysis to Process Networks

Table of Contents

Foreword

During one of the visits that I made to KTH Stockholm recently, my hosts were so kind to show me of one the most visited museums in Scandinavia: the Vasa Museum. In a large ship hall stands the warship Vasa, the17th century ship that sank tragically at its maiden voyage on August 10, 1628, only after a few minutes of sailing.

Reflecting on the 40 years of history of Information Systems, I cannot help thinking of this disaster. Not that I would call this history itself a disaster in any sense. As the chapters in this book show as well, substantial progress has been made both in practice and on the research level. The contribution of the Scandinavian school of which Benkt Wangler is one representative, has been quite significant. We all know that one of the first theorists of information was Bjorn Langefors, who is famous for his infological equation that relates *and* distinguishes "data" and "information", I = i (D, S, T), where I stands for information, D data, S the recipient prior knowledge as result of the individual's life experience, T the time, and i the interpretation process. Langefors defined an information system as "a technologically implemented medium for recording, storing, and disseminating linguistic expressions, as well as for drawing conclusions from such expressions". The Swedish IS tradition has always emphasized the essential human involvement in the information system.

In the early 70's, Ted Codd (IBM), Sjir Nijssen (Control Data), Peter Chen and others introduced and worked out the idea of data independence and, directly related to that, *conceptual modeling*. Conceptual modeling, using formal or semi-formal graphical representations, has been a successful innovation that has not only been adopted in various fields of Computer Science but also in some other disciplines.

Admittedly, the history of Information Systems so far had a high pioneering character, but it cannot be called as disaster. However, in the introduction of information systems in organizations, disasters, not as appealing as the Vasa but often with huge financial and organizational impact, have not been rare, unfortunately. To some extent, these disasters are the raison d'être for the discipline itself. What went wrong? What went wrong with the Vasa? A lot of ink has been written on this question.

Some blame the King Gustavus Adolphus who was anxious to acquire a ship as glorious as possible and demanded riskful changes in the original design. Similarly, the IS people have often been forced to deal with staggering expectations. We have also given rise to them ourselves. "MIS is a mirage" (John Dearden, 1972) was one of the first articles to expose this habit. There was and there will always be a need for healthy critical thinking.

Some blame the Dutch shipbuilder who built the hull too narrow. The problem was that in the 17th century there were no scientific methods of calculating a ship's stability. Instead shipbuilders used "reckonings" which recorded certain ship-measurements. However, the Vasa was much bigger than normal ships and so the usual reckonings did not apply. Similarly, many of the IS failures can be explained by the lack of good design theory and the temptation to apply methods beyond the realm in which they had been developed. According to IS researcher Roger Clark, "there is a predilection for 'reference frameworks', which is a pre-theoretic construct used as a means of organizing limited numbers of largely ad hoc observations or clusters of apparently interdependent variables, preparatory to conducting pilot studies". However, Clark does not want to be only negative about this. "The rate of change in the phenomena under study is sufficiently high that it can be argued that neither the paucity of established theories nor the prevalence of 'exploratory studies' and 'research frameworks' are defects: the IS discipline is in a permanent state of accumulating evidence about new and significantly changed phenomena, in order to enable existing theories to be adapted and new theories to be postulated" (Roger Clarke, 2006: A Retrospective on the Information Systems Discipline in Australia). Nevertheless, it would surely contribute to the maturity of the field when IS researchers would spend some more time and effort on evaluation research and on sharpening their validity criteria. One chapter in this book is about validating conceptual models.

According to a new theory, the captain of the Vasa was to blame by sailing right from the start with open gun ports. Similarly, in many cases IS disasters can be explained by pointing at the users, or, more generally, the insufficient attention to the alignment of the technical system and the social system. The Swedish socio-technical design approach, represented in several chapters of this book, seeks to mitigate this risk by the direct participation of end-users in the information system design process.

Some blame Admiral Fleming who was in charge of the project and could have stopped the ship after the stability test that had been performed prior to the maiden voyage, a test that gave rather worrying results. Similarly, many IT projects suffer from lack of good management. Fortunately, Management of IT is an established field nowadays, although I do have the impression that still much more of industrial experience could be explored and accumulated in sound theory than is currently the case yet.

Perhaps the blame for the Vasa disaster is not to be given to any individual, but to the system in which they were caught, in which each actor just played its role. As such, this cautionary tale should remind us all never to stop thinking, to keep aware of the limitations of models and methods – technical and managerial — and never to reduce our human responsibility to role-playing.

According the Vasa Museum website, the ship is now surrounded by permanent exhibitions, cinemas, a shop and a restaurant. Here I see another parallel to developments in our field, but IS researchers who have been active in European projects and conference organizations, like Professor Wangler, will be able to work it out for themselves, I guess.

Paul Johannesson did a great job in bringing together an interesting collection of articles on modeling and design. I expect that this book will offer the reader many new insights and much reading pleasure.

Hans Weigand
Tilburg University

Preface

Information systems are becoming ubiquitous in our lives. They are used to pay our salaries, they co-ordinate the activities of international companies, and they link the world together in global networks. The purpose of an information system is to support communication and work within and between organisations. An information system must provide accurate and up-to-date information that satisfies the information needs of enterprises, thereby supporting their routine operations as well as their decision making. In their most basic forms, information systems process and store large amount of data from routine business transactions, such as payrolls, invoicing, and stocktaking. They support the day-to-day activities of a business by relieving people from the tedious and time-consuming aspects of performing operational transactions. An information system can also provide managers and decision makers with information about the activities of their organisation, thereby helping them in spotting business opportunities, detecting long-term trends, and monitoring the performance of the organisation. An information system can also include more advanced tools for analysis and decision making, e.g. for optimisation and data mining. In order to take strategic decisions, external information about the environment of an organisation is at least as important as internal information. Information systems, therefore, also have the role of supporting management with such external information, known as business intelligence.

Information systems belong to the most complex artifacts built in today's society. Developing, using, and maintaining an information system raises a large number of difficult problems, ranging from purely technical to organizational and social ones. Many of these problems are ill-structured, meaning that there are no algorithms or mechanical methods for solving them, or that they cannot even be precisely formulated. The problems are ill-structured mainly because the development and use of an information system involve many kinds of stakeholders with different and conflicting interests and perspectives, which need to be sorted out and negotiated. This is a difficult task as information systems and services are notoriously hard to illustrate and describe in terms that are easily understandable to non-experts. Communication problems are rather the rule than the exception. There is no panacea for these problems, but there are aids by which the problems can be described more clearly, in a more structured way, and sometimes even be formally represented. These aids have been investigated within the area of information systems engineering. They consist of solid conceptual frameworks and clear notations to be used when describing and designing systems at the conceptualization and problem formulation level. Such frameworks and notation as well as associated methods, called enterprise modeling, can significantly improve the dialogue and cooperation between stakeholders in information systems design and use.

An enterprise model is a "computational representation of the structure, activities, processes, information, resources, people, behavior, goals, and constraints of a business, government, or other enterprises", as defined in (Enterprise Modeling, 2007). Enterprise models have been used in information systems design, and it is possible to identify three main ways of utilising enterprise models, (Fowler, 2003):

- **Models as sketches**. Models are used as sketches to describe possible solutions to problems or to document existing solutions in order to facilitate communication among stakeholders. The idea is to use the models as informal support for communication and description.

- **Models as blueprints**. Models are used as blueprints for implementing information systems and services. The idea is that the models shall be sufficiently precise and formal for programmers, database designers and other IT experts to build a functioning system.

- **Executable models**. Executable models take the idea of models as blueprints one step further. The models shall be formal enough to be automatically translatable into executable code. In this way, the coding step is eliminated, thereby reducing cost and risk for introducing errors.

Enterprise models have been used in these ways for a long time in business and systems design, but they have not yet been put to their full potential. Typically, they have been used only as sketches for limited tasks in systems design and then discarded. To realise the full potential of enterprise models, there is a need to use models as blueprints and taking advantage of executable models. This can be realised by a business and technology architecture that places the models firmly in the centre and let them be the driving force in analysis, design, implementation, deployment and use of systems and services. There is a need for a business and model driven information systems architecture. Such an architecture will serve to enact the software specification contained in the models by composing the software executable at the time of need. This will remove the lag between changes in the model and changes in the software system driven by that model, and will create software systems that evolve seamlessly to adapt to the rapidly changing business and organisational practices. Dynamic composition will enable the delivery of fine-grained software as services personalised to the user needs at the point of delivery. This will create unique working environments tailored to, and controlled by people. A business and model driven information systems architecture will thus put people at the centre of new working environments supported by model-driven software services.

Much research is still needed before a business and model driven information systems architecture can be realised. A number of key issues in current enterprise modelling research are the following:

What is the right balance between expressiveness and usability in enterprise modelling languages? A language for enterprise modelling can be highly expressive, allowing for preciseness and reasoning support, often through some logic based formalism. This is fine for building advanced and comprehensive models, but the drawback is that the modelling process becomes more difficult, in particular for business experts with limited time and experience of modelling. A closely related question is how to improve the usability of enterprise modeling languages through adequate graphical notations.

- Which are the right concepts for modelling enterprises? There exist many different types of enterprise models: information models, conceptual models, activity models, process models, role models, goal models, business models, and so on. For each type of enterprise model, there also exist many alternative languages and notations based on different concepts. There is an ongoing search for the most appropriate concepts for capturing all the different aspects of enterprises, and how the resulting models are to be related to each other. While early enterprise models focused on data and information analysis, we see today a move towards modelling processes and value exchanges in networks of organisations.

- How should enterprise models be developed? Building enterprise models is a complex undertaking as it requires the contribution from many stakeholders with different perspectives, ranging from end users and business experts to management and information systems designers. Therefore, methods for building enterprise models are needed, and there is today more and more consensus that these methods need to be agile as well as participatory.

• How are enterprise models to be managed? As enterprise models become more and more wide-spread, there is a need to manage their relationships, maintenance, and evolution. Enterprise models are to be integrated, harmonised, made interoperable with each other, and related to standards. Thus, there is a need for methods, techniques, and tools that can help in these efforts.

This book identifies current trends as well as emerging and future areas in enterprise modeling and information systems engineering. The book also presents recent research results and experiences from applications in industry. The chapters in the book cover all of the issues introduced above ranging from analysis of data models over methods for participative modeling to the design of process and value networks.

The chapter entitled "Translating Schemas Between Data Modelling Languages" by Peter McBrien addresses the classical but still essential issues of data analysis and mapping. The chapter focuses on data modelling languages, and the challenges faced in mapping schemas in one data modelling language into another data modelling language. The chapter reviews the ER, relational and UML modelling languages (the later being representative of object oriented programming languages), highlighting aspects of each modelling language that are not representable in the others. The chapter introduces a nested hypergraph data model that may be used as an underlying representation of data models, which shows the differences between the modelling languages in a more precise manner. Finally, the chapter proposes a platform for the future building of an automated procedure for translating schemas from one modelling language to another.

The chapter entitled "Intention Driven Conceptual Modelling" by Colette Rolland discusses how classic conceptual modelling notions need to be complemented with intention and strategy driven modelling. The chapter argues that while conceptual models succeeded in telling us how to represent some excerpt of the world in informational terms, they failed to guide system analysts in conceptualising purposeful systems, i.e. systems that meet the expectations of their users. The chapter investigates the issue of conceptualising purposeful systems and discusses the role that goal driven approaches can play to resolve it. It considers the challenge of new systems having a multifaceted purpose and shows how intention/strategy maps help facing this challenge.

The chapter entitled "Integrated Goal, Data and Process Modeling: From TEMPORA to Model-Generated Work-Places" by John Krogstie also addresses the issue of extending and combining modelling approaches including goals, data, and processes. Goals and rules on different levels ranging from visions, to strategies, tactics, and operational goals have been acknowledged for a long time. In the information systems engineering field, the interest in goals and rules has come from two directions, requirements engineering and rule based systems. Based on perspectives from these areas, the chapter proposes an approach to combining goal, data, resource and process modeling, in the support of the development and user-led evolution of what is called Model-generated Work-places.

The chapter entitled "Value and Intention Based Information Systems Engineering" by Paul Johannesson and Prasad Jayaweera investigates the problem of relating and structuring enterprise models of different types. The authors propose a light-weight enterprise architecture framework based on linguistic theories and organizational metaphors and argue that it provides a number of advantages in terms of flexibility, traceability and business orientation. The authors show how basic notions in enterprise modelling can be organised by three organisational metaphors - the organisation as machine where the focus is on the production and exchange of resources, the organisation as negotiated order where the focus is on commitments and contracts, and the organisation as power structure where the focus is on authorities and roles.

The chapter entitled "Pragmatic-Driven Approach for Service-Oriented Analysis and Design" by Remigjius Gustas and Prima Gustiené investigates novel modelling concepts for managing services and presents a pragmatic-driven approach for service-oriented information systems analysis and design. Services are viewed as dynamic subsystems, where outputs depend not only on inputs, but on a service state as well. Intentions of various business process experts are represented in terms of a set of pragmatic dependencies, which are driving the overall system engineering process. It is demonstrated how the pragmatic aspects are linked to the conceptual representations, which define the semantics of business design. In contrast to the traditional system development methodologies, the main difference of the service-oriented approach is that it integrates the static and dynamic aspects into one type of diagram.

The chapter entitled "The Practice of Participatory Enterprise Modelling – a Competency Perspective" by Anne Persson addresses the question of how to develop enterprise models in a participatory way, in particular which competencies that are required for this purpose. The chapter presents the two main ways of working when it comes to involving stakeholders in the modelling process, the participatory and the non-participatory, and then focuses on the participatory approach. The author describes the desired competencies of domain experts and method experts, which are two of the most crucial actors in the participatory modelling process. The author further argues that although competency is one of the most critical success factors in modelling it is an overlooked topic in modelling research. The chapter is illustrated with quotes from an interview study that the author has carried out.

The chapter entitled "How to Support Agile Development Projects with Enterprise Modelling" by Janis Stirna and Marite Kirikova also addresses the issue of how to design enterprise models and discusses the role of enterprise models in the context of agile systems development, which has much in common with participatory design approaches. The chapter analyses the potential of using enterprise modelling in agile information system development projects on the basis of a number of empirical findings. The authors outline the current issues and challenges that projects using agile development approaches are facing. To address these challenges, they analyse what are the objectives of using enterprise modelling in agile development projects and give recommendations concerning modelling process as well as tool support.

The chapter entitled "Experiences with Modelling Early Requirements" by Pericles Loucopoulos investigates the early stages of systems development when requirements are to be identified and agreed upon. The chapter argues that a key challenge in the development of systems is the engagement of domain experts in their articulation, agreement, and validation of require-ments. This challenge is particularly pronounced at the early requirements phase when multiple stakeholders from different divisions and often different organisations need to reach agreement about the intended systems. Decisions taken at this stage have a profound effect on the technical and economic feasibility of any project. The chapter introduces an approach that advocates the use of a modelling process expressed in terms of strategy-service-support dimensions, augmented by appropriate simulation techniques that enable experimentation with different scenarios. The chapter provides insights from a large project, in which the author played an active and interventionist part, on the utility of the approach in facilitating stakeholder engagement in early requirements specification.

The chapter entitled "Determining Requirements for Management Support Systems" by Sven Carlsson also addresses the management of requirements, but here focused on management support systems (MSS). The chapter presents a methodology that can be used as a guide for MSS design, with a primary focus on MSS requirements determination and how requirements can be fulfilled using information and communication technologies. The methodology builds on Quinn and associates' competing values model of organizational effectiveness and current MSS knowledge. The methodology can guide MSS designers in designing MSSs that support different managerial roles, i.e. the development of MSSs that support managerial cognition and behavior.

The chapter entitled "Towards a Holistic Approach to Validating Conceptual Models" by Jörg Becker, Björn Niehaves, and Daniel Pfeiffer moves into the issue of how to validate conceptual models. The chapter introduces a holistic approach to semantically validating conceptual models. The quality and thus the validation of conceptual models are of high economic importance, but only little empirical work has focused on their evaluation so far. This raises the question how a holistic approach for determining the quality of conceptual models should be designed. In order to describe the current state of research the authors develop a two dimensional framework and use it to identify a notable shortcoming on conceptual model evaluation, the lack of an approach that covers all aspects of the framework. To remedy this situation, the authors propose a procedure model that integrates different evaluation techniques, which provides a starting point to further elaborate on a holistic evaluation approach.

The chapter entitled "New Software Methodologies and Techniques for Business Models with Evolutionary Aspects" by Hamid Fujita proposes a language and an architecture for flexible information systems with a focus on eliciting and representing user intentions and requirements. The chapter also introduces a methodology, Lyee, for managing a development process moving from fuzzy intentions to formal and executable specifications. The results presented in the chapter are based on a large international project, which has resulted in numerous applications including the management of legacy software and the diagnosis of programs in imperative languages. The chapter gives an overview of the project and shows how its results have been developed and applied in industrial practice.

The chapter entitled "Refining the Concept *Syndicate Data* – Categories and Characteristics, Definitions, and a View Ahead" by Mattias Strand focuses on data management and introduces the concepts of external data and syndicate data. It contributes a conceptual discussion regarding different categories of syndicate data, as well as definitions and applications thereof. In addition, the chapter gives a view ahead for syndicate data, with respect to organizational as well as technological challenges and trends. Thereby, it increases the understanding of syndicate data as a vital component in business intelligence initiatives and explains why external data in general and syndicate data in particular have become prerequisites in modern information systems.

The chapter entitled "Interconnecting E-Business Model Components" by Eva Söderström and Vinay Kumar Mandala concerns electronic business (e-business) models that have emerged and altered the traditional ways in which to do business. An e-business model is a specialisation of a business model, and is an organisational plan for how to work with the products or services intended to bring profit and revenue, and using ICT and the Internet in doing so. E-business models consist of components that constitute a business concept, i.e. an idea that an organisation wants to bring into reality. The analysis of the e-business model components and their interconnections results in a framework in the form of a model displaying the connections between the clustered components. The purpose of the chapter is to explain an overview of e-business model components and show how value is created and added at each component level.

The chapter entitled "Experiences from Technology Transfer Initiatives at SISU" by Janis Bubenko and Eva Lindencrona addresses the industrial uptake of information systems engineering and includes reflections on the authors' experiences from an initiative to technology transfer in the field of information systems in Sweden. The authors discuss transfer of knowledge as well as of technical prototypes from academic research to product development, exploitation, and practical use in organisations. Their experiences emanate from their work in SISU – the Swedish Institute for Systems Development. The authors describe, firstly, which are the main products of technology transfer, and, secondly, which are the main factors that influence, or hinder, the success of a technology transfer initiative.

The chapter entitled "On IT-modelling in a cross-competence world" by Arne Sølvberg takes a broad perspective and discusses how IT in general and enterprise modelling in particular will become integrated into other disciplines. The author starts from the observation that the deep penetration of computers in all realms of society makes technological change the key driver for changing our lives. This will result in a change in our view of IT, from viewing the role of IT to mainly support other disciplines, to the integration of IT concepts, tools and theory into the modelling theories of the supported disciplines. The chapter discusses the opportunities and challenges of this integration.

This book is dedicated to Benkt Wangler, at his retirement from Högskolan Skövde, who has been a portal figure of the information systems area in Sweden for decades. Benkt Wangler is appreciated by his colleagues, fellow researchers and PhD students as a man of integrity, great knowledge on a wide variety of subjects, and with an ability to put complex problems into an understandable form. As a PhD supervisor, Benkt Wangler is dedicated and caring, for the actual research as well as for the students. As a colleague in the academic workplace, Benkt Wangler is known for his commitment to a wide variety of issues, both in the research group, the community of research leaders, the departments, and the university as a whole. Furthermore, his knowledge and interest in art, literature and gourmet food has inspired many interesting conversations and excursions. Although not always strictly research oriented, these conversations have contributed to the widened knowledge and interest of all those participating. One highly valuable quality Benkt Wangler possesses is the ability to take new pieces of knowledge and research results and integrate them with his already existing vast knowledge into a comprehensive knowledge web. The results are new ideas, new research streams, new projects and a living and always evolving research community.

Paul Johannesson

Eva Söderström

References

Enterprise Modelling (2007). From http://en.wikipedia.org/wiki/Enterprise_modeling.

Fowler, M., & Scott, K. (2003). *UML Distilled: A Brief Guide to the Standard Object Modeling Language.* Addison-Wesley.

List of Reviewers

Beatrice Alenljung, University of Skövde

Birger Andersson, Stockholm University

Per Backlund, University of Skövde

Maria Bergholtz, Stockholm University

Ananda Edirisuriya, University of Colombo

Martin Henkel, Royal Institute of Technology

Tharaka Ilayperuma, University of Ruhuna

Björn Lundell, University of Skövde

Erik Perjons, Royal Institute of Technology

Anne Persson, University of Skövde

Jelena Zdravkovic, University of Gävle

Rose-Mharie Åhlfeldt, University of Skövde

Acknowledgments

The editors would like to acknowledge the help of all involved in the authoring and review process of the book, whose valuable support was necessary for the successful completion of this project. Some of the authors of chapters included in the book also served as referees for chapters written by other authors. Additionally, the following people provided comprehensive and insightful reviews: Beatrice Alenljung, Birger Andersson, Per Backlund, Maria Bergholtz, Ananda Edirisuriya, Martin Henkel, Tharaka Ilayperuma, Björn Lundell, Erik Perjons, Jelena Zdravkovic, and Rose-Mharie Åhlfeldt. Many thanks go to all of them.

Special thanks also go to the publishing team at IGI Global, whose support throughout the whole process from initial idea to final publication has been invaluable. In particular, many thanks to Deborah Yahnke, Meg Stocking and Kristin Roth for their continuous assistance and prompt replies to all questions that have appeared during the work on this project.

Finally, we wish to thank all of the authors for their enthusiasm, insights and excellent contributions to this book.

Paul Johannesson and Eva Söderström
Stockholm, Sweden
July 2007

Chapter I

Translating Schemas Between Data Modelling Languages

Peter McBrien, Imperial College London, UK

Abstract

Data held in information systems is modelled using a variety of languages, where the choice of language may be decided by functional concerns as well as non-technical concerns. This chapter focuses on data modelling languages, and the challenges faced in mapping schemas in one data modelling language into another data modelling language. We review the ER, relational and UML modelling languages (the later being representative of object oriented programming languages), highlighting aspects of each modelling language that are not representable in the others. We describe how a nested hypergraph data model may be used as an underlying representation of data models, and hence present the differences between the modelling languages in a more precise manner. Finally, we propose a platform for the future building of an automated procedure for translating schemas from one modelling language to another.

Introduction

Data held in information systems is modelled using a variety of languages, where the choice of language may be decided by functional concerns (such as using a language suited to a particular database system, or using a language with modelling constructs suited to modelling a particular domain) or non-technical concerns (such as following organisation or national standards, or simply reusing a model from some other application).

This chapter focuses on data modelling languages, and the challenges faced in mapping schemas in one data modelling language into another data modelling language. In *model management* (Bernstein, 2003), this mapping process is called ModelGen, and a mapping process that restructures schemas within one modeling language is called Mapping. To illustrate the issues faced in implementing ModelGen, consider the ER schema in Figure 1(a), which describes details of students and the departments in which they study. The cardinality constraints in the ER model, which in our version of the ER model use *look-here* semantics (Song, Evans, & Park, 1995), state that each student studies in exactly one department, and that each department must have at least one student.

When mapped into a relational schema, some ER to relational mapping techniques would produce the relation schema shown in Figure 1(b). This makes the "obvious" mapping between entities in the ER model, and tables in the relational model. The relationship between the student and dept is modelled by a did column in the student table in the relational model, together with a foreign key from that attribute pointing at the did column in the dept table.

Whilst apparently an exact representation of the ER schema in the relational model, Figure 1(b) contains one semantic difference, in that the relational schema allows instances of the dept table to exist that are not related to any student instances, whilst the ER schema forbids this. In practice, such changes in the semantics of the schema when translated between modelling languages means that applications may exhibit unexpected behaviour. In this particular case, it would be the case that the relational schema allows departments to be created without any students, which was disallowed when the application was modelling in the ER modelling language. The purpose of

Figure 1. Alternative representations of a schema for students and their department

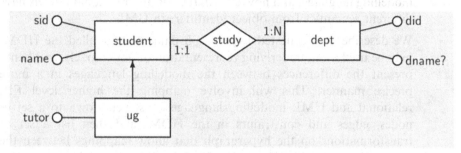

(a) ER modelling language

student(<u>sid</u>,name,did)   ug(<u>sid</u>,tutor)   dept(<u>did</u>,dname?)
student.did → dept.did   ug.did → student.did

(b) Relational modelling language

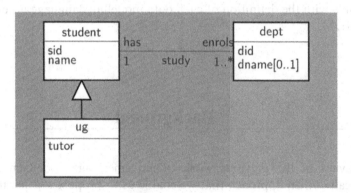

(c) UML modelling language

this chapter is to report on some existing work that allows these differences in modelling languages to be described in a precise manner, and to point the direction for work that might semi-automate or fully-automate the generation of mappings that specify ModelGen. There will be three areas covered:

- We review the ER, relational and UML modelling languages (the later being representative of object oriented programming languages), highlighting aspects of each modelling language that are not represen-table in the others. In particular, we consider how cardinality constraints of ER and UML models may not be enforced in the relational model, how the notion of generalisation hierarchies in the ER and UML models may only be partially modelled in the relational modelling language, and how keys in the ER and relational models have different semantics from object identifiers in UML.

- We describe how a nested hypergraph data model (called the HDM) may be used as an underlying representation of data models, and hence present the differences between the modelling languages in a more precise manner. This will involve mapping the higher level ER, relational and UML modelling language constructs down to a set of nodes, edges and constraints in the HDM, and then list a set of transformations on the hypergraph that allow mappings between the higher level modelling languages to be written that clearly identify which aspect of one language is not represented in the another language.

- We discuss how the previous work being reported on in this chapter forms a platform for the future building of an automated procedure for translating schemas from one modelling language to another, supplied only with the definition of each data modelling language in terms of the HDM.

Background

Our review of the previous work to implementing ModelGen will focus specifically on an approach that we enable us to propose a general direction of work towards automating the implementation of ModelGen.

A Comparison of Data Modelling Languages

First we review data modelling languages and data schemas in a notation that will suit development into a system for comparing and mapping between schemas held in different modelling languages. A *modelling language x* contains a set of modelling constructs, where each construct y is used to represent some set, bag or list of data values, and/or constraints on sets, bags or lists of data values. A *schema s* comprises of a set of schema objects, where each schema object *so* is typed to a construct y of modelling language m, which in the AutoMed (AutoMed, 2007) notation we write as *m:c:«so»*. To date, almost without exception, researchers have considered that any given information system uses a single modelling language, and hence schemas of data sources $s = \{m:c_1:\text{«}so_1\text{»}, m:c_1:\text{«}so_2\text{»}, ..., m:c_n:\text{«}so_{m-1}\text{»}, m:c_n:\text{«}so_m\text{»}\}$.

Let us now review the examples in Figure 1 using this notation. The ER schema has the following schema objects, which we have equated to sets of values that might form the extent of a data source that the ER schema models. Note that we assume that each ER entity is identified by its key attributes. The extent of an ER relationship has tuples of values formed from a subset of the product of the extent of the entities the relationship connects.

er:entity:«student» = {1, 12, 17, 24}

er:attribute:«student,sid,key» = {⟨1,1⟩, ⟨12,12⟩, ⟨17,17⟩, ⟨24,24⟩}

er:attribute:«student,name,notnull» = {⟨1,Peter⟩, ⟨12,Nikos⟩, ⟨17,Duc⟩, ⟨24,Andrew⟩}

er:entity:«ug» = {12, 24}

er:attribute:«ug,tutor,notnull» = {⟨12,John⟩, ⟨24,Simon⟩}

er:isa:«ug,student»

er:relationship:«study,student,dept,1:1,1:N» = {⟨1,100⟩, ⟨12,101⟩, ⟨17,101⟩, ⟨24,100⟩}

er:entity:«dept» = {100, 101, 102}

er:attribute:«dept,did,key» = {⟨100,100⟩, ⟨101,101⟩, ⟨102,102⟩}

er:attribute:«dept,dname,null» = {⟨100,CS⟩, ⟨101,EE⟩}

Note that there is intentionally no extent associated with «ug,student», since it is a constraint schema object, which in this case enforces the fact that the extent of «ug» is a subset of the extent of «student». The relational schema has the schema object listed below. Despite being a superficially quite distinct modelling language, the relational table construct is analogous to the ER entity construct, and the relational column construct is roughly analogous to the ER attribute construct. There is no direct representation of the ER relationship construct in the relational model. For the one-many cardinality relationship in our ER example, the representation in the relational model is to have a column on the table at the "one" end of the relationship, together with a foreign key that states that the constraint that values in the column must also appear in the column of another table.

rel:table:«student» = {1, 12, 17, 24}rel:column:«student,sid,key» = {⟨1,1⟩, ⟨12,12⟩, ⟨17,17⟩, ⟨24,24⟩}

rel:column:«student,name,notnull» = {⟨1,Peter⟩, ⟨12,Nikos⟩, ⟨17,Duc⟩, ⟨24,Andrew⟩}

rel:column:«student,dname,notnull» = {⟨1,100⟩, ⟨12,101⟩, ⟨17,101⟩, ⟨24,100⟩}

rel:table:«ug» = {12, 24}

rel:column:«ug,sid,key» = {⟨12,12⟩, ⟨24,24⟩}

rel:column:«ug,tutor,notnull» = {⟨12,John⟩, ⟨24,Simon⟩}

rel:foreign_key:«student,dname,dept,dname»

rel:foreign_key:«ug,did,student,did»

rel:table:«dept» = {100, 101, 102}

rel:column:«dept,did,key» = {⟨100,100⟩, ⟨101,101⟩, ⟨102,102⟩}
rel:column:«dept,dname,null» = {⟨100,CS⟩, ⟨101,EE⟩}

Note that as foreign keys «student,dname,dept,dname» and «ug,did,student,did» are constraints, they have no extent. Now turning our attention to Figure 1(c), we find that the UML schema again is superficially quite distinct from the ER and relational schemas, but the UML class is roughly analogous to the ER entity and relational table constructs, and the UML attribute construct roughly analogous to the ER attribute and relational column constructs. However, there is a significant difference in that UML identifies instances of the classes by *unique object identifiers* (UID), whilst the relational model, and our ER modelling language use *natural keys*. Natural keys are values that have some significance in the real world being modelling by the information system, whilst UIDs are arbitrary values chosen by the information system to identify objects, and have no meaning in the real world being modelled. Hence the extents the UML schema objects are quite distinct from their analogous ER and relational counterparts.

uml:class:«student» = {343, 123, 770, 24}
uml:attribute:«student,sid,notnull» = {⟨343,1⟩, ⟨123,12⟩, ⟨770,17⟩, ⟨24,24⟩}
uml:attribute:«student,name,notnull» = {⟨343,Peter⟩, ⟨123,Nikos⟩, ⟨770,Duc⟩, ⟨24,Andrew⟩}
uml:class:«ug» = {123, 24}
uml:attribute:«ug,tutor,notnull» = {⟨123,John⟩, ⟨24,Simon⟩}
uml:association:«student,dname,dept,dname,1,1..*» = {⟨343,100⟩, ⟨123,101⟩, ⟨770,101⟩, ⟨24,100⟩}
uml:class:«dept» = {432, 188}
uml:attribute:«dept,did,notnull» = {⟨432,100⟩, ⟨188,101⟩}
uml:attribute:«dept,dname,notnull» = {⟨432,CS⟩, ⟨188,EE⟩}

Despite the differences in UML using UIDs, and our ER model not using UIDs but instead natural keys, there is a strong similarity between the two in terms of the schemes that form the description of the schema. However, the UML has quite distinct data instances, which make mapping between the schemas in the two modelling languages a complex task as we will see in Section 3.

So far, we have identified two significant differences between the modelling capabilities of ER, relational and UML models. Firstly, the relational model is unable to represent the mandatory inclusion of a schema object in the "one" end of a one-many relationship (for example student in the study relationship of the ER schema), and secondly that UML has hidden extra values used to model objects, and does not enforce the uniqueness of natural key attributes (for example, there could be two different student instances with the same value for sid in the UML schema). More complex example schemas would reveal other differences. For example, a generalisation hierarchy in the ER schema dividing students into pg and ug students, or a similar disjoint generalisation in UML is often represented in a relational schema by two separate foreign keys between pg and student and between ug and student. However this fails to enforce that no single student can be both a member of ug and of pg.

Mapping Schemas into a Different Data Modelling Language

Most work that has considered the problem of mapping a schema between data modeling languages has considered the problem of just mapping between two specific modeling languages. For example, (Anderson, 1994) considered mapping relational schemas to ER schemas, and (Halpin, 2001) considered mapping ORM to both relational schemas and UML schemas. In (McBrien & Poulovassilis, 1999) it was proposed that a simple nested *hypergraph data model* (HDM) be used as an underlying represention of schemas, and that this would form the basis for the ModelGen operator. This approach was elaborated upon in (Boyd & McBrien, 2005) to give a version of the HDM with constraint primitives that we summarise now, and give an overview of in Figure 2.

We will use the HDM as an intermediate representation in two examples of intermodel mapping presented in the following subsections.

ER to UML Mapping

To enable as many details to be presented of the mapping process, let us for this discussion consider the simple example illustrated in Figure 3. The ER

Figure 2. A short overview of the HDM

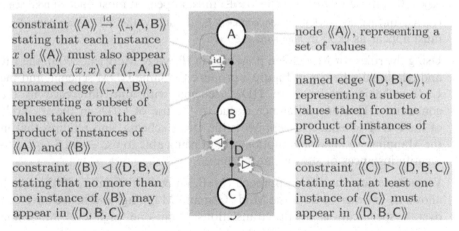

constraint $\langle\!\langle A \rangle\!\rangle \xrightarrow{id} \langle\!\langle \_, A, B \rangle\!\rangle$ stating that each instance x of $\langle\!\langle A \rangle\!\rangle$ must also appear in a tuple $\langle x, x \rangle$ of $\langle\!\langle \_, A, B \rangle\!\rangle$	node $\langle\!\langle A \rangle\!\rangle$, representing a set of values
unnamed edge $\langle\!\langle \_, A, B \rangle\!\rangle$, representing a subset of values taken from the product of instances of $\langle\!\langle A \rangle\!\rangle$ and $\langle\!\langle B \rangle\!\rangle$	named edge $\langle\!\langle D, B, C \rangle\!\rangle$, representing a subset of values taken from the product of instances of $\langle\!\langle B \rangle\!\rangle$ and $\langle\!\langle C \rangle\!\rangle$
constraint $\langle\!\langle B \rangle\!\rangle \lhd \langle\!\langle D, B, C \rangle\!\rangle$ stating that no more than one instance of $\langle\!\langle B \rangle\!\rangle$ may appear in $\langle\!\langle D, B, C \rangle\!\rangle$	constraint $\langle\!\langle C \rangle\!\rangle \rhd \langle\!\langle D, B, C \rangle\!\rangle$ stating that at least one instance of $\langle\!\langle C \rangle\!\rangle$ must appear in $\langle\!\langle D, B, C \rangle\!\rangle$

Figure 3. Relating UML and ER schemas via schema in the HDM

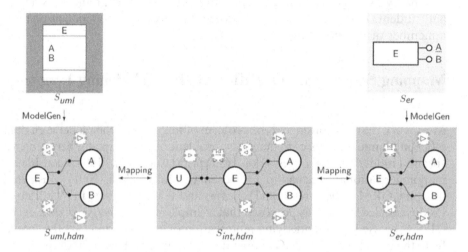

S_{uml} S_{er}

ModelGen ↓   ↓ ModelGen

$S_{uml,hdm}$ Mapping $S_{int,hdm}$ Mapping $S_{er,hdm}$

schema has an entity labelled er:entity:«E» that we represent by a node hdm:node:«E» in the HDM schema (represented by a black outlined circle), and the attributes er:attribute:«E,A» and er:attribute:«E,B» of er:entity:«E» are also represented as nodes in the HDM, together with edges (the thick black lines) associating them hdm:node:«E». The fact that each entity instance has only one associated attribute instance in each of er:attribute:«E,A» and er:attribute:«E,B» is represented by constraint rules in the HDM (the ◁, ▷, and → symbols in grey boxes), as is the fact that er:attribute:«E,A» is a key attribute of er:entity:«E». Informally, we say that hdm:node:«E» ▷ hdm:edge:«_,E,A» if each value of hdm:node:«E» must appear at least once in hdm:edge:«_,E,A», hdm:node:«E» ◁ hdm:edge:«_,E,A» if each value of hdm:node:«E» must appear at most once in hdm:edge:«_,E,A», and hdm:node:«E» □ hdm:edge:«_,E,B» if each value ⟨x⟩ of hdm:node:«E» must appear as ⟨x,x⟩ in hdm:edge:«_,E,A».

Using the rules for ModelGen presented in (Boyd & McBrien, 2005), the ER and relational schemas in Figure 3 produce the same HDM schema, and the UML schema produces an HDM schema with one difference in the constraints. This one difference is due to the use of UIDs in the «E» node of the HDM schema that represents the UML schema, and requires that in the Mapping we make assumptions about being able to use «A» in $S_{uml,hdm}$ to identify instances of «E» in that schema.

We now review the BAV approach (McBrien & Poulovasillis, 2003), which allows us to describe both the ModelGen and Mapping, and hence have one overall specification of the translations from one high-level modelling language schema to another via a representation of each in the HDM. In the BAV, the translation of schemas can be expressed by a series of transformation steps, where incrementally, a new schema is built from an old schema using queries over the old schema to define what is the extent of constructs in the new schema, and queries over the new schema to define schema objects in the old schema. This leads to two important classes of BAV transformation that either add or delete schema objects from a schema listed below. The third class renames a schema object without altering its other characteristics:

- The transformation add(so,q) applied to schema S produces a new schema S', differing from S in that it contains schema object so, the extent of which can be derived by a query q over S. If and only if so can not be derived from S, the transformation extend(so) is used instead of add.

- The transformation delete(so,q) applied to schema S produces a new schema S', differing from S in that it does not contain schema object so, the extent of which can be recovered by a query q over S. If and only if so can not be derived from S, the transformation contract(so) is used instead of delete.

- The transformation rename(so,so') applied to schema S produces a new schema S' where the name of schema object so in S has been changed to so in S'.

The execution of ModelGen involves building a representation of a schema in a high-level modelling language as a schema in the HDM.

The execution of Mapping involves constructing a sequence of BAV transformations that map one HDM schema into another. Let us suppose we wish to convert $S_{uml,hdm}$ (the HDM schema version of the UML schema) in Figure 3 into $S_{er,hdm}$ (the HDM schema version of the ER schema). The first difference to deal with is that «E» in $S_{uml,hdm}$ contains UIDs, whilst «E» in $S_{er,hdm}$ contains natural key values. We deal with this by applying schema transformation macros. First, we make the UID in the $S_{uml,hdm}$ schema appear as a another node «U» in the HDM graph, which we represent as a macro identity_node_split, the application of which produces the following transformations in this particular case (the details of how the macros are defined may be found in (Boyd & McBrien, 2005)):

identity_node_split(«E»,«U»)

(A1) add(hdm:node:«U»,«E»)

(A2) add(hdm:edge:«_,E,U»,[⟨x,x⟩ ⎮ ⟨x⟩ <- «E»])

(A3) add(hdm:cons:(hdm:node:«E» ▷ hdm:edge:«_,E,U»))
(A4) add(hdm:cons:(hdm:node:«E» ◁ hdm:edge:«_,E,U »))
(A5) add(hdm:cons:(hdm:node:«E» ☐ hdm:edge:«_,E,U »))
(A6) add(hdm:cons:(hdm:node:«U» ▷ hdm:edge:«_,E,U »))

We then need to assume that hdm:node:«A» is a key for hdm:node:«E», and hence move the reflexive constraint ☐ from the hdm:edge:«_,E,U» to hdm:edge:«_,E,A», and change the extent of hdm:node:«E» to be that of hdm:node:«A», using another macro called node_reindentify which results in the following transformations:

node_reidentify(«E»,«_,E,A»)
(B1) add(hdm:node:«E'»,«A»)
(B2) add(hdm:edge:«_,E',A»,[⟨x,x⟩ ⎮ ⟨x⟩ <- «A»])
(B3) add(hdm:cons:(hdm:node:«E'» ▷ hdm:edge:«_,E',A»))
(B4) add(hdm:cons:(hdm:node:«E'» ◁ hdm:edge:«_,E',A»))
(B5) add(hdm:cons:(hdm:node:«E'» ☐ hdm:edge:«_,E',A»))
(B6) add(hdm:cons:(hdm:node:«A» ▷ hdm:edge:«_,E',A»))
(B7) add(hdm:edge:«_,E',U»,[⟨y,x⟩ ⎮ ⟨x,y⟩ <- «_,E,A»])
(B8) add(hdm:cons:(hdm:node:«E'» ▷ hdm:edge:«_,E',U»))
(B9) add(hdm:cons:(hdm:node:«E'» ◁ hdm:edge:«_,E',U »))
(B10) add(hdm:cons:(hdm:node:«U» ▷ hdm:edge:«_,E',U »))
(B11) add(hdm:edge:«_,E',B»,[⟨y,z⟩ ⎮ ⟨x,y⟩ <- «_,E,A»; ⟨x,z⟩ <- «_,E,B»])
(B12) add(hdm:cons:(hdm:node:«E'» ▷ hdm:edge:«_,E',B»))
(B13) add(hdm:cons:(hdm:node:«E'» ◁ hdm:edge:«_,E',B»))
(B14) add(hdm:cons:(hdm:node:«B» ▷ hdm:edge:«_,E',B»))
(B15) delete(hdm:cons:(hdm:node:«E» ▷ hdm:edge:«_,E,B»))
(B16) delete(hdm:cons:(hdm:node:«E» ◁ hdm:edge:«_,E,B»))
(B17) delete(hdm:cons:(hdm:node:«B» ▷ hdm:edge:«_,E,B»))
(B18) delete(hdm:edge:«_,E,B»,[⟨y,z⟩ ⎮ ⟨x,y⟩ <- «_,E',A»; ⟨x,z⟩ <- «_,E',B»])
(B19) delete(hdm:node:«E»,«U»)
(B20) rename(hdm:node:«E'»,hdm:node:«E»)

Note that in (B1)-(B20) (which for brevity has some transformations omitted from the listing), only information preserving transformations add, delete and rename are used, and hence the *information capacity* (Miller, Ioannidis, & Ramakrishnan, 1994) of the schema is preserved. The process creates a new node under the temporary name E', that has all the properties of the node named with E moved over to it, before the node named E is deleted, and E' renamed to E.

Finally, we need discard in transformations (C1)-(C5) hdm:node:«U» and hdm:edge:«_,E,U» as they do not have significance in the ER schema using BAV contract transformations. The use of contract makes explicit the fact that the UIDs (in «U») are not derivable from the information held in the ER schema.

(C1) contract(hdm:cons:(hdm:node:«E» ▷ hdm:edge:«_,E,U»))

(C2) contract(hdm:cons:(hdm:node:«E» ◁ hdm:edge:«_,E,U»))

(C3) contract(hdm:cons:(hdm:node:«U» ▷ hdm:edge:«_,E,U»))

(C4) contract(hdm:edge:«_,E,U»)

(C5) contract(hdm:node:«U»)

What results is schema Ser,hdm to the right of Figure 3, which is equivalent to Ser. The fact that we used in (C1)-(C5) some contract transformations indicates the Ser has less information capacity than Suml since we have removed a node and edge that we present in the UML schema, and could not be derived from information in the ER schema (which is indeed the case, since the UIDs of the UML model can not be derived from the natural keys of the ER schema.

ER to Relational Mapping

We now return to the example of intermodel mapping in Figure 1 to illustrate the conversion between ER and relational models. In this example we still have a change in the information capacity due to the cardinality constraints of the ER model not being represented in the relational model. Comparing the HDM schemas in Figure 4 for the ER and relational schemas of Figure 1 reveals that translating the schemas from high-level modelling languages into the HDM has "for free" performed some of the process of mapping between the ER and relational schemas. In particular, the notion of ER entity maps to relational table via a single HDM node, and an ER attribute maps to a relational column via an HDM node and an HDM edge, which connects the "attribute" node to the HDM node representing the table.

In the fragment of the pathway of transformations below that defines a mapping from our example ER schema into an equivalent HDM schema, the first transformation (D1) will define that the schema object hdm:node:«student» has the extent {1, 12, 17, 24}, then (D2) will define that the schema object hdm:node:«student:sid» has the extent {1, 12, 17, 24}, and so on, and (D3) defines that the edge between those two nodes has the extent {⟨1,1⟩, ⟨12,12⟩, ⟨17,17⟩, ⟨24,24⟩}. The net consequence of transformations (D4)-(D7) is to add constraints that enforce the fact that hdm:node:«student» and hdm:node:«student:sid» should always have the same extent, and hdm:edge:«_,student,student:sid» should contain just the identity mapping between the two nodes. Taken together, (D2)-(D7) form a complete definition of a key ER attribute in the HDM; other attributes have a similar pattern of transformations, varying in which constraints are added.

(D1) add(hdm:node:«student»,er:entity:«student»)

(D2) add(hdm:node:«student:sid»,[⟨y⟩ı ⟨x,y⟩ ← er:attribute:«student,sid»])

Figure 4. HDM schemas representing high level modelling language schemas

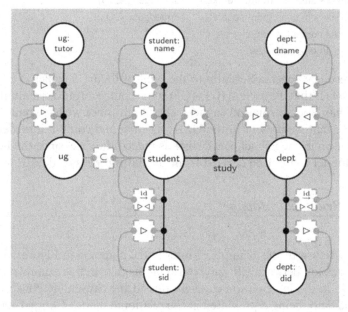

(a) HDM schema representation of ER schema

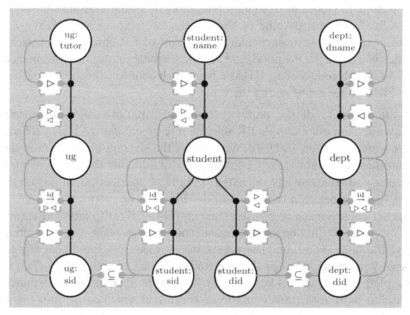

(a) HDM schema representation of relational schema

(D3) add(hdm:edge:«⌐student,student:sid»,er:attribute:«student,sid»)

(D4) add(hdm:cons:(hdm:node:«student» ▷ hdm:edge:«⌐student,student:sid»))

(D5) add(hdm:cons:(hdm:node:«student» ◁ hdm:edge:«⌐student,student:sid»))

(D6) add(hdm:cons:(hdm:node:«student» □ hdm:edge:«⌐student,student:sid»))

(D7) add(hdm:cons:(hdm:node:«student:sid» ▷ hdm:edge:«⌐student,student:sid»))

(D8) add(hdm:node:«dept»,er:entity:«dept»)

(D9) add(hdm:edge:«study,student,dept»,er:rel:«study,student,dept»))(D10)

add(hdm:cons:(hdm:node:«student» ▷ hdm:edge:«study,student,dept»))

(D11) add(hdm:cons:(hdm:node:«student» ◁ hdm:edge:«study,student,dept»))

(D12) add(hdm:cons:(hdm:node:«dept» ▷ hdm:edge:«study,student,dept»))

The result of the transformations is to create a schema that contains schema objects from both the ER and HDM modelling languages (i.e. a combination of Figures 1(a) and 4(a)). Once this stage has been reached, the ER schema objects can be deleted, with each transformation containing queries over the HDM schema, defining what the extent of ER schema objects in terms of the HDM schema objects, as illustrated by a few of the transformations listed below.

(E1) delete(er:attribute:«student,sid»,hdm:edge:«⌐student,student:sid»)

(E2) delete(er:attribute:«student,name»,hdm:edge:«⌐student,student:name»)

(E3) delete(er:subset:«ug,student»)

Once the high level schemas are converted into the HDM, the execution of the following macros will convert the relationship HDM schema of Figure 4(b) into the ER HDM schema of Figure 4(a), with one exception which we will return to discuss later. For conciseness, we present just the macros without their expansion (details of this process can be found in (Boyd & McBrien 2005)):

inclusion_merge(hdm:node:«dept:did»,hdm:edge:«⌐student:did,student»)

move_dependents(hdm:node:«student:sid», hdm:node:«student», hdm:edge:«⌐student:did,student»)

move_dependents(hdm:node:«dept:did», hdm:node:«dept», hdm:edge:«⌐dept:did,dept»)

identity_node_merge(⌐hdm:edge:«⌐ug:sid,ug»)

Once executed, the HDM schema that results will miss only the name of the relationship and the constraint for each department holding one student, that may be added by

(F1) rename(hdm:edge:«⌐student,dept»,hdm:edge:«study,student,dept»)

(F2) extend(hdm:cons:(hdm:node:«⌐dept» ▷ hdm:edge:«study,student,dept»))

The use of extend indicates that the constraint is additional information not derivable from the relational schema.

Future Directions: Automated Mapping between Modelling Languages

Using the HDM as an intermediate representation, combined with BAV transformations discussed in the previous section, gives us a method of specifying the relationship between schemas held in different high level modelling languages in terms of transformations on the HDM. Furthermore, we have illustrated that these transformations on the HDM can be generated by the application of functions such as inclusion_merge and identity_node_merge. If we identify the set of such transformation generating functions as F, then we can define $L(F)$ to be the power list of F, i.e. the list of all possible lists drawn from elements of F. Each member t of $L(F)$ defines the template of mapping from one schema to another. Denoting $t(S)$ as applying t to some schema S, we note that the application will require choosing which schema objects t applies to, and hence may generate more that one output BAV transformation m. Based on these definitions, we can now define a (very naive) algorithm for finding the mapping that relates schema S_x in modelling language x to an equivalent schema S_y in modelling language y as:

1. $S_{x,hdm} = \mathrm{ModelGen}_{x,hdm}(S_x)$
2. $S_{y,hdm} = \mathrm{ModelGen}_{y,hdm}(S_y)$
3.   foreach $t \in L(F)$: foreach $m \in t(S_{x,hdm})$: if $S_{y,hdm} = m(S_{x,hdm})$ then return m

Note that this algorithm requires that we know the target schema S_y in order to determine $S_{y,hdm}$ Hence in the more normal situation where we wish to find S_y given S_x, we would need to develop a $\mathrm{ModelGen}_{hdm,y}$, (i.e. an algorithm to generate from schema expressed in the HDM an equivalent schema expressed in modelling language y if it exists, and returns $\varnothing$ otherwise), which is the subject of some current research work, and then run the following process:

1. $S_{x,hdm} = \mathrm{ModelGen}_{x,hdm}(S_x)$
2.   foreach $t \in L(F)$: foreach $m \in t(S_{x,hdm})$:

$\qquad S_{y,hdm} = \mathrm{ModelGen}_{hdm,y}(m(S_{x,hdm}))$

$\qquad$ if $S_{y,hdm} \neq \varnothing$ then return m

To build a practical algorithm, we need to direct the selection of t from $L(F)$ such that is produces output that is acceptable to ModelGen$_{hdm,y}$, rather than simply enumerate all cases. The practically of this proposition will need to be the subject of future work. One major challenge is the insertion of additional transformations that rename, extend or contract objects when there is a mismatch in the HDM schemas produced by ModelGen, for example the addition of transformations (F1) and (F2) in the example of the previous section.

References

Anderson, M. (1994). Extracting an entity relationship schema from a relational database through reverse engineering. In *Proc ER94* (pp. 403-419), LNCS.

AutoMed (2007). From www.doc.ic.ac.uk/automed.

Bernstein, P. A. (2003). Applying model management to classical meta data problems. In *Proc CIDR03*.

Boyd, M., & McBrien, P. J. (2005). Comparing and transforming between data models via an intermediate hypergraph data model. *Journal on Data Semantics IV*, Springer-Verlag. pp. 69-109.

Halpin, T. (2001). *Information modeling and relational databases*. Academic Press.

McBrien, P. J., & Poulovassilis, A. (1999). A uniform approach to inter-model transformations. In *Proc. CAiSE'99*. Springer Verlag (LNCS 1626, pp. 333-348).

McBrien, P. J., & Poulovassilis, A. (2003). Data integration by bi-directional schema transformation rules. In *Proc ICDE 2003*, pp. 227-238.

Miller, R. J., Ioannidis, Y. E., & Ramakrishnan, R. (1994). Schema equivalence in heterogeneous systems: Bridging theory and practice. *Information Systems*, *19*(1), 3-31.

Song, I. Y., Evans, M., & Park, E. K. (1995). A comparative analysis of entity-relationship diagrams. *Journal of Computer & Software Engineering*, *3*(4), 427-459.

Chapter II

Intention Driven Conceptual Modelling

Colette Rolland, Université Paris1 Panthéon Sorbonne, France

Abstract

Conceptual modelling aims to capture the relevant aspects of the world on which it is necessary to provide information. Whereas conceptual models succeeded in telling us how to represent some excerpt of the world in informational terms, they failed to guide system analysts in conceptualising purposeful systems, i.e. systems that meet the expectations of their users. This chapter aims to investigate the issue of conceptualising purposeful systems and to discuss the role that goal driven approaches can play to resolve it. It considers the challenge of new systems having a multifaceted purpose and shows how intention/strategy maps help facing this challenge.

Introduction

Traditionally Information System (IS) engineering has made the assumption that an information system captures some excerpt of world history and hence has concentrated on modelling information about the Universe of Discourse. This is done through conceptual modelling that aims at abstracting the specification of the required information system i.e. the conceptual schema, from an analysis of the relevant aspects of the Universe of Discourse about which the users' community needs information (Dubois, 1989). This specification concentrates on what the system should do, that is, on its functionality. Such a specification acts as a prescription for system construction.

Whereas conceptual modelling allowed our community to understand the semantics of information and led to a large number of semantically powerful conceptual models, experience demonstrates that it failed in supporting the delivery of systems that were accepted by the community of their users. Indeed, a number of studies show (Standish group, 1995; European Software Institute, 1996; META Group, 2003) that systems fail due to an inadequate or insufficient understanding of the requirements they seek to address. Further, the amount of effort needed to fix these systems has been found to be very high (Johnson, 1995).

To correct this situation, it is necessary to address the issue of building *purposeful systems*, i.e. information systems that are seen as fulfilling a certain purpose in an organisation (Ackoff, 1972). Understanding this purpose is a necessary condition for the conceptualisation of these purposeful systems. The foregoing suggests to go beyond the functionality based view of conceptual modelling and to extend the '*what is done by the system*' approach with the '*why is the system like this*'. This why question is answered in terms of organisational objectives and their impact on information systems supporting the organisation. The expectation is that as a result of a refocus on the *why* question, more acceptable systems will be developed in the future. The field of requirements engineering has emerged to meet this expectation.

The first objective of this chapter is to deal with the above issue of conceptualising purposeful systems and to show how goal-driven approaches can help to this end.

The second objective is to consider new challenges raised by emerging conditions of system development. Whereas in the 'from scratch' type of development, a system needs to meet the purpose of a single organisation, systems of today need to be conceived in a larger perspective, to meet the purpose of several organisations and to be adaptable to different usage situations/customers sets (Hui, 2003; van Gurp, 2001; Bosch, 2001; Bachmann, 2001; Halmans, 2003). The new issue is therefore, to deal with the *multi-purpose nature* of information systems of today. We will discuss this issue in the second part of the chapter.

This chapter is organised as follows: In section 2 we focus on the issue of conceptualizing purposeful systems. We argue that the goal concept is central to resolving this issue and demonstrate the various roles that goals can play in conceptualizing purposeful systems. In section 3 we discuss the emerging trend of building multi-purpose systems. We show that the multi-purpose nature of information systems leads to introduce variability in their conceptualization and present a particular goal model called goal/strategy map to illustrate how to model variability.

Conceptualising Purposeful Systems

In this section we first propose a system engineering framework that helps understanding the source of the IS purpose and justifying goal-driven approaches towards the conceptualisation of purposeful systems. In the second part, we present the state-of-the art in goal-driven approaches and their roles in IS conceptualisation.

System Engineering Framework

To support the view of system engineering being proposed in this chapter, we present an engineering framework composed of three interrelated worlds as shown in Fig. 1.

In this framework, the traditional system environment is split into two worlds, the *subject world and the usage world,* respectively. The *usage world* describes the tasks, procedures, interactions etc. performed by agents and how systems are used to do work. It can be looked upon as containing the objectives that are to be met in the organisation and which are achieved by the activities carried out by agents. Therefore, it describes the activity of agents and how this activity leads to useful work.

The second part of the Universe of Discourse, the *subject world*, contains knowledge of the real world domain about which the proposed system has to provide information. It contains real world objects that are to be represented in the conceptual schema.

Figure 1. Relationships between the worlds of usage, subject and system

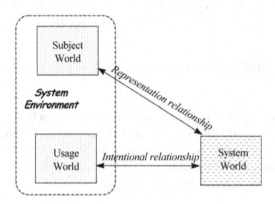

There is a third world, the *system world* which is the world of system specifications. This world holds the modelled entities, processes, and events of the subject and usage worlds as well as the mapping from these conceptual specifications to the design and implementation levels of the software system. All these worlds are interrelated as shown in Fig. 1.

The framework helps us understanding that traditional conceptual modelling has been concentrating on the *representation relationship* between the *subject* and *system world*. This permits to capture the domain-dependent characteristics that need to be conceptualised. Reasoning on this relationship allowed our community to understand the meaning of information and to develop semantically rich models able to represent the real world facts and constraints on the designed system implied by laws of physics independently of user's needs or wishes. However, the focus on this relationship has drawn our attention away from another equally important relationship, namely the *intentional relationship* between the usage world and the system world.

The point developed in this chapter is that the usage world is the one which provides the rationale for building a system. The purpose of developing an information system is to be found outside the system itself, in the *enterprise,* or in other words, in the context in which the system will function. The social relationship between the usage and system world addresses the issue of the system purpose and relates the system to the goals and objectives of the organisation. This relationship explains *why* the system is developed. Modelling this establishes the conceptual link between the envisaged system and its changing environment.

The aforementioned suggests an augmentation of conceptual modelling to deal with the description of the context in which the system will function. Along this line we propose the use of *goal-driven approaches* to directly model organisational objectives and relate them to system functions. These approaches have been developed to address the semiotic, social link between the usage and the system world with the hope to construct systems that meet the needs of the organization and fulfil its purpose.

Goal Modelling Approaches

The concept of a goal is central to goal-driven approaches; its benefit being to support heuristic, qualitative or formal reasoning scheme during the IS conceptualization process. In this section we successively introduce the notion of a goal, present goal models and discuss the various roles that these models play in conceptualising purposeful systems.

What are Goals?

According to Axel van Lamsweerde (2001) "a goal corresponds to an objective the system should achieve through the cooperation of agents in the software To-Be and in the environment". Goals refer to intended or optative (Jackson, 1995) properties of envisioned system or of its environment. They are expressions of intent and thus, declarative with a prescriptive nature, by opposition to descriptive statements (Jackson, 1995) which describe real facts. For instance, *Transport passengers safely* is a goal whereas *if doors are closed, they are not opened* is a descriptive statement. The goal expresses what is wanted i.e. a state that is expected to be reached or maintained. *Make Room Booking* is a goal to make to make a reservation for rooms in a hotel. The achievement of this goal leaves the system in the state, *Booking made*. This intentional nature of a goal is essential to hide the details of how the goal will be achieved to concentrate on what is aimed to be achieved. This is an important property to understand the purpose of the system before specifying in the conceptual schema the solution for fulfilling the goal.

Goals can be formulated at *different levels of abstraction* ranging from high–level, e.g. strategic results that an enterprise wants to achieve, down to low level, e.g. technical concerns on precise situations that a system component should help to reach. *Transport passengers safely* is an example of high level goal whereas *Keep doors closed when moving* is a goal of a lower level of abstraction. This property of the concept of a goal is fundamental to understand the IS purpose in the broader context of the environment in which it will function. Relating the strategic goal *Transport passengers safely* to the operationalisable goal *Keep doors closed when moving* provides the rationale for the latter and the subsequent conceptual schema elements such as the class 'door', the 'close' operation on doors, the event 'start' on the train etc.

Goals cover *different types of concerns, functional* and *qualitative* (also called *non functional)*. Functional goals refer to functionalities that will be provided by the system or its environment whereas quality goals refer to qualities of the system behaviour in its environment. *Provide cash* is a functional goal whereas *Serve customer quickly* is a quality goal. Traditionally, conceptual modelling has concentrated on functional aspects of the system To-Be. However, experience has shown that a differed consideration of qualitative aspects to a later phase of IS development can lead to cost intensive errors. Indeed, the discovery of the inability of a given functionality to cope with some qualitative constraint can imply a complete revision and re-implementation of functions. Goals have this advantage to provide a mechanism to express functional and qualitative considerations in the same way, at the same time.

Unlike system requirements, goals are usually achieved by the *cooperation of multiple agents*. The goal *Transport passengers safely* requires for example, the cooperation of agents such as the train transportation system, the software system, the tracking system and the passengers. A goal under the responsibility of a single agent in the software becomes a requirement. One important decision in the conceptualisation process is therefore, to decide which goals will be automated and which ones will not. Whereas the actual situations met in the system environment (e.g. physical laws, regulations, norms and behaviours, etc) are usually not controlled by the system, it is possible to control the satisfaction of requirements by implementing them into the system. *Maintain doors while moving* is a goal leading to a requirement for the system that will ensure its satisfaction whereas *Get in when doors open* is an assumption (Dardenne, 1993) about agents out of the system control.

Goal Modelling

Whereas each goal captures part of the purpose, the assembly of goals provided by a *goal model* allows to capture and reason about the purpose in its entirety.

The most common form of a goal model is an AND/OR graph. AND/OR relationships (Bubenko, 1994; Dardenne, 1993; Rolland, 1998; Loucopoulos, 1997; Mylopoulos, 1999) directly borrowed from problem reduction methods in Artificial Intelligence (Nilsson, 1971). Such a goal graph aims at capturing situations where goals positively or negatively support other goals. AND-links relate a goal to a set of sub-goals. This means that satisfying all the sub-goals is sufficient for the parent goal to be achieved. For example, in a book lending system as shown in Fig. 2, *Satisfy borrower request* is *ANDed* (has an AND relationship) with *Satisfy Bibliography request, Satisfy book request* and *Provide long borrowing period*. These three goals are sub-goals of the former that will be satisfied if its sub-goals are themselves satisfied.

OR-links relate a goal to a set of alternative refined goals; this means that if one of the alternative goals is achieved, then the parent goal is satisfied. *Maintain as many copies as needed* and *Maintain regular availability* are alternatives to satisfy the goal *Satisfy customer request*. The former is *ORed* (has an OR relationship) with the latter and will be satisfied if one of the two alternative goals is satisfied.

AND relationships and OR relationships play different roles in a goal model and support different types of reasoning. The AND link introduces goal decomposition and helps understanding how strategic goals can be satisfied through the fulfilment of more tactical goals which, in turn are decomposed into operationalisable goals that imply system requirements. Thus, clearly the AND decomposition is a means to reason about the rationale of system requirements and to establishing a conceptual link, the pre-traceability link (Gotel, 1994) between high level, strategic goals of the IS organizational context and the IS requirements.

Figure 2. A goal graph

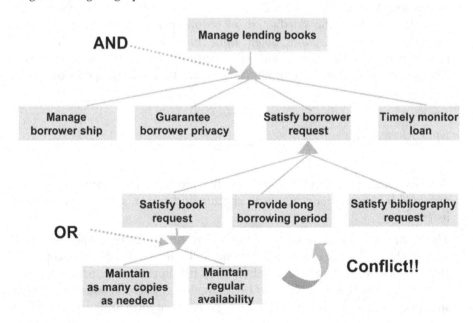

OR relationships introduce goal refinement and help reasoning about different alternative ways to satisfy a goal. Each alternative leads to different requirements and therefore, modelling these different possibilities is important to consciously decided what the system should be. Evidently, ORed goals call for qualitative and/or quantitative techniques to deliberate and make decision about which alternative is the most appropriate to the situation at hand.

As shown in Fig.2 goal models help discovering *conflict* between goals. A conflict between two goals is when the satisfaction of one might prevent the other to be satisfied. This ability of goal models to make conflicts explicit is an important characteristic. That helps resolving conflict among stakeholders at a low cost compared to traditional situations in which conflicts arise when the system is installed and require expensive changes to be performed. Nuseibeh (1994), Easterbrook (1994) and Robinson (1996) explain how conflicts arise from multiple viewpoints and concerns. Various forms of conflict have also been studied in (Darimont, 1998). Ivankina (2004), Sutcliffe (1999a) and Sutcliffe (1999b), generalize the notions of obstacle, conflict and other system menace into the notion of threat because they all correspond to the partial or total hindering of one or several system goals.

In (Mylopoulos, 1999; Mylopoulos, 1992; Chung, 2000), the inter-goal relationship is extended to support the capture of negative/positive influence between goals. A sub-goal is said to contribute partially to its parent goal. This leads to the notion of goal *satisfycing* instead of goal *satisfaction*. For example, *Ensure confidentiality of accounts* and *Ensure security of accounts* are ANDed to *Secure accounts*. Both contribute positively to satisfycing the father goal *Secure accounts*. By opposition to goal satisfaction, which can be verified quantitatively, using some criterion (Robinson, 1989), goal satisfycing cannot be established in a clear-cut sense. Goal satisfaction expressed in AND/OR graphs of *hard* goals is referred to as the *quantitative framework* whereas goal satisfycing expressed with *soft* goals is part of the so- called *qualitative framework*. The 'motivates' and 'hinders' relationships among goals in (Bubenko, 1994) are similar in the sense that they capture positive/ negative influence among goals. Clearly soft goals are dealing with non functional aspects whereas hard goals are referring to functional ones.

One promising direction of is to couple the quantitative and the qualitative frameworks in order to use the reasoning schemes of the latter to select an alternative refinement of hard goals in the former. The selected alternative will be the one that contributes the best to the satisfycing of soft goals related to cost, reliability, performance etc. Multi-criteria analysis techniques could be helpful in this selection process.

In addition to inter-goals relationships, goals are also related in goal models to other elements. This provides support for other forms of reasoning with the ultimate aim to understand the purpose better and explore all aspects of the ways it can be achieved through the use of an information system.

There has been a massive amount of work on coupling goals with *scenarios* (Potts, 1995; Cockburn, 1995; Leite, 1997; Kaindl, 2000; Sutcliffe, 1998; Haumer, 1998; Anton, 1998, Lamsweerde, 1998). This is understandable because scenarios and goals complement each other. Goals are declarative whereas scenarios are procedural. Goals exhibit intentions whereas these are implicit in scenarios. Goals are abstract in the sense that they abstract from details of the processes to achieve the expected results whereas scenarios are concrete descriptions of behaviours to obtain the results. Combining goals and scenarios can be therefore, seen as a way to mitigate limitations that each concept has when used in isolation. Potts (1995) for example, says that it is *"unwise to apply goal based requirements methods in isolation"* and suggests complementing them with scenarios. This combination has been used mainly, to make goals concrete: scenarios can be interpreted as containing information on how goals can be achieved. In (Dano, 1997; Jacobson, 1995; Leite, 1997; Pohl, 1997), a goal is considered as a contextual property of a use case i.e. a property that relates the scenario to its organizational context. Therefore, goals play a documenting role only.

Cockburn (1995) goes beyond this view and suggests to use goals to structure use cases by connecting every action in a scenario to a goal assigned to an actor. In this sense a scenario is discovered each time a goal is. Clearly, all these views suggest a unidirectional relationship between goals and scenarios. Rolland (1998) further extends this view by suggesting a *"bi-directional relationship between goals and scenarios"*. In the forward direction from goal to scenario, the scenario represents a possible behaviour of the system to achieve the goal, and therefore, scenarios help making the goal concrete and detecting unrealistic goals. In the backward direction, from scenario to goal, the relationship is used to discover new goals using mining techniques. As the scenario represents a concrete, realistic behaviour of the system to be, the goals inferred from it should themselves be realistic ones. In (Lamsweerde, 1998), a similar approach is developed that takes scenarios as examples and counter examples of the intended system behaviour and generates goals that cover positive scenarios and exclude the negative ones. Anton (2001) takes similar position to derive goals from use-case specifications.

Relationships with *agents* have been emphasized in (Yu, 1994; Yu, 1997) where a goal is the object of the dependency between two agents. Such type of link is introduced in other models as well (Dardenne, 1993; Lamsweerde, 1991; Letier, 2001) to capture who is responsible of a goal.

Aside from the relationships with scenarios and agents, goals might have links with other concepts of requirements models. For example, as a logical termination of the AND/OR decomposition, goals link to *operations* which operationalize them (Dardenne, 1993; Anton, 1998; Kaindl, 2000; Lamsweerde, 1998). Relationships between goals and system *objects* have been studied in (Lee, 1997) and are for instance, inherently part of the KAOS model (Lamsweerde, 1991; Dardenne, 1993). In (Bubenko, 1994), goals are related to a number of concepts such as *problem*, *opportunity* and *threat* with the aim to understand better the context of a goal. Finally the interesting idea of *obstacle* introduced by Potts (1995) leads to obstructions and resolution relationships among goals and obstacles (Lamsweerde, 2000; Sutcliffe, 1998).

Roles of Goals

It can be seen from the aforementioned that in this movement towards the 'whys' of the system To-Be, goal models play a leading role. They provide the basis for modelling the intentionality of the system and establishing a link between the objectives of the organization and the functionalities of the system implied by these objectives. They allow to consider the multiple view points of the various stakeholders to explore alternative design choices and reason about them so as to make conceptual decisions on the basis of rational arguments in favour or against the different alternatives. Recording these help to deal with changing objectives and requirements. In the following we sum up the different roles that goal models play towards the conceptualization of purposeful systems.

- Goal modelling proved to be an effective way to *elicit requirements* (Potts, 1994; Rolland, 1998; Dardenne, 1993; Dubois, 1998; Potts, 1994; Kaindl, 2000; Lamsweerde, 2000). The pros of goal-based requirements elicitation is that the rationale for developing a system must be found outside the system itself, in the enterprise (Loucopoulos, 1994) in which the system shall function. As a consequence (a) elicitation of the requirements of a system is done with respect to their purpose in organizations and (b) only organizationally purposeful systems are conceptualized.

- In this movement from the 'whats' to the 'whys', it becomes mandatory to consider multiple view points of the various stakeholders, to explore alternative design choices and reason about them so as to make conceptual decisions on the basis of rationale arguments in favour and against the different alternatives. Alternative goal refinement proved helpful in the systematic *exploration of system choices* (Rolland, 1998; Loucopoulos, 1994; Rolland, 1999a; Hui, 2003) leading to conceptual solutions aligned with the organization priorities and decisions.

- Recording these shall help to deal with changing organisation objectives. Goals provide a means to ensure *conceptual schema pre-traceability* (Gotel, 1994; Ramesh, 1995; Pohl, 1996). They establish a conceptual link between the system and its environment, thus facilitating the propagation of organizational changes into the conceptual schema and related system functionality. This link provides the rationale for the conceptual functionality (Bubenko, 1994; Sommerville, 1997; Ross, 1977; Potts, 1994) and facilitates the explanation and justification of it to the stakeholders.

- Stakeholders provide useful and realistic viewpoints about the system To-Be expressed as goals. *Negotiation* techniques have been developed to help choosing the prevalent one (Hoh, 2002; Boehm, 1994). *Prioritization* techniques aim at providing means to compare the different viewpoints on the basis of cost and value (Karlsson, 1997; Moisiadis, 2002). Multiple viewpoints are inherently associated to conflicts (Nuseibeh, 1994) and goals have been recognized to help in the *detection of conflicts* and their resolution (Lamsweerde, 2000; Robinson, 1996; Robinson, 1998; Easterbrook, 1994).

Facing the New Challenge of Multi-Purpose Systems

In this section, we discuss the case of particular type of goal model, the intention/strategy map. We first justify the move from traditional *AND/OR goal models* to *Intention/Strategy maps* as a response to the challenge posed by the multi-purpose nature of emerging information systems and the need to depart from goal modelling to model goal achievement through strategies to fulfil goals. We introduce the concept of a map, illustrate it with an example of an Electricity Supply Management system and discuss how the model meets the aforementioned challenge.

New Challenges and Trends in Goal Modelling

Goal modelling approaches have been conceived with the traditional software system life cycle in mind: high strategic goals are captured to elicit software requirements and build the software functionality that fulfils these requirements. However, in recent years, development 'from scratch' became the exception and a new context in which software systems are developed has emerged. Whereas earlier, a system met the purpose of a single organization and of a single set of customers, a system of today must be conceived in a larger perspective, to meet the purpose of several organizations and to be adaptable to different usage situations/customer sets. The former is typical of an ERP-like development situation whereas the latter is the concern of product-line development (van Gurp, 2001; Bosch, 2001) and adaptable software (Mostow, 1985). In the software community, this leads to the notion of software variability which is defined as the ability of a software system to be changed, customized or configured to a specific context (van Gurp, 2000). Whereas the software community studies variability as a design problem and concentrates on implementation issues (van Gurp, 2001; Bosch, 2001; Bachmann, 2001), we believe like Halmans (2003) that capturing variability at the goal level is essential to meet the multi-purpose nature of new information systems.

Our position is that variability implies a move from systems with a *mono-facetted purpose* to those with a *multi-facetted purpose*. Whereas the former concentrates on goal discovery, the multi-facetted nature of a purpose extends it to consider the many different ways of goal achievement. For example, for the goal *Purchase Material*, earlier it would be enough to know that an organization achieves this goal by forecasting material need. Thus, *Purchase Material* was mono-facetted: it had exactly one strategy for its achievement. However, in the new context, it is necessary to introduce other strategies as well, say the Reorder Point strategy for purchasing material. *Purchase Material* now is multi-facetted, it has many strategies for goal achievement. These two strategies, among others, are made available, for example, in the SAP Materials Management module (Rolland, 2000).

The foregoing points to the need to balance *goal-orientation* with the introduction of *strategies for goal achievement*. This is the essence of *intention/strategy maps* which we present here.

A *intention/strategy map*, or *map* for short, is a graph, with nodes as *intentions* and *strategies* as edges. An edge entering a node identifies a strategy that can be used for achieving the intention of the node. The map therefore, shows which intentions can be achieved by which strategies once a preceding intention has been achieved. Evidently, the map is capable of expressing variability in goal achievement and therefore, can help modelling the multi-facetted purpose of a system.

Modelling a Multi-Facetted Purpose with MAP

In this section we introduce the key concepts of a map and their relationships and bring out their relevance to model multi-facetted purposes. We use the ESM (Electricity Supply Management) map as an example.

The Map Representation Formalism

Map is a representation system that was originally developed to represent a process model expressed in intentional terms (Rolland, 1999b). It provides a representation mechanism based on a non-deterministic ordering of *intentions* and *strategies* that we will use here as a means for modelling the multi-facetted purpose of a To-Be system.

A map is represented as a labelled directed graph with *intentions* as nodes and *strategies* as edges between intentions. An edge enters a node if its strategy can be used to achieve the intention of the node. There can be multiple edges entering a node.

- An *Intention* is a goal that expresses what is wanted, i.e. a state that is expected to be reached or maintained. For example, in the ESM of Fig.3, *Sell Electricity* and *Serve Customer Request* are two intentions. Furthermore, ach map has two special intentions, *Start* and *Stop*, associated to the initial and final states respectively.

- A *Strategy* is an approach, a manner to achieve an intention. A strategy S_{ij} between the couple of intentions I_i and I_j represents the way I_j can be achieved once I_i has been achieved. In Fig.3 *Credit strategy* is a strategy to *Sell Electricity* which refers to the conventional solution where the electricity company provides electricity to its customers and gets paid after consumption.

- A *Section* is a triplet $<I_i, I_j, S_{ij}>$ as for example $<Serve\ Customer\ Request,\ Sell\ Electricity,\ Credit\ strategy>$ and represents a way to achieve the target intention I_j, *Electricity* from the source intention I_i, *Serve Customer Request* following the strategy S_{ij}, *Credit strategy*. Each section of the map captures the situation needed to achieve an intention and a specific manner in which the target intention can be fulfilled.

Sections in a map are related to each other by three kinds of relationships namely *thread, bundle* and *path* relationships.

- *Bundle relationship*: Several sections having the same pair of source and target intentions, which are mutually exclusive, are in a *bundle relationship*. For example in Fig.3, the *Payment strategy* is a bundle consisting of the *Credit strategy* and *Advance payment strategy*.

- *Thread relationship*: It is possible for a target intention to be achieved from a source intention in many different ways. Each of these ways is

Figure 3a. The ESM map example. Figure 3b. $_{Mbc2}$ map refining bc2 section

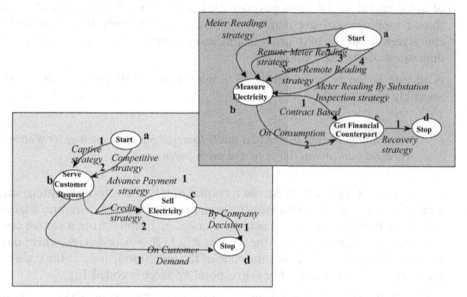

expressed as a section in the map and these sections are in a *thread relationship* with one another. In Fig.3 the *Captive strategy* and the *Competitive strategy* are in a *thread* relationship. The difference between a *thread* and a bundle relationship is that of an exclusive OR of sections in the latter versus an OR in the former.

- *Path relationship*: This establishes a precedence/succession relationship between sections. For a section to succeed another, its source intention must be the target intention of the preceding one. For example the two sections, <*Start, Serve Customer Request, Captive strategy* >, < *Serve Customer Request, Sell Electricity, Credit strategy* > constitutes a path.

Finally, it is possible to *refine* a section of a map into an entire map at a lower level of abstraction. For example, Fig.3b shows the refinement of the section <*Serve Customer Request, Sell Electricity, Credit strategy*> as a map. This refinement mechanism leads to a hierarchy of maps that will be used to model the multi facetted purpose at different level of details.

Modelling the Multi-Facetted Purpose with Maps

In its totality, a map captures the main system *purpose*. For example, the ESM system can be seen to meet the purpose, *Manage Electricity Supply Efficiently* and this is the intention of the root map shown in Fig.3a.

Evidently, the map is able to present a global perspective of the diverse ways of achievement of the main purpose; this is based on the path, bundle and thread topologies of the map. We will show in the following, how these characteristics of the map provide a means to represent of the multi-facetted dimension of the main purpose.

A section is the basic construct of a map which itself can be seen as an assembly of sections.

- *When a map is used to model a multi-facetted purpose, each of its sections represents an atomic facet of the main purpose.*

For the sake of conciseness, we use a textual notation in which intentions are named by letters of the alphabet, strategies are numbers and therefore, a facet named ab_i designates a way to achieve a target intention b from a source one a following a strategy i. Thus, the section $<I_i, I_j, S_{ij}>$ is coded ab_1 where a is the code of the intention I_i, b is the code of the intention I_j and 1 is the code of the strategy S_{ij} (see Fig.4). The corresponding facet is coded F_{ab1}.

A facet highlights a consistent and cohesive characteristic of the system that stakeholders want to be implemented through some functionality. A facet in our terms is close to the notion of feature defined in FODA (Kang, 1990) as a 'prominent or distinctive user-visible aspect, quality or characteristic of a system". However, our view of a facet emphasizes the intention that the underlying functionality allows to achieve and to support this view, we name a facet by referring to the intention it supports. For example, the F_{ab1} facet above is named F_{Ij}. We believe that a facet is a useful abstraction to express variability in intentional terms and show this in the following.

The ESM root map (Fig.3a) contains 6 facets, F_{ab1}, F_{ab2}, F_{bc1}, F_{bc2}, F_{cd1}, F_{bd1} with the following names:

F $_{Serve\ Customer\ Request\ with\ Captive\ Strategy,}$

F $_{Serve\ Customer\ request\ with\ Competitive\ Strategy,}$

F $_{Sell\ Electricity\ with\ advance\ Payment\ strategy,}$

Figure 4. The ab1 section and F_{ab1} facet

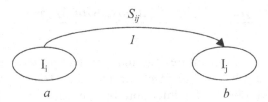

F *Serve Customer request with Credit Strategy,*

F *Stop on Company Decision,*

F *Stop on Customer Demand.*

Given the fact that a section identifies a system purpose facet, let us show now, how relationships between sections of a map lead to a detailed view of each intention achievement and thus, to the representation of the multi-facetted dimension of each intention of the main purpose.

A *thread* relationship between sections in a map (Fig.5) highlights various ways to achieve the same intention b starting from a source intention a. Each way offers a *choice* to attain the target intention and the set of threaded sections can been seen as representing the multi-facetted dimension of the target intention.

- *A thread relationship expresses a variability by grouping optional facets from which one or many of them can be selected. We call* **Choice Facet** *a facet detailing the multi-facetted nature of an intention by offering a choice of facets to achieve it. We denote the choice using the 'v' symbol.*

The choice facet F_{ab} in Fig.5 designated F_{Ij} is defined as, $F_{ab1} \ v \ F_{ab2}$.

In the ESM root map (Fig.3a) the thread relationship between ab1 and ab2 introduces a choice to achieve the intention *Serve Customer Request*. The corresponding choice facet F_{ab} captures the multi facetted dimension to achieve the intention *Serve Customer Request* by offering two alternative strategies to achieve this intention, namely the *Captive strategy* and the *Competitive strategy*. The former applies to customers that are not yet entitled to buy their electricity to the supplier of their choice whereas the competitive strategy is tailored to those customers who are free to select their supplier. However, the competitive strategy might be applied to captive customers too as a means to secure their loyalty in the scope of the market liberalization.

Figure 5. A choice *between facets*

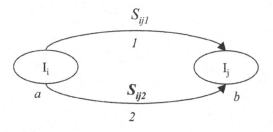

The *bundle* relationship is used in the case where the several ways to satisfy the same intention b are exclusive. It implies that only one way can be selected to achieve the target intention. Fig. 6 shows an example of a bundle relationship.

- *A bundle relationship expresses a variability by grouping alternative facets that are mutually exclusive. We call **Alternative Facet**, a facet that offers an exclusive choice among its components facets. We denote the exclusive choice using the '$\otimes$' symbol.*

The *alternative* facet F_{ab} in Fig. 6 designated F_{Ij} is defined as, $F_{ab1} \otimes F_{ab2}$. In the root ESM map (Fig. 3a) there is only one alternative facet F_{bc} based on the bundle of sections bc1 and bc2. Named $F_{Sell\ Electricity}$, this facet is defined as: $F_{Sell\ Electricity} = F_{SE\ with\ advance\ Payment\ strategy} \otimes F_{SE\ with\ Credit\ strategy}$. This alternative facet details the multi-faceting of the intention *Sell Electricity* by offering two exclusive strategies namely, the *Advance Payment strategy*, and the *Credit strategy* to achieve it. These strategies identify two rather different business strategies to get the customer to pay for his electricity consumption. Indeed the *Advance Payment strategy* refers to a solution based on the use of payment cards to energize the customer meter whereas the *Credit strategy* refers to the more conventional solution where the electricity company provides electricity to its customer and gets paid after consumption.

The *path* relationship in a map is when the achievement of a target intention b from a source intention a requires the satisfaction of intermediary intentions. It establishes a precedence/succession relationship between facets. In general, a path is a composition of facets (some being possibly *choice* or *alternative* facets) or of other paths. Fig. 7 presents a path between the intentions I_i and I_k, denoted respectively by a and c, which is composed of a *choice facet* containing F_{ab1}, F_{ab2}, F_{ab3} and the facet denoted F_{bc1}. It expresses that, in order to achieve the intention I_k, it is necessary to select one or several facets among F_{ab1} v F_{ab2} v F_{ab3} and then execute the facet F_{bc1}.

Figure 6. An alternative between facets

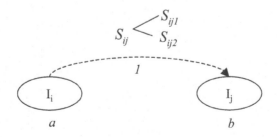

Figure 7. A path *facet*

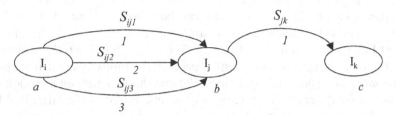

- *A **path facet** is a composite facet that can include variability and provides the basis for expressing variability on a higher granularity. We denote the composition of facets in a path with the . symbol.*

The path facet $F_{a, \{b\}, c}$ in Fig.7 is defined as $(F_{ab1} \vee F_{ab2} \vee F_{ab3}) \cdot F_{bc1}$.

Given the three relationships between sections namely path, bundle and thread, an intention of a map can be achieved by several combinations of sections. Such a topology is called a *multi-path*. In general, a map from its *Start* to its *Stop* intentions is a multi-path. For example, Fig.8 shows a multi-path composed of two alternative paths to satisfying the intention I_k (denoted c) starting from the intention I_i (denoted a). The first path achieves I_k through the intermediary intention I_j whereas the second path achieves I_k directly from I_i.

- *A multi-path relationship is a means to express variability by grouping the alternative paths satisfying the same intention. We call **multi-path facet** a facet offering a choice of paths to achieve an intention and denote this choice using the "∪" symbol*

The multi-path facet $F_{a, \{b\}, c}$ in Fig.8 is defined as $((F_{ab1} \vee F_{ab2} \vee F_{ab3}) \cdot F_{bc1}) \cup F_{ab1}$.

Figure 8. A multi-path *facet*

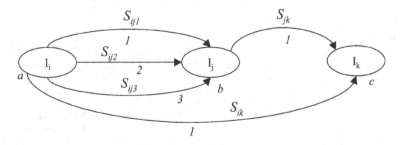

In the ESM map, there is a multi-path to achieve the intention *Stop* from the *Serve Customer Request* intention. Either the path from *Serve Customer Request* to *Stop* via *Sell Electricity* can be followed or the direct path from *Serve Customer Request* to *Stop* can be used. This leads to the multi-path facet $F_{b,\{c\},d}$ defined as $F_{bd1} \cup ((F_{bc1} \otimes F_{bc2}) \cdot F_{cd1})$. A *multi-path* facet such as $F_{b,\{c\},d}$ highlights a different aspect of the multi-facetted purpose than *alternative* and *choice* facets, namely the one showing that an intention can be achieved by different combinations of facets. Whereas the latter highlight a *local faceting* (variations of strategies to achieve an intention), the former exhibits *global faceting* (variations of paths to achieve an intention).

Table 1 sums up the results of the ESM root map faceting. It shows that the map is based on 6 atomic facets and two path facets that support the expression of three variants, one of each of the three types, *alternative*, *choice* and *multi-path*.

Multi-faceting is also based on the refine relationship that exists between a section in a map and an entire map. For example the section bc2 of the ESM root map is modelled as the map M_{bc2} presented in Fig. 3b.

- *From the point of view of multi-faceting, refinement allows to look to the multi-facetted nature of a facet. It introduces levels in the representation of the multi-facetted purpose which is thus, completely modelled through a hierarchy of maps.*

As an illustration, Table 2 shows the facets and variants embedded in the refined map of Fig. 3b.

To sum up

- The purpose of the system To-Be is captured in a *hierarchy of maps*. The intention associated to the root map is the high level statement about the purpose. Using the refinement mechanism each section of the root map can be refined as a map and the recursive application of this

Table 1. ESM facets

Facet types	Facets
Variant Facets	$F_{\text{Sell Electricity}} = F_{\text{SE with advance Payment strategy}} \otimes F_{\text{SE with Credit strategy}}$
	$F_{\text{Serve Customer Request}} = F_{\text{SCR with Captive Strategy}} \vee F_{\text{SCR with Competitive Strategy}}$
	$F_{\text{Stop Electricity Supply}} = F_{\text{Stop on Company Decision}} \cup F_{\text{Supply Electricity \& Stop Provision}}$
Atomic facets	$F_{\text{Serve Customer Request with Captive Strategy}}$, $F_{\text{Serve Customer request with Competitive Strategy}}$, $F_{\text{Sell Electricity with advance Payment strategy}}$, $F_{\text{Sell Electricity with credit strategy}}$ $F_{\text{Stop on Customer Demand}}$, $F_{\text{Stop on Company Decision}}$
Path facets	$F_{\text{Manage Electricity Supply}} = F_{\text{Serve Customer Request}} \cdot S_{\text{Stop Electricity Supply}}$
	$F_{\text{Supply Electricity \& Stop Provision}} = F^{*}_{\text{Sell Electricity}} \cdot F_{\text{Stop on Customer Demand}}$

Table 2. Facets in M_{bc2}

Facet types	Facets
Variant facets	F *Measure electricity* $= F$ *Measure electricity by meter readers* $\vee F$ *Measure electricity by remote meter readers* $\vee F$ *Measure electricity by semi-remote meter readers* $\vee F$ *Meter reading by substation inspection strategy*
	F *Get financial Counterpart* $= F$ *Get financial counterpart on contract* $\otimes F$ *Get financial counterpart on consumption*
Atomic facets	F *Measure electricity by meter readers,* F *Measure electricity by remote meter readers,* F *Measure electricity by semi-remote meter readers,* F *Meter reading by substation inspection strategy,* F *Get financial counterpart on contract,* F *Get financial counterpart on consumption,* F *Recover financial counterpart*
Path facets	F *Sell electricity with credit strategy* $= F$ *Measure electricity* $\cdot F$ *Get financial Counterpart* $\cdot F$ *Recover financial counterpart*

mechanism results in a map hierarchy. At successive levels of the hierarchy the purpose stated initially as the intention of the root map is further refined.

- At any given level of the hierarchy, the multi-facetted dimension is based on the *bundle, thread* and *multi-path* topologies. Bundle and thread introduce local faceting in the sense that they allow to represent the different ways for achieving an intention directly. Multi-path introduces global faceting by representing different combinations of intentions and strategies to achieve a given map intention. Any path from Start to Stop represents one way of achieving the map intention, therefore the purpose represented in this map.

Adapting the Purpose to the Situation at Hand

Since a map captures a full range of facets of a main purpose, the adaptation issue is of determining which facets and which combination of facets are relevant to situation at hand. One can think of two kinds to adaptation:

- *Design time adaptation* permits a selection of a combination of facets that results in only one path from Start to Stop.

- *Run time adaptation* allows to leave a large degree of variability in the adapted map and the desired facets can then be selected dynamically at enactment time of the system.

We believe that is possible for business people to perform this adaptation. This is because a knowledge of the business characteristics and an analysis based on these is enough to make the adaptation decision. To illustrate this aspect, we perform pay-off analysis on M_{bc2} (Fig. 3b). The facets that form part of the adapted map are determined by an analysis of the benefits that accrue from facets standing alone and in combination with other related facets.

To adapt section bc2 of the ESM root map (Fig.3a), one has to decide on how electricity should be measured and how the financial counterpart should be obtained. This leads to selecting the appropriate facets and facet combinations of the map M_{bc2} presented in Fig.3b. Each facet selection has however, a payoff that can be analysed in the view of its combination to another one. The pay-off analysis for M_{bc2} facets is summarized in the Table 3 below.

Let us consider the case where it is necessary to get financial counterparts both contract based and on consumption. The table shows that remote readings are a cost effective way to handle electricity measurement in both cases. Indeed, it is real time and therefore, adapted to payment on consumption. Besides, the cost of installing remote readers can be included in the contract prices and recovered in the long term. However, the payoff table also says that remote reading, as it is automated, is not fully reliable and should be double-checked, e.g. by using substation inspection. One possible adaptation of section bc2 is then to keep the facets ab2 and ab4 along with bc1 and bc2 of M_{bc2}.

In addition to the electricity project (Rolland, 1999b) used in this section, maps have been used in several large industrial projects; for example, to represent the multi-purpose of an ERP system (Rolland, 2001) and to align its functionalities to the specific needs of an organisation (Rolland, 2006) as well as to support organisational changes required by the harmonisation of

Table 3. Pay-off summary

		Get financial counterpart	
		Contract based	On consumption
Measure electricity consumption	Meter reading by meter reader	Can be envisaged at sustainable cost if visits are achieved at a low frequency e.g. (once or twice a year)	Excluded because too difficult to organise all visits at the required pace.
	Remote reading	Cost effective combination that can be done in real time. However, remote reading is not completely secure. A complementary check of electricity measurement is thus needed, e.g. by meter reader, or by substation inspection.	
	Semi-remote reading	Cost effectiveness is a linear function of the number of contracts per cluster of semi-remote reader.	Very costly if the number of customers paying on consumption, per cluster of remote reader is low.
	Substation inspection	Only possible if the connected meter readers relate to single contract. Otherwise, calls for individual reading.	Cost effective way to handle the verification of consumers invoiced by remote reading clustered on the same substation.

an upgraded information system in the different branches of a company across Europe (Rolland, 2004).

Conclusion

In this chapter we *first* argued that it is necessary to go beyond the traditional way of conceptualising an envisioned information system in order to understand and model its purpose. The hope is that more acceptable systems will be developed in the future. Goal-driven approaches proved to be well suited for capturing the rationale of the system To-Be and have been discussed in this chapter. Beyond this, we have seen that there are some other advantages:

- Goals bridge the gap between organizational strategic objectives and system conceptualisation thus providing a conceptual link between the system and its organisational context;

- AND/OR graphs provide pre-traceability between high level strategic concerns and low level technical constraints, therefore facilitating the propagation of business changes onto system functionalities;

- ORed goals introduce explicitly design choices that can be discussed, negotiated and decided upon;

- ANDed goals facilitate the decomposition of high level goals into more tactical goals and thus, ease the discovery of system requirements;

- Relationships between goals and concepts such as objects, events, operations etc. traditionally used in conceptual modelling facilitates the mapping of goal graphs onto conceptual schemas

The chapter *then* argued that goal-driven approaches are now facing the challenge of forthcoming multi-purpose systems, i.e. systems that incorporate variability in the functionality they provide and will be able to self adapt to the situation at hand. The intention/strategy maps have been introduced and discussed as an example of goal model that has been conceived to meet the aforementioned challenge. It was showed that:

- The map expression provides a synthetic view of variability in a relatively easy to understand way. Variations are revealed by the alternative strategies and alternative paths available in the map. The former capture local faceting (different ways to achieve a goal) whereas the latter provide global faceting (different combinations of goals and strategies to attain a goal).

- The complexity of the multi-purpose of an information system requires the use of a refinement mechanism. Using maps, the multi-purpose is captured through a hierarchy of maps, thus allowing a progressive understanding of variability at different levels of granularity;

- Variations are then, revealed in two ways, by the gradual movement down the different levels of a map hierarchy, and by the alternative strategies/paths available at a given map level.

- Product variations as shown with the ESM map, express the multi purpose behind systems. Their expression relates more closely to the organizational stakeholders as different from system developers. Yet, this expression acts as a specification of what the new system should achieve.

References

Antòn, A. I., & Potts, C. (1998). The use of goals to surface requirements for evolving systems. *International Conference on Software Engineering (ICSE '98),* Kyoto, Japan, (pp. 157-166).

Antòn, A. I., Carter, R., Dagnino, A., Dempster, J., & Siege, D. F. (2001). Deriving Goals from a Use-Case Based Requirements Specification. *Requirements Engineering Journal, 6,* 63-73.

Ackoff, R. L., & Emery, R. E. (1972). *On purposeful systems,* Aldine-Atherton, Chicago.

Bachmann, F., & Bass, L. (2001). Managing variability in software architecture. *ACM Press,* NY, USA.

Boehm, B., Bose, P., Horowitz, E., & Lee, M. J. (1994). Software requirements as negotiated win conditions. In *1st International Conference on Requirements Engineering* (pp. 74-83), USA.

Bosch, J., & Svahnberg, M. (2001). Variability Issues in Software Product Lines. *4th International Workshop on Product Family Engineering (PEE-4),* Bilbao, Spain.

Bubenko, J., Rolland, C., Loucopoulos, P., & de Antònellis, V. (1994). Facilitating fuzzy to formal requirements modelling. In *IEEE 1st Conference on Requirements Enginering, ICRE'94* (pp. 154-158).

Chung, K. L., Nixon, B. A., Yu, E., & Mylopoulos, J. (2000). Non- Functional Requirements in Software Engineering. *Kluwer Academic Publishers* (pp. 440).

Cockburn, A. (1995). *Structuring use cases with goals* (Tech. Rep). Human and Technology, 7691 Dell Rd, , Salt Lake City, UT 84121, HaT.TR.95.1.

Dano, B., Briand, H., & Barbier, F. (1997). A use case driven requirements engineering process. *In 3rd IEEE International Symposium On Requirements Engineering RE'97,* Antapolis, Maryland, USA.

Dardenne, A., Lamsweerde, A. V., & Fickas, S. (1993). Goal-directed Requirements Acquisition. *Science of Computer Programming, 20,* Elsevier, 3-50.

Darimont, R., van Lamsweerde, A., & Letier, E. (1998). Managing Conflicts in Goal-Driven Requirements Engineering. *IEEE Transactions on Software Engineering, 24*(11), 908-926.

Dubois, E., Yu, E., & Pettot, M. (1998), From early to late formal requirements: a process-control case study. In *Proc. IWSSD'98- 9th International Workshop on software Specification and design* (pp. 34-42). IEEE CS Press.

Dubois, E., Hagelstein, J., & Rifaut, A. (1989). Formal Requirements Engineering with ERAE. *Philips Journal of Research, 43*(4).

Easterbrook, S. M. (1994). Resolving Requirements Conflicts with Computer-Supported Negotiation. In M. Jirotka & J. Goguen (Eds.), *Requirements Engineering: Social and Technical Issues* (pp. 41-65), London: Academic Press.

European Software Institute (1996). *European User Survey Analysis.* Report USV_EUR 2.1, ESPITI Project.

Gotel, O., & Finkelstein, A. (1994). Modelling the contribution structure underlying requirements. In *1st Int. Workshop on Requirements Engineering: Foundation of Software Quality,* Utrech, Netherlands.

Halmans, J. (2003). Communicating the variability of a software product family to customers. *Software and System Modeling,* Springer-Verlag.

Haumer, P., Pohl, K., & Weidenhaupt, K. (1998). Requirements elicitation and validation with real world scenes. *IEEE Transactions on Software Engineering, Special Issue on Scenario Management,* In M. Jarke, R. Kurki-Suonio (Eds.), *24*(12), 1036-1054.

Hoh, P. (2002). Multi-Criteria Preference Analysis for Systematic Requirements Negotiation. In *26th Annual International Computer Software and Applications Conference* (pp. 887), Oxford, England.

Hui, B., Liaskos, S., & Mylopoulos, J. (2003). Requirements Analysis for Customizable Software: A Goals-Skills-Preferences Framework. *In IEEE Conference on Requirements Engineering* (pp. 117-126), Monterey Bay, USA.

Ivankina, E., & Salinesi, C. (2004). An Approach to Guide Requirement Elicitation by Analysing the Causes and Consequences of Threats. *In 14th*

European - Japanese Conference on Information Modelling and Knowledge Bases, Skövde, Sweden.

Jackson, M. (1995). Software Requirements & Specifications – a Lexicon of Practice, Principles and Prejudices. *ACM Press.* Addison-Wesley.

Jacobson, I. (1995). The Use case construct in object-oriented software engineering. In J. M. Carroll (Ed.), *Scenario-Based Design: Envisioning Work and Technology in System Development* (pp. 309-336).

Johnson, J. (1995). Chaos: the Dollar Drain of IT project Failures. *Application Development Trends,* 41-47.

Kaindl, H. (2000). A design process based on a model combining scenarios with goals and functions. *IEEE Trans. on Systems, Man and Cybernetic, 30*(5), 537-551.

Kang, K., Cohen, S., Hess, J., Novak, W., & Peterson, A. (1990). *Feature-Oriented Domain analysis (FODA) Feasibility Study (Tech. Rep. CMU/ SEI-90-TR-21),* Pittsburgh, PA, Software Engineering Institute, Carnegie Mellon University.

Karlsson, J., Olsson, S., & Ryan, K. (1997). Improved Practical Support for Large-scale Requirements Prioritizing. *Journal of Requirements Engineering,* Springer-Verlag, 51-60.

Lamsweerde, A. V., Dardenne, B., Delcourt, &Dubisy, F(1991). The KAOS project: knowledge acquisition in automated specification of software. *Proc. AAAI Spring Symp. Series, Track: "Design of Composite Systems",* (pp. 59-62), Stanford University.

Lamsweerde, A. V. (2001). Goal-oriented requirements engineering: a guided tour. In *RE'01 International Joint Conference on Requirements Engineering* (pp. 249-263), Toronto.

Lamsweerde, A. V., & Letier, E. (2000). Handling obstacles in goal-oriented requirements engineering. *IEEE Transactions on Software Engineering, Special Issue on Exception Handling, 26*(10), 978-1005.

Lamsweerde, A. V., & Willemet, L. (1998). Inferring declarative requirements specifications from operational scenarios. *In IEEE Transactions on Software Engineering, Special Issue on Scenario Management. 24*(12), 1089-1114.

Lee, S. P. (1997). Issues in requirements engineering of object-oriented information system: a review. *Malaysian Journal of computer Science, 10*(2).

Leite, J. C. S., Rossi, G., Balaguer, F., Maiorana, A., Kaplan, G., Hadad, G., & Oliveros, A. (1997). Enhancing a requirements baseline with scenarios. *In 3rd IEEE International Symposium On Requirements Engineering RE'97* (pp. 44-53), Antapolis, Maryland.

Letier, E. (2001). *Reasoning about agents in goal-oriented requirements engineering.* Ph. D. Thesis, University of Louvain.

Loucopoulos, P., Kavakli, V., & Prakas, N. (1997). Using the EKD approach, the modelling component. *ELEKTRA project internal report.*

Loucopoulos, P. (1994). The f³ (from fuzzy to formal) view on requirements engineering. *Ingénierie des systèmes d'information, 2*(6), 639-655.

META Group (2003). Research on Requirements Realization and Relevance, *report.*

Moisiadis, F. (2002). The Fundamentals of Prioritising Requirements Systems Engineering. *Test & Evaluation Conference,* Sydney, Australia.

Mostow, J. (1985). Towards better models of the design process. *AI Magazine, 6,* 44-57.

Mylopoulos, J., Chung, K. L., & Yu, E. (1999). From object-oriented to goal-oriented requirements analysis. *Communications of the ACM, 42*(1), 31-37.

Mylopoulos, J., Chung, K. L., & Nixon, B. A. (1992). Representing and using non- functional requirements: a process-oriented approach. *In IEEE Transactions on Software Engineering, Special Issue on Knowledge Representation and Reasoning in Software Development 18*(6), 483-497.

Nilsson, N. J. (1971) *Problem Solving Methods in Artificial Intelligence.* McGraw Hill.

Nuseibeh, B., Kramer, J., & Finkelstein, A. (1994). A framework for expressing the relationships between multiple views in requirements specification. *In IEEE Transactions on Software Engineering, 20,* 760-773.

Pohl, K., & Haumer, P. (1997). Modelling contextual information about scenarios. *Proceedings of the Third International Workshop on Requirements Engineering: Foundations of Software Quality REFSQ'97* (pp. 187-204), Barcelona, Spain.

Pohl, K. (1996). Process centred requirements engineering. J. Wiley and Sons Ltd.

Potts, C. (1995). Using schematic scenarios to understand user needs. *ACM Symposium on Designing interactive Systems:Processes, Practices and Techniques,* University of Michigan, USA.

Potts, C., Takahashi, K., & Antòn, A. I. (1994). Inquiry-based requirements analysis. *In IEEE Software 11*(2), 21-32.

Ramesh, B., Powers, T., Stubbs, C., & Edwards, M. (1995). Implementing requirements traceability: a case study. *In Proceedings of the 2nd Symposium on Requirements Engineering (RE'95)* (pp. 89-95), UK.

Robinson, W.N., & Volkov, S. (1998). Supporting the Negotiation Life-Cycle. *Communications of the ACM,* 95-102.

Robinson, W. N., & Volcov, S. (1996). Conflict Oriented Requirements Restructuring. *Working Paper CIS-96-15.*

Robinson, W. N. (1989). Integrating multiple specifications using domain goals. *Proc. IWSSD-5 - 5th Intl. Workshop on Software Specification and Design* (pp. 219-225), *IEEE.*

Rolland, C. (2006) *Aligning Business and System Functionality Through Model Matching,* Systèmes d'Information et Management (SIM), Editions ESKA.

Rolland, C., Salinesi, C. &Etien, A. (2004). Eliciting Gaps in Requirements Change. *Requirement Engineering Journal, 9,* 1-15.

Rolland, C., & Prakash, N (2001). Matching ERP System Functionality to Customer Requirements. *In Procs of the 5th IEEE International Symposium on Requirements Engineering,* Toronto, Canada. August 27-31.

Rolland, C., & Prakash, N. (2000). Bridging the gap between Organizational needs and ERP functionality. *Requirements Engineering journal 5.*

Rolland, C., Grosz, G., & Kla, R. (1999a). Experience with goal-scenario coupling in requirements engineering. *In Proceedings of the Fourth IEEE International Symposium on Requirements Engineering,* Limerik, Ireland

Rolland, C., Prakash, N., & Benjamen, A. (1999b). A Multi-Model View of Process Modelling. *Requirements Engineering Journal (REJ),* 169-187.

Rolland, C., Souveyet, C., & Ben Achour, C. (1998). Guiding goal modelling using scenarios. *IEEE Transactions on Software Engineering,* Special Issue on Scenario Management, *24*(12).

Ross, D. T., & Schoman, K.E. (1977). Structured Analysis for Requirements Definition. *IEEE Transactions on Software Engineering, 3*(1), 6-15.

Sommerville, I., & Sawyer, P. (1997). Requirements engineering. *Worldwide Series in Computer Science,* Wiley.

Standish Group (1995). The Chaos. *Standish Group Internal Report.*

Sutcliffe, A. G, & Minocha, S (1999a). Analyzing Socio-Technical System Requirements. *CREWS project Report* 98-37.

Sutcliffe, A. G., Galliers, J., Minocha, S. (1999b). Human Errors and System Requirements. *International Symposium on Requirements Engineering, RE'1999.* Limerick, Ireland.

Sutcliffe, A. G., Maiden, N. A., Minocha, S., & Darrel, M. (1998). Supporting scenario-based requirements engineering. *IEEE Trans. Software Engineering 24*(12), 1072-1088.

van Gurp, J., Bosch, J., & Svahnberg, M. (2001). On the notion of variability in Software Product Lines. *In Procs of the Working IEEE/IFIP Conference on Software architecture.*

van Gurp, J. (2000). *Variability in Software Systems, the key to Software Reuse.* Licentiate Thesis, University of Groningen, The Netherlands.

Yu, E. (1997). Towards Modelling and Reasoning Support for Early-Phase Requirements Engineering. *In Procs of the 3rd IEEE International Symposium on Requirements Engineering (RE'97).*

Yu, E. (1994). *Modelling strategic relationships for process reengineering.* Ph.D. Thesis, Dept. Computer Science, University of Toronto.

Chapter III

Integrated Goal, Data and Process Modeling:
From TEMPORA to Model-Generated Work-Places

John Krogstie, Norwegian University of Science and Technology, Norway

Abstract

In organizations, goals and rules on different levels ranging from visions, to strategies, tactics, and operational goals have been expressed for a long time. In the IS-field, the interest on goals and rules has come from two directions. A) Business goals for use in requirements specification. B) Rule-based (expert) systems, focusing on automation of rule-execution. We were already 15 years ago involved in an EU-project Tempora together with Benkt Wangler and others where we tried to combine these worlds. Although able to produce interesting prototypes, the approaches we used then proved to be difficult to scale to an industrial setting. 15 years later we are involved in taking these approaches to a new level. We will in this paper present our approach to combining goal, data, resource and process modeling, in the support of the development and user-led evolution of what we term Model-generated Workplaces (MGWP), with an emphasis on the use of goal and rule-modeling in combination with process modeling. A case study extending an ongoing industrial trial of production rule systems is provided to illustrate some of the benefits of the approach.

Introduction

Goal-oriented modeling focuses on goals and rules. A *rule* is something which influences the actions of a set of actors. A rule is either a rule of necessity or a deontic rule (Wieringa, 1989). A rule of necessity is a rule that must always be satisfied. A deontic rule is a rule which is only socially agreed among a set of persons and organizations. A deontic rule can thus be violated without redefining the terms in the rule. A deontic rule can be classified as being an obligation, a recommendation, permission, a discouragement, or a prohibition (Krogstie and Sindre, 1996).

The general structure of a rule is

"if *condition* then *expression*"

where *condition* is descriptive, indicating the scope of the rule by designating the conditions in which the rule apply, and the *expression* is prescriptive. According to Twining & Miers (1982) any rule, however expressed, can be analyzed and restated as a compound conditional statement of this form.

Representing knowledge by means of rules is not a novel idea. According to (Davis & King, 1977), production systems were first proposed as a general computational mechanism by Post in 1943. Today, goals and rules are used for knowledge representation in a wide variety of applications.

Several advantages have been experienced with a declarative, rule-based approach to information systems modeling (Krogstie and Sindre, 1996):

- Problem-orientation. The representation of business rules declaratively is independent of what they are used for and how they will be implemented. With an explicit specification of assumptions, rules, and constraints, the analyst has freedom from technical considerations to reason about application problems. This freedom is even more important for the communication with the stakeholders with a non-technical background.

- Maintenance: A declarative approach makes possible a one place representation of the rules, which is a great advantage when it comes to the maintainability of the specification and system.

- Knowledge enhancement: The rules used in an organization, and as such in a supporting computerized information system (CIS), are not always explicitly given. In the words of Stamper (1987) ¨Every organization, in as far as it is organized, acts as though its members were conforming to a set of rules only a *few of which may be explicit* . This has inspired certain researchers to look upon CIS specification as a process of rule reconstruction, i.e. the goal is not only to represent and support rules that are already known, but also to uncover de facto and implicit rules which are not yet part of a shared organizational reality, in addition to the construction of new, possibly more appropriate ones.

On the other hand, several problems have been observed when using a simple rule-format.

- Every statement must be either true or false, there is nothing in between.

- It is usually not possible to distinguish between rules of necessity and deontic rules

- In many goal and rule modeling languages it is not possible to specify who the rules apply to.

- Formal rule languages have the advantage of eliminating ambiguity. However, this does not mean that rule based models are easy to understand. There are two problems with the comprehension of such models, both the comprehension of single rules, and the comprehension of the whole rule-base. Whereas the traditional operational models (e.g. process models) have decomposition and modularization facilities which make it possible to view a system at various levels of abstraction and to navigate in a hierarchical structure, rule models are usually flat. With many rules such a model soon becomes difficult to grasp, even if each rule should be understandable in itself. They are also seldom linked to other models of the organization used to understand and develop the information systems, such as data and process models.

- A general problem is that a set of rules is either consistent or inconsistent. On the other hand, human organizations may often have more or less contradictory rules, and have to be able to deal with this.

We will in the next section give an overview of related work in the area. We will then present a case study in the realm of student loan support, where one are looking at automating parts of the case processing using current rule engine technology. The experiences from this case is evaluated using SEQUAL, a semiotic quality framework (Krogstie, Sindre & Jørgensen, 2006), and we outline how a more integrated modeling approach can address some of the weaknesses identified.

Related Work

Goals and rules have been used for knowledge representation in a wide variety of applications. An early example was the so-called expert-systems, which received great interest in the eighties. Unfortunately, these systems did not scale sufficiently well for large-scale general industrial applications. Lately, these approaches has reappeared and are in fact now able to deal with the processing of large databases (e.g. experiences with tools like Blaze Advisor www.fairisaac.com/rules , which is an extension of the Nexpert Object system that goes back to the late eighties have shown this. See http://www.brcommunity.org for an overview of current industrial solutions on this marked). Although being an improvement as for efficiency, they still have limited internal structuring among rules, and few explicit links to the other models underlying large industrial information systems. They seldom differentiate between deontic rules and rules of necessity, although this might be changing after the development of the OMG SBVR-standard which focuses on deontic rules (OMG, 2006). On the other hand, since the way of representing deontic notions in SBVR is not executable, it is possible that theses aspects will be ignored by vendors of rule-based solutions such as Blaze Advisor since these largely focus on the execution of formal rules, and not the representation of more high-level strategic and tactical aspects of the organization.

On the other hand, high-level rules *are* the focus on application of goal-oriented modeling in the field of requirements specification. Over the last 15 years, a large number of these approaches have been developed, as summarized in (Kavakli & Loucopoulos, 2005). They focus on different parts of requirements specification work, including

- Understanding the current organizational situation
- Understanding the need for change

- Providing the deliberation context of the RE process
- Relating business goals to functional and non-functional system components
- Validating system specifications against stakeholder goals

The existing approaches do not bridge the areas of requirements specification and rule-based systems. Few differentiate between deontic rules and rules of necessity. A notable contribution of these techniques, are the structuring of goals and rules in hierarchies and networks. Some of the approaches also link rules to other models, but with limited support of following up these links in the running system. An early example of such an approach was Tempora (Loucopoulos et al, 1991) which was an ESPRIT-3 project that finished in 1994. It aimed at creating an environment for the development of complex application systems. The underlying idea was that development of a CIS should be viewed as developing the rule-base of an organization, which is used throughout development and evolution of the system. Tempora had three closely interrelated Languages for conceptual modeling. ERT being an extension of the ER language, PID being an extension of the DFD in the SA/RT-tradition, and ERL, a formal language for expressing the rules of an organization, which was also extended with deontic notions. The basic modeling construct of ERT where: Entity classes, relationship classes, and value classes. The language also contains the most usual construct from semantic data modeling, such as generalization and aggregation, and derived entities and relationships, as well as some extension for temporal aspects particular to ERT. It also has a grouping mechanism to enhance the visual abstraction possibilities of ERT models. The PID language is used to specify processes and their interaction in a formal way. The basic modeling constructs were processes, ERT-views being links to an ERT-model, external agents, flows (both control and data flows), ports to depict logical grouping of flows as they enter or leave processes, and timers, acting as either clocks or delays.

A way to combine models in these languages as a basis for generating prototypes where developed (Krogstie et al, 1991, Lindland & Krogstie, 1993). In addition to linking PID to ERT-models and ERL-rules to ERT-models and PIDs, one had the possibility of relating rules in rule hierarchies. The relationships available for this in Tempora were (McBrien et al, 1994):

- Refers-to: Used to link rules where definitions or the introduction of a necessary situation can be found in another rule.
- Necessitates and motivates: Used to create goal-hierarchies.
- Overrules and suspends: These deals with exceptions.

As will be described below, we have worked further based on these ideas in connection to develop the modeling language used as a basis for the MGWP-approach EEML (Krogstie & Jørgensen, 2004).

Case Study: Loan Administration System

In Norway, one attempt to make it possible for everyone with the appropriate skills and competence to afford pursuing higher studies. In connection to this, a specific organization within the public sector, State Education Loan Fund (Statens Lånekasse) is established to manage student financing. This involves accepting application for student financing, evaluating these, and ensuring loans are paid back according to the regulations. Whereas the Parliament decides the overall laws for the area, the relevant department (currently named the 'Knowledge Department') produces more detailed regulations. The guidelines for how to follow-up of the laws and regulations are further detailed by experts in the Loan Fund to be followed in case processing.

One is currently testing out a new solution for the Loan Fund in a Proof of Concept-study (PoC), where the production rules used in the case processing are to be represented in a rule engine (Blaze Advisor). Several goals for the representation of rules explicit have been identified.

a.   Support a quick implementation of new rules, as these are changed regularly through the political process.

b.   Be able to analyze the consequences of proposed changes in the laws and regulations (with the politicians and department officials)

c.   Make it easier to maintain and evolution of the rule base, including the more detailed internal rules.

d.   Support the education and training of the employees at the Loan Fund.

In connection to the PoC, areas a and c were chosen as the main targets, whereas we are here also investigating areas b and d.

The architecture of the approach is to have the administrative case-processing system to be in charge of the overall workflow, calling the rule engine on a case by case basis. It is possible to call the rule engine with incomplete data, in which case it gives an overview of the lacking data. The case processing system then have to support getting the missing data, either from internal or external data sources, before calling the rule engine again. We will below evaluate the chosen approach relative to the above mentioned goals, but first we will describe the chosen evaluation approach.

Evaluation Framework

There are a number of approaches and frameworks available for evaluating modeling approaches (including models, modeling languages, and modeling tools). Early proposals for quality goals for conceptual models and requirement specifications as summarized by Davis (Davis, 1993) included many useful aspects, but unfortunately in the form of unsystematic lists (Lindland, 1994). They are also often restricted in the kind of models they regard (e.g. requirements specifications (Davis, 1993)) or the modeling language (e.g. ER-models (Moody, 1994) or process models (Sedera, Rosemann, and Doebli 2003)). Few have specifically targeted goal-modeling. Another limitation of many approaches to evaluating modeling languages, is that they focus almost entirely on the expressiveness of the language (e.g. relative to some ontology, such as Bunge-Wand-Weber (Wand and Weber, 1993)). We have earlier developed a more comprehensive and generic framework for evaluating modeling approaches, called SEQUAL (Krogstie, Sindre & Jørgensen, 2006). SEQUAL has three unique properties:

- It distinguishes between goals and means by separating what you are trying to achieve from how to achieve it.

- It is closely linked to linguistic and semiotic concepts. In particular, the core of the framework including the discussion on syntax, semantics, and pragmatics is parallel to the use of these terms in the semiotic theory of Morris (see e.g. (Nöth, 1990) for an introduction).

- It is based on a constructivistic world-view, recognizing that models are usually created as part of a dialogue between the participants involved in modeling, whose knowledge of the modeling domain and potentially the domain itself changes as modeling takes place.

We have used the SEQUAL framework to evaluate the current results of the PoC, and also the applicability of this approach to the full set of goals. The main concepts of the framework and their relationships are shown in Fig. 1 and are explained below. Quality has been defined referring to the correspondence between statements belonging to the following sets:

Figure 1. SEQUAL: Framework for discussing the quality of models

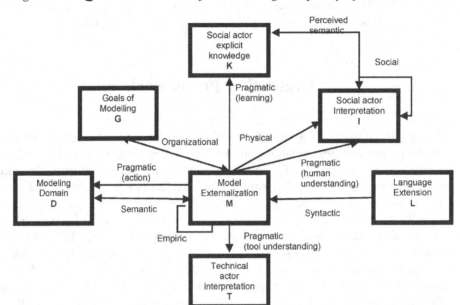

- G, the goals of the modeling task.
- L, the language extension, i.e., the set of all statements that are possible to make according to the graphemes, vocabulary, and syntax of the modeling languages used.
- D, the domain, i.e., the set of all statements that can be stated about the situation at hand.
- M, the externalized model itself.
- K, the relevant explicit knowledge of those being involved in modeling.
- I, the social actor interpretation, i.e., the set of all statements that the audience thinks that an externalized model consists of.
- T, the technical actor interpretation, i.e., the statements in the model as 'interpreted' by modeling tools.

The main quality types are indicated by solid lines between the sets, and are described briefly below:

- Physical quality: The basic quality goal is that the externalized model M is available for the audience.

- Empirical quality deals with predictable error frequencies when a model is read or written by different users, coding (e.g. shapes of boxes) and HCI-ergonomics for documentation and modeling-tools. For instance, graph layout to avoid crossing lines in a model is a mean to address the empirical quality of a model.

- Syntactic quality is the correspondence between the model M and the language extension L.

- Semantic quality is the correspondence between the model M and the domain D. This includes validity and completeness.

- Perceived semantic quality is the similar correspondence between the audience interpretation I of a model M and his or hers current knowledge K of the domain D.

- Pragmatic quality is the correspondence between the model M and the audience's interpretation and application of it (I). We differentiate between social pragmatic quality (to what extent people understand and are able to use the models) and technical pragmatic quality (to what extent tools can be made that interpret the models). In addition, we focus under pragmatic quality on the extent that the participants after interpreting the model learn based on the model and that the audience after interpreting the model and learning from it are able to change the domain (preferably in a positive direction relative to the goal of modeling).

- The goal defined for social quality is agreement among audience members' interpretations I.

- The organizational quality of the model relates to that all statements in the model contribute to fulfilling the goals of modeling (organizational goal validity), and that all the goals of modeling are addressed through the model (organizational goal completeness).

Language quality relates the modeling language used to the other sets. Six quality areas for language quality are identified, with aspects related to both the language meta-model and the notation as illustrated in Fig. 2.

- Domain appropriateness. This relates the language and the domain. Ideally, the conceptual basis must be powerful enough to express anything in the domain, not having what (Wand & Weber, 1993) terms construct deficit. On the other hand, you should not be able to express things that are not in the domain, i.e. what is termed construct excess (Wand & Weber, 1993). Domain appropriateness is primarily a mean to achieve semantic quality.

Figure 2. Language quality in SEQUAL

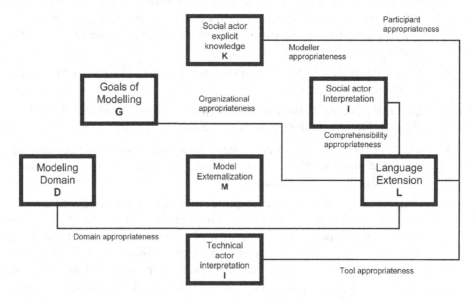

- Participant appropriateness relates the social actors' explicit knowledge to the language. Do the participants have the necessary knowledge of the modeling language to understand the models created in the language. Participant appropriateness is primarily a mean to achieve pragmatic quality.

- Modeler appropriateness: This area relates the language extension to the participant knowledge. The goal is that there are no statements in the explicit knowledge of the modeler that cannot be expressed in the language. Modeler appropriateness is primarily a mean to achieve semantic quality.

- Comprehensibility appropriateness relates the language to the social actor interpretation. The goal is that the participants in the modeling effort using the language understand all the possible statements of the language. Comprehensibility appropriateness is primarily a mean to achieve empirical and pragmatic quality.

- Tool appropriateness relates the language to the technical audience interpretations. For tool interpretation, it is especially important that the language lend itself to automatic reasoning. This requires formality (i.e. both formal syntax and semantics being operational and/or logical), but formality is not necessarily enough, since the reasoning must also be efficient to be of practical use. This is covered by what we term analyzability (to exploit any mathematical semantics) and executability (to exploit any operational semantics). Different aspects of tool appropriateness are means to achieve syntactic, semantic and pragmatic quality (through formal syntax, mathematical semantics, and operational semantics).

- Organizational appropriateness relates the language to standards and other organizational needs within the organizational context of modeling. These are means to support organizational quality.

Evaluation of Current Approach to Loan Administration System

In connection to the case study the sets can be described as follows:

Model M: The model underlying the total system can be divided in three

- Data model (as a basis for the database-application, but also as basis for data definitions used in the case processing system and rule engine)
- Process model (as a basis for the case processing system called SAM)
- Rule model (as a basis for the rule engine)

The rule model can be looked upon as four interrelated models:

- The laws and regulation as they are written in juridical terms. Here we look upon this as part of the domain (see below).
- Rule documentation. A word-document for communication of rules to people in the loan fund. Links are provided here to the relevant laws and regulations and to the detailed implementation in the rule engine.
- The rules as implemented in the rule engine (Blaze Advisor). Not all rules are implemented (these are only found in the rule documentation). All implementable rules in the documentation match 1:1 to rules in Blaze Advisor, but also more technically oriented rules are included in the rule engine.
- Some rules are made available through a web interface (called RMA – Rule Maintenance Application) so they can be changed by domain experts in the loan fund directly.

The models in 3 and 4 relates to the same rule repository.

Finally, the implementation in Blaze Advisor can be looked upon as three models:

- Rule-flows, a simple decomposable process modeling notations to illustrate the implementation structure of rule sets.

- Rule model: per rule/rule set (rules are put in rule sets that are evaluated together).

- Data model internally in Blaze Advisor that needs to be consistent with the data model in SAM. Can be imported automatically based on the data-model used there.

Domain D: As indicated above, this is primarily described through the laws and regulation for study financing. Whereas the Parliament decides the overall laws for the area, the education department produces more detailed regulations. The guidelines for how to follow-up of the laws and regulations are further detailed by experts in the Loan Fund. Also other relevant laws and regulations are part of the domain. Although the domain seems to be fully externally given, in practice a large number of the resulting rules to follow are based on internal deliberations within the Loan Fund, thus there is a need to support quick changes, and not only the yearly revisions coming from parliament.

In connection to the audience of the model, two main roles are identified: Rule modeler and rule interpreter

Rule modeler (as a basis for K): The rules were modeled in Blaze Advisor by professional rule designers and loan fund professionals in cooperation. For defined changes the loan fund professionals could do this through the RMA.

Rule interpreter (vs. I): The rules in Blaze were to be understood by those involved in the modeling. All loan fund personal were to be able to understand the rule documentation. RMA-rules being easier to understand were to be available for all. Through rule execution, texts including the reasoning of the decision made were produced, which are meant to be understandable by everyone.

Language used for rule modeling was partly the proprietary rule language SRL (Structured Rule Language) and rule-flows both found in Blaze Advisor.

Tool: Blaze Advisor, Word.

Based on SEQUAL, we looked at the following areas in the evaluation relative to the goals for the representation of rules highlighted above

- Quality of the rule modeling language
- Quality of the existing rule model

Quality of Modeling Language

- Domain appropriateness: It was possible to express all the execution rules in the PoC formally in SRL. In some cases one had to implement parts of these in functions being programmed procedurally, but this was an exception. More generally, one can evaluate the language relative to emergent standards for rule languages. In connection to this there are a number of initiatives particularly within OMG and W3C
    - OMG's PRR – Production Rule Representation (OMG, 2003)) – this group is working towards a proposal for a standard early 2007 which Blaze expect to support. The standard is focused on the management of production rule sets e.g. the kinds of rules that execute in Blaze Advisor, JRules etc.

    - W3C's RIF– Rule Interchange Format (W3C, 2005) - this standard has a very large number of companies involved and is trying to decide how much detail about the rules to manage in the interchange format. This is being coordinated with PRR .This would allow the interchange format for PRR to be RIF.

    - OMG's SBVR – Semantics of Business Vocabularies and Rules (OMG, 2006) - this standard is supposedly closing in on a final specification, but it is struggling to resolve large numbers of open issues. It is a standard designed to manage source rules and is a very thorough/complex standard. The linkage from SBVR to PRR has yet to be defined, but both teams are working on the assumption that traceability will be the key, rather than transformation.

Whereas Blaze will probably support PRR rules, one does not support many aspects of SBVR rules including support of deontic operators. For more high-level rules this is an important limitation. Higher level rules are specifically important for a broader understanding and discussion on rules as mandated by goal b and d above.

- Modeler appropriateness: The loan fund professionals were together with rule designers able to express the rules in SRL. Loan fund professionals were also able to use the RMA for rule maintenance.

- Participant appropriateness: SRL was only known by rule designers in external companies, and it is found that it presents a steep learning curve both for Loan Fund professionals as well as system developers internally.

- Comprehensibility appropriateness: Those closely involved in the process appeared to understand the rules, especially since navigation was supported through the rule-flows. Since the execution rules ended up as a mix of English keywords and Norwegian concepts used in the data model, they are somewhat hard to comprehend. The need for the separate word-document model also acknowledges problems with the comprehension in general.

- Tool appropriateness: The tool was appropriate for rule execution, and other tests have been done supporting the scalability of the approach based on the possibility of executing the rules in the rule-base in different ways.

- Organizational appropriateness: A positive aspect here is that the language used is according to an emerging standard (PRR). More high-level organizational issues are difficult to represent.

Quality of Rule Model

- Physical quality: The rules are primarily available through the tool, which limits the availability. It is also possible to generate html-reports from the tools for wider availability, but it seems not appropriate for widespread dissemination, which is why the separate word-document is produced. RMA includes standard authorization mechanisms, ensuring that only authorized personnel can change the rules.

- Empirical quality: The rule-flow visualization is a useful way of getting an overview of the rule-base, being an improvement of just having a 'flat' rule-base.

- Syntactical quality: The word-document has currently a number of syntactic errors. The rules implemented in the rule engine are syntactically correct

- Semantic quality: All the production rules are included, but very few of the rules as expressed in the underlying laws and regulations are included directly. Also we notice that links across data, process and rule models are mostly implicit, and has to be manually checked and maintained.

- Pragmatic quality: It is relatively easy to keep an overview of the implemented rules and how they are related to the laws and regulations (through expressed meta-data). It is hard to understand the underlying intention of the rules, since this is not captured specifically.

- Social quality: On some of the detailed rules there are discussions on the appropriate interpretation of these. This does not apply to the rules and regulations itself, but rather to how they should be follow up in practice in the Loan Fund.

- Organizational quality: The approach appears to support goal a and c, and partly d, but give little support to address goal b, a more high-level discussion on the rules to have for the area. On the other hand, having the rules implemented in this way, makes it possibly to simulate different scenarios. The rule engine support that only certain rules are enforced at a certain time, thus one can easily simulate the effects of new rules (or alternatively, see how a case would be handled with a previous set of rules).

Thus whereas the approach support the implementation of business rules in a combined way with a case processing system with its underlying process model and data model, there are certain improvements possible for a more integrated representation of rules with the overall process model, data model, and goal model. We will look at an approach for supporting aspects of this in the next section.

MGWP and EEML

Building on among other the approach originally developed in Tempora, we have over the last five years been developing a model-driven approach to be able to quickly support the development of model-driven solutions both within and across networked organization (Krogstie & Jørgensen, 2004). Our main approach to achieve this is the use of model-generated work-places (MGWP), which is a working environment for the business users involved in running the business operations of the enterprise. It is a user platform that provides the graphical front-end for human users to interact with software services supporting their day-to-day professional activities.

The workplace can be tailored to meet the specific requirements of different roles or persons within an enterprise, providing customized presentation and operation views. This is achieved through model-configured and user-composable services (MUPS). These services make use of knowledge models developed in our EEML-language (Krogstie & Jørgensen, 2004) to generate business-oriented and context-aware graphical user interfaces.

We will here provide an examples on how the underlying modeling language for this approach (EEML - Extended Enterprise Modeling Language), which combines structural modeling, process modeling, goal modeling with goal hierarchies, and resource modeling is used in practice to bridge the type of goal modeling used in common requirements engineering to other modeling approaches. We will also compare this approach to the related work, both in requirements specification and rule-based systems. The focus is on how we can extend the rule modeling with goal modeling to better support goal b and d outlined in the above case-description.

The kernel EEML-concepts are shown in Fig. 3 as a simplified conceptual meta-model. The process logic is mainly expressed through nested structures of *tasks* and *decision points*. The sequencing of the tasks is expressed by the *flow* relation between decision points. Each task has an input port and an output port being decision points for modeling process logic, *Roles* are used to connect resources of various kinds (persons, organizations, information, material objects, software tools and manual tools) to the tasks. In addition, data modeling (using UML class diagrams), goal modeling and competency modeling (skill requirements and skills possessed) are supported. We will discuss specifically the goal modeling in more detail below.

In figure 4, we have included parts of the overall goal-model for this case (note that since the models are originally in Norwegian, we have here redrawn only parts of this).

The top-level goals are taken from the law on study financing (Including the need to ensure sufficient knowledge and skills in society, and because of this, that everyone should be able to pursue a higher education). All goals and rules can be expressed both informally and formally, and all kind of rules can be expressed. A deontic modality can be added to each rule (indicating if the rule is a rule of necessity, or a deontic rule i.e. an obligation, recommendations etc.). For executable rules, a formal expression of the rule can be included, as illustrated below. The relationships between rules are also deontic. An example is on the top left of the model, where it can be read that to ensure sufficient knowledge and skills in the society, it is obligatory that everyone is able to take a higher education. Note that although you will find rules at this level in the laws and regulations, the relationships between rules are not represented explicitly anywhere and have appeared through detailed discussions. Relationships between rules can also be more complex, i.e. it is the combination (and) of that one want everyone to be able to study, and that they should be able to study efficiently (so-called full-time students not having to work on the side to finance the studying) that mandate the need for study financing arrangements.

Whereas the law goes down to the level in the goal-hierarchy where it is stated that 'if little income, no interest should be paid' the detailing of this (e.g. that you need not pay interest if you are serving military duty), is taken from the departmental regulations which provide the details for the laws.

Figure 3. Conceptual meta-model of EEML

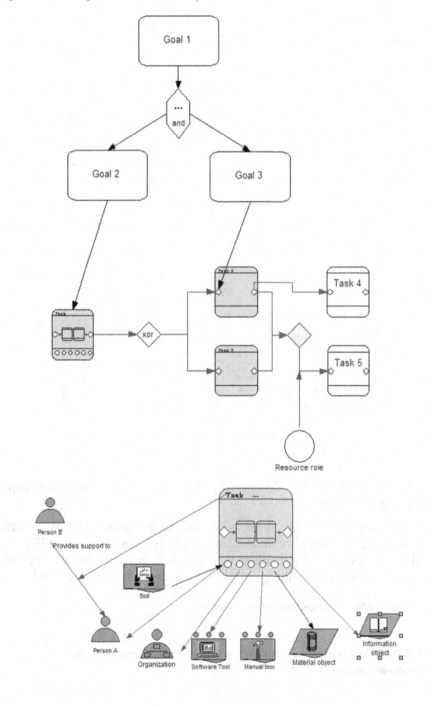

Figure 4. Part of goal model for loan fund case

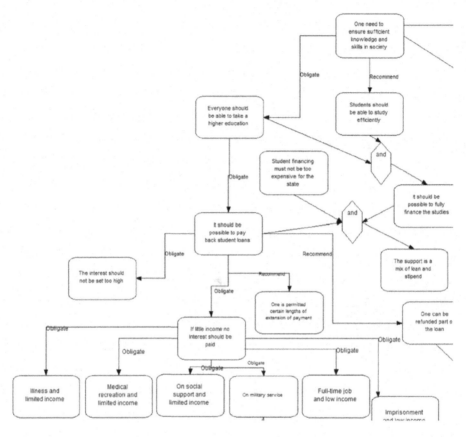

In Fig. 5, we have further decomposed this rule, into the rules used to enforce this in the Loan Fund.

The relationship between these rules and the evaluation task is as 'action rules', using the formal representation of the rule (in this case in SRL to be able to include directly in Blaze advisor). For instance the rule 'Period in application larger than three months' is expressed as follows in SRL:

rule FR.ST07.VPL01.Ingen.periode.storre.enn.3mnd

is

if (vernepliktPeriode.tilDato as a date).subtractInDays(vernepliktPeriode.fraDato) <
Rentefritaksperioden

Figure 5. Implementation of rules, linked to the process model

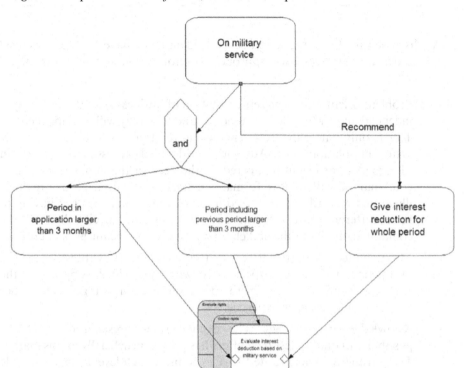

then {

    returData.merknader.add(lagMerknad("VPL01")).

    returData.returKode = Returkoder.AVSLAG as a string.

}

The task also maps to the same task in the Blaze rule-flow, but the overall-process model includes both these tasks and the other tasks in the case processing system in an integrated manner. The links to the data model is not shown. The rules at this level is influenced both by the regulation from the department (where it is stated that you will get exemption from interest if you are in the military for three months or more), but also the local rules in the loan fund, indicating that even if you only ask for say 4 months exemption, and you serve for 12 months, you will get the exemption for the full 12 months.

Conclusion

As discussed in the introduction several advantages have been experienced with a declarative, rule-based approach to information systems modeling:

- Problem-orientation: The representation of business rules declaratively is independent of what they are used for and how they will be implemented. This is only partly the experience using the traditional production rule system in isolation (Blaze Advisor). The detailed expression of the rules in SRL is to some extent hampered by the need of the implementation. A combination with a less formally defined rule language as we have illustrated with EEML is looked upon as beneficial instead of having to have different, not integrated representation, specifically for the communication with the stakeholders with a non-technical background.

- Maintenance: The benefits on this account is witnesses in the production-rule system, specifically with the added support of the RMA, although for many of the perceived needed changes to the rules one need rule designer expertise.

- Knowledge enhancement: The explicit rule-representation, and the possibility to quickly test their effect has proved beneficially in this matter. The possibility to also relate the rules to more high-level goals in the rule hierarchy is believed to enable an even broader debate on these issues.

As for the identified limitations, many of these can be addressed by EEML including:

- Every statement must be either true or false, there is nothing in between: EEML rules can be partly fulfilled.

- Possible to distinguish between rules of necessity and deontic rules: EEML rules can include deontic operators.

- In many goal and rule modeling languages it is not possible to specify who the rules apply to: EEML-rules can be explicitly related to organizational actors.

- Flat rule-bases: Development of a rule hierarchy is supported, and it is also possible to link the rules to a hierarchical process model.

- Link to other models of the organization used to understand and develop the information systems, such as data and process models: Provided in EEML.

- Support contradictory rules and goals: Possible in EEML. This is not shown in the case, but since the full range of deontic operators is also possible to use between rules, it is possible to e.g. represent that the fulfillment of one rule forbids the fulfillment of another.

Thus in addition to be instrumental for the development of a rule-based system for rule automation, the combined approach can also support goal-oriented modeling as part of requirements specification work, including

- Understanding the current organizational situation: through the overall enterprise model.

- Understanding the need for change: E.g. if there are high-level goals that are not met by the current system.

- Providing the deliberation context of the RE process: Since it is possible to change and simulate changes in the environment.

- Relating business goals to functional and non-functional system components: Relating the goals to e.g. the implemented processes of the system.

- Validating system specifications against stakeholder goals: Ensure that specification fulfill the goals of the stakeholders, making it easier to trace them.

Further work is planned to be done on this approach in parallel to the implementation of the rule engine technology in the Loan Fund. We would also like to get more experience on the approach in other domains, especially in networked organization where the goal structures emerges much quicker than in the public sector. As SVBR is standardized, we will also look at aligning the goal-modeling part of EEML to this.

References

Davis, A.M., Overmeyer, S., Jordan, K., Caruso, J.,Dandashi, F., Dinh, A., Kincaid, G., Ledeboer, G., Reynolds, P., Sitaram, P., Ta, A., &Theofanos, M. (1993) Identifying and measuring quality in a software requirements specification. In *Proceedings of the First International Software Metrics Symposium* (pp. 141-152.)

Davis, R., & King, J. (1977). An overview of production systems. In E.W. Elcock and D. Mitchie (Eds.) *Machine Intelligence* (pp. 300-332)

Kavakli, E., & Loucopoulos, P. (2005). Goal Modeling in Requirements Engineering: Analysis and critique of current methods In *Information Modeling Methods and Methodologies*, In J. Krogstie, K. Siau, and T. Halpin(Eds.) Idea Group Publishing

Krogstie, J., Seltveit, A. H, McBrien, P., & Owens, R. (1991). Information Systems Development Using a Combination of Process and Rule Based Approaches. In *Proceedings of the Third International Conference on Advanced Information Systems Engineering (CAiSE'91)*. Trondheim, Norway: Springer-Verlag

Krogstie, J., & Sindre, G. (1996). Utilizing deontic operators in information systems specifications. *Requirement Engineering Journal, 1*, 210-237.

Krogstie, J., & Jørgensen, H. D. (2004). Interactive Models for Supporting Networked Organisations. *In 16th Conference on advanced Information Systems Engineering.* Riga, Latvia: Springer Verlag.

Krogstie, J., Sindre, G., & Jørgensen, H. D. (2006). Process models representing knowledge for action: A revised quality framework. *European Journal of Information Systems 15,* 91-102

Lindland, O. I., & Krogstie, J. (1993). Validating Conceptual Models by Transformational Prototyping. *In 5th International Conference on Advanced Information Systems Engineering (CAiSE'93).* Paris, France: Springer-Verlag.

Lindland, O.I., Sindre, G., & Sølvberg, A. (1994) Understanding Quality in Conceptual Modeling, *IEEE Software 11*(2):42-49

Loucopoulos, P., McBrien, P., Schumacker, F., Theodoulidis, B., Kopanas, V., & Wangler, B. (1991) Integrating database technology, rule-based systems and temporal reasoning for effective information systems: the TEMPORA paradigm. *Journal of Information Systems 1*, 129-152

McBrien, P., Seltveit, A. H., & Wangler, B. (1994). Rule Based Specification of Information Systems, *International Conference on Information Systems and Management of Data*, Madras, India.

Moody, D. L. & Shanks, G. G. (1994) What makes a good data model? Evaluating the quality of entity relationship models, In *Proceedings of the 13th International Conference on the Entity-Relationship Approach (ER'94)*, (pp. 94-111), Manchester, England.

OMG (2003) PRR – Production Rule Representation- Request for Proposal, Retrieved January 1 2006 from http://www.omg.org/cgi-bin/doc?br/2003-9-3

OMG (2006).Semantics of Business Vocabulary and Rules Interim Specification. Retrieved January 1 2006 from http://www.omg.org/cgi-bin/doc?dtc/06/03/02

Nöth, W. (1990) *Handbook of Semiotics* Indiana University Press

Sedera, W., Rosemann, M. & Doebeli, G.(2003) A Process Modelling Success Model: Insights From A Case Study. *11th European Conference on Information Systems,* Naples, Italy

Stamper, R. (1987). Semantics. In R.J. Boland and R.A. Hirschheim (Eds.) *Critical issues in Information Systems Research* (pp. 43-78) John Wiley & Sons.

Twining, W., & Miers, D. (1982) *How to do things with rules.*Weidenfeld and Nicholson.

Wand, Y., & Weber, R. (1993). On the Ontological Expressiveness of Information Systems Analysis and Design Grammars. *Journal of Information Systems 3*(4), 217-237.

W3C (2003) RIF – Rule Interchange Format, Retrieved January 1 2006 from http://www.w3.org/2005/rules/

Wieringa, R. (1989) Three roles of conceptual models in information systems design and use. I E. Falkenberg and P. Lindgren (Eds.) *Information Systems Concepts: An In-Depth Analysis* (pp. 31-51) North-Holland, 1989.

Chapter IV

Value and Intention Based Information Systems Engineering

Paul Johannesson, The Royal Institute of Technology, Sweden

Prasad Jayaweera, University of Ruhuna, Matara, Sri Lanka

Abstract

In order to cope with increasingly complex business and IT environments, organisations need effective instruments for managing their knowledge about these environments. Essential among these instruments are models, i.e. representations of aspects of reality including the domain of work, the processes, and their context. Models come in a variety of forms, formal or informal; describing static or dynamic aspects; representing agents, data, goals, processes, or resources; focusing on business or IT aspects. A major question is how to organise and relate the different models that are needed for representing and visualising enterprises and their environments, and this issue has been addressed within the area of enterprise architecture. In this chapter, we propose a light-weight enterprise architecture framework based on linguistic theories and organizational metaphors. The concepts and entities of an organization are categorized into three groups concerning resources and resource exchanges, contracts and commitments, and authorities and roles. The activities and processes in organizations are divided into three levels based on how they affect physical, communicative and social aspects of organizations.

Introduction

A number of current trends, including globalisation, specialisation, and customisation, require enterprises and their IT systems to become ever more adaptive in order to handle changes in a complex environment. Enterprises need to be able to quickly set up networks to cope with tasks they cannot handle alone. They need to manage an environment that is constantly changing and where lead times, product life cycles, and partner relationships are shortening. In order to cope with such increasingly complex business and IT environments, organisations need effective instruments for managing their knowledge about these environments. Essential among these instruments are enterprise models, i.e. representations of aspects of reality including the domain of work, the processes, and their context. Models come in a variety of forms, formal or informal; describing static or dynamic aspects; representing agents, data, goals, processes, or resources; focusing on business or IT aspects. Models have been around for a long time in business and systems design, but they have not been put to their full potential. Typically, they have been used only for limited tasks in systems design and then discarded. To realise the full potential of models, there is a need for a business and technology architecture that place the models firmly in the centre and let them be the driving force in analysis, design, implementation, deployment and use of systems and services.

A major question is how to organise the different models that are needed for representing and visualising enterprises and their environments. This question has been addressed within the area of enterprise architecture. Enterprise architecture can be defined as "the practice of applying a comprehensive and rigorous method for describing a current and/or future structure and behavior for an organization's processes, information systems, personnel and organizational sub-units, so that they align with the organization's core goals and strategic direction", see (Enterprise

Architecture, 2007). The most well-known framework for enterprise architecture is the highly structured Zachman framework, presented in (Sowa, 1992), which can be visualized as a grid around 6 basic questions (What, How, Where, Who, When, and Why) that are asked to five different roles in an enterprise (Planner, Owner, Designer, Builder and Subcontractor). A strong point of Zachman's framework is its complete coverage, but a consequence of this completeness is a high complexity that makes the framework difficult and time-consuming to apply. In this Chapter, we propose a light-weight enterprise architecture framework based on linguistic theories, see e.g. (Dietz, 2006), and organizational metaphors. The concepts and entities of an organization are categorized into three groups concerning resources and resource exchanges, contracts and commitments, and authorities and roles. The activities and processes in organizations are divided into three levels based on how they affect physical, communicative and social aspects of organizations. Together, these divisions form a matrix that helps to organize the models required by an enterprise.

The chapter is structured as follows. In the next section, Three Metaphors of Organisations, we introduce three views of organizations: organisations as machines, organisations as negotiated orders, and organisations as power structures. In the following section, Three Worlds of Human Actions, we discuss how human actions can be structured into three layers depending on their effects on the environment. Based on these views of organisations and layers of actions, we suggest a framework in the form of a matrix for structuring enterprise models. In the following three sections, we elaborate on this matrix by investigating the concepts, actions, and processes of each organisation view. In the final section, we outline benefits and applications of the proposed framework.

Three Metaphors of Organisations

There exists a large number of views and theories of organisations including "Taylorism and time and motion studies; organisational needs analysis, open systems and contingency theory; organisational ecology; cybernetic and holographic thinking; corporate culture; organisations as a collection of interests, conflicts and power; psychoanalytic theory; self-organising systems; Marxian dialectics; or framing and reframing", (Lawley, 2001). One way to approach this plethora of theories is to use metaphors for understanding different aspects of organizations. Five such metaphors, called perspective frameworks, are identified in Reed's work on organizational sociology,

(Reed, 1992). The first metaphor views *organizations as social systems* composed of social units that are integrated through structural relationships and properties within an environment placing constraints on the system. The second metaphor views *organizations as negotiated orders* that are the products of interactions between agents, individuals as well as organizations. The third metaphor views *organizations as structures of power and domination* used to protect the power and interests of agents. The fourth metaphor views *organizations as symbolic constructions* and focus on the myths, rituals and narratives that exist in an organization, while the fifth metaphor views *organizations as social practices* that regulate and control performance. Another set of metaphors have been proposed by Gareth Morgan, (Morgan, 1997), who identifies organizations as machines, organisms, brains, cultures, political systems, psychic prisons, flux and transformation, and instruments of domination.

Taking these organizational metaphors as a starting point, we will in this Chapter make use of three of them, though in a more restricted sense than in the work referenced above.

- *Organisations as machines.* In this view, an organization is seen as a machine that transforms input to output in order to create value for an environment. The focus is on production and exchanges of resources, efficiency, measurement, and control.

- *Organisations as negotiated orders.* In this view, an organization is seen as a network of commitments that binds agents together in mutual obligations. The focus is on agreements, contracts, and establishing and fulfilling commitments.

- *Organisations as power structures.* In this view, an organization is seen as a distribution of powers and authorities over agents. The focus is on what actions that agents are authorised or have a duty to carry out.

Although these are three different views of an organization, they are closely related. The contracts and commitments of the negotiated orders view typically concern the resources of the machine view, and the authorities of the power structure view concern carrying out actions that affect resources, contracts and other objects in the other two views. These three views on organizational phenomena will help in categorizing and relating enterprise models, but before describing this in detail, we will discuss how human action can be divided into different layers in the next section.

Three Worlds of Human Action

In this section, we will discuss how human actions can be structured into layers depending on their effects on the environment; this layering is based on (Searle, 1997) and (Dietz, 2006). In order to make this layering more intuitive, we start with a motivating example.

Understanding Soccer

Imagine a person who watches a soccer game for the first time in her life and knows nothing about the purpose or rules of the game. What kind of report of her watching experience could she be expected to give? Maybe something like the following: "I saw about twenty people running around on a large field of grass. They kicked a ball back and forth across the field and shouted to each other. At a couple of times the ball hit a net, and then some of the people on the field started jumping and yelling enthusiastically as well as many in the audience, while others looked quite unhappy. There was a specially dressed guy who many times blew a whistle and then people stopped kicking the ball. This guy also handed out some red and yellow pieces of paper to some of the people on the field who then looked sad and angry."

The account above of a soccer game is in some sense correct and faithful, but at the same time it is a poor description missing most of the essential features of soccer. If we would like to make clear to the viewer what is really happening on the field and why there are so many emotions around, what kinds of explanations would make sense? Giving explanations based on physics, like describing possible trajectories of the ball, would not be very helpful. Psychological explanations that focus on the inner state of the players might be a bit more useful but would still give only a small piece of the picture. Instead, the key to understanding the game is to realize that it has a social dimension. Through the game, people interact with each other, create relationships, and try to achieve common goals, i.e. they engage in a social activity. Explaining soccer means to describe this social activity, and we would probably start by explaining the objectives of a soccer game. The main objective for a soccer team is to win the game by scoring more goals than the opponent team. This would make them the winner of the game and the other team the loser – a social relationship between the teams.

While scoring the largest number of goals is the top objective of a soccer team in a game, there are also many other objectives, like getting free-kicks, passing the ball to other players in good positions, avoid getting yellow and red cards, etc. All these objectives, actions, and concepts can only be understood in a social setting as they concern relationships between people. For example, getting a free-kick means that one player is allowed to kick a ball from a certain spot without interference from other players who are obliged to stay at a certain distance from that spot. Thus, the concept of free-kick is understood in terms of relationships between people, in particular how they are allowed to interact with each other. Similarly, a player getting a red card means that he or she is not allowed to participate in the rest of the game, i.e. the player's relationships with other people are restricted. The social dimension of soccer is also what makes it such an engaging game, often causing strong emotions among players as well as audience.

The social actions in soccer are carried out by means of physical actions. Soccer is clearly a very physical activity where the players run, kick and nick the ball, tackle each other, and so on. Some of these physical actions can under certain circumstances have a direct effect on the social dimension of a soccer game. For example, if a player kicks a ball into the goal net, this physical action will count as scoring a goal. While some physical actions have a social effect, others have not. For example, if a player kicks his or her shoe into the goal net, this action will not count as anything. A physical action must also be carried out under the right circumstances in order to have a social effect. If a player kicks a ball into the goal net after the judge has blown the whistle, this will not count as scoring a goal. A goal can only be scored when the game is ongoing. Summarizing, a physical action may *count as* a social action *when* performed under the right circumstances. For example, kicking the ball into the goal net *counts as* scoring a goal *when* the game is ongoing. Another example is that tackling a player *counts as* a violation *when* that player does not have the ball.

When a physical action has taken place, it is often obvious whether it can count as a certain social action, but in some cases there is a need for human judgment to determine whether it really can do so. For example, consider a situation where a player has kicked the ball towards the goal, the goalkeeper kicked away the ball, but it seemed as if the ball for a fraction of a second was inside the goal. Should this count as scoring a goal or not? Different people could have different opinions on this, but the one who decides whether a goal really was scored or not is the judge. The judge makes a judgment and communicates it, and thereby he decides whether the kicking of the ball should count as scoring a goal or not. Thus, a physical action itself is not sufficient for producing a social effect – there is also a need for a communicative action, where someone states that the physical action really can count as a certain social action. The performance of the communicative action thereby brings about the social action.

Returning to our soccer game viewer, she was only able to observe the physical actions of the game. In order to understand what goes on in soccer, she needs to know about the social and communicative actions of the game and how they are related to the physical ones. In the next section, we will generalize the notions introduced above by classifying human actions into three categories.

Actions Occur in Three Worlds

Human actions can be divided into three categories: physical actions, communicative actions, and social actions, (Bergholtz, 2003). Physical actions directly influence the physical world, like painting a car or tying a shoe lace. Communicative actions are about expressing intentions and feelings, e.g. people talking to each other, placing orders, complaining about deliveries, asking for information, and so on. Social actions are about changing social and institutional relationships among people. Two main questions about communicative actions concern their purpose and form, i.e. why communicative actions are performed and how they are performed. To begin answering the why-question, it can be noted that many communicative actions simply have the intention to convey some piece of information from one agent to another, e.g. one person may tell another person the time. However, there are many communicative actions that do not convey information, but instead intend to change the social world, i.e. the relationships between agents. For example, when someone says "I apologise", "I promise...", or "I name this ship...", the utterance immediately changes the social reality. An apology takes place when and only when someone admits to having been at fault, and a ship is named when and only when the act of naming is complete. In cases like these, to speak is to perform. Statements that change the social world differ in many respects from statements that just convey information, particularly in that they are neither true nor false. For example, if someone says "I name this ship...", it would be unreasonable to comment "That is not true". To summarise, the answer to the why-question about communicative actions is that agents use them to inform each other and to change the social reality, i.e. to carry out social actions.

In order to answer how communicative actions are performed, the key idea is that certain physical actions, often called message actions, are used to express communicative actions. When a judge in a soccer game shows a red card (a message action), he does so to express that the player should not be allowed to participate in the rest of the game (a communicative action).

One way to see the relationships between physical, communicative, and social actions is to view them as taking place in three different "worlds":

- *The physical world.* In this world, people carry out *physical actions* that have direct physical effects, e.g. opening a package or repairing a machine. A special class of physical actions are the *message actions* – people utter sounds, wave their hands, show differently coloured cards, send electronic messages, etc.

- *The communicative world.* In this world, people express their intentions and feelings. They tell other people what they know, and they try to influence the behaviour of other agents by communicating with them. People perform such *communicative actions* by performing message actions in the physical world.

- *The social world.* In this world, people change the social and institutional relationships among them. For example, people become married or they acquire possession of property. People perform *social actions*, i.e. change social and institutional relationships, by performing communicative actions in the communicative world.

The relationship between actions in the three worlds are shown pictorially in Figure 1, which illustrates how an action in the physical world can count as an action in the communicative world, i.e. putting ink on a piece of paper

Figure 1. Actions in the physical, communicative, and social worlds

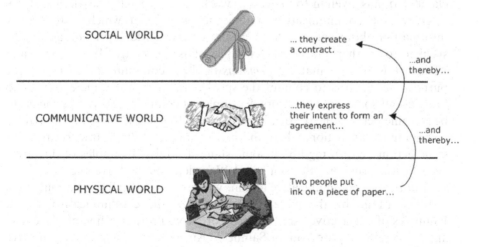

counts as expressing an intention to form an agreement. Furthermore, an action in the communicative world counts as a social action, i.e. by expressing an intention to form an agreement a contract is created. In the following subsections, we will discuss the three worlds and their actions in more detail.

Physical and Message Actions

A physical action is any action that changes the physical world. Some examples are driving a car, eating a meal, baking a loaf of bread, and saving a computer file. Most physical actions have no other effect than changing the physical world, but some of them are intended to change the communicative world. Such physical actions are called message actions. In principle, any physical action can work as a message action, e.g. a spy wearing a flower of a certain colour may signal something to her colleagues. However, in practice message actions have a special form, often including linguistic symbols, that makes them easy to distinguish from other physical actions. Typical examples are waving a hand, making vocal sounds, showing letters on a piece of paper, and sending text through email.

Communicative Actions

Communicative actions can be divided into different categories depending on the way in which they intend to change the social world. A well known classification is given in John Searle's work on speech acts, (Searle, 1970). An *assertive* is a communicative action, the purpose of which is to convey information about some state of affairs of the world from one agent, the speaker, to another, the hearer. Examples of assertives are "It is raining" and "The cat is on the mat". A *commissive* is a communicative action, the purpose of which is to commit the speaker to carry out some action or to bring about some state of affairs. Examples of commissives are "I promise to be at home before nine o'clock" and "I swear to bring it back". A *directive* is a communicative action, where the speaker requests the hearer to carry out some action or to bring about some state of affairs. Examples of directives are "Please bring me the salt" and "I order you to leave the room". A *declarative* is a communicative action, where the speaker brings about some state of affairs by the mere performance of the communicative action. Examples of declaratives are "I hereby order you to pay a fine of 500 euro" and "I hereby baptise you to Samuel". An *expressive* is a communicative action, the purpose of which is to express the speaker's attitude about some state of affairs. An example is "I like coffee".

When someone performs a communicative action, she thereby expresses that she has some intention with respect to some subject matter. This means that a communicative action can be viewed as consisting of two parts, the intention that the speaker has (often called *illocution*) and the subject matter (often called *propositional content*). The illocution is one of the categories introduced above, i.e. assertive, commissive, directive, declarative, and expressive. The propositional content can be any proposition. Two communicative actions may have the same propositional content but different illocutions. Examples are "I want you to do the dishes tonight" and "I promise to do the dishes tonight", which have the same propositional content (do the dishes tonight) but different illocutions (directive and commissive, respectively). Analogously, two communicative actions may have the same illocution but different propositional contents.

A simple way to write down a communicative action is to use a tuple

<Speaker, Hearer, Illocution, Propositional content>.

Some translations to this format are the following:

- John asks Peter to buy a paper – <John, Peter, directive, buy a paper>
- John promises Peter to buy a paper – <John, Peter, commissive, buy a paper>
- John tells Peter that it is raining – <John, Peter, assertive, it is raining>

In the examples above, it is implicitly assumed that an agent can change the social world by unilaterally performing a communicative action. However, this is not true in general. In most cases, the social world is not changed unless several agents together perform communicative actions in a particular order. An example is a wedding ceremony where the priest cannot himself marry two people just by saying "I hereby pronounce you husband and wife" – this statement must have been preceded by appropriate questions to and answers from the couple to be married. In order for the couple to become married, three people (the priest, the woman, and the man) have to join in performing correct communicative actions, choreographed in a certain way. This example illustrates that it is not sufficient to study communicative actions in isolation, as their relationships and context are essential to understand when and how they influence the social world. In the following subsection, we will discuss how communicative actions can be combined and choreographed into larger units, called transactions, processes, and collaborations.

Communicative Processes

A communicative process consists of a sequence of communicative actions that are carried out in order to obtain some goal. When an organisation enacts a communicative process, some activities will take place within the organisation itself while other activities will require interactions with other organisations. In the latter case, two processes in different organisations may become interlocked with each other, i.e. they need to synchronise some of their activities. Pictorially, this can be visualised as in Figure 2, which shows a procurement process in an organisation A, a sales process in an organisation B, and the points of interactions between these two processes. There are three points of interactions where the processes need to synchronise:

- Ask for price – Answer price request
- Ask for delivery conditions – Answer delivery conditions request
- Request order – Accept/reject order

In between these points, each process can include one or many other activities that are internal to the organisation enacting the process.

An interaction between two communicative processes always takes the same form – a request/reply pair, where an initiating actor requests something and a responding actor provides some reply to the request. An example from Figure 2 is organisation A asking for some price information (request) and organisation B providing this information (reply). Thus, the basic units in

Figure 2. Synchronised procurement and sales processes

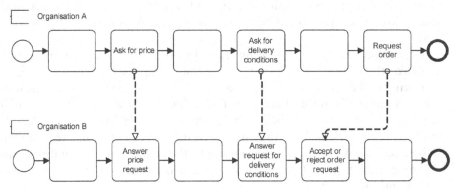

communication between business processes are request/reply pairs, often called *business transactions,* e.g. in (UMM, 2007).

The business transactions that occur in the communication between two business processes can themselves be viewed as forming a new process. Such a process, commonly called a *business collaboration,* consists of a set of business transactions and a control flow describing how they are ordered. A business collaboration describes how two parties are to synchronise their individual processes in order to carry out a joint process. An example of a simple business collaboration is shown in Figure 3, which specifies how the concurrent business processes in Figure 2 interact. This business collaboration consists of three business transactions ordered in sequence. Note that each activity in this business collaboration is a business transaction consisting of one request action carried out by organisation A and one reply action carried out by organisation B.

Social Actions

Social actions change social and institutional relationships between people. These relationships may be about anything people come up with, e.g. one person being married to another, one person being king of other people, one soccer team defeating another soccer team, and one person being employed by a company. The list of such relationships is open ended and new types of relationships are invented all the time. Thus, the list of social actions is also open ended and constantly changing. As a social action changes the relationship between two or more people, it is always required that several people participate in a social action. They do this by carrying out communicative actions in a process that results in, or counts as, a social action, (Searle, 1997). For a given social action, there may exist several different ways of performing it. In other words, different communicative processes may result in the same social action. For example, a couple can choose to be married through many different ceremonies, but they all result in the same social relationship, a marriage.

Based on the classifications in this and the previous section, we can now design a matrix for structuring enterprise models, see Table 1. The column

Figure 3. A business collaboration

Table 1. A lightweight enterrprise model framework

	Machine	Negotiation	Power
Concepts	Resource	Commitment	Authority
	Right	Contract	Role
Social Actions	Conversion	Contract establishment	Assignment
	Transfer	Contract fulfilment	
	Conversion process	Commitment establishment	
	Transfer process	Commitment fulfilment	
	Resource life cycle		
Communication Actions	Conversion transaction	Contract negotiation	Assignment transaction
	Transfer transaction	Contract execution	
Physical Actions	Message actions using different channels, including voice, paper, and hypertext	Message actions using different channels, including voice, paper, and hypertext	Message actions using different channels, including voice, paper, and hypertext

headings give the three metaphors of organisations: as machine, as negotiated order, and as power structure. The first row specifies the most important concepts for each organisational metaphor, while the following rows give the actions used to manage these concepts, divided into the social, communicative and physical world. In the following sections, we will discuss in detail the contents of this matrix.

The Organisation as Machine

In this section, we describe the basic concepts and actions of the *organisation as machine* view, where an organization is seen as a machine that transforms input resources to output resources in order to create value for an environment. The most important concept is that of resource, and the actions are primarily about producing, consuming, transforming, and exchanging resources.

Machine View Concepts

Resource

A *resource* is an object that is considered valuable by some agent, (Geerts, 1999; Gordijn, 2004). A resource is always scarce; otherwise an agent would not consider it valuable. For example, ice would not count as a resource at the North Pole where it is abundant, neither would sand in Sahara. These examples illustrate that in order to determine whether an object is a resource, it is not sufficient to consider the object in isolation – its context must also be taken into account. Ice may not count as a resource at the North Pole, but at other places it may be a highly valuable resource.

An agent views a resource as something that can provide value for her, and this value can be provided in three different ways. First, an agent can use a resource to get a pleasurable experience, e.g. reading a book, listening to music, or watching a movie. Secondly, a resource may be used in a production process, where another and more valuable resource is produced as output. Thirdly, an agent may use a resource for exchanging it for another resource that the agent finds more valuable. An example is a person buying a painting not for viewing it but for putting it in a safe and selling it for a high price at some time in the future.

As any object potentially can be a resource, it is not possible to give any complete classification of resources. However, there are some categories of resources that occur frequently:

- *Goods.* Physical objects, like cars, refrigerators, and cell phones.
- *Information.* Information objects, like customer and product databases.
- *Services.* Services are resources that encapsulate other resources and are used to increase the value of some other resource. Examples are hair cuts and transportation.

When modelling resources, there is often a need to distinguish between a class Resource and a class Resource Type. A Resource Type is the abstract classification or definition of a Resource. An example of a Resource Type could be a car model, such as "Skoda Octavia", while a Resource is a specific, concrete car, which can be classified as being of the Resource Type "Skoda Octavia". Typically, the class Resource Type is used when describing the planning of activities, since in planning it is known that certain kinds of resources will be used, but it is seldom of interest to know exactly which individual resources that will be used. When executing activities, on the other hand, the actual resources used are known, which can be modelled by the Resource class.

The class Resource is used to model actual, concrete resources, such as specific cars. The class Resource Type is used to model abstract descriptions that apply to a set of concrete resources, e.g. a car model. This distinction between these two model levels is relevant not only for resources but also for practically any phenomena. The lower level, often called the operational level, (Fowler, 1996), models concrete, tangible individuals in a domain. The upper level, often called the knowledge level, models information structures that characterise categories of individuals at the operational level. Distinguishing between the operational and the knowledge level enables a separation of concerns in modelling, which makes the resulting models more robust and easy to understand. Stable information about categories of individuals resides on the knowledge level, while ever-changing information about individual activities and objects resides on the operational level.

Right

In order to understand why the notion of right will become central, we start by considering the question stated in (Weigand, 2006) "What is transferred in an exchange?" This question may seem trivial, as the answer could just be "a resource". For example, if someone buys a book at a book store, then a book (goods, a resource) is transferred to him. Similarly, if someone borrows a book at a library, then again a book is transferred to him. However, these examples indicate that the simple answer may in fact be too simple. There is clearly a difference between buying a book and borrowing a book. If you buy a book, you are entitled to read it or use it for any other purpose, give it to someone else, or even destroy it. In contrast, if you borrow a book, you are still entitled to read it, but neither to give it away nor destroy it. So, just saying that a book is transferred when you buy a book is not sufficient – we need to spell out how you are allowed to use the book, i.e. what rights you hold on it. In other words, buying a book means to get certain rights on it.

Having a right on a resource means to be entitled to use it or benefit from it in some way, to do something with it. For any resource, there can be many different rights associated to it. For a car, there may be the right to drive it, the right to clean it, the right to sell it, the right to dispose of it, as well as many other rights. For a computer file, there may be the right to read the file, the right to update the file, the right to delete the file, etc. What rights that can exist on a resource depends on the resource itself as well as its type – there are different rights for goods and for information objects. Thus, it would be pointless to try to give a complete classification of all possible rights. However, there are three broad categories that capture most rights:

- *Use rights.* Rights to use resources in different ways. To read a book, to copy a file, to eat a meal, to drive a car.

- *Income rights.* Rights to earn income from resources. To rent a house, to lend DVDs.

- *Transfer rights.* Rights to transfer (rights on) resources to other agents. To sell a book.

Returning to the question "What is transferred in an exchange?" we can now give the more precise answer "a right to a resource". When someone buys a book, he gets the ownership right to the book, which is a bundle of use rights, income rights, and transfer rights. Likewise, when he borrows a book, he gets a restricted set of use rights, no transfer rights, and probably no income rights.

Machine View Actions

In this section, we will look into the actions of the *organisation as machine* view. We will first discuss the social actions and then move to the communicative ones.

Actions in the Social World

Like any other objects, resources and rights are created and modified. We will start by describing the atomic social actions that create and change resources and rights, and then discuss how these can be combined into processes.

Transfer – Affecting Rights

Agents can exchange resources with each other, meaning that they acquire some resources by giving up others. For example, John pays 100 euros to a store in order to get a new jacket. In other words, John transfers 100 euros to the store, and the store transfers the ownership of the jacket to him. There are two natural questions to ask about resource transfers: "What is transferred?" and "Why do transfers happen?"

We have already looked at the question "What is transferred?", and suggested the answer "a right to a resource". When someone buys a book, he gets the ownership right to the book, which is a bundle of use rights, income rights, and transfer rights. Likewise, when he borrows a book, he gets a restricted set of use rights, no transfer rights, and probably no income rights. Transfers are about affecting rights.

Moving to the question "Why do transfers happen?", the starting point is that rights on resources are transferred between agents. An agent receives rights on one resource and gives up rights on some other resource. For example, when a person buys a car, she gets the ownership right to the car and gives up the ownership right to some amount of money. By acquiring rights on a resource through the exchange, an agent can increase the value that resource has for her. This can most easily be understood through an example. Suppose you see a nice car in a car store and consider buying it. Before you buy the car, it really has no value for you, as you cannot drive it, take it home, put it into your garage, lend it to friends, etc. You are not allowed to do these things, because you do not have any rights on the car. However, when you have bought the car, you have got the ownership right to the car, and thereby you can use the car as you please. This means that the car now has value for you, as you are allowed to use it. In other words, buying the car means that the value of the car for you has increased. Thus, a precise answer to the question "Why do exchanges happen?" is that an agent wants to increase the value some resource has for her.

Looking from one agent's perspective, an exchange means that the value of some resource for the agent is increased, while the value of some other resource is decreased. An agent buying a car means that the value of the car for the agent is increased, while the value of the money she has to pay is decreased. This means that we can distinguish between two kinds of value changes in an exchange – increments and decrements. An increment increases the value of some resource for an agent, while a decrement decreases the value of a resource for an agent.

Conversion – Affecting Resources

A conversion changes or modifies some resource. For example, a car can be painted, a TV can be repaired, or bread can be baked. There are two natural questions to ask about conversions: "What is modified in a conversion?" and "Why do conversions happen?".

A conversion may change any *feature* of a resource, i.e. any of its properties, characteristics, or associations, (Hruby, 2006). A feature may be physical as the weight of a table, the color of a car, or the size of a box. A feature may also be mental as the happiness or interest of a person. Furthermore, a feature may represent economic or social facts as the salary of a person, whether a company accepts credit cards, or the number of shops that accepts a certain credit card. In short, a feature is anything that can be stated about a resource.

There is one special feature that any resource can have, namely existence, which is a boolean feature telling whether a certain resource exists at a certain point in time. The reason for including this feature is to enable modelling the history of a resource. When a resource ceases to exist, we change its existence feature to "false", thereby specifying that the resource does not exist anymore. This is often a better solution than removing the resource from an information system, as it makes it possible to keep historical information about the resource. Summarising, the answer to the question "What is modified in a conversion?" is "a feature of a resource". A conversion can change the color of a car, it can increase the salary of a person, or it can bring a pizza into existence, i.e. change its existence feature. A conversion changes resource by changing their features.

In the previous section, we stated that agents carry out exchanges in order to increase the value some resource has for them. Agents carry out conversions for exactly the same reason – they want to increase the value of some resource. By modifying some feature of a resource through a conversion, an agent can make a resource more valuable for her. For example, by painting a car and thereby changing its colour feature, the car becomes more valuable for an agent. Thus, we can increase the value some resource has for us not only by acquiring rights on the resource but also by changing features of the resource.

In the subsection Communicative Actions, we discussed communicative processes that existed in the communicative world. However, it is also meaningful to consider processes in the social world that are composed of social actions, e.g. a set of transfers and conversions; such processes will here be called *business processes*. It is often useful to identify special kinds of business processes, and below we introduce exchange processes, conversion processes, and resource life cycles.

Exchange process

A transfer never comes alone, as people do not transfer resources to others without expecting anything in return. In other words, if someone wants to get rights on a resource she must be prepared to give up rights on some other resource. As the saying goes, "one good turn deserves another". This means that there is a relationship between increment transfers and decrement transfers, often called a *duality* relationship, expressing that a decrement transfer is carried out as a counterpart to an increment transfer. For example, a person receives a jacket (an increment transfer) and pays 100 euros (a decrement transfer) for it. There may also be cases where one increment transfer is related to several decrement transfers and vice versa.

Transfers that are related to each other via a duality relationship form an exchange process. (We use the term "exchange" here instead of "transfer" to emphasize that rights on resources are exchanged, not only transferred.) An example of an exchange process is shown in Figure 4 below, which expresses that a person receives a jacket in exchange for some amount of money.

Conversion process

Just as for transfers, a conversion never comes alone. If you want to produce or improve some resource, you need to use or consume some other resource in the process. As the saying goes, "there is no such thing as a free lunch". Thus, there is a duality relationship between increment conversions and decrement conversions, just as there is a duality relationship between increment transfers and decrement transfers. For example, if you are going to produce marzipan, you will have to consume almonds and sugar, as illustrated in Figure 5 below. This is also an example of a conversion process – a set of increment and decrement conversions that are related via a duality relationship.

Resource Lifecycle

Lifecycles of objects are often useful to view as business processes. In contrast to the exchange and conversion processes introduced above, a lifecycle is not only a set of actions but also a temporal structure on this set. The lifecycle shows how an object is born, what happens to it during its life time, and how it comes to an end.

Figure 4. An exchange process

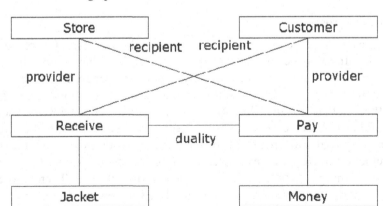

Figure 5. A conversion process

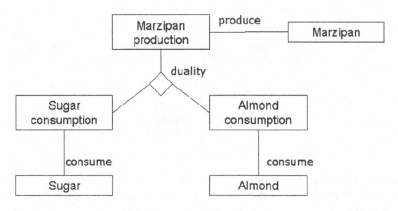

Actions in the Communicative World

Transfers and conversions in the social world are brought about by means of communicative processes where actors state and accept that rights are transferred and resources are produced or modified. These processes are often quite simple and usually include only the actors directly involved in the transfers and conversions.

Communicative Process for a Transfer

In the simplest case, a transfer can be brought about by two communicative actions in sequence. First, one actor declares that rights on a resource has been transferred from her to another actor. Then, the other actor accepts this declaration, and thereby the transfer has been completed. Expressed in the notation introduced in the previous section, this becomes:

1.   <Provider, Receiver, declarative, transfer rights on resource from P to R>

2.   <Receiver, Provider, declarative, transfer rights on resource from P to R>

Graphically, this simple example is shown in Figure 6 below.

In some cases, it may also be required to include a third actor, e.g. a legal authority, who has to confirm the transfer before it becomes legally binding.

Figure 6. A communicative process for a transfer

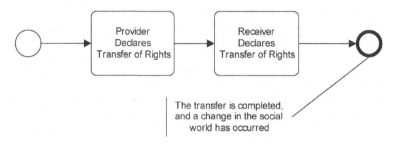

The example above shows the happy path, where the transfer is completed. However, there is also a possibility that the receiving actor refuses to accept the transfer. In such a case, no transfer takes place, see Figure 7 below.

Communicative Process for a Conversion

The communicative process for a conversion is very similar to the one for a transfer. In the simplest case, one actor first declares that some resource has

Figure 7. A communicative process for a transfer with a failure path

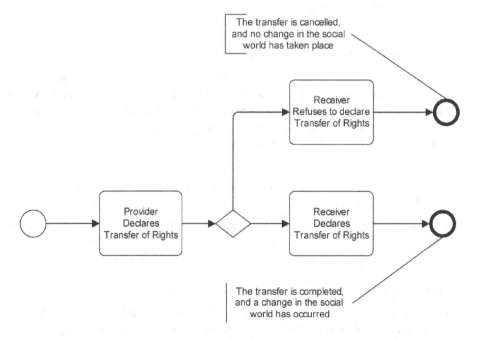

been produced or that some feature of a resource has been modified. Then, the actor for whose benefit the conversion has been carried out accepts this declaration, and thereby the conversion has been completed.

The Organisation as Negotiated Order

In this section, we describe the basic concepts and actions of the *organisation as negotiated order* view, where an organization is seen as a network of commitments that binds agents together in mutual obligations. The most important concepts are those of commitments and contracts, and the actions are primarily about establishing, modifying and fulfilling these commitments and contracts.

Negotiated Order View Concepts

Commitment

Actions that are performed in organisations have to be co-ordinated so that agents and resources are always available when requested or needed. The basic mechanism for co-ordinating actions is the *commitment,* as defined in (Geerts, 1999). A commitment ties together two agents in that one of the agents has an obligation of some form towards the other agent. This means that the first agent is bound to behave in a certain way for the benefit of the other agent. For example, one agent may have a commitment to pay an amount of money to another agent.

It is possible to distinguish between two kinds of commitments: to-do commitments and to-see-to-it-that commitments. A to-do commitment means that an agent is obliged to carry out a specific action, e.g. to deliver a product or pay an invoice. A to-see-to-it-that commitment means that an agent has to ensure that some condition is satisfied, e.g. that the balance of a bank account never goes below zero. In the following, we will focus on to-do commitments, as these are the most basic ones. In particular, we will consider commitments for carrying out transfers and conversions.

A commitment is typically related to three other kinds of objects. First, there are always two agents involved in a commitment – one agent who has an obligation to carry out an action, and another agent for whose benefit the action is to be carried out. In other words, a commitment is always directed –

from one agent, the debtor, to another agent, the creditor. Secondly, the commitment is related to an action type telling what kind of action that is to be carried out. This action type will be either a transfer type or a conversion type. Thirdly, the commitment may be related to one or several resource types indicating what kinds of resources, and in which quantities, that are affected by the commitment. An example is a commitment from Acme Inc. (an agent) to John Doe (another agent) to carry out a delivery (an action type, a transfer type) of 500 chocolate bars (a resource type) before 31 Dec 2008. A commitment typically concerns a resource type, but in some cases it may concern a specific resource. For example, if you order a new car, the commitment is for a car model (a resource type) because you only care about getting a car of a certain car model, not a specific physical car. On the other hand, if you order a used car, the commitment is for a certain physical car (a resource).

Commitments are related through an association reciprocity, which is the analogue of the association duality between transfers and conversions. This means that a commitment never exists in isolation – if one agent has a commitment to another agent, the latter agent also has a reciprocal commitment towards the former. For example, if a company has a commitment to deliver a product to a customer, then the customer has a reciprocal commitment to pay an amount of money to the company. Note that the association reciprocity is many-to-many. To see why this is the case, consider a situation where a company has several commitments to deliver different products to a customer, while the customer has just one commitment to make a single payment for all the products together.

Contract

It is often convenient to group together a number of similar commitments into one group. Such a group of commitments is called a *contract*. In addition to function as a container for a set of commitments, a contract also includes a collection of rules that govern its commitments. These rules tell in what ways commitments may be modified, i.e. if, when, and how they may be cancelled, released, delegated, and assigned. Furthermore, the contract rules specify how violations of commitments should be managed, i.e. what to do when an agent has not fulfilled a commitment in a satisfactory way. Typically, some compensating action is to be performed when a violation has occurred.

An example of a contract is a purchase order, where the commitments are the order lines. Each order line specifies a product type, a quantity, and a due date. The contract rules of the purchase order may tell when an order line may be cancelled, e.g. "an order line may be cancelled within three days of the due date". Another contract rule may specify what will happen when a violation occurs, e.g. "if a product has not been delivered at the due date, the seller has to pay $1000 to the buyer".

Negotiated Order View Actions

In this section, we will look into the actions of the organisation as negotiated order view. We will first discuss the social actions and then move to the communicative ones.

Actions in the Social World

Like any other objects, commitments and contracts are created and modified. We will first consider the atomic social actions that create and change commitments and contracts, and then discuss how these can be combined into processes.

Contract Establishment

A contract is established between two or more agents. When a contract is established, the contract is created as well as all the commitments it contains. A contract is established in order to coordinate the activities of the partners of the contract.

Contract Execution

When a contract has been established, its commitments are to be fulfilled, i.e. the transfers and conversions associated to the commitments are to be carried out. In the simplest case, this means that the commitments are fulfilled one after the other, typically in some predetermined sequence. An example of the execution of a contract containing two commitments, one for transferring some goods and one for payment, is shown in Figure 8. In this example, the

Figure 8. A simple contract execution

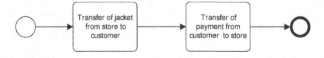

commitments are about transfers, and the contract execution will therefore consist of a number of transfers.

In more complex cases, the execution of a contract may include additional social actions. In particular, when a commitment has not been fulfilled, a compensating action may be required, which means that a commitment is created for one agent to carry out a compensating transfer or conversion. An example of such a case is shown in Figure 9 below.

Actions in the Communicative World

Contracts are established and executed by means of communicative processes where actors create and fulfil commitments. These processes range from simple ones to complex that may include negotiations and biddings.

Communicative Process for Establishing a Contract

In the simplest case, a contract can be established by two communicative actions in sequence. First, one actor requests that a contract and its commitments shall be established. Then, the other actor accepts this request, and thereby the contract has come into existence. Expressed in the notation used above, this becomes:

- <Provider, Receiver, directive, establish contract between P and R>
- <Receiver, Provider, commissive, establish contract between P and R>

In many cases, a contract is established through a more complex negotiation process with bids and counter bids. Figure 10 below shows such a case.

Figure 9. A contract execution with a compensating action

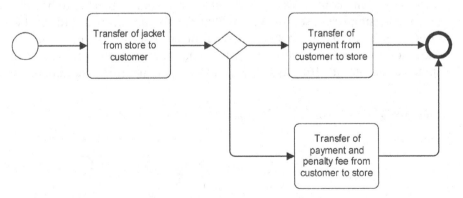

Figure 10. A contract execution process

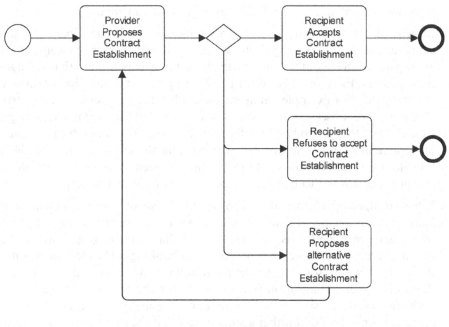

Power Structure View

In this section, we describe the basic concepts and actions of the organisation as power structure view, where an organization is seen as a distribution of powers and authorities over agents. The focus is on what actions that agents are authorised or have a duty to carry out.The most important concepts are those of commitments and contracts, and the actions are primarily about establishing, modifying and fulfilling commitments and contracts.

Power Structure Concepts

Agent

Actions are performed by agents. In an organisational setting, it is possible to distinguish between three types of agents: human agents, organisational agents, and artificial agents. A human agent is a person, who is capable of performing actions. An organisational agent is an organisational unit, e.g. a company or a department in a company. An artificial agent is a man-made artefact that has been given the capability to perform actions on behalf of its owner, who may be either a human or an organisational agent. An example is a software agent that makes bids and negotiates contracts.

In general, an agent may have a large range of capabilities, like reasoning, expressing emotions, taking decisions, carrying out physical actions, etc. In an organisational context, there are three main capabilities that an agent must possess. First, an agent must be able to perceive events that occur in its environment. For example, an agent should be able to receive an order from a customer or observe that a delivery has been made. Secondly, an agent should have the capability to affect its environment, either by performing physical actions or communicative actions. Thirdly, an agent must be able to take decisions on how to act. For example, an agent may need to be able to compute the answer to queries or decide when to issue an alert.

When an agent performs an action, it can do so on its own behalf or on behalf of another agent. The latter case occurs frequently in organisations, where an agent performs an action on behalf of the organisation. For example, a clerk in a hotel may accept room bookings. The clerk does not do this as a private person but as a representative of the hotel, which means that the hotel as an organisation is responsible for the room booking, not the individual clerk. In situations like these where one agent is a representative of, or acts on behalf of another agent, we say that the first agent is an internal agent with respect to the other agent. In the example, the clerk is an internal agent with respect to the hotel.

An internal agent may be allowed to perform certain kinds of actions for its organisation, while being disallowed to carry out other kinds of actions. For example, the hotel clerk may be allowed to accept and cancel room bookings, but may not be allowed to hire people for the hotel. In order to specify what rights and duties an internal agent has in an organisation, it is convenient to use the notions of Authority and Role.

Authority

In sociology, authority has been defined as "power which is recognised as legitimate and justified by both the powerful and the powerless" in (Authority, 2007). In an organizational setting, authority means that an organization has allowed an agent to carry out some physical or communicative action. In other words, an agent may be authorized by an organisation to carry out a physical or communicative action. Note that an agent cannot be authorised to carry out a social action, as such an action materialises as a consequence of several communicative actions carried out by at least two agents. Thus, a single agent can never perform a social action herself but only in interaction with other agents. Some examples are that an agent can be authorised to place purchase orders, to withdraw purchase orders, or to accept sales orders.

Role

When distributing authorities over agents in an organisation, it is often convenient to use roles. A role groups together a number of authorities, and when an agent is assigned a role, she will get all its authorities. In addition to authorities, a role may also include duties to react to certain events, and duties to fulfil certain commitments. For example, a hotel clerk (a role) may have the authority to accept room bookings (the right to perform an action), she may have the duty to answer incoming phone calls from hotel guests (the duty to react to an event), and she may have the duty to provide her superior with a weekly report on accepted and cancelled room bookings (the duty to fulfil a commitment).

Power Structure Actions

Actions in the Social World

The structure of the processes for managing authorities and roles are straight forward in the social world, while they can be much more complex in the communicative world.

An authority or a role is created by some agent for another agent who will then be authorised to perform a number of actions. The authority or role can at a later point in time be revoked from the agent. Even if the processes in the social world are simple they may be regulated through complex business rule that determine under what circumstances a role or authority can be created or revoked.

Actions in the Communicative World

The communication needed for assigning authorities and roles may become quite complex, in particular when many agents need to be involved. The minimal process for assigning an authority or role is that some representative of an organisation declares that an agent is assigned that authority or role followed by the acceptance of that declaration by the agent. In many cases it is also required that at least one other agent in the organisation, typically at a higher level, accepts the assignment.

Concluding Remarks

The framework outlined in this chapter can be used to structure the models of any business domain. The concepts of the three views of an organisation form a foundation for the object models. The concepts need to be specialised for specific situations, like introducing purchase orders and sales orders as specialisations of contracts. Furthermore, there is a need for additional concepts that are to be included in these models, e.g. concepts addressing time points, locations, and product structures. One approach for adding these kinds of concepts is through aspect oriented patterns as suggested in [Hruby06]. For the dynamic aspects, the framework provides a structure for the process models through the three worlds of human action.

The framework provides a number of benefits:

- Flexibility. The levels given by the three worlds provide an effective instrument for flexible designs. While the social world level is typically stable, the lower levels are more volatile. This makes it possible to leave models on the highest level unmodified while changing models at lower levels, thus facilitating flexible design solutions.

- Traceability. The framework facilitates traceability from systems to business levels. First, all process activities are clearly motivated by being related to the concepts they affect. Secondly, process activities on the lower, physical level are directly related to higher level activities on the communicative or social levels.

- Business orientation. The framework provides a clear business orientation by being based on three established views of organisations. This makes the framework easy to understand and apply for domain experts as well as systems designers.

- Abstraction. The framework supports process views on different abstraction levels. A highly abstract view of a process can be obtained by focusing on the social world, while more concrete and detailed views of the same process would include activities in the communicative and physical worlds.

The framework proposed can be used for methodology, architecture, and knowledge management purposes. For methodologies, the framework can be used for ways of working that separate concerns by layering human actions into the three worlds. For architectures, the framework can support model driven approaches that successively add details according to the matrix in Table 1 and derive executable code from the resulting models. For knowledge management, the framework can provide mechanisms for structuring and searching repositories of generic enterprise models.

References

Authority (2007). From http://en.wikipedia.org/wiki/Authority.

Bergholtz, M., Jayaweera, P., Johannesson, P., & Wohed, P. (2003). Reconciling Physical, Communicative, and Social/Institutional Domains in Agent Oriented Information Systems – A Unified Framework. In *Conceptual Modeling for Novel Application Domains.* Springer.

Dietz, J. (2006). *Enterprise Ontology: Theory and Methodology.* Springer.

Enterprise Architecture (2007). From http://en.wikipedia.org/wiki/Enterprise_architecture

Fowler, M. (1996). *Analysis Patterns: Reusable Object Models.* Adison-Wesley.

Geerts, G., & McCarthy, W. (1999). An Accounting Object Infrastructure for Knowledge-Based Enterprise Models. *IEEE Intelligent Systems, 14*(4), 89-94.

Gordijn, J. (2004). E-business value modelling using the e3-value ontology. In W. L. Curry (Ed.), *Value creation form e-business models* (pp. 98-127). Oxford, UK: Elsevier.

Hruby, P. (2006). *Model-Driven Design Using Business Patterns.* Springer.

Johannesson, P., Wangler, B., & Jayaweera, P. (2000). Application and Process Integration-Concepts, Issues, and Research Directions. In *Information Systems Engineering Symposium CAiSE, 2000.* Springer.

Lawley, J. (2001). Metaphors of Organisation, from http://www.cleanlanguage.co.uk/Metaphors-of-Orgs-1.html.

Morgan, G. (1997). *Images of Organisation.* Sage.

Reed, M. (1992). *The Sociology of Organisations: Themes, Perspectives and Prospects. Harvester Wheatsheaf.* Hemel Hempstead, Hertfordshire.

Sowa, J., & Zachman, J. (1992). Extending and formalizing the framework for information systems architecture. *IBM Systems Journal, 31*(3), 590-616.

Searle, J. (1970). *Speech Acts: An Essay in the Philosophy of Language.* Cambridge University Press.

Searle, J. (1997). *The Construction of Social Reality.* Free Press.

UMM (2007). From http://www.unece.org/cefact/umm/umm_index.htm.

Weigand, H., Johannesson, P., Andersson, B., Bergholtz, M., Edirisuriya, A., & Ilayperuma, T. (2006). On the Notion of Value Object. In *Proceedings of the 18th Conference on Advanced Information Systems Engineering.* Springer.

Chapter V

Pragmatic-Driven Approach for Service-Oriented Analysis and Design

Remigijus Gustas, Karlstad University, Sweden

Prima Gustiene, Karlstad University, Sweden

Abstract

This chapter presents a pragmatic-driven approach for service-oriented information system analysis and design. Its uniqueness is in exploiting a design foundation for graphical description of the semantic and pragmatic aspects of business processes that is based on the service-oriented principles. Services are viewed as dynamic subsystems. Their outputs depend not only on inputs, but on a service state as well. Intentions of business process experts are represented in terms of a set of pragmatic dependencies, which are driving the overall system engineering process. It is demonstrated how pragmatic aspects are mapped to conceptual representations, which define the semantics of business design. In contrast to the traditional system development methodologies, the main difference of the service-oriented approach is that it integrates the static and dynamic aspects into one type of diagram. Semantics of computation independent models are expressed by graphical specifications of interactions between service providers and service consumers. Semantic integrity control between static and dynamic dependencies of business processes is a one of the major benefits of service-oriented analysis and design process. It is driven by pragmatic descriptions, which are defined in terms of goals, problems and opportunities.

Introduction

Service-orientation is an approach of designing an integrated business process as a set of loosely coupled services. The concept of service-oriented architecture (SOA) can be used in different contexts such as products, technologies or design (Erl, 2005) style, methods and principles. In this chapter, we focus on SOA aspects that are related to system analysis and design style for engineering of enterprise and information system architectures that exploit service-oriented approach. The most fascinating idea about service concept is that it applies equally well to organizational as well as technical components, which can be viewed as service requestors and service providers. Despite of this fact, there is no complete agreement on the specific modeling principles of service architectures. Many approaches are focussing on design of services from software components by using object-oriented methods (Ambler, 2002), (Gustas & Jakobsson, 2004). Since the object-oriented models are based on computation dependent constructs, they increase complexity of a system specification. It results in difficulties for business process analysis experts to validate the design solutions and therefore, makes service architectures prone to inconsistencies, discontinuities and ambiguities.

Enterprise models (Gustas & Gustiene, 2004; Gustas, 2005) can be graphically defined by using a set of organizational and technical components, which are viewed as service requesters and service providers. Such components are represented by people, organizations, hardware or software. For instance, information systems could be viewed as a set of services that retrieve, store, remove and update information. If enterprise business processes are not aligned with IT services, then information systems do not always deliver what users really need. SOA starts from the premise that a business process has a design (High et al., 2005). An ambition of service-orientation is to provide designers with a constructive way of integrating businesses as a set of linked services. Pragmatism (Gustas & Gustiene, 2002) and question "why" should drive a system engineering process from business goals to IT solutions. The pragmatic aspects can also be used for the semantic consistency control of business design. Goal modeling activity is linking the "why" and the "what" aspects (Zachman, 1996) and it helps in building more purposeful products (Rolland, 2005).

Service-orientation in business design should guide engineering of the supporting information technologies, manage commitments for achievement of customer satisfaction (Denning & Medina-Mora, 1995). One of the problems with the traditional semantic models and methods applied for system analysis is that they are implementation oriented. The consequence is that enterprise models are difficult to comprehend for most business experts, who determine the goals of organization. Many business engineering approaches either rely on black-box models or on modeling data flows. Such models do not embody an appropriate understanding of the notion of business design. Consequently they do not provide effective support (Dietz, 2001). Pragmatic descriptions should be also used for motivation of information system architectures, which can be defined as compositions of information and software services.

Service-oriented engineering is a new emerging approach that has evolved from the object-oriented (Blaha & Rumbaugh, 2005) and component-based software engineering (Szyperski, 1998). Services can be represented as autonomous descriptions that are defined and published on the Internet by using machine readable formats. Experience from Service-Oriented Architecture (SOA) implementation projects (Zimmerman, 2005) states that traditional information system modeling methods cover just a part of required modeling notations that are currently emerging under the service - oriented analysis and design (SOAD) approaches. Since most of the existing approaches are using the Unified Modeling Language (UML) notation (Gottschalk et al., 2002), (Zimmerman, 2005), there is no complete agreement on the fundamentals of SOAD.

Conventional methods of information system development divide system specifications into separate parts such as representations of business processes, data architecture, application architecture and technology architecture. It is difficult to keep track of interdependencies among various types of models, which are used to define different perspectives. Computation Independent Models (CIM) of service architectures should not be influenced by possible technical solutions. They can be used both by information system designers as well as non-technicians (strategy planners, owners, users, system analysts), who play a key role in semantic information system integration and business design change management. Most of conventional system analysis and design methodologies, address the logical design phase. For instance, UML primitives, which are used for conceptual modeling, abstract from concrete implementation artifacts and therefore they are more comprehensible for software designers. Semantics of the individual UML diagram types is quite clear. However, its modeling foundation has inherent integrity problems when the static and behavioral aspects are analyzed together. Another weakness of UML is a notation for defining pragmatics of a system is missing.

The idea of CIM was introduced by the Object Management Group (Object Management Group Architecture Board, 2001). Computation independent representations that can be used by non-technicians in SOAD methodologies are a major focus in this study. Sometimes, we will refer to computation independent type of diagrams as Enterprise Models (Finkelstein, 2004). CIM play a key role for semantic system integration. It is recognized that UML support for such task is quite vague (Perrone et al., 2005), because semantic integration principles of different diagram types are still lacking (Harel & Rumpe, 2004). Enterprise models (Gustas & Gustiene, 2004) are implementation agnostic, they are built on an integrated set of semantic and pragmatic dependencies. Semantic level is guided by the pragmatic principles that are placed on the higher level of abstraction. Despite of the fact that every business process is a goal driven activity, there could be different alternative ways to achieve the same goal (Rolland, 2005). Semantic level should have to have capacity to describe such alternative solutions in a clear and sufficiently rich way.

Elements of Service-Oriented Analysis and Design

SOA represents a set of design principles that enable business processes to be analyzed in terms of services. SOAD is based on the assumption that business process models are composed of loosely coupled components, which are viewed as service requestors and service providers. To achieve ultimate flexibility, this essentially simple idea can be used at all levels of the enterprise architecture (Lankhorst et al., 2005), including component based software engineering. Service propositions, requests and service provision within a value chain or within a business process can be defined by pragmatic patterns (Moor, 2005), which are refined in terms of communication actions (Dietz, 2001). Service-orientation is an architectural style that structures business processes as compositions of services. It establishes a set of design principles such as loose coupling, minimization of dependencies encapsulation, re-use and composability (Zimmerman et al., 2005).

The concept of service is understood and used in different domains. Therefore, it might be useful for bridging a communication gap between business experts and information system designers. Service orientation promotes interoperability by minimizing requirements for shared understanding. Business processes can be changed by replacing or recomposing services. Service oriented enterprise architectures allow to define business processes in terms of more specific services. At the bottom level of abstraction a service is implemented as a business process function that is packaged as a reusable software component. It either provides information or changes business data from one consistent state to another (Colan, 2004). This does not exclude the object-oriented analysis and design (OOAD) point of view adopted by RUP, but rather suggests an additional level of abstraction above it. Semantic descriptions are constraining computation dependent models (CDM) at the syntactic level. Characteristic features of SOAD model types and levels are presented in Table 1.

Models of the syntactic level should define implementation-oriented details, which explain the data processing needs of a specific application or software component (Davis, 1989). Syntactic elements are considered to be the basic building blocks that define the implementation perspective. All three SOAD levels are interrelated. The pragmatic level prescribes and motivates the static and dynamic architecture of services at the semantic level. Enterprise model semantics can be analyzed in the context of pragmatics. Implementation related details of software components, which can be defined at the syntactic level by using object-oriented principles, are constrained by enterprise models at the semantic level.

Services are internally characterized by state changes (Hull et al., 2003). At the same time, service semantics cannot be described independently of how these self-contained business and technical components are externally used (Moor, 2005). Separation of the internal and external behavior, which is encapsulated in service concept with a clear purpose, creates big challenges for the conventional object-orientated methods and for business process modeling approaches such as Business Process Modeling Notation (Business

Table 1. Characteristic features of SOAD

Model Types	Modeling Foundation	Levels
Enterprise Model (CIM)	Business Process Analysis	Pragmatic level
	Service-Oriented Analysis	Semantic level
Computation Dependent Model (CDM)	Component-Oriented Design	Syntactic level
	Object-Oriented Design	

Process Modeling Notation working Group, 2004). Various types of object-oriented models are widely used as a basis for semantic modeling of services. Every model typically focuses on a single perspective. Since different perspectives are highly intertwined, it is crucial to maintain integrity across multiple diagrams. If the dispersed views and perspectives are defined in isolation, then traceability from one diagram type to another becomes a bottleneck in the conventional information system modeling approaches.

Services are implemented as organizational and technical system components, which can be used by various actors to achieve their goals. A service from the information system analysis point of view can be viewed as a function, which is defined by a number of flows into opposite directions between a service requester and service provider. Each *Service Response* is a function of a *Service Request*. Service providers are actors that typically receive service requests, over which they have no direct control, and transform them into responses that are sent to service requesters. This idea illustrated graphically in Figure 1.

Service can be analyzed as a business process component, which provide information or change business data from one consistent state to another (Colan, 2004). Our definition of service architecture is based on a similar understanding, which is rooted in the system analysis and design tradition. Service architecture is a composition of various types of enterprise actors, which are viewed as service requesters and service providers. Actors are the organizational and technical subsystems. Their outputs depend not only on inputs, but on service states as well. The dynamic aspect of service is characterized by service states, which are defined for every interaction between service requester and service provider by using the precondition and post-condition classes. States represent service objects and restrict service responses to the present and future inputs. Requests, responses and states are crucial to understand the semantic aspects of services. A precondition state and the input flow should be sufficient for determining a service output flow and a post-condition state. In this way, an enterprise system can be defined by using service architecture that is represented as a set of interacting loosely connected subsystems, which are able to perform specific services on request. Subsystems can be viewed as technical or organizational components.

Figure 1. Service as an interaction loop

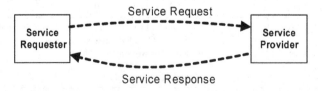

Organizational components can be individuals, companies, divisions or roles, which denote groups of people. Technical components are subsystems that can be represented by software and hardware.

Understanding of the semantic aspects is not sufficient for discovering and composing web services. Comprehensive business system engineering cannot separate pragmatic details of service usage from the semantic description of services. The pragmatic aspects (Singh, 2002; Moor, 2005) are very important, because service requesters may use services in unexpected ways. Holistic understanding of semantic and pragmatic dependencies between service requesters and service providers would include analysis of service objectives and conceptualization of their interaction links. Pragmatic aspects can be characterized by a possibility to avoid a problem or to achieve a goal. Every interaction loop between service requester and service provider adds value to business processes.

Every business process of an organization includes many purposeful activities. From the pragmatic point of view, a service function could be viewed as a problem, opportunity or a goal. Business activities can be defined in terms of interaction loops that together form a purposeful business process. Behind a business process is a clear motivation or goal, which should be analyzed together with a final process state. Achievement of this state should bring customer satisfaction. SOAD requires defining course grained business processes as a service choreography or composition of fine-grained services. Every business process has the beginning and the end. The end of the business process is characterized by goal. If a goal can not be achieved, then the business process boundaries were not correctly stated. This would result in semantic incompleteness of business process specification. Pragmatic notions such as goals, problems and opportunities provide guidance about incompleteness of semantic descriptions of service oriented architectures.

Semantic descriptions of services must follow the basic conceptualization principle (Griethuisen, 1982) by representing only computation independent aspects. Such representations are less complex and more comprehensible for business process experts, because they are not influenced by possible implementation solutions. Additionally, SOAD notation should support a flexible interpretation of semantic roles various concepts play in graphical descriptions of services. The problem of strict classification of semantic roles (Gustiene & Gustas, 2002) is one of the main reasons of severe difficulties in the area of view integration (Batini et al., 1986). Strict classification of concepts is a reason of structurally different, but semantically equivalent representations (Johanesson, 1993). The structural differences are justifiable in the information system design phase, because they show important implementation details. The conventional methods of system analysis and design enforce early design decisions, which result in strict interpretation of concept role. Computation independent representations of services should allow flexible interpretation of semantic roles. It will be demonstrated below that the interpretation of roles various concepts are playing in diagrams depend on the pragmatic and semantic dependency links they are connected.

Pragmatic Dependencies

Pragmatics is supposed to motivate and drive the overall service-oriented analysis and design process. Pragmatic dependencies are used to analyze business processes in terms of goals, problems and opportunities. One of the main challenges of SOAD process is mapping graphical descriptions at the pragmatic level into the semantic specifications, which are defined in terms of the static and dynamic relationships among concepts. Refinement of goals in terms of semantic representations is viewed as a driving force in the enterprise modeling and integration process. The pragmatic dependencies address the 'why' perspective. An important part of the business process analysis is the ways in which different goals, opportunities and problems are related. Goals can be interpreted at the semantic level as business process states that should be reached or desirable parts of specifications that system architects are striven for. State changes are triggered by interactions between service consumers and service providers. It does not suffice to talk about the possible prior and next states surrounding a particular business process state. Why a certain combination of service interactions is chosen must be accounted for. The pragmatic dependencies are used to define intentions of actors that are involved in business processes. Goals, problems and opportunities may be referred to either as the desirable and not desirable situations (Gustas et al., 1996), or desirable or undesirable properties of business processes. Graphical notation of the pragmatic dependencies is presented in Figure 2.

We briefly describe the set of pragmatic dependencies:

- Goal dependency is used to specify either the desirable situations or desirable structural properties in a system. It links enterprise actors to the intentional notions such as goals or objectives.

- Problem dependency is used to specify undesirable situations. Restrictive notions such as problems or causes of problems express either not desirable properties of a system or undesirable situations that enterprise actors are intend to avoid.

Figure 2. Legend of the pragmatic dependencies

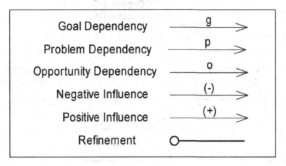

* Opportunity dependency can be used to refer to future situations that can be taken advantage to improve a current situation. Opportunities also can be viewed as strength in the existing system or a business process.

* Negative influence dependency (-) and positive influence dependency (+) are used to denote influences among goals, problems and opportunities. Negative influence dependency from A to B indicates that A can be regarded as a problem, because it hinders the achievement of goal B. The positive influence dependency from A to B would mean that A can be viewed as an opportunity for the achievement of goal B.

* Refinement dependency is used as a means of pragmatic decomposition of goals, problems and opportunities. Pragmatic entities are typically refined by referring to other more specific situations.

The presented set of pragmatic dependencies can be viewed as modeling basis to reason about intentions of designers on new system architecture. An opportunity is a desirable fragment of an existing semantic specification that is intended to be maintained in a new system. The desirable features of a problematic situation can be indicated as opportunities by using refinement links. A meta-model of an opportunity that is represented as a desirable organizational strength in a problematic situation is illustrated in Figure 3.

Opportunities represent fragments of the semantic specification that are intended for reuse in the desirable situation. Such fragments typically represent an organizational strength. Another type of opportunity can be defined as a situation that negatively influences at least one of the problems and positively influence at least one of the organizational goals. A meta-

Figure 3. Opportunity as strength

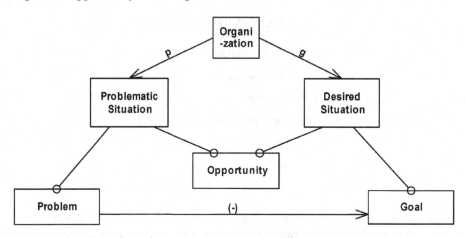

model of opportunity that negatively influences a problem can be represented by a diagram, which is illustrated in Figure 4.

One way to improve an existing problematic situation is by eliminating the semantic fragment of specification that is represented as a problem at the pragmatic layer. Another way for improving a current situation is weakening a problem by introducing a new opportunity, which has a negative affect on a problem. Such opportunities represent new features of a desired situation that should be maintained in system re-engineering process. A role of designer has a responsibility to enforce semantic integrity among all fragments, which referred to as opportunities and goals.

Figure 4. Opportunity contributing to the achievement of an organizational goal

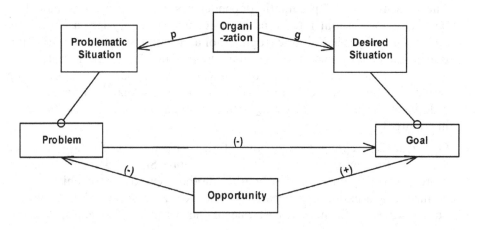

Goals, problems and opportunities are introduced by using pragmatic links. The pragmatic entities can be refined by using more specific elements. For instance a goal can be refined into sub-goals and a problem can be refined by representing its sub-problems. Refinement of A into B is denoted be B∘– A. It states that B satisfies A, where B can be partially used for the achievement of A. The *refinement* link is characterized by the following condition:

B ∘– A if and only if S(B) ⊆ S(A) and P(A) ⊆ P(B),

Here: P(A), P(B) correspondingly denote sets of pragmatic dependencies of concept A and concept B, S(A), S(B) correspondingly denote sets of the semantic dependencies that define pragmatic entity A and B. The presented formal condition consists of two parts:

1. A set of the semantic dependencies that define pragmatic entity B is a subset of a set of the semantic dependencies of A, and

2. A set of the pragmatic influence dependencies of entity A is propagated to B. The second part of the condition is defined as follows:

if B ∘– A and A $\dashrightarrow$ C then B $\dashrightarrow$ C,

if B ∘– A and A $\dashrightarrow$ C then B $\dashrightarrow$ C.

Many requirements engineering researchers recognize that it is not enough to describe semantics of information system. The lack of methods with ability to define the pragmatic issues in a clear and sufficiently rich way is crucial in many areas including software engineering, object oriented system design, system analysis, conceptual modeling, e-service composition (Hull et al., 2003), semantic web (Daconta et al., 2003) and information system engineering. Very often system designers tend to start by focusing on the static concept dependencies or on behavior, by concentrating on the activity triggering effects. This tradition tends to neglect the pragmatic aspects, which are important part of requirements about how business processes can be improved. Another problem is that the goal models often are analyzed in isolation from the semantic models.

Semantic Dependencies

Usefulness of a great number of semantic relations (Snoeck et al., 1999), (Storey, 1993) in enterprise modeling and system design is an open problem.

Some of semantic relations have quite complex nature and are mostly studied by theoreticians. One example is a multivalued dependency that is defined in relational database theory (Codd, 1990). Multivalued dependency is not so often used in data base design practice. Another problem is that principles of interplay between the static and dynamic dependencies are not clear. That is the reason why the semantic integrity control is very difficult in information system development methodologies. As a consequence the semantic quality of system specifications is often compromised. Most information and software system development methodologies have adopted purely process driven or purely data driven approaches. Even if object oriented paradigm is capable to tie the static and behavioral aspects together, the interplay among the semantic dependencies in different diagram types is not clear enough.

Let us try to take look at the fundamentals of conceptual dependencies in system analysis and design. There are two major classes of semantic dependencies in conceptual models: static and dynamic. These dependencies are typically used in isolation for representing design solutions in different types of static and dynamic diagrams. In this chapter we will survey the basic types of semantic dependencies. The legend of dependencies is presented in Figure 5.

Classification dependency is used to define instances of classes. An instance can be viewed as an element of a set that is defined by a concept it belongs to. Sometimes classification dependency is referred to as instantiation, which is reverse of classification. In object-oriented approaches it is representing a link between an object and a class. Inheritance dependency is used for sharing similarities from more general concepts. It predefines inheritance of the static as well as dynamic dependency links for the more specific concepts. It should be noted that in object oriented approach inheritance is applied just for attributes and operations. In our service-oriented approach, we additionally define inheritance of interaction, composition, transition and computation dependencies.

Figure 5. Legend of the semantic dependencies

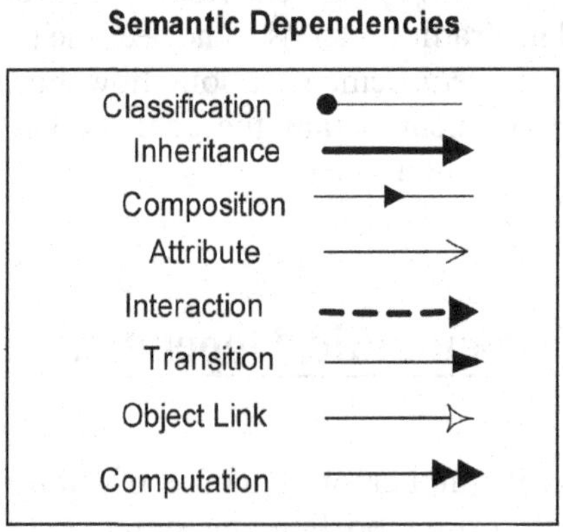

Semantic Dependencies

Classification	●———
Inheritance	——➤
Composition	—▶—
Attribute	——→
Interaction	━ ━ ━▶
Transition	——▶
Object Link	——▷
Computation	——▶▶

Static differences in various classes are represented in terms of dependent concepts that are connected by the attribute dependencies. The attribute dependencies are stemming from the traditional semantic models. Semantics of static dependencies in object-oriented approaches are defined by multi-plicities. They represent a minimum and maximum number of objects in one class that can be associated to objects in another class. In our approach, just a subset of all variety of static associations is used for defining attributes of classes. Two different notations of the attribute dependencies and their cardinalities are represented in Figure 6.

The first way is used in non-graphical conceptual specifications that are typically presented in a text form. The second - is the graphical notation, which corresponds a classical way for representing associations (Hoffer et al., 2004), (Martin & Odell, 1998). Cardinalities of each dependency are represented on the right hand side. One significant difference of this notation from the traditional approaches is that the association ends are nameless. The dependencies are never used to denote the association mappings in two opposite directions. Whether a concept is regarded as an instance, class, attribute, relationship, flow or an actor depends upon types of the static and dynamic dependencies they are related to other concepts. Every noun is captured by a box and a verb is captured by an ellipse (see Figure 8). Possible interpretations of concepts are represented in Figure 7.

The meta-model demonstrates that any concept can be interpreted in different ways. This diagram should be analyzed together with the meta-model of a relationship (see next figure). Relationships are two types: static and dynamic. Actions and rules represent two subsets of the dynamic relationships. Actions are defined in terms of interaction dependencies between different types of actors. Depending on the nature of a flow element in action, the communication flows can be information and physical. Flows represent messages or physical objects to be transferred from agents to recipients. Computation dependencies are used to define the dynamic relationships among attributes of various classes in terms of computation rules and constraints. For a reason of space limitations, we are not going into a discussion on computation rules any further.

Figure 6. Graphical representation of the attribute dependencies

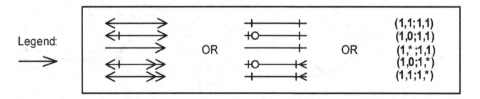

Figure 7. Meta-model illustrating flexible interpretation of concept

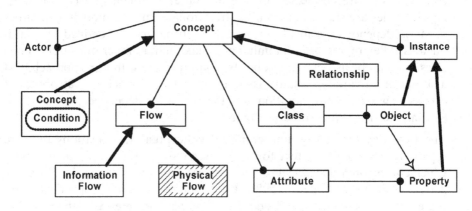

Composition dependency is useful for formation of a new static relationship as a whole from other concepts that might be viewed as parts. This type of composition is more restrictive as compared to the traditional definition of aggregation and composition (Maciaszek, 2001). A part cannot simultaneously belong to more than one whole of the same concept. If it does belong to more then one whole, then it must be a whole that is an instance of another concept. A part and a whole are created at the same time. Once a part is created, it can be terminated at the same time the whole is terminated. This definition is stricter as compared to a composition that is used in the object - oriented approaches. It means that the life spans of instances for compositionally dependent classes must be identical.

Figure 8. Meta-model of relationships

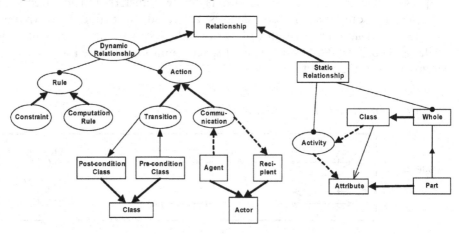

Interaction dependency (----►) can be viewed as a static and as a dynamic relationship. Static interaction relationship can be interpreted as an activity that characterizes a static dependency between a class and an attribute. For instance, employee (class) works for (relationship) company (attribute). Interactions also can be defined between any types of concepts that represent an individual, group of people, organization, machine, and software or hardware component. A complete definition of the interaction as a dynamic relationship would include specification of actions, which are carried out by dependent actors. Every action is characterized by the transition dependency (→) from a precondition class to a post condition class. A dynamic interaction link in reality is viewed as a physical, information or a decision flow between actors involved. A meta-model of various types of relationships is presented in Figure 8.

Interaction as a dynamic relationship is defined by a communication action. An action is capable to change a state of an object by reclassifying it. Attribute dependencies of the precondition and post-condition classes represent the semantic difference of object link changes, which necessary to implement during the transition from one class to another. States can be also represented by Boolean conditions that are associated to concepts. State changes are important to service requesters and service providers. Without the ability to represent noteworthy state changes, we would have difficulties to understand the rational and effect of every action. Graphical notation of the interaction dependency between an agent and a recipient is presented in Figure 9.

Actions express the permissible ways in which state changes may occur. In the conventional approaches, state changes are specified by using state-transition links in a finite state machine (Harel & Rumpe, 1987). Interaction dependency is similar to a communication action (Dietz, 2001) between two actors. It indicates that one actor depends on another actor. At the same time

Figure 9. Graphical representation of the interaction dependency

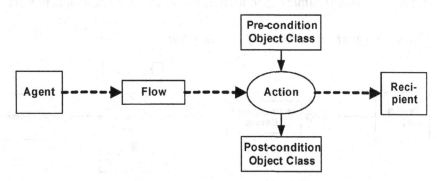

interaction is a strategic flow dependency link (Yu & Mylopoulos, 1994) between agent and recipient. Therefore, it can be used as a basic building block in the SOAD process. Interaction is considered at the same time to be an action and a communication flow. An agent initiates a flow by using a communication action to achieve his goal (Gustas & Gustiene, 2004). The achievement of goal will depend on a service provider, which should deliver a service flow into the opposite direction. Any action is typically related to a state change that can be defined as a reclassification of object from one class to another. Otherwise, an action is not purposeful. If there is an instantiated object in the precondition class, then, by using action, the transition of an object to the post-condition class can be performed. For instance, if a person has applied for a job, then he expects to be employed. If so, then Employment Details are sent by the Personnel Department to a Person by using the action of Employ. A reclassification example is illustrated in Figure 10.

Fundamentally, two kinds of changes occur during any transition: declassification of object from the precondition class and classification of the same object to the post-condition class. Sometimes, objects are passing several states, and then are removed. A removal can be defined by an action with a missing post-condition object class. It is a special case of an interaction dependency, which is representing a termination event. Since a next state makes no sense for a termination event, it is not included in a specification of action. Creation is an opposite of a removal. It is a special case of the communication action with a missing precondition object class. An example of the creation action is presented in Figure 11.

The effect of every action is considered as a creation, termination or transition event. Compositions of various communication actions result in a diagram, which represents a continuous or finite lifecycle. A finite lifecycle of object has an initial, intermediate and last state. A creation event corresponds to a starting point and removal action – to the end point in object lifecycle. The most critical issue in modeling of interaction details is semantic integrity of the static and dynamic dependencies. For instance, a removal action that is

Figure 10. Graphical example of a reclassification

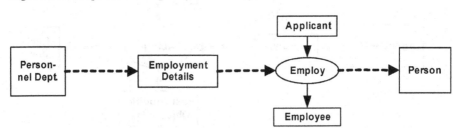

Figure 11. Example of the creation action

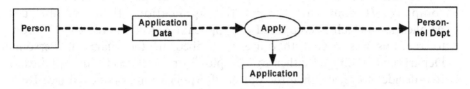

connected to a class indicates termination of all object association links whose types are connected by the attribute dependencies. A creation action must bring into existence all object association links whose types are connected by the attribute dependency. Semantics of various kinds of object links are defined by cardinality constraints.

Presented set of semantic dependencies plays an important role in defining interactions between service requestors and service providers. Understanding interactions is critical in various business modeling approaches, because they serve as a basis to analyze obligations and authorizations among actors involved. State changes that take place in various interaction loops can be represented by combining reclassification, creation and termination events. These events are fundamental for definition of different types of communication actions. A typical action workflow loop can be defined in terms of two or even three interaction dependencies between two actors. By matching the actor dependencies from agents to recipients, one can explore opportunities that are available to these actors. We shall illustrate the basic semantic dependencies in one action workflow loop between two actors (Person and Personnel Dept.) together with the creation, termination and reclassification events, which are illustrated in Figure 12.

Figure 12. Integrated example of static and dynamic description

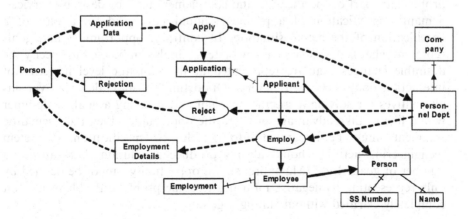

This diagram illustrates that a person is authorized to apply for a new employment by sending an application to personnel department of a company. If company accepts the application, then an object of Application, which is composed of Applicant object, is created. According to the business events that are prescribed in the diagram, Personnel Department is obliged either to "Employ" or to "Reject" an Application. If it decides to reject, then the object of Application is removed (see Reject action), otherwise it must be reclassified to an employee (Employ action is triggered). Please note that these two actions are exclusive for the same application object. According to the presented static dependencies, removal of any Applicant at the same time would cause destruction of a correspondent Application object and vise versa. The two attributes of class Person (Name and SS Number) must be instantiated at the time when the applicant is created. If an Employee object would be terminated by another action (not legal in the context of this diagram), then the object association links to the Employment object should be removed as well. The attributes of Employee and Applicant are essential to characterize the semantic difference between two kinds of Person. The concept of Employee is characterized by the additional attribute of Employment. The concept of Applicant defined by using composition link to Application In such a way, sequences of communicative actions prescribe sequences of create, remove and update operations, which should be coded at the computation dependent modeling phase.

Operations at the Pragmatic Level

Enterprise re-engineering can be regarded as a process of eliminating the problematic part of specification and complementing it by desirable services. Semantic specification of a problem should be considered a part of a specification of the actual situation. In contrary, opportunities and goals represent what is desirable in a new system. Goals can be used to specify the desirable changes that are represented at the semantic level in terms of interaction loops between actors. Opportunities may describe various alternatives for solving a specific problem and reaching a goal. If designer would like to take advantage of a specific opportunity, then their semantic fragments must be integrated into the desired specification. A system reengineering activity should always produce a solution that satisfies a number of goals. In SOAD approach, an opportunity cannot be defined by only representing its negative influence to some problem. Problems are not completely clarified without stating a goal.

Enterprise reengineering activities at the semantic level should be driven by predefined specifications at the pragmatic level. And vice versa, operations with goals, problems and opportunities should have consequences on specification fragments at the semantic level. A predefined goal can be achieved by avoiding a problem or using some opportunity for reaching a goal. It should be noted that the notion of a problem and a goal is relative. Achievement of some goal for one enterprise actor can be regarded as a problem for another actor. There is very little or no support in conventional information system engineering methodologies for bridging from the pragmatic to the static and behavioral aspects. Typically, various perspectives such as the "what", "who", "where", "when" and "how" (Zachman, 1996) are defined in isolation. This situation results in various requirement traceability problems when reasoning about new data, process and technology architecture.

Pragmatic dependencies can be used for reasoning about completeness of system descriptions at the semantic layer. Business process descriptions in terms of goals, problems and opportunities should be used as a driving force of enterprise modeling at the semantic level. We will clarify this idea by using a hypothetical semantic difference operation, which is supposed to compute a semantic difference between two graphical descriptions. In conventional system development approaches, formalization of such operation is very difficult, because the static and dynamic aspects are analyzed in isolation.

Let S_D is a computation independent definition of the desired situation and S_A denotes a semantic description of the actual situation. Then a specification of an overall design goal S_G can be defined as a semantic difference between S_D and S_A: $S_G = S_D - S_A$. Here "-" is the semantic difference operation. Any specific goal can be viewed as a further refinement of S_G. It denotes a conceptual description, which represents what is desirable in a new system.

The opposite of a goal is a problem. A computation independent definition of a problem can be defined as a semantic difference between the actual situation S_A and the desired situation S_D: $S_P = S_A - S_D$. Any specific problem describes what is not desirable in a new system and can be regarded as a further refinement of S_P.

Such interpretation of problem and goal has some implications on how different pragmatic notions are perceived by stakeholders. In the initial phase of modeling, the goals and problems can be analyzed in isolation. Nevertheless, consensus on a specific problem or goal cannot be reached without a detail analysis of a set of semantic dependencies in the actual and in the desired situation. Semantics of a problem can not be stated without complete understanding what is desired in a new system. On the other hand, the semantics of a goal cannot be specified without understanding what is undesirable in a problematic situation. Sometimes, a problem makes sense even if the goals are not completely understood, but the reasons of problems can not be fully comprehensive unless they are refined in terms of the semantic dependencies in a problematic situation.

Similarity of goals, problems and opportunities is an important character-istic. Similar pragmatic entities can be placed in the same hierarchy and they are characterized by compositionability of interaction loops. Compatible interaction loops are defined in terms of: (a) at least one identical or similar actor involved and (b) at least one identical or similar either precondition or postcondition object classes. Similar concepts are connected by one of the basic static dependency links and similar actors are connected by either by inheritance or composition link. Formalization of operations on semantic fragments is an interesting and challenging research problem.

Similarity of pragmatic entities is useful, because it allows performing two pragmatic operations, such as the operation of union and the operation of intersection. Since interpretation of goal, problem and opportunity is relative and depended on a judgment of an actor, in this section we will sometimes refer to all these pragmatic categories as goals. Any two similar goals B and C have their greater common specialization denoted by intersection (B ⊓ C) and their least common generalization denoted by union (B ⊔ C). The *union of goals* (⊔) is defined as the semantic union of their specifications.

Operation of the union of similar goals is characterized by the following properties:

B ∘− (B ⊔ C),

C ∘− (B ⊔ C),

(B ⊔ C) ∘− A if and only if B ∘− A , C ∘− A.

If any two goals B and C are refinement of the goal A then their union is the specialization of the same goal A as well.

Intersection of goals (⊓) is defined as an intersection of the semantic specifications of goals. Intersection is represented by a common interaction loops. If any goal A is refinement of two goals, B and C, then it is a refinement of the intersection of those goals. Operation of the intersection of similar goals can be characterized by the following properties:

A ∘− (B ⊓ C) if and only if A ∘− B , A ∘− C,

(B ⊓ C) ∘− B,

(B ⊓ C) ∘− C.

Figure 13. Graphical representation of the union and intersection operations

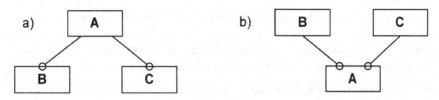

Graphical notation of the pragmatic union is presented in Figure 13 (a), and the intersection is presented in Figure 13 (b).

The refinement dependency can be characterized by the following axioms:

if A $\circ-$ B, B $\circ-$ C then A $\circ-$ C ,

if A $\circ-$ B then A $\dashrightarrow$ B ,

A $\circ-$ B , B $\circ-$ A if and only if A $\circ-\circ$ B .

Here $\circ-\circ$ is the satisficing dependency. Satisficing dependency means attaining a certain minimum quality in describing a goal that is sufficient to solve a problem (Skytter, 2001).

A *satisfice* B if and only if A is a refinement (i.e. B satisfy A) of B and a set of semantic dependencies of B is sufficient for the specification of a goal A. The notion of satisficing has been introduced by Simon (Simon, 1993). It is made up from two words: satisfy and suffice. This dependency very important as it is used to bridge enterprise models fragments that are defined at the semantic level to goals, problems and opportunities.

Pragmatic entities are *independent* if and only if they have no common interaction loops and they have neither negative, nor positive influence to each other. If any two goals A and B are independent, then their intersection empty ($\perp$), i.e. (A $\sqcap$ B) = $\perp$. Here: $\perp$ is empty element. The criterion of independence is useful for identification of the decomposition links among goals. A is decomposition of elements B and C if and only if the

Figure 14. Composition of A by using B and C

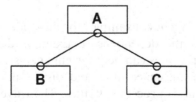

components B and C are independent and their semantic union satisfice the goal A, i.e.

$(B \bigtriangledown C) \circ\!\!-\!\!\circ A$ if and only if$(B \sqcup C) \circ\!\!-\!\!\circ A$ and $(B \sqcap C) = \perp$.

Here $\bigtriangledown$ is the pragmatic composition operation. Graphical representation of pragmatic composition is presented in Figure 14.

A goal decomposition hierarchy is usually formed of satisficing goals on the neighboring levels of abstraction. Objectives at the bottom level are defined in terms of the basic semantic dependencies. Goal decomposition hierarchy describes how the various high-level objectives are going to be achieved.

Compositions of service descriptions that represent goals, problems or opportunities can be formed by using the operation of intersection. A semantic fragment of goal C can be specified as an intersection of two other pragmatic entities A and B by using the following expression: $(A \sqcap B) \circ\!\!-\!\!\circ C$. According to this expression, C can be formed if and only if A and B are similar and consistent. It should be noted that the intersection $(A \sqcap B)$ can not be formed, if A and B are inconsistent. Inconsistency situation at the pragmatic level is characterized by conflicting or contradictory goals. If A $\dashrightarrow$ B, then A is *conflicting* with goal B. If A $\dashrightarrow$ B and A $\dashrightarrow$ B, then A is *contradictory* for the achievement of B. If *sub-goals of the same goal are conflicting,* then a global goal is *contradictory.* Any contradictory goal has at least two sub-goals that are conflicting.

Operations on goals create big challenges for the traditional approaches, because integration of the static and dynamic aspects is quite problematic. In our approach, semantic fragments of computation independent specifications are defined by using service-oriented concept of an interaction loop. Interaction dependencies specify services in terms of communication actions, which play an integrating role in binding the static and dynamic aspects together. Since semantic integrity rules of static and dynamic aspects are missing in the traditional information system analysis and design models, they are difficult to apply for computing the semantic difference, union or intersection of goals.

Case Study: A Travel Agency Example

We use a Travel Agency example to illustrate interplay between the pragmatic and semantic dependencies. Example demonstrates how goals, problems and opportunities can help system analysis experts to reason about advantages (positive influence link) and disadvantages (negative influence dependency) of business process activities. The travel Agency has identified two problems: "Sloppy Selling Process for Low Cost Trips" is an internal problem and "Sharp Competition among Travel Agencies" can be viewed as external problem. Both problems hinder to the achievement of the goal "First Choice of Customers", which characterizes the overall *desired situation*. It is the goal to attract and retain customers by finding the best ways in redesigning business processes in the Travel Agency. Two opportunities can be used to improve the *current situation*. The first opportunity "Offer Discounts for Returning Customers" represents system functionality, which is not available in the *problematic situation*. The second opportunity "Sell a Trip" characterizes functionality, which represents strength of the current situation. It is always desirable to maintain the strength in the future situation. If one of the goals can be reached, then the problematic situation will be improved. Goals problems and opportunities are represented graphically in Figure 15.

The decomposition and refinement links help a business designer to see the structure of the main goal. It is not sufficient to represent specification of every subgoal in terms of interaction loops in different services. Interactions must be integrated, because they belong to the same goal. The goal "First Choice of

Figure 15. Pragmatic dependencies of a Travel Agency

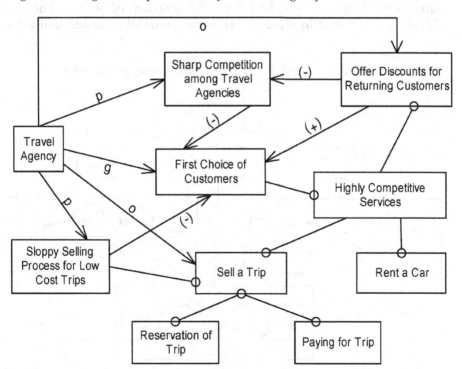

Customers" is refined into sub goal "Highly Competitive Services", which consists of three sub goals "Sell a Trip", "Rent a Car" and "Offer Discounts for Returning Customers". In this example we are not going into further details of subgoal "Rent a Car" for the reason of space limitations.

Opportunity "Sell a Trip" represents fragment of functionality that is viewed as a strength of the organization, because it is a refinement of both the problem "Sloppy Selling Process for Low Cost Trips" and the goal "Highly Competitive Services". This opportunity is decomposed into two activities "Reservation of Trip" and "Paying for Trip". It is the only alternative to "Sell a Trip" at the Travel Agency in the current situation, which is viewed as a problematic. Goal decomposition process could be seen as a means of eliminating the problematic fragments of specification at the semantic level and complementing them by the desirable fragments. Decomposition hierarchy motivates the strategies and the ways in which the high-level objectives are achieved. At the bottom level of abstraction, it is necessary to refine goals in terms of interaction loops between service requesters and service providers. This is represented in Figure 16.

Subgoal "Reservation of Trip" is decomposed into three activities: "Searching for Trips", "Selecting Trips", and "Create Reservation". This decomposition is complete, because the semantic union of these three interaction loops is sufficient for "Reservation of Trip". The goal decomposition hierarchy represents two actors (service requesters and service

Figure 16. Decomposition of the goal in terms of interaction loops

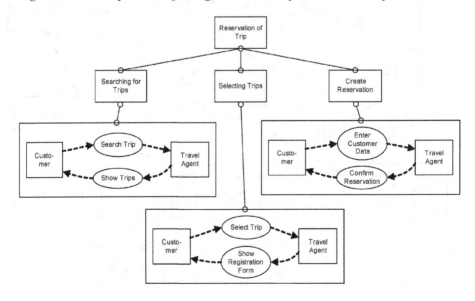

provider) that are involved in each business process step. Refinement of every goal at the bottom level is defined in terms of input and output flows that define atomic interactions in different service steps. Composition of interaction loops should result in an integrated business process or service. "Reservation of Trip" consists of three interaction loops for that are represented in Figure 17.

As it is indicated in the graphical description in the first interaction loop a Customer initiates the action Search Trip, which is viewed as a service request. Travel Agent is a service provider, which is supposed to "Show

Figure 17. 'Reservation of Trip' description at the semantic level

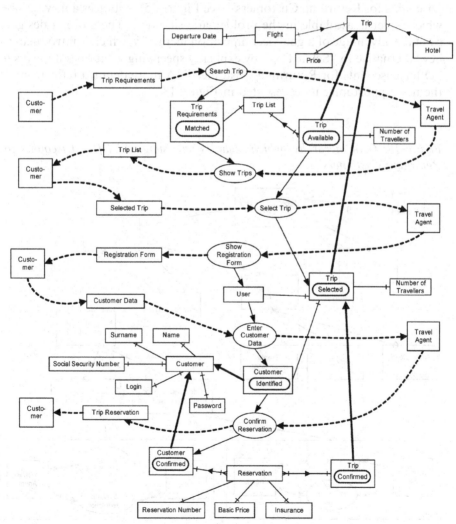

Trips". In the next interaction loop, a Customer selects a trip from a Trip List by initiating the communication action "Select Trip". When a trip is selected, a Travel Agent shows registration form. In the third interaction loop a customer is supposed to "Enter Customer Data". If so, then Travel Agent will be obliged to "Confirm Reservation".

New opportunities, which positively affect the goal of organization, should be fully integrated into the overall business process. If a designer is willing to take advantage of an opportunity, then it is not sufficient to represent it on the diagram by using refinement dependency. Enterprise model must unambiguously demonstrate how an opportunity is integrated both at the semantic and at the pragmatic levels. For instance, the opportunity "Offer Discounts for Returning Customers" (see Figure 15) embraces a new service, which is yet unavailable in the problematic situation. Therefore, a designer can take advantage of a goal decomposition hierarchy, which is introducing a new alternative to "Sell a Trip" by explicitly specifying what does it means to "Offer Discounts for Returning Customers". A more detailed refinement of the new opportunity is represented in Figure 18.

Figure 18. Goal hierarchy, which includes new subgoal "Offer Discounts for Returning Customers"

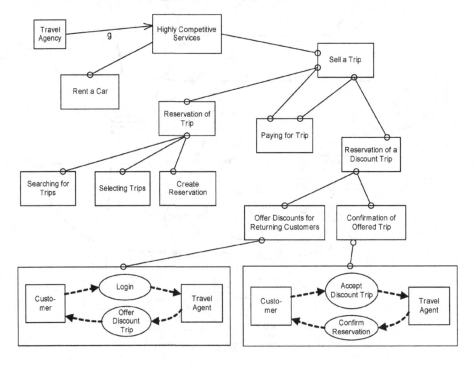

Figure 19. Two strategies for the achievement of goal "Sell a Trip"

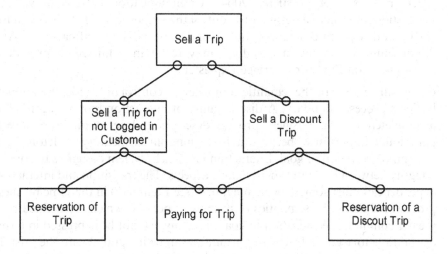

Eventually, a new opportunity must be integrated into the existing enterprise model at the semantic level. It means that "Offer Discounts for Returning Customers" functionality must be consistent with the other subgoals in the hierarchy of "Highly Competitive Services". Since both pragmatic entities "Offer Discounts for Returning Customers" and "Reservation of Trip" belong to the same hierarchy of "Highly Competitive Services", they must satisfy conditions that apply for the greater common specialization "Sell a Trip". "Sell a Discount Trip" is a new alternative of selling, which can be used by the returning customers. Discounts can be offered just to those customers, which have possibility to login. A new alternative for the achievement of goal "Sell a Trip" is explicitly introduced by extending the goal hierarchy. Two alternatives are represented in Figure 19.

The alternative way to "Sell a Trip" is represented by using satisficing dependency link. Please note that two subgoals "Sell a Trip for not Logged in Customer" and "Sell a Discount Trip" can be interpreted as two different strategies (Roland, 2005), which are expressed in terms of decomposition. This hierarchy tells a designer that the same "Paying for Trip" functionality is used in both alternatives. Semantics of "Reservation of Trip" differs significantly from "Reservation of a Discount Trip". It consists of "Offer Discounts for Returning Customers" and "Confirmation of Offered Trip". The subgoal "Paying for Trip" represents an overlapping part, which can be represented as an intersection of two alternative goals (strategies) for the achievement "Sell a Trip" goal. It is not difficult to see that a content of interaction loops is prescribed by the pragmatic part of the enterprise model. Goal hierarchies help a designer to control the semantic completeness of specifications. The transition and interaction dependencies must somehow go together (Gustas & Gustiene, 2004). Communication actions in various interaction loops help a designer to control the semantic integrity between the static and dynamic aspects of business process specifications. Any discontinuity of an interaction loop may result in a failure to provide a communication flow for a service requester.

Goals can be used for the semantic completeness control or for identification of business process boundary. A discontinuity of interaction loop is regarded as incompleteness in a business process description. Interaction loop have a paramount importance, because it is defining an elementary skeleton for a semantic description of goal. Interaction loops help system designers to control integrity between the static and dynamic aspects. The transition and interaction dependencies must somehow be integrated (see Figure 17) in the same business process. Additionally, semantics of business processes, which are defined by a greater common specialization in goal hierarchy, cannot be expressed in terms of contradictory goals. If new opportunities can be integrated with the existing business process descriptions, then they are viewed as subgoals. In our example, the opportunity "Offer Discounts for Returning Customers" is viewed as a subgoal for a Trip Agency. Thus, it cannot be contradictory in the "Sell a Trip" goal hierarchy. All semantic integrity issues in the context of "Highly Completive Services" must be resolved. We are not going into the semantic integrity details for "Reservation of a Discount Trip" any further for the reason of space limitations.

Concluding Remarks and Outlook

We presented a new pragmatic-driven approach for service-oriented analysis. Engineering of enterprise models at the semantic level is driven by the pragmatic descriptions, which are defined in terms of goals, problems and opportunities. Semantic integrity of static and dynamic dependencies in various interaction loops is viewed as one of the major benefits of Service-Oriented Analysis and Design. Pragmatic descriptions aim to provide motivation for conceptual representations of enterprise components, which are defined by elementary interactions between service consumers and service providers. Enterprise models at the pragmatic level are crucial for success of information systems projects. The underlying assumption is that system services are worthwhile if they meet the goals of the organization.

The success of SOAD approach depends much on finding the appropriate fitness between pragmatic level, which defines the overall business strategy, and the semantic level that defines business processes across organizational and technical system boundaries. An integrated set of the static and dynamic dependencies is used for service-oriented modeling of semantic aspects of business process architectures. The graphical example is presented for demonstration of bridging from the pragmatic to semantic specifications, which are defined in terms of computation independent notation. Semantic and pragmatic models are defining just essential aspects of service-oriented architectures that are not influenced by possible technical solutions. The concept of service is quite unique, because it is well understood by business managers and by system development experts. Elementary interactions can be applied equally well for conceptual modeling of organizational as well as technical components.

Any business process fragment can be defined as a service. A service from the pragmatic point of view can be regarded as a problem, opportunity or a goal. Pragmatic dependencies are used for the analysis of actor intentions. They express contradictions between actors, what is desirable or what actors try to avoid. Goal hierarchies can also help to identify new business process boundaries and provide a basis for reasoning about semantic completeness of specifications. Every service is defined in terms of interaction loops, which add value and together form a purposeful business activity. It was illustrated that evolution or change of business process fragments can be supported by using operations of semantic difference, union and intersection on goals, problems and opportunities.

A new service-oriented foundation for information system analysis and design is heavily centered on modeling of the semantic and pragmatic aspects of business processes. The computation independent modeling of business processes in terms of services gives possibility to define SOAD as an engineering discipline, which provides a basis for semantic integrity and semantic completeness control. Computation independent diagrams are represented as enterprise models at the pragmatic and semantic levels. The semantic level provides motivation for technical and organizational system components. The pragmatic specifications can be characterized as strategy-oriented. They are useful for several reasons: motivating service events and can be used as a driving force in service-oriented engineering of business process patterns.

References

Ambler, S. W. (2002). Deriving web services from UML models. From www-106.ibm.com/ developerworks/webservices/library/ws-uml1

Batini, C., Lenzerini, M., & Navathe, B. L. (1986). A comparative analysis of methodologies for data base schema integration. *ACM Computing Surveys, 18*(4), 323-363.

Blaha, M., & Rumbaugh, J. (2005). *Object-oriented modelling and design with UML*. London: Pearson.

Business Process Modeling Notation Working Group (2004). Business process modeling notation. Retrieved June 09, 2005, from http://www.bpmn.org

Codd, E. F. (1990). The relational model for database management. Addison_Wesley.

Colan, M. (2004). Service-oriented architecture expends the vision of web services, Part 1, Characteristics of service-oriented architecture, IBM Corporation. Retrieved April 21, 2004, from http://www-106.ibm.com/developerworks/library/ws-soaintro.html

Daconta, M. C., Obrst, L. J., & Smith, K. T. (2003). *The semantic web: A guide to the future of XML, web services, and knowledge management*. Indianapolis: Wiley.

Davis, G. B., & Olson, M. (1989). *Management information systems*. New York: McGraw Hill.

Denning, P. J., & Medina-Mora, R. (1995). Completing the loops. *Interfaces, 25*, 42-57.

Dietz, J. L. G. (2001). DEMO: Towards a discipline of organisation engineering. *European Journal of Operational Research (128)*, Elsevier Science, pp. 351-363.

Erl, T. (2005). *Service-oriented architecture: Conceprs, technology, and design*. Crawfordsville, IN: Pearson Prentice Hall.

Finkelstein, C. (2004). Enterprise integration using enterprise architecture. In H. Linger et al. (Ed.), *Constructing the infrastructure for the knowledge economy*. Kluwer Academic/Plenum Publishers.

Gottschalk, K., Graham, S., Kreger, H., & Snell, J. (2002). Introduction to web services architecture. *IBM Systems Journal, 41*, 170-177.

van Griethuisen, J. J. (1982). Concepts and terminology for the conceptual schema and information base. Report ISO TC97/SC5/WG5, No 695.

Gustas, R. (2005). Inference rules of semantic dependencies in the enterprise modelling. In H. Fujita, & M. Mejri (Eds.), *New trends in software methodologies, tools and techniques* (pp. 235-251), IOS Press.

Gustas, R., Bubenko, J., & Wangler, B. (1996). Goal driven enterprise modelling: Bridging pragmatic and semantic descriptions of information systems. *Frontiers in Artificial Intelligence and Applications: Information Modelling and Knowledge Bases VII, 34*, IOS Press, pp. 73-91.

Gustas, R., & Gustiene, P. (2002). Extending lyee methodology using the enterprise modelling approach. *Frontiers in Artificial Intelligence and Applications* (pp. 273-288). Amsterdam: IOS Press.

Gustas, R., & Gustiene, P. (2004). Towards the enterprise engineering approach for information system modelling across organisational and technical boundaries. *Enterprise Information Systems V* (pp. 204-215). Netherlands: Kluwer Academic Publisher.

Gustas, R., & Jakobsson, L. (2004). Enterprise modelling of component oriented information system architectures. *New trends in software methodologies, tools and techniques,* IOS Press, pp. 88-102.

Gustiene, P., & Gustas, R. (2002). On a problem of ambiguity and semantic role relativity in conceptual modelling. In *Proceedings of International Conference on Advances in Infrastructure for e-Business, e-Education, e-Science, and e-Medicine on the Internet,* ISBN 88-85280-62-5, L'Aquila, Italy.

Harel, D., & Rumpe, B. (2004, October). Meaningful odeling: What's the semantics of 'semantics'?, *IEEE Computer,* pp. 64-72.

High, R., Kinder, S., & Graham, S. (2005). IBM's SOA foundation, IBM Corporation, version 1.0. Retrieved November 02, 2005, from http://download.boulder.ibm.com/ibmdl/pub/software/dw/webservices/ws-soa-whitepaper.pdf

Hoffer, J. A., George, J. F., & Valacich, J. S. (2004). *Modern system analysis and design.* New Jersey: Pearson Prentice Hall.

Hull, R., Christophides, V., & Su, J. (2003). E-services: A look behind the curtain. *ACM PODS,* San Diego, CA.

Johanesson, P. (1993). Schema transformations as an aid in view integration. In *Proceedings of the Fifth International Conference on Systems Engineering.* Paris: Springer.

Lankhorst, M. et al. (2005). *Enterprise architecture at work.* Berlin: Springer.

Maciaszek, L. A. (2001). *Requirements analysis and system design.* Addison Wesley.

Martin, J., & Odell, J. J. (1998). *Object-oriented methods: A foundation (UML edition).* Englewood Cliffs: Prentice-Hall.

de Moor, A. (2005). Patterns for the pragmatic web. In *Proceedings of the 13th International Conference on Conceptual Structures* (pp. 1-18). LNAI, Berlin: Springer.

Object Management Group Architecture Board (2003). *MDA guide.* version 1.0.1, J. Miller, & J. Mukerji (Eds.), Retrieved November 20, 2006, from http://www.omg.org/ docs/omg/03-06-01.pdf

Perrone, V., Mainetti, L., & Paolini, P. (2005). A UML extension for designing usable user experiences for web applications. In *Proceedings of the CAISE*05 Workshop on Web Oriented Software Technologies, 153.*

Rolland, C. (2005). Modelling multi-facetted purposes of artefacts. In H. Fujita, & M. Mejri (Eds.), *New trends in software methodologies, tools and techniques* (pp. 3-16). IOS Press.

Simon, H. A. (1996). *The sciences of the artificial.* MIT Press.

Singh, M. P. (2002, May–June). The pragmatic web. *IEEE Internet Computing,* pp. 4-5.

Skyttner, L. (2002). *General system theory ideas and applications.* Singapore: World Scientific Publishing.

Snoeck, M., Dedene, G., Verhelst, M., & Depuydt, A. M. (1999). *Object-oriented enterprise modelling with merode.* Leuven University Press.

Storey, V. C. (1993). Understanding semantic relationships. *VLDB Journal,* F. Marianski (Ed.), *2,* 455-487.

Szyperski, C. (1998). *Component software – Beyond object-oriented programming.* Reading, MA: Addison-Wesley.

Yu, E., & Mylopoulos, J. (1994). From e-r to 'a-r' - modelling strategic actor relationships for business process reengineering. In *Proceedings of 13th International Conference on the Entity - Relationship Approach,* Manchester, U.K.

Zachman, J. A. (1996). Enterprise architecture: The issue of the century. *Database Programming and Design Magazine.*

Zimmerman, O., Krogdahl, P., & Gee, C. (2004). Elements of service-oriented analysis and design. Retrieved June 9, 2005, from www-128.ibm.com/developerworks/library/ws-soad1/.

Chapter VI

The Practice of Participatory Enterprise Modelling:
A Competency Perspective

Anne Persson, University of Skövde, Sweden

Abstract

This chapter discusses competency aspects of participatory Enterprise Modelling. It presents the two main ways of working when it comes to involving stakeholders in the modelling process, the participatory and the non-participatory and then focuses on the participatory approach. The author describes the desired competencies of domain experts and method experts, two of the most crucial actors in the participatory modelling process. The author argues that in spite that competency is one of the most critical success factors in modelling it is an overlooked topic in modelling research. The chapter is illustrated with interview quotes from an interview study that the author has carried out.

Introduction

Enterprise Modelling (EM) is an activity where an *integrated* and *negotiated* model describing different aspects of an enterprise is created. An Enterprise Model consists of a number of related "sub-models", each describing the enterprise from a particular perspective, e.g. processes, business rules, goals, actors and concepts/information/data.

Enterprise Modelling (EM), or Business Modelling, has for many years been a central theme in information systems engineering research. There are two main reasons for using EM (Persson and Stirna, 2001):

1) *Developing the business* – This entails developing business vision, strategies, redesigning the way the business operates, developing the supporting information systems, etc.

2) *Ensuring the quality of the business* – Here the focus is on two issues: 1) sharing the knowledge about the business, its vision, the way it operates and 2) ensuring the acceptance of business decisions through committing the stakeholders to the decisions made.

Examples of EM methods can be found in Bajec and Krisper (2005), Dobson, Blyth and Strens (1994), Castro, Kolp, Mylopoulos and Tropos (2001), Johannesson, Boman, Bubenko, and Wangler (1997), Willars et al (1993), Bubenko, Persson, and Stirna (2001), Bubenko (1993), F3 Consortium (1994), Fox, Chionglo and Fadel, (1993), Krogstie, et al (2000), Loucopoulos et al (1997), and Yu and Mylopoulos (1994).

Examples of application domains for EM can be found in Wangler, Persson, Johannesson, and Ekenberg (2003), Niehaves and Stirna. (2006), Stirna, Persson, and Aggestam (2006), Wangler and Persson (2002), Wangler, Persson and Söderström (2001), Gustas, Bubenko and Wangler (1995), and Kardasis et al (1998).

A large amount of research has been dedicated to the development of new modelling languages and to the refinement of existing ones, while their use in practice has attracted less attention.

EM practice can be discussed from a number of alternative perspectives, such as e.g.:

- the ability of modelling languages to express aspects of the domain being modelled,
- the usability of modelling languages,
- the role of enterprise models in information systems engineering,
- the effect on the systems development process of using conceptual models, and
- the applicability of modelling languages in different contexts.

In this paper we focus on a perspective that has been very little discussed in the literature: the competency of the stakeholders involved in the modelling process and how it influences the quality of the modelling outcome. Our research has shown that this is a critical success factor for the effective use of EM. A factor that we claim could be more critical than e.g. the features of the modelling language used.

The paper builds on a series of case studies that were carried out in European and Swedish research projects as well as an interview study targeting experienced EM practitioners. A large portion of these studies are reported in Persson (2001). The case studies involved more than 100 modelling sessions during the years 1993–2006 and the interview study involved 11 EM practitioners with 10-25 years of experience. The competency profiles of interviewees are included in Appendix 1. The paper compiles the research results concerning competency issues in enterprise modelling gathered from the case studies and interviews. Throughout the paper, quotations from the interview study have been included to illustrate the findings. A similar approach to writing can be found in Orlikowski (1993).

One of the interviewees in the interview study that has provided input to this paper made quite a pointed remark about the quality of models being produced in current practice:

"I claim that 30 % of what is produced today is at all acceptable as a platform to stand on [for further development work] … Most of what is done today, especially with regard to business processes, is garbage." [Interviewee 1]

This interviewee and several others in our interview study emphasised that there is a shortage of method user competency in current EM practice.

The concept of competency is complex and can be defined in a number of ways. For the purposes of this paper we state that competency has four main aspects:

1) *Knowledge*
   A person's factual knowledge about a specific subject matter, as a result of e.g. education.

2) *Skills*
   A person's ability to actually use the knowledge to achieve goals.

3) *Individual properties*
   A wide range of personal characteristics e.g. social skills, intelligence, flexibility, integrity, ability to co-operate, courage etc.

4) *Willingness to contribute competency*
   A person's attitude towards actually contributing her/his knowledge and skills to the achievement of goals other than her/his own.

The remainder of the paper targets the competencies of method and domain experts because these are claimed to have the heaviest influence on the modelling process.

The paper is organised as follows. Section 2 discusses the two main ways of working when it comes to involving stakeholders in the modelling process, the participatory and the non-participatory. In the remainder of the paper we focus on the participatory approach. The stakeholders of the participatory modelling process are described in section 3. Section 4 and 5 discusses the desired competencies of domain experts and method experts, two of the most critical actors in the modelling process, while section 6 focuses on training of these two stakeholder categories. Finally, the findings are discussed in section 7.

Ways of Working in Enterprise Modelling – Advocating a Participatory Approach

There are different ways of working in the EM process, when it comes to gathering domain knowledge to be included in Enterprise Models. Some of the more common ones are:

- Interviews with domain experts
- Analysis of existing documentation
- Observation of existing work practices
- Facilitated group modelling

These ways of working can be categorised according to the degree of participation by the domain experts. Mumford (1983) distinguishes between three levels of participation in the systems development process:

1) *Consultative participation*
    Leaves the main design tasks to the systems developer but the affected stakeholders are consulted about the design decisions.

2) *Representative participation*
    Here the "design group" consists of systems developers *as well as* user representatives.

3) *Consensus participation*
    At this level the systems development process is intended to be user-driven.

These levels are applicable also to the ways of working in EM. Interviews can be consultative and also representative. In observation and document analysis domain experts do not participate actively. Facilitated group modelling is the way of working that in a participatory manner involves the domain experts.

Method developers have advocated a participatory way of working (see e.g. Bubenko, Persson and Stirna, 2001; F³ Consortium, 1995; Nilsson, Tolis and Nellborn, 1999). In facilitated group modelling, participation is *consensus-driven* in the sense that it is the domain stakeholders who "own" the model and govern its contents. In contrast, *consultative* participation means that analysts create models and domain stakeholders are then consulted in order to validate the models.

In the participatory approach to modelling, stakeholders meet in modelling sessions, led by a facilitator, to create models collaboratively. In the modelling sessions, models are often documented on large plastic sheets using paper cards. The "plastic wall" is viewed as the official "minutes" of the session, for which every participant is responsible.

In order to achieve consensus-driven participation, some additional goals must also be achieved:

- To achieve active communication and lively discussion between individuals and between groups of individuals. Functioning human communication and lively discussion increase the chances of identifying different views on the problem to be discussed.

- To create a group, i.e. to make people feel that they work towards the same goal. Chances of achieving a good modelling result increases if the group works in the same direction.

More on the participative approach to modelling can e.g. be found e.g. in F^3 Consortium (1995) and Willars et. al. (1993).

The goal of conceptual modelling is often to describe the current or future state of some domain. This description is then used as important input in the process of systems development. For conceptual modelling in general the product of modelling, namely conceptual models are the main target. *Participatory* modelling has an additional target, namely to achieve some effect on the *thinking* of the people participating in the modelling process. In fact, some practitioners claim that the *real* model resides in the minds of the participants of the modelling process (See e.g. Willars, 1999).

Our interview study shows that there are three main reasons why an approach that focuses on stakeholder participation (a participatory approach) should be used, if possible:

- The quality of the Enterprise Model is enhanced.
- Consensus is enhanced.
- Achievement of acceptance and commitment is facilitated.

The *quality of a model is enhanced* if the models are created in collaboration between stakeholders, rather than resulting from a consultant's interpretation of interviews with domain experts. This was explained by two of the interviewees:

"... I usually claim that the knowledge is not collected in one brain. We need to bring in many different people. OK, then it could work with interviews, but it is different knowledge, which cannot be easily integrated. Kalle says something and Lisa says something. How do I know what is the difference between their statements when I don't know anything about the domain. This is why I need to bring Kalle and Lisa together so that they together can explain to me that they mean the same thing or that they do not mean the same thing." [Interviewee 2]

"... but if you are going to design something for the future you can not collect one piece here and one piece there and then say that I choose this one because it seems right. They [the stakeholders] need to come together and decide what they want. ..." [Interviewee 5]

Another aspect of this is that ideas are validated and improved when a group works with them:

"The next important thing is that ideas grow when they are "juggled" by a group. This is the really strong argument, which supports the view that a group of people can achieve so much more if they work together. … But this "juggling" of ideas … I see it daily that ideas improve when they are discussed openly between people" [Interviewee 2]

An interesting and illustrative anecdote related to this idea was told by one of the interviewees:

"Perhaps you have heard about the exercise about emergency landing on the moon, that is often used in seminars about group dynamics. It's about imagining that you have travelled with a space ship to the moon together with some other people. Unfortunately you have crash-landed. You cannot start again. However, help is on the way in a rescue ship. However, it cannot land where you have landed. You have to transport yourselves about 10 km over the moon surface to the place where the rescue ship can land. You can bring no more than 10 things from your ship. What do you choose to bring to maximise the probability of survival? This exercise is first carried out individually. Everyone writes his own list. Then you work out your list in pairs. Little by little the groups grow bigger and finally all the people have to agree on one list. Then you compare with the "right" answer provided by NASA and then it shows that the two lists converge. You get the right solution with more people. Of course, none of the participants have the truth, since no one is an expert in moonwalks. … This is a good example of how it works in participative EM. That's why I emphasise the importance of having a heterogeneous collection of competencies in the sessions. Because, often the truth can be found in the meeting between different competencies." [Interviewee 6]

Even if modelling does not result in a concrete solution, the collaboration itself can have a positive effect on future work:

"As I had understood it, there were some conflicts between different projects and departments. Preferably they should produce a use case model, but they did not agree on how to co-operate. I saw that this was an impossible mission, but I thought that the most important thing is to have a common view on the world. Then we can start producing something, and this was something that they absolutely wanted. I felt that I got them to talk about things that they hadn't been able to talk about before. They got an understanding that we do this and the others do that. The modelling result was not used as such, but they had created a value in that they had begun to gain a common view. It had become easier to talk to each other." [Interviewee 8]

One interviewee had found - much to his surprise - that people in organisations, especially large ones, do not talk to each other about their work as much as one may think:

"Well, it is not unusual that people really talk to each other for the first time in a modelling session. You expect that people do it every day. In a large organisation there are high walls everywhere, I find. It is often difficult. .... People say they don't have the time; they only do their work. They sub-optimise their little piece of the work." [Interviewee 7]

Here, the fact that people communicate actively during a modelling session is a contribution in itself.

Consensus is enhanced when a participative approach is adopted.

"... where you need to obtain agreement in a group. There participative enterprise modelling is effective." [Interviewee 4]

"The participative way of working forces people to collectively expose their thinking and somehow either establish a direct conflict or strive towards consensus." [Interviewee 1]

The adoption of a participative approach involves stakeholders in the decision making process, which facilitates the *achievement of acceptance and commitment.* This is particularly important if the modelling activity is focused on changing some aspect of the domain, such as its visions/strategies, business processes and information system support.

"Active involvement from stakeholders is a contributing factor for successful implementation of the modelling result." [Interviewee 1]

This view of why participatory modelling is used clearly influences the competency requirements for a method expert, particularly the facilitator.

The Stakeholders of the Participatory Enterprise Modelling Process

There are a number of roles in the participatory EM process. They fall into two main categories: *domain experts* and *method experts* (Figure 1).

An Enterprise Model comprises knowledge regarding different aspects of some organisation. Domain experts provide this knowledge. To create the

Figure 1. Some roles in a participatory EM project

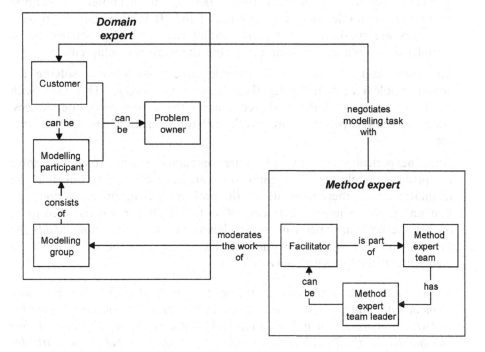

Enterprise Models, using a participative approach, a *method expert* is needed. The method expert is expected to have the necessary knowledge with regard to the EM method used and the participatory approach to modelling.

The *customer* is the main responsible party for the modelling project on the domain expert side. In the modelling sessions, the *modelling groups* consist of *modelling participants*, which are stakeholders concerned with the problem at hand. These stakeholders may also be involved in other projects that are related to the one being planned. The customer may also participate in modelling groups. The main problem being addressed has a *problem owner*, which mostly is the customer. For sub-problems, there can be also other problem owners, e.g. other modelling participants.

The method expert negotiates and plans the modelling activity together with the customer. A *facilitator* moderates each modelling session. In a session there can be more than one facilitator. A larger modelling activity will typically have several facilitators forming a *method expert team*, which is headed by a *method expert team leader*. The team leader is often an experienced facilitator.

The responsibilities of actors in the EM process are described in Figure 2. The main responsibility of the method expert is that the chosen EM method is suitable for modelling the problem at hand. It is also that the project resources are used in a way that enables the modelling activity to be completed on time and in such a way that the goals are achieved.

The main responsibility of the domain experts is towards solving the actual problem at hand using their domain knowledge. This view with regard to responsibilities is shared among the experienced interviewees, whereas the less experienced are less clear about the distinct roles of these two actors.

Some inexperienced report that they are sometimes expected to actually solve the problem, while the experienced ones are very clear in stating that the facilitator is *only* there to moderate the problem solving process among the domain experts. The issue here is whether the facilitator is considered to be one of the domain experts in the modelling group or an actor *outside* the domain expert group. One of the interviewees explains the risk involved in being one of the "problem solvers":

"You tend to think that you are pretty smart yourself. And when you have done 15 models of billing, you start to believe that you know how such a thing works, and when you are assigned to do it the 16th time with a group that is a bit slow and inactive ... it's difficult to pick up the pace ... then you help them a little bit by asking very leading questions which come from your own idea of what billing is. And then, since you are a nice guy and an external consultant with some authority, they buy what you are saying ... just like that. This mistake I've done a number of times ... that I more or less unconsciously use my knowledge ... or assumed knowledge ... in their models instead of drawing out their knowledge. Which has turned out, a few steps later ... "but it was you who said that it should be like that" [interviewee speaks in the voice of the modelling participants] And that is educative, that you somehow must be intellectually humble ... something that is not very easy when you think you know. It's part of the trick in this job to quickly adapt to a new environment and sometimes you do it too well. You think that you know things too good, better than the modelling participants." [Interviewee 6]

The competency of domain experts and method experts is identified by the most experienced interviewees as *the* most crucial resources in a participatory modelling activity.

"It has happened that I have cancelled sessions where I don't get enough good people. In that case it's not worth either the money or the effort." *[Interviewee 6]*

Figure 2. Responsibilities of actors in participatory EM

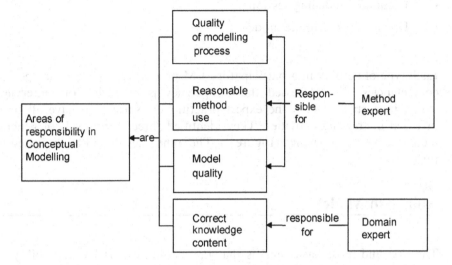

The Competency of Method Experts

In the literature, very little is said about the competency of the method expert. Some references exist (see e.g. F[3] Consortium, 1995; Nilsson, Tolis and Nellborn, 1999; Bubenko, Persson and Stirna, 2001 and Astrakan, 2001), which mainly focus on the method expert in her/his capacity as facilitator. We have not found references, which take a broader perspective considering the competency required throughout a whole EM project. This broader perspective is emphasised in this paper. Furthermore, the references focus on the *individual* method expert, while we consider that one individual may possess the competency or several individuals in a team of method experts can represent it. Therefore we focus our discussion of method expert competency not on the individual but on which competency that is required for the different activities in a participatory EM process.

The competency of the method expert is a critical resource, being responsible for the effective adoption of the chosen method and for the modelling activity reaching its goals using the assigned resources. The activities carried out by a method expert reflect the EM process:

- Define the project
- Negotiate resources

- Prepare modelling sessions
- Facilitate modelling sessions
- Document and refine models

Each type of activity in a participatory EM process requires certain specific competencies. We addressed the competency issue during our interview study, in particular with the expert practitioners since they have all been involved in training activities. They identified three main levels of general method expert competency (Figure 3). These three levels will be discussed in turn.

Ability to Model

The *first* and most basic level is that the method expert has the ability to model, i.e. to choose a suitable formalism for the problem at hand, to use the EM method's meta-model in order to represent some chunk of knowledge. Furthermore, the knowledge should be represented in such a way that the model actually reflects the knowledge.

This ability does not only rely on knowledge about specific modelling formalisms. It is very much based on knowledge about the ideas behind conceptual modelling in general and on the ability to compare different modelling formalisms and choose one that is suitable for a specific situation (Astrakan, 2001).

Figure 3. Three levels of method expert competency

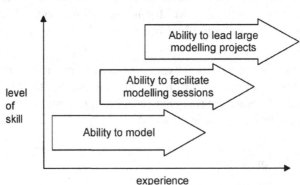

This ability is reasonably well covered in terms of literature and courses, but still it seems that part can be learnt and part of it comes from the individual personality:

"Surprisingly often the basic model quality was really low for most modelling facilitators. Basic model quality sucks. And this can't everybody detect. There are some people that are completely blind to this." [Interviewee 1]

The ability to model can in itself have different levels:

"One has to do with bread and butter modelling in normal situation. There you can often make do with ordinary craftsmanship. Then there is what I call highly qualified modelling, where you operate on processes at a generic level, where you make relatively heavy abstractions in the models to reach substantial efficiency improvements. Where you want to make a break-through in the business. Then craftsmanship is not enough. It's just a fact. There are only a few people who can do this. I have unfortunately seen a number of Business Process Reengineering projects that wanted to do this and failed because they didn't realise the potential in what they had done. ... It's about having some sort of composer's talent." [Interviewee 1]

The situation described in this quote is about radical business change. From our own experience and also from some interviewee statements we conclude that modelling the present state is very different from modelling the future state in the sense that an unknown arena is entered in future state modelling. This requires from the modelling participants that they can think creatively about the future but it also requires a higher degree of skill in the method expert so that the group keeps up their creativity.

Ability to Facilitate Modelling Sessions

The *second* level of competency focuses on the ability to facilitate a modelling process, i.e. to lead/facilitate a modelling group in the process of collaboratively creating an Enterprise Model. This ability is very much based on knowledge about the effects of modelling, the principles of human communication and socialisation, especially in groups, as well as the conditions of human learning and problem solving (cognition) (Astrakan, 2001).

Facilitation is a general technique used in group processes for a wide variety of purposes, also within EM (see further International Association for Facilitators (IAF) http://www.iaf-world.org/i4a/pages/index.cfm?pageid=1).

In participatory EM facilitation we include the activities of preparing modelling sessions, facilitating them and documenting the result.

When talking to practitioners about competency requirements for facilitation of modelling sessions they often mention "social skills" as one such requirement. These "social skills" are personal characteristics, which can be further described as follows (Astrakan, 2001):

Listening Skills

Listening is not only about listening to what is actually being said. Listening behind the words for what is really meant is essential here. One of the interviewees actually talked about taking on his "elephant ears".

Group Management and Pedagogical Skills

The leader role is facilitated by the ability to motivate and keeping the modelling facilitators interested. The ability to detect and solving potential conflicts is also part of this skill

Act as an Authority

To be an authority in this context is not the same as being authoritative. To act as an authority is to create trust for your own competency and to make the modelling participants feel that you know what you are talking about.

Courage and Ability to Improvise

Several of the interviewees emphasise courage as a desired personal characteristic in a modelling facilitator.

Courage and ability to improvise were particularly emphasised by the interviewees.

"Instead of knowing everything you top it off with courage..." [Interviewee 4]

It is also helpful to be interested in and curious about the problem domain in question.

"Part of the talent is to be extremely curious. You need to like diving into other truths than the ones that you know for the moment. And you have to like doing it with the help of other people. Preferably with integrity, but you have to respect that there are actually other people than you, kid, who know this." *[Interviewee 6]*

Courage in participatory EM is about not being afraid of the unknown. Not everyone accepts entering into the unknown, owing to her/his personality. Others are too inexperienced to cope with this type of situation:

"I think it's a matter of personality if you accept to enter into unknown situations. With hidden parameters. If you know from the start what the parameters are, then you can start juggling them about and go into problem solving. But if you don't even know which they are you have to do something to get them out ... this is not something for the novice." *[Interviewee 4]*

This situation relates to the issue of problem complexity, particularly the notion of "wicked problem". A wicked problem has many unknown variables.

Some may think that being a skilled facilitator is to know a large number of "tricks" to make the work group. It may work for a time, but the facilitator also needs give some of her/himself to achieve useful results with a group.

Several interviewees talked about the advantages of having more than one facilitator in a modelling session. Two of the interviewees always work as a facilitator team and several others prefer being more than one if possible. We have tried this way of working ourselves and it has several advantages. Some facilitator teams share the work in that one person documents and one facilitates. Others take turns facilitating the group. However, the team relationship must be completely equal in order to function properly. Every member of the facilitator team must be considered by the group to be an authority.

"We have thought a lot about this because we have seen different constellations that have tried to work together but failed. We have also tried to work with other people where it didn't work. [The interviewee normally works with a particular person]. If I'm allowed to be a bit categorical I have to say that it's difficult with masculine types who always have to have the last word. It doesn't work if one of the facilitators always has to have the last word. We normally use gestures and mimicry. We have a wordless dialogue. You need to be able to communicate without words and without the group noticing that something is happening." *[Interviewee 5]*

Ability to Lead Modelling Projects

The *third* and top level emphasises the ability to co-ordinate and lead modelling projects, involving a team of method experts, toward achieving project goals. Leading a modelling project involves negotiating the project as well as monitoring it and reporting the results.

If facilitation of modelling sessions is considered to be the micro process in participative EM, then the whole project is the macro process. Managing the macro process, especially in large projects, requires a significant amount of experience. The usual project management skills are evidently needed, but apart from that, EM project leaders need to be able to see how the whole set of modelling sessions and their results hold together and how they contribute to achieving the project goals.

"You have a different focus. There is only one thing to think about really and that is does the complete thing work. How do we integrate the different results [models]? It's all about how we keep the different results together so that they don't diverge? ... I still believe that we have between a dozen and twenty really skilled people in Sweden who can really run this macro process." [Interviewee 1]

A critical task in leading a project is negotiating the project definition and resources as well as judging which approach to modelling is appropriate in that situation. Difficult tasks, such as assessing the organisational culture and looking for hidden agendas must be carried out. It is clear from the interviews that beginners in the field should not make these assessments. It is advisable that and experienced method expert negotiate the project while the less experienced focus on other tasks, such as facilitating modelling sessions.

In current participatory EM practice it seems to be fairly common that the role of facilitator and that of leader for the overall project is not clearly separated. In particular this seems to be the case in smaller projects, where a single person is the method expert. The interviews indicate that a significant amount of experience is required to properly negotiate a participatory EM project, a task that is commonly included in that of a project leader. We have not found a difference between small and large projects, when it comes to the project negotiation. A small project can be as critical to an organisation as a large project. It can also contain as difficult "political" issues as a large project. This places a great responsibility on the person negotiating the project in that she/he has to be able not only to define the scope and resources for the project but also assess the applicability of participatory EM. Considering this, we find it disturbing that most of the less experienced interviewees report that the project negotiations are carried out by people who are not experienced in participatory EM and that the facilitators in most cases cannot influence these negotiations.

Another way of looking at the increasing method expert competency that comes with experience was introduced by one of the interviewees. He described it as a maturity model for EM practitioners (Figure 4). He claimed that the typical EM method user reaches new levels of maturity and insight with increased experience. The novice focuses mainly on the formalism (meta-model). Notation and expressiveness of a modelling language is important to the novice. Once the method user gains more experience she/he realises that an effective process is necessary to actually create the models. The next level of maturity is reached. With even more experience method users often start to become concerned about different quality aspects of the product resulting from the modelling process. However, focus is still very much on the tangible product of modelling, the model itself. The highest level of maturity is when the method user is mostly concerned with achieving some positive effect of modelling in the organisation in question. At this level of maturity the method user is able to reflect on the desired effect in a certain situation and choose a suitable formalism as well as design a process that will produce the necessary model quality required to reach the desired effect.

The Competency of Domain Experts

From the domain expert side, customer and modelling participants are the main actors. In this section we focus on the modelling participants, of which

Figure 4. Participatory EM – from formalism to effect [Interviewee 1]

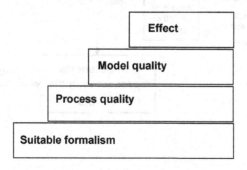

the customer can be one. In a participatory EM project, the project plan commonly includes a series of modelling sessions. Each modelling session has a goal or several goals that are to be achieved. These goals contribute to fulfilling the project definition. The goals of each modelling session define the requirements on the competency that should be represented by the participants in the modelling group. The willingness or opportunity of people to contribute their competency is constrained by a number of different situational factors such as organisational culture, authority of involved actors, management support, time resources, method acceptance and conflicts. These relationships are shown in Figure 5.

In the following we will discuss how these relationships influence: 1) the required competency of individual modelling participants and 2) the composition of the modelling group

Figure 5. Competencies of a modelling group - relationships between requirements and constraints

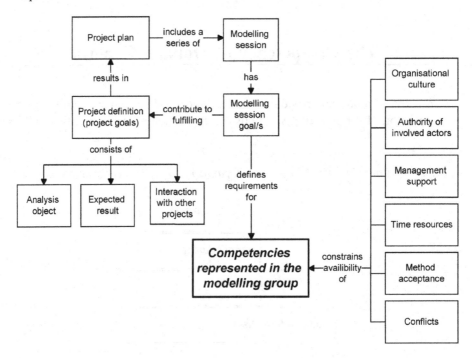

The Competency of Individual Modelling Participants

The modelling participants need to possess knowledge that is pertinent to the problem that the modelling session addresses. Otherwise they will have no possibility to contribute an opinion on the subject matter.

"The right competency in relationship to the problem to be solved. It has to be people that know the problem, understand the problem, and feel for the problem. They should have enough knowledge about the part of the organisation where the problem belongs, so that they can understand how to solve the problem." [Interviewee 3]

In addition to knowledge about the problem addressed, some personal characteristics are desired in an "ideal" modelling participant.

"It must be people with the ability of abstract reasoning … of generalisation … to look at things at a more general level. [Interviewee 1]

Personal characteristics, such as social skills, ability to verbalise and communicate, creativity etc., are also on the wish list of the interviewees. However, one of the most important requirements for an individual modelling participant is the motivation to participate and to contribute to solving the problem at hand. This can make up for lack of some personal characteristics.

Composition of the Modelling Group

The composition of the modelling group is instrumental to the achievement of the goals for the modelling session. Aspects to consider are described by one of the interviewees:

"There are some rules of thumb. Preferably different areas of knowledge should be represented so that you cover the problem from different flanks. Then it's good that you not only cover the problem domain in terms of scope but also regarding depth, so that you have people that know about the details and also people who have overview." [Interviewee 3]

The "direction" of the analysis, i.e. if the analysis concerns the current state of affairs or the future state, also defines requirements for the group's composition.

"It is often the case that the people that are deeply involved in the job can describe the current state. But when it comes to the future, you need a different type of people. The visionaries, perhaps those that are a bit higher in the organisation and see more than just the little piece of the puzzle, see the whole chain." [Interviewee 2]

In addition, people may not feel that they are authorised to have an opinion about the future.

Another aspect of group composition is the number of participants in a group. It seems that an ideal number is between 5 and 10–12 (the number 10–12 given by one of the interviewees). If the group is too large it is difficult for the facilitator to manage the group process, but a really small group can also have a negative influence on the modelling result.

"If there are only four people in a meeting then the critical mass is too small to actually get the analysis going. Then it becomes more of a discussion ... you don't get the proper "pressure". You don't feel the participation is distributed with four people. You don't get that effect ... and by the way you can't use the trick of dividing the group into sub-groups and play them against each other, which often creates an extra driving force." [Interviewee 4]

It is evidently an ideal situation if all of these requirements are fulfilled. However, reality does often prove to be something completely different.

"One of my rules of thumb is that the people I need is probably not the people I can get. It sounds a bit harsh, but it is very often the situation. Not always though. Sometimes the organisation is mature and understands that you need the best and then you get them, but sometimes you get the people that they don't have any use for." [Interviewee 3]

This is related to the issue of resources, in particular with regard to management support and time resources.

One thing to make sure is that the participants are there with the task of actually contributing to solving the problem at hand.

"We say that there's no point in having deadweight in a group. To send people that are expected to learn or people they want to get rid of. It has happened that I was with a group of 10 people, one contributed and the others were there to learn. It's impossible to do a good job." [Interviewee 2]

Another issue is concerning different "political" views regarding who should participate or not. Sometimes this is related to the authority of involved actors or conflicts between stakeholders.

"Political decision conflicts can sometimes cause problems. Some people demand to be included ... people are taken hostage ... or they don't let the people participate that actually have the knowledge. Sometimes you know that there are different opinions and if you want the result to be accepted all the different parties should be represented. But they don't show up. They choose to be excluded." [Interviewee 2]

The status or rank of certain stakeholders can also restrict the possibilities of composing a group that represents the best available competency.

"Someone explained it to me that when people reach a certain military rank they are considered [sometimes falsely], both by themselves and the environment, to automatically possess a certain competency. Therefore it can be difficult to demand the participation of those who are really competent." [Interviewee 4]

For further details about the dynamics of a modelling group, see e.g. Willars et.al. (1993), Nilsson, Tolis and Nellborn (1999), Astrakan (2001), Bergquist and Heide (1999) and Bubenko, Persson and Stirna (2001).

The view of the interviewees is that it is highly desirable that method experts have a strong influence on the composition of the modelling group. One of the most experienced interviewees even claims that he is reluctant to take on an assignment where he does not have this influence. The less experienced say that they need to become better in making their requirements clear to the customer in this respect. At present they are very seldom given the opportunity to influence the choice of modelling participants.

If the method expert is able to influence the choice of modelling participants, how can that be done and which kind of influence is relevant? One of the interviewees has some advice regarding this issue:

"You can help the customer to find these people [to pick out who will participate in the modelling seminar]. Often it's better that the customer himself picks out who should participate, provided that you have made the requirements clear to him. He knows his organisation and his staff much better than you. Sometimes you can help him by doing a short PEM session where you look at the goals, what to achieve, which problem is in focus and we analyse the problem domain. Then you ask which people are most suitable to solve this problem in a group. You get a list of potential people but then you do interviews to pick out the most suitable ones. [Interviewee 1]

As we can see from the quote, the interviews with individual modelling participants are emphasised once again. This indicates the importance of letting the method expert learn about the organisation before the modelling activity, not only on a superficial level but also on the level of the involved modelling participants. This enables her/him to better control the quality of the result and to evaluate what can be achieved.

An ideal modelling group has the following characteristics:

- The knowledge represented in the group covers the full scope of the problem domain as well as detail and overview.

- The group is authorised to address the problem at hand and suggest a suitable solution to the problem.

- The number of modelling participants is 5–12.

- The group consists *only* of people that are expected to actively contribute to the modelling work.

- The group consists of people without personal animosity between themselves.

Once the modelling participants to be included in the different modelling sessions have been chosen, they need to be prepared for what will happen during the sessions. This is particularly critical in organisations where the employees are not used to modelling in general and particularly to modelling in a group. Before the modelling session each individual modelling participant has to (Lindström, 1999):

- understand the objective of the modelling session,

- agree upon the importance of this objective,

- feel personally capable to contribute to a positive result, and

- be comfortable with the rest of the team (including the facilitator).

The best way of preparing the participants is to carry out individual interviews. There are several goals with these interviews, which have emerged from our interview study. They fall into three categories related to the subject matter, the motivation of modelling participants and the group process.

Goals Related to the Subject Matter

In order to prepare the modelling seminar as concerns issues to cover, driving questions etc. the method expert needs to understand the views of the modelling participants regarding the problem, in particular focusing on goals and possible hinders to achieve the goals. Their views regarding how other stakeholders might think about the problem at hand are also important. This might reveal potential conflicts of interest and also personal animosities between stakeholders and stakeholder groups. If resolution of potential conflicts of interest is essential for solving the problem at hand, driving questions can be posed to the group during the modelling session, in order to make the conflict surface. However, bringing personal conflicts to the surface during a modelling session should be avoided.

Goals Related to the Motivation of the Modelling Participants

In order for the goals of the modelling session to be accomplished, the group process should have the highest possible quality so as to capitalise on the fullest potential of the competencies in the group. Therefore, one goal is to prepare the modelling participant with regard to what will happen during the modelling session and why. It is also necessary that modelling participants understand in what way their particular competency contributes to the goals of the session and of the project, i.e. why they are important. This clarifies what is expected from them during the session and motivates them to participate actively. To ensure motivation, the attitudes of the modelling participants towards the modelling method and the participative approach should also be investigated.

Goals Related to the Group Process

The personalities in a group govern how the facilitator runs the modelling session. The facilitator will e.g. need to neutralise dominant persons and encourage more shy persons in order to accomplish full and consensus-driven participation from everyone of the modelling participants. The facilitator will also need to ensure that the models produced are the result of consensus between the views represented in the session. Therefore, the method expert/facilitator will try to understand as much as possible of each individual's personality during the interview. She/he will then be better equipped to facilitate the communication between the members of the modelling group.

The less experienced seldom do this type of preparation. It would be interesting to study more carefully the daily work of the less experienced to see which kind of problems they experience during the sessions. This may reveal particular problems caused by lack of preparation. Some of the less experienced are aware of their lack of preparation and claim that they need to become more skilled in negotiating project resources for this purpose.

The Challenge of Training in Participatory Enterprise Modelling

It is clear that participatory EM is not a trivial process. It is demanding both for method experts and domain experts. The issue of which is the necessary training should therefore be relevant to discuss.

Training for Method Experts

The expert interviewees in our study have all been involved in training activities, trying to increase the number of skilled method experts. They report that training somebody for reaching the level tree competency - ability to lead modelling projects (Figure 3) - is a long and complicated process where the risk is evident to lose many candidates along the way.

"We interviewed 73 or 74 potential facilitators. Out of these we chose 15 who we thought were at least reasonably good. Towards the end we had 7 left. This is the real situation. We lost some on the first level. They didn't really have the ability to model. Some we lost on the second step. They didn't have the ability to facilitate modelling sessions. Then we lost some because ... well all facilitators are exhibitionist prima donnas ... but some had too many co-operation problems." [Interviewee 1]

It is self-evident that training to become a skilled participatory EM method expert involves acquiring knowledge that is provided in the literature or by taking courses. However, most of the training must be focused on actually practising to become more and more skilled.

"It is practice that gives mastery. It is the same with military education. You can practice your drills back home on the exercise field but it takes a real war to see if it really works." [Interviewee 6]

One of the interviewees recommends that practitioners systematically collect their experiences in order to share them with others and in order to make their own learning more efficient.

"I believe in the power of the example and to refer to real cases, to do evaluations after projects and note down important stuff. You can learn from other people's mistakes. I have done it myself. Somebody should write a casebook with good and bad examples. It's valuable to know what works, but it's at least as valuable to know what goes to XXX." [Interviewee 4]

According to Interviewee 6 it is difficult to organise "learning by doing", with feedback loops in a systematic and practical way, for a large group of people. A complicating factor here is that the person being trained needs to be subjected to a variety of situations, in order to be prepared for future assignments. Also, since the situation in real projects is often sensitive, there is no room for critical mistakes. This means that the number of skilled participatory method experts increases very slowly.

A practical way of learning, which the author of this paper has experience with, is to work together with more experienced facilitators. Novices should never facilitate alone, since the errors made during modelling will negatively influence the outcome of the process where modelling is used. With reference to the maturity levels of method experts, a common mistake that novices make is that they believe that just because they have learned to master a modelling language, they will be able to carry out a participatory modelling process.

Training for Domain Experts

When it comes to training the domain experts, there are two predominant views. One that claims that all domain experts need to be trained in the method used before taking part in modelling and one that claims that this is not necessary.

Enterprise Modelling languages can be semantically "simple" and self-instructive but some are more semantically "rich". The question to be asked here is whether the problem at hand requires a semantically rich language. In our opinion, which is based on our empirical experience, simple languages are preferable for solving most organisational problems. Participatory EM relies on the domain experts to understand the models during the modelling session in order to be able to contribute their critical domain knowledge. Therefore, we suggest that a modelling language is chosen that suits the previous modelling experience of the domain experts.

It seems from the interviews that this is not something that the interviewees see as a problem. According to our understanding their view is that method experts are expected to be able to construct the model and that the domain experts should focus on the subject matter. Our empirical experience is that in most situations, simple notations are sufficient for the modelling session itself, which decreases the need for training. In fact, during our case studies we did not train the modelling participants at all and we could not detect any problems caused by that. Training was by doing, without too much focus on the notation itself.

Concluding Remarks

Little research has been spent the practice of Enterprise Modelling and even less on defining what modelling competency is and how it can be developed. The research presented in this paper takes a step towards systematising portions of the method application knowledge of expert practitioners. Giving advice in written form is difficult, since the motivation for the advice is difficult to convey. Therefore, we believe that the way that this paper is written, with illustrating quotes from expert practitioners is a fruitful way forward.

What are then the implications of the results presented in this paper when it comes to further research? We perceive that there are a number of issues that needs to be addressed, such as e.g.:

1) How do developers of modelling languages take into consideration the learnability of their languages, if at all they do?

2) How can we increase our knowledge about the various complex aspects of the modelling process?

3) Why is it so difficult to become a skilled facilitator?

4) How can training in modelling be improved so that model quality can be enhanced in general?

References

Astrakan (2001). *Högre kurs i modelleringsledning* (in Swedish). Course notes Version 1.1, Astrakan Strategisk Utbildning AB, Stockholm, Sweden.

Bajec, M., & Krisper, M. (2005). A methodology and tool support for managing business rules in organisations. *Information Systems, 30*(6), 423-443.

Bergquist, S., & Eide. H. (1999). *Team Games –snabbaste vägen mot högpresterande arbetsprocesser* (in Swedish). Frontec AB, Sweden.

Bubenko Jr., J. A. (1993). *Extending the Scope of Information Modelling*. Fourth International Workshop on the Deductive Approach to Information Systems and Databases, Lloret, Costa Brava (Catalonia), Sept. 20-22, 1993. Department de Llenguatges i Sistemes Informatics, Universitat Politecnica de Catalunya, Report de Recerca LSI/93-25, Barcelona.

Bubenko, J. A. Jr., Persson, A., & Stirna, J. (2001). *User Guide of the Knowledge Management Approach Using Enterprise Knowledge Patterns*. Deliverable D3, IST Programme project Hypermedia and Pattern Based Knowl-edge Management for Smart Organisations, project no. IST-2000-28401, Royal Institute of Technology, Sweden.

Castro, J., Kolp, M., Mylopoulos, J., & Tropos, A. (2001). A Requirements-Driven Software Development Methodology. *Proceedings of the 3rd Conference on Advanced Information Systems Engineering (CAiSE 2001)*, 108-123, Springer LNCS 2068, Interlaken, Switzerland.

Dobson, J., Blyth, J., & Strens, R. (1994). Organisational Requirements Definition for Information Technology. *Proceedings of the International Conference on Requirements Engineering 1994*, Denver/CO

F3 Consortium (1994). *F3 Reference Manual*. ESPRIT III Project 6612, SISU, Stockholm.

Fox, M. S., Chionglo, J. F., & Fadel, F. G. (1993). A common-sense model of the enterprise. *Proceedings of the 2nd Industrial Engineering Research Conference*, Institute for Industrial Engineers, Norcross/GA.

Gustas, R., Bubenko, J. A. jr, & Wangler, B. (1995). *Goal Driven Enterprise Modelling:* Bridging Pragmatic and Semantic Descriptions of Information Systems. *5th European - Japanese Seminar on Information Modelling and Knowledge Bases*, Sapphoro, May 30-June 3, 1995.

Johannesson P., Boman, M., Bubenko, J., & Wangler, B. (1997). *Conceptual Modelling*. Prentice Hall International Series in Computer Science, Prentice Hall, 1997.

Kardasis P., Loucopoulos P., Scott B., Filippidou D., Clarke R., Wangler B., Xini G. (1998). *The use of Business Knowledge Modelling for Knowledge Discovery in the Banking Sector*. IMACS-CSC'98, Athens, Greece, October, 1998.

Krogstie, J., Lillehagen, F., Karlsen, D., Ohren, O., Strømseng, K., Thue Lie, F. (2000). *Extended Enterprise Methodology*. Deliverable 2 in the EXTERNAL project, available at http://research.dnv.com/external/deli-verables.html.

Lindström, C-G, (1999). Lessons Learned from Applying Business Modelling: Exploring Opportunities and Avoiding Pitfalls. In Nilsson, A. G., Tolis, C. and Nellborn, C. (Eds.), *Perspectives on Business Modelling: Understanding and Changing Organisations*, Springer-Verlag.

Loucopoulos, P., Kavakli, V., Prekas, N., Rolland, C., Grosz, G., & Nurcan, S. (1997). *Using the EKD Approach: The Modelling Component*, UMIST, Manchester, UK.

Mumford, E. (1983). *Designing Participatively*, Manchester Business School, Manchester, UK, 1983.

Niehaves, B., & Stirna, J. (2006). *Participative Enterprise Modelling for Balanced Scorecard Implementation, 14th European Conference on Information Systems (ECIS 2006)*, Gothberg, Sweden

Nilsson, A. G., Tolis, C., & Nellborn, C. (Eds.) (1999). *Perspectives on Business Modelling: Understanding and Changing Organisations*, Springer-Verlag.

Orlikowski, W. J. (1993). CASE Tools as Organizational Change: Investigating Incremental and Radical Changes in Systems Development. *MIS Quarterly*, September 1993.

Persson, A. (2001). *Enterprise Modelling in Practice: Situational Factors and their Influence on Adopting a Participative Approach*. Ph.D. thesis, Department of Computer and Systems Sciences, Stockholm University, ISSN 1101-8526.

Persson, A., & Stirna, J. (2001). An explorative study into the influence of business goals on the practical use of Enterprise Modelling methods and tools. *Tenth International Conference on Information Systems Development (ISD2001)*, Royal Holloway, University of London, 5-7 September 2001.

Stirna, J., Persson, A., & Aggestam, L. (2006). Building Knowledge Repositories with Enterprise Modelling and Patterns - from Theory to Practice. *Proceedings of the 14th European Conference on Information Systems (ECIS 2006)*, Gothenburg, Sweden, June 2006.

Wangler, B., Persson, A., Johannesson, P., & Ekenberg, L. (2003). Bridging High-level Enterprise Models to Implemenation-Oriented Models. In Fujita, H., and Johannesson, P. (Eds.), *New Trends in Software Methodologies, Tools and Techniques,* IOS Press, Amsterdam, Netherlands.

Wangler, B., & Persson, A. (2002). Capturing Collective Intentionality in Software Development. In Fujita, H. and Johannesson, P. (Eds.), *New Trends in Software Methodologies, Tools and Techniques,* IOS Press, Amsterdam, Netherlands, pp 262-270.

Wangler, B., Persson, A., & Söderström, E. (2001). Enterprise Modeling for B2B integration. *International Conference on Advances in Infrastructure for Electronic Business, Science, and Education on the Internet,* August 6-12, L'Aquila, Italy (CD-ROM proceedings)

Willars, H. et al (1993). *TRIAD Modelleringshandboken N 10:1-6.* (in Swedish), SISU, Electrum 212, 164 40 Kista, Sweden.

Willars, H (1999). Business Modeller's Checklist: "Dos" and "Don'ts" in Hands-on Practice". In Nilsson, A. G., Tolis, C. and Nellborn, C. (Eds.),

Perspectives on Business Modelling: Understanding and Changing Organisations, Springer-Verlag.

Yu, E. S. K., & Mylopoulos, J. (1994). From E-R to "A-R" - Modelling Strategic Actor Relationships for Business Process Reengineering. *Proceedings of the 13th International Conference on the Entity-Relationship Approach,* Manchester, England.

Zorgios, Y. (Ed.), (1994). *Enterprise State of the Art Survey, Part 3, Enterprise Modelling Methods.* DTI ISIP Project Number 8032, AIAI, The University of Edinburgh.

Appendix 1.
Competency Profiles of Interviewees

Interviewee 1	Senior business and IS development consultant at a commercial consultancy company. More than 25 years of experience with EM and business development in a wide variety of domains. An expert in managing large projects. A number of publications on EM and business modelling subjects, experience from method development and research.
Interviewee 2	EM consultant at a commercial consultancy company. About 25 years of experience from business and IS development as well as teaching. Experience from method development and testing of methods. Several publications, including reports on model quality and model integration. Author of several books on programming languages.
Interviewee 3	Business consultant at a commercial consultancy company. About 10 years of experience with EM, mostly involving medium size to large organisations, public as well as private. A number of publications on EM and business modelling subjects. Experience from method development.
Interviewee 4	Business consultant and strategy developer for a commercial consultancy company, more than 25 years of experience in the area of EM and business development, has publications in the area, experience from method development.
Interviewee 5	EM consultant with a commercial consultancy company, about 20 years of experience both from consulting and research. Experience from method development and takes a particular interest in integration and quality assurance of Enterprise Models.
Interviewee 6	Senior business consultant with more than 25 years of experience from business and IS development in the public sector as well as in the private sector. Has worked for different companies, including a large telecommunications company and a private consultancy company. Experience with method development. Publications on EM related subjects.
Interviewee 7	Employed as an internal IT method consultant in one of Sweden's largest industrial corporations. Has worked with business modelling in strategic business and IT development for about 10 years in different companies. Involved in method development.
Interviewee 8	Employed as a consultant with a large software house in Sweden. Systems development consultant for about 15 years. Mentor for systems development project. Experience with facilitated group sessions.
Interviewee 9	Employed at the IT subsidiary of a large industrial international corporation. Involved in process analysis and feasibility studies using facilitated group sessions for about 5 years.
Interviewee 10	Employed at the IT subsidiary of a large international industrial corporation. Acts as method support mostly in Process Engineering. More than 10 years of experience from business development in small and large companies. Has worked with facilitated group sessions since the beginning of the 1990ies.
Interviewee 11	Employed as a systems development consultant with a large international consultancy company. About 15 years experience with systems development and about 5 years with facilitated group sessions.

Chapter VII

How to Support Agile Development Projects with Enterprise Modelling

Janis Stirna, Jönköping University, Sweden

Marite Kirikova, Riga Technical University, Latvia

Abstract

This paper analyses the potential of using Enterprise Modelling (EM) in agile information system development projects on the basis of a number of empirical findings. We outline the current issues and challenges that projects using agile development approaches are facing. To address these challenges we analyse what are the objectives of using EM in agile development projects and give recommendations concerning the modelling process and tool support.

Introduction

In the recent years the Information System (IS) development community has been trying out and adopting various agile development approaches such as eXtreme Programming (Beck, 2004), SCRUM (Schwaber & Beedle, 2002), DSDM (Stapleton, 2003). One of the strengths of agile development approaches is their flexibility and ability of dealing with change efficiently. The underlying philosophy of these approaches is development of only those artefacts that are directly related to the software product. These approaches are best suited for small-to-medium size teams and projects. Agile development approaches typically do not prescribe which methods, languages, and tools are to be used. Instead, the main emphasis is on choosing the simplest, most effective and, therefore, the most cost effective ones. In spite of the common misconception that agile development approaches mostly advocate ad hoc coding in a "program first, ask questions later" way, IS requirements are gathered and analysed and system architecture is designed in agile projects. These processes might only look different from the outset, but their main goals are similar to the plan driven system development approaches. Consequently, modelling of requirements and architectures is common in agile development projects.

To support the modelling process on a macro level within the agile development teams Agile Modeling (AM) (Ambler, 2002a) was developed. Agile Modeling provides a set of best practices of "light-weight" modelling. Agile Modeling also requires active stakeholder involvement, which is similar to Participative Enterprise Modelling (Bubenko et al, 2001).

However, gathering requirements in agile methods is targeted exclusively to software development needs (Leffingwell, 2002; Ambler, 2006). The relationship between knowledge of enterprise stakeholders and software artefacts is tacit and contributes only to the software development process, not to the enterprise knowledge development on a larger scale. This phenomenon does no permit to utilize all possible benefits of requirement gathering exercise. Nowadays agility is needed not only in software development processes but in all aspects of organisational performance. Therefore a method that transparently relates software development to other organisational processes is needed.

In this paper we analyse the potential of using Enterprise Modelling (EM) in agile development projects. We have based our findings on a number of qualitative research studies (Persson, 2001; Stirna, 2001; Persson & Stirna, 2001; Jönsson, 2004; Lagerquist et al., 2006).

Enterprise Modelling (EM) is an activity where an integrated and negotiated model describing different aspects of an enterprise is created. An Enterprise

Model comprises a number of related "sub-models", each focusing on a particular aspect of an organisation. Examples of such aspects are processes, business rules, concepts/information/data, goals, and actors. Typically these models are developed in a series of facilitated modelling seminars with a group of stakeholders. Such a participative way of working improves quality, consensus, acceptance and agreement on the business decisions made and organisational designs produced during the seminar. EM developers have suggested that EM is applicable for a variety of purposes, e.g. business process standardisation and reengineering, strategy planning, sharing corporate knowledge and organisational learning, enterprise integration, as well as information systems development (Fraser et al., 1994; Persson & Stirna, 2001). Examples of EM approaches are reflected in (Yu & Mylopoulos, 1994; Fox et al., 1993; Zorgios et al., 1994; Dobson et al., 1994; Bubenko et al., 2001; Castro et al., 2001).

A combination of Enterprise Modelling and Agile software development thus suggests a new paradigm in agile project development where software development relevant knowledge is derived from overall organisational development knowledge, captured in an Enterprise Model. Such approach not only utilizes all knowledge created in requirements gathering process, but also provides transparency of relationships between software development process and other organisational development processes.

The rest of the paper is structured as follows. Chapter II provides background to EM and Agile Development. Chapter III outlines the current issues and challenges that projects using agile development approaches are facing. Chapter IV discusses the potential of the use of Enterprise Modelling in agile development projects. More specifically, we analyse what are the objectives of using EM in agile development projects and give recommendations concerning the modelling process and tool support. Chapter V briefly discusses future trends, while chapter VI presents concluding remarks.

Background

In this chapter we outline the basic concepts of Enterprise Modelling, Agile development approaches and Agile Modeling in particular.

Enterprise Modelling

EM is a method for developing, acquiring, and communicating early, enterprise knowledge, such as strategies, goals, or requirements, by a structured, iterative, working and modelling approach (Bubenko et al., 2001). The Enterprise Model consists of set of structured, goal/problem - driven models to be used for structuring and representing organisational knowledge. The modelling process is guided by a set of guidelines for conducting the knowledge acquisition, analysis, and representation process. The basic assumptions are that knowledge acquisition is strongly participatory and consensus about the decisions made during the modeling seminar contributes to their implementation in reality. Hence, all involved actor and stakeholder types in an organisation are assumed to actively contribute.

In Scandinavia, Business or Enterprise Modelling were introduced in the eighties by Plandata, Sweden (Willars, 1988), and later refined by SISU (The Swedish Institute for System Development). This approach introduced business goals as part of an Enterprise Model, complementing traditional model component types such as entities, relationships, and processes. The SISU framework was later extended in the ESPRIT projects TEMPORA (c.f. Theodolidis, Loucopoulos & Wangler, 1991; TEMPORA Consortium, 1994) and F3 – "From Fuzzy to Formal" (F3 Consortium, 1994). The current framework is denoted EKD – "Enterprise Knowledge Development" (Loucopolous et al., 1997; Bubenko et al., 2001). A significant contribution of the TEMPORA project to EKD was the notion and typology of business rules (Wangler, 1993).

Apart from the "Scandinavian" strand of EM, a variety of other methods have been suggested. C.f. e.g. Yu and Mylopoulos (1994), Fox et al. (1993), Zorgios et al. (1994), Dobson et al. (1994), Castro et al (2001), Bajec and Krisper (2005).

The rest of this section will outline EM taking EKD as a representative of widely used and accepted participative EM methods developed Scandinavia. We will present the EKD modelling language, the EKD modelling process, and the applicability issues of EKD.

The EKD Modelling Product

The EKD Enterprise Model contains a number of interrelated sub-models (see Figure 1). Each of them represents some aspect of the enterprise. The types of sub-models and issues they address are: Goals Model, Business Rules Model, Concepts Model, Business Process Model, Actors and Resources Model, as well as Technical Components and Requirements Model.

Goals Model (GM) focuses on describing the goals of the enterprise. Here we describe what the enterprise and its employees want to achieve, or to avoid,

Figure 1. Sub-models comprising the EKD enterprise model

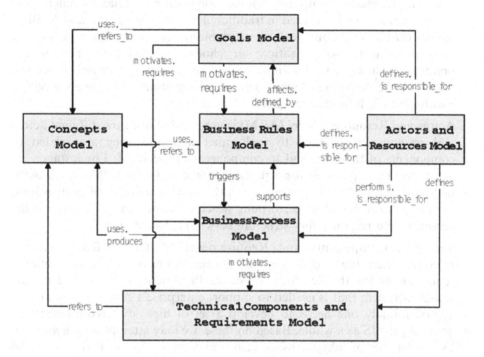

and when. GM usually clarifies questions, such as: where should the organisation be moving, what are the goals of the organisation, what are the importance, criticality, and priorities of these goals, how are the goals related to each other, which problems are hindering achievement of the goals.

Business Rule Model (BRM) is used to define and maintain explicitly formulated business rules consistent with the GM. Business rules may be seen as operationalisation or limits of goals. BRM usually clarifies questions, such as: which rules affect the organisation's goals, are there any policies stated, how a business rule is related to a goal, how can goals be supported by rules.

Concepts Model (CM) is used to strictly define the "things" and "phenomena" one is talking about in the other models. In CM we represent enterprise concepts, attributes, and relationships. CM usually clarifies questions, such as: what concepts are recognised in the enterprise (including their relationships to goals, activities and processes, and actors), how are they defined, what business rules and constraints monitor these objects and concepts.

Business Processes Model (BPM) is used to define enterprise processes, the way they interact, and the way they handle information as well as material. A business process is assumed to consume input in terms of information and/or material and produce output of information and/or material. In general, the BPM is similar to what is used in traditional data-flow diagram models. BPM usually clarifies questions, such as: which business activities and processes are recognised in the organisation, or should be there, to manage the organisation in agreement with its goals; how should the business processes, tasks, etc. be performed (workflows, state transitions, or process models); which are their information needs.

Actors and Resources Model (ARM) is used to describe how different actors and resources are related to each other and how they are related to components of the GM, and to components of the BPM. For instance, an actor may be responsible for a particular process in the BPM or, the actor may pursue a particular goal in the GM. ARM usually clarifies questions, such as: who is/should be performing which processes and tasks, how is the reporting and responsibility structure between actors defined?

Technical Components and Requirements Model (TCRM) becomes relevant when the purpose of EKD modelling is to aid in defining requirements for the development of an IS. Attention is focused on the technical system that is needed to support enterprise's goals, processes, and actors. Initially one needs to develop a set of high level requirements or goals, for the IS as a whole. Based on these, we may attempt to structure the IS in a number of subsystems, or technical components. TCRM is an initial attempt to define the overall structure and properties of the IS to support the business activities, as defined in the BPM. TCRM usually clarifies questions, such as: what are the requirements for the IS to be developed, which requirements are generated by the business processes, what is the potential of the emerging information and communication technologies for process improvement.

The ability to trace decisions, components and other aspects throughout the enterprise is dependent on the use and understanding of the relationships between the different sub-models shown in Figure 1. When developing a full enterprise model, these relationships between components of the different sub-models play an essential role. For instance, statements in the Goals Model allow different concepts to be defined more clearly in the Concepts Model. A link is then specified between the corresponding Goals Model component and the concepts in the Concepts Model. In the same way, goals in the Goals Model motivate particular processes in the Business Processes Model. The processes are needed to achieve the goals stated. A link therefore is defined between a goal and the process. Links between models make the model traceable. They show, for instance, why certain rules, processes and information system requirements have been introduced.

The EKD Modelling Process

During the EKD modelling process different ways of working are applied in order to elicit and develop the knowledge of business stakeholders or domain experts. Typical examples of ways of working are facilitated group sessions and interviews.

The Sub-models are developed iteratively and in parallel, meaning that they are on different levels of "completeness" at a certain point in time. In the participative approach to EM the stakeholders collaboratively develop Enterprise Models in facilitated group sessions. This type of participation is *consensus-driven* in the sense that it is the stakeholders who "own" the model and hence decide its contents. In contrast, consultative participation means that analysts create models and that stakeholders are then consulted in order to validate the models. In the EKD EM method the participative approach to EM is preferred.

More about setting up and carrying out participative EM seminars is available in (Bubenko et al., 2001) and in (Persson, 2001).

Applicability of Participative Enterprise Modelling

Person and Stirna (2001) show that EM can be used for a number of purposes. The two main types of objectives are (1) developing the business, e.g. developing business vision, strategies, redesigning the way the business operates, developing the supporting information systems (e.g. eliciting business requirements), or (2) ensuring the quality of the business, e.g. sharing the knowledge about the business, its vision, the way it operates, or ensuring the acceptance of business decisions through committing the stakeholders to the decisions made.

Earlier research (Persson & Stirna, 2001; Persson, 2001) shows that applicability of the participative approach depends on the existing organisational culture, which defines how people communicate between each other. Two types of cultures have been identified – consensus oriented culture and authoritative culture. In consensus oriented cultures subordinates can question higher managers, the dialogue between levels of the organisation is open and direct, and reward systems encourage initiatives from all levels. In authoritative cultures management is done by directives only, the dialogue is indirect and initiatives from different levels of the organisation are not encouraged. In participative EM the dialogue is extremely direct. Opinions are weighed against each other to obtain consensus. Also, the "minutes" of the session are visible to everyone present. In an authoritative culture it is extremely difficult to achieve a "good" modelling result, since hidden agendas and fear of retaliation obstruct the creative effort. The advice is against using a participative approach in authoritative organisational cultures (Persson & Stirna, 2001).

EM has proven to be useful in a variety of contexts and in different organisations. For instance, versions of methods from the "Scandinavian school" of EM have been successfully applied in six EU funded research projects and in numerous European organisations, such as British Aerospace (UK), Capital Bank (UK), National Bank of Greece, Public Power Corporation (Greece), Sema Group (France), Telia (Sweden), Vattenfall (Sweden), Volvo (Sweden), Verbundplan (Austria), Riga City Council (Latvia).

Agile Development Approaches

Agile development approaches such as Agile Modeling (Ambler, 2002), eXtreme Programming (Beck, 2004), Crystal Clear (Cockburn, 2005), Scrum (Schwaber & Beedle, 2002), and DSDM (Stapleton, 2003) all share the same values, e.g. to be flexible and to be able to deal with changes during the course of a software project. The highest goal of the agile methods is to deliver value to the customer early and continuously. Based on these assumptions the agile methods then provide a set of principles, techniques and best practices for IS development. Some of them focus on providing support for different phases of the IS development and some of them can easily be combined with other methods, techniques and practices to further support IS development (c.f. e.g. Abrahamssson et al., 2003).

Agile approaches suggest delivering solutions to customer requirements (software components) in smaller parts on a frequent basis before the whole product is delivered. These small deliveries allow for early customer feedback (c.f. e.g. Stapleton, 2003). Because changes are generally unavoidable the agile methods require close cooperation with the customer to determine which features are going to add the most business value to the product at the end of the next iteration (Boehm & Turner, 2004).

According to (Boehm & Turner, 2004) an agile development method must have the following characteristics – (1) iterative (several cycles), (2) gradually growing (not to deliver the whole product at once), (3) self-organizing (the team in cooperation with the customer decides and prioritises the tasks and organizes themselves along with the decisions taken), and (4) adaptive (processes, principles, work structures are adapted as needed when identified during the project instead of being fixed early or before the need is identified).

The following four agile approaches may be considered as a representative sample of agile approaches:

- eXtreme Programming (Beck, 2004) is a collection of well known software development best practices, such as short iterations, pair programming, test-driven development, refactoring, continuous integration, close customer participation during the whole development project, and rapid feedback, etc. The core values of XP are communication, simplicity, feedback, courage, and respect which clearly states the purpose and the goal of each activity in XP projects.

- Scrum (Schwaber & Beedle, 2002)is a method for managing software development projects. Projects are divided in short iterations (called "sprints") to allow for feedback and flexibility. The developers are encouraged to choose the techniques and tools that suit the team in the development process in order to achieve the expected results. The team synchronizes their job every day in a stand-up meeting lasting 15 minutes. Every team member answers three questions – What did you do since last meeting, what will you do before next meeting, and do you have any obstacles? The answers help to control if the work is proceeding as planned.

- Dynamic Systems Development Method (Stapleton, 2003) is a method developed by a consortium where all the members can participate in the further development and refinement of the method. The main approach of DSDM is to fix the project resources and the time. The requirements are then prioritised according to what can be done within the time and resource constraints. DSDM defines project participant roles that are set by the customer – the orderer, visionary, ambassador user, and reference user.

- The Crystal family (Cockburn, 2005) consists of a number of different methods that depend on the team's size. Each method is named after a colour – Clear, Yellow, Orange, Red, etc. Crystal Clear is a method for small project groups including up to eight members which therefore needs less coordination than lager teams.

The above development approaches do not explicitly address modelling in terms of specific guidelines how to model and what. These issues are addressed by Agile Modeling.

Agile Modeling

Agile Modeling (Ambler, 2002a) as a method was developed during the 90's with the goal to integrate more traditional modelling approaches with the thoughts of agile development. Agile development has earlier been associated with no or very little modelling in development work, and Agile Modeling is essentially an approach to modelling in connection with other development activities.

The method Agile Modeling focuses on modelling and documentation. To have complete support for a software and/or system development process it has to be combined with another development method

Main Concepts of Agile Modeling

Some of the main concepts in Agile Modeling are: *agile models* and *agile documentation*. Agile models are models that are easy to understand, fulfil their purpose and are just detailed and advanced enough (Ambler, 2002a). In addition to this, agile models should be kept up to date to ensure consistency and accuracy (Jönsson, 2004). Agile documentation is about creating the documentation that is really needed, and the focus of agile documentation often lies on how a system is used, not how it was constructed.

The philosophy of AM relies heavily on *communication* between project members and stakeholders. This puts heavy requirements on the *individuals* involved in AM, on their ability to communicate and their skills in systems engineering. To reach a high level of communication, the workspaces have to be suitable for this type of work, with open offices and accessible whiteboard areas.

Practices

AM has several practices, concerning modelling, teamwork, simplicity of work and validation. The modelling in AM should be iterative and incremental. To achieve this, several models should be created in parallel, and the increments should be relatively small. For the teamwork to be as effective as possible modelling should be participative and the models made should be displayed publicly. Every artefact that is created should be kept simple and the simplest tools should be used. To validate the work in AM, everything should be testable and proven with code (Ambler, 2002a).

Application

AM can be applied as a supporting method to almost any development process. Best suited are projects with low demands on security and rapidly changing requirements. Evidence about the suitability of AM in practice is available i.e. in (Jönsson, 2004).

Current Issues in Agile Projects

Agile development approaches mostly focus on the development of a software system. The underlying assumption of these projects is that the customer is more or less certain about what kind of system is to be built, what are its features at least in general, and how and by whom the new system will be used once delivered. In practice, however, information system development often is an integral part of some business development, reengineering or change management project. Moreover, in the course of the project a number of ill-structured or wicked problems (Rittel & Webber, 1984) may surface at any time and need to be resolved. In such projects the organisations assess and explore various alternatives of business development, which needs to be taken into account when developing the supporting IS, because there often are several ways of achieving or supporting the same business goal.

A common situation is to set up business goals of an IS system to be built before the development project is commissioned. In some cases this is done independently without involving the people or the supplier that will develop the new IS. These business goals might be vague and obscure. They might communicate only the official information about the project, but valuable knowledge about existing problems, challenges and hidden agendas is left out. Hidden agendas will further undermine the possibility of achieving the project goals (e.g. develop the functionality that is really needed by the business), since different stakeholders will try to steer the project towards their own goals. This immediately puts the IS development team at a disadvantage because not all information is properly communicated to them. The agile development approaches try to address this challenge by active stakeholder involvement and having a customer representative on the development site. However, these practices might not be enough because the agile team has to re-acquire the knowledge about who are the stakeholders and what their intentions are, and then rediscover the real business objectives of the system. Furthermore, the agile team might need to access stakeholders who are high level managers and are either too busy or disinterested in engaging in IS development projects.

Agile development teams do not use business or enterprise modelling, which means that they do not require the business people to think systemically about their business and connect their business needs to the IS that is being developed. Changing the organisation, e.g. its business goals or business processes, independently of the IS development often lead to excessive communication overhead because different stakeholders are involved in both projects. In some cases the IS development team might even be unaware of some of the decisions made at the business level, which leads to unnecessary development iterations.

A lot of the knowledge about the IS being built, e.g. about the desired functionality, and the future (to-be) business context in which it will be used, is scarce and tacit – it lays in heads of a few stakeholders. They may also have different opinions about the same issue, especially concerning the future plants of the organisation, which, therefore, need to be consolidated, made explicit, and transferred to the agile development team. A successful practice, suggested by e.g. XP (Beck, 2004), is "customer on site". In reality, however, only a few stakeholder types can be kept on site. High level managers such as CEO or CFO need to be reached differently.

Using Enterprise Modelling in Agile Development

This chapter analysed the potential of using EM in agile development project. We discuss the objectives of using EM in agile projects and give recommendations about the modelling process and the tool support.

Objectives of Using EM in Agile Development Projects

EM can be used for various business development purposes (Persson & Stirna, 2001). In this section we will deal only with those that are related to information system development. In particular, we will investigate how EM can contribute to agile development projects.

Agile development projects commonly use Agile Modelling or at least a part of its recommendations, principles and practices. The purpose of Agile Modeling is to support the process of analysis and design. More specifically, the purpose is to discover, understand, illustrate, and describe some development artefact and to facilitate communication about this artefact between developers and stakeholders. In this process both parties should eventually reach consensus, so that the development process can go on. The emphasis is on models that are of manageable size. As one practitioner of AM explains:

"... the purpose [of AM is] to create few and manageable concepts and manageable entities and to develop a language, to create a conception of your project, so that you, when you say customer, know what you mean by that." – *Interviewee i7 in (Jönsson, 2004)*

Similarly, in IS development, the objectives of EM are to capture business or stakeholder requirements for the IS. Since the modelling process is participative, only those aspects of the problem domain that are relevant and important to the project and product are modelled. This directly contributes to the core principles of AM "travel light" and "model with purpose". See the citation below:

"...it depends what you want to do with [Enterprise] models, because depending on what you do, you can throw them away, they might just have been sort of drawing for planning your work and afterwards the value of them is already consumed. But in other cases you have made a design for an organisation which is in the progress of changing step by step and you want to use (Enterprise Models) as a basis for the next step." – *Interviewee i1 in (Stirna, 2001)*

Since the enterprise models are developed in a group seminar, one of the main outcomes is also increased understanding and commitment of the team, thus contributing to the values of AM "communication", e.g.

"Active participation leads to commitment. So, by creating active participation you make it impossible for people to escape commitment." – *Interviewee i5 in (Persson and Stirna, 2001)*

One can see that in both modelling approaches (AM and EM) the group work is used to achieve consensus, understanding and commitment concerning the scope of the development project. However, there is an essential difference between EM and modelling methods currently used in agile development, especially with respect to the gathering requirements. In essence, AM differs from EM regarding the following issues:

- "Project stakeholders do not know what they want. Project stakeholders are unable to see beyond the current situation" (Ambler, 2006).

AM just presents these issues as challenges of the agile development projects. EM addresses these problems directly by providing helpful means for discovering the requirements not only with respect to the current situation but also with respect to further organisational situations.

- It is not the goal of AM to document the requirements (Ambler, 2006). EM provides the means for model based requirements documentation.

- AM uses tacit enterprise knowledge and utilizes the tacit relationship between enterprise level knowledge and software development knowledge. EM supports externalization of knowledge and helps creating explicit enterprise models thus achieving transparency between enterprise knowledge, requirements knowledge and software models (Kirikova, 2004; Bubenko & Kirikova, 1999).

- AM puts emphasis only on requirements prioritization in change management (Ambler, 2006) while EM supports reusable explicit domain knowledge, i.e., it enables to create engineered vision of a new way of working (Kirikova, 2003; Kirikova, 2000b).

Similarities between AM and EM suggest that EM is suitable for use in projects taking an agile development approach. Moreover, the differences in both approaches suggest that using EM in agile development projects can contribute to achieving a new level of agility, where agility is based on the use of both tacit and explicit knowledge and is explicitly addressed not only at the level of software product development but also at the level of enterprise development per se.

The Table 1 shows the relationship between candidate artefacts for modelling requirements (Ambler, 2006) in AM and EKD enterprise model sub-models.

Table 1 shows that all candidate artefacts for modelling requirements currently used in agile development projects can be supported by Enterprise Model elements. The following four types of support are possible:

- The enterprise sub-model element is equal to the agile requirements modelling artefact, e.g. business rule definition can be represented as an element of the Business Rules Model.

- The agile requirements modelling artefact is an aggregate of the EKD enterprise model's elements belonging to one or several sub-models, i.e., it can be derived from the enterprise model. For instance, a Data Flow Diagram potentially can be derived from a Business Process Model; an essential use case can be derived from elements belonging to Actors and Resources Model, Business Process Model and Goals Model.

Table 1. Correspondence between the candidate artefacts for modelling requirements and EKD enterprise model's components

Candidate artefact	EKD enterprise model sub-model where it can be incorporated
Acceptance test	Technical Components and Requirements Model.
Business rule definition	Business Rules Model and Technical Components and Requirements Model
Change case	Goals Model and Technical Components and Requirements Model
Class Responsibility Collaborator	Concepts Model, Actors and Resources Model, Business Process Model, and Technical Components and Requirements Model.
Constraints definition	Business Rules Model
Data flow diagram	Business Process Model
An essential use case	Business Process Model, Actors and Resources Model, and Goals Model
An essential user interface prototype	Actors and Resources Model, Business Process Model, Technical Components and Requirements Model.
Feature	Goals Model
Technical requirement	Technical Components and Requirements Model
Usage scenario	Goals Model and Technical Components and Requirements Model
Use case diagram	Goals Model, Business Process Model, and Technical Components and Requirements Model
User story	Technical Components and Requirements Model

- An agile requirements artefact can be partially integrated in the Enterprise Model by related elements of several EKD sub-models, e.g. a user story can be partially represented by elements of Goals Model, Business Rules Model, Business Process Model, and Actors and Resources Model.

- An enterprise model element can serve as a reference to a particular agile requirement modelling artefact, e.g. an element of the Technical Components and Requirements Model may refer to a user story which is documented as a text or a video/audio record.

Integration of AM and EM suggests new emergent properties of the systems development approach that would be achieved by utilising strength of both methods. There are development dimensions at which both methods are strong and dimensions where one or the other method may be considered as superior. For instance, agile methods handle software development at both, - theoretical and practical levels of development - while EM does it only at theoretical level. On the other hand, EM can be considered as more powerful than AM with respect to the following dimensions (Conboy, 2006, p. 213):

- Dimension of holistic learning: AM facilitates software developers learning about the expected performance of the system to be introduced (Nerur & Balijepally, 2006), EM facilitates business level

learning about strategic and operational alignment and correspondence between business system and software system. Integration of
AM and EM suggests an emerging development property: holistic
organisational learning during the systems development process. This
is achieved by better understanding of business goals, idea generation,
tests and experiments, as well as to information storage and distribution.

- Dimension of contingency: Expert opinions show that contingency is
  not a built-in feature of agile systems development methods. Systemic
  explicit models provided by EM on the other hand compensate this
  weakness of AM in case of integration of both methods.

- Dimension of disciplined and educated tailoring: An Enterprise Model
  may serve as a useful map for tailoring systems development efforts and
  thus bring in more assurance in systems development process than in
  other AM cases.

- Dimension of measurement of output: Expert opinions show that this
  dimension is not supported by AM, while EM provides means for
  application of at least partial measurement of output on the basis of
  measurable objectives and goals in the Goals Model and Technical
  Components and Requirements Model.

Consequently, utilisation of EM in agile development aims at systemic
enterprise level agility by providing explicit knowledge based means for
change management, enterprise and software systems configuration management and other activities, which are essential constituents of enterprise
agility, i.e. ability to change rapidly not only in terms of software processes
but also in terms of business goals, processes and concepts (Browning et al.,
2006; Conboy & Fitzgerald 2004).

Recommendations Concerning the Modelling Process

Agile development projects using EM should focus on the business vision and
business requirements. The main objective should be to fulfil the business
requirements. This can be done by integrating prototyping approaches with
business modelling in order to explore various alternatives of supporting
business goals and processes by IS components and features. Using EM to
capture the business knowledge pertinent to the IS development project is not
the same as BDUF (big design up front) which is argued against by many
practitioners, e.g. Ambler (2002b).

Recommendation: Develop an Enterprise Model in Parallel

Developing an enterprise model that answers various questions from the perspective of multiple stakeholders ensures that the agile team has a repository of explicit knowledge needed for the development of an IS. Such a repository/model should address questions such as what are the goals of the customer organisation, what are the business and/or organisational problems that the new IS attempts to solve, what are the business processes and actors that need to be supported, what are the business rules and policies that affect the new IS, what resources are available/necessary, what are the IS goals and problems, etc.

To address the aforementioned issues we recommend holding a series of participative EM seminars in the early stages of agile projects. The EM process should proceed according to guidelines in (Bubenko et al., 2001). The agile team should not however aim at developing a complete enterprise model first and only then begin developing software as the following citation warns against:

"...if you see [the model] as our mutual opinion right now, in this question, then you are working agile. As soon as you start talking about freezing stuff and to itemize ... by that you mean that (something) is decided ... but that would almost be seen as failure and not as ... the right way to get the knowledge." – Interviewee i8 in (Jönsson, 2004)

The initial version of the Enterprise Model can serve as a starting point for IS development, but the team has to keep in mind that changes may and most likely will occur.

"You do more modelling in the beginning of project, because when you start implementing, the model has to have reached certain maturity, otherwise you have nothing to work towards. Then, of course, if you are working really agile, you have to be prepared to remodel and do more modelling, because it might be so that you are not doing all the modelling at one time." – Interviewee i9 in (Jönsson, 2004)

The developers of the agile team should also be involved in the EM process in order to be familiar with the modelling product and with the stakeholders. The modelling facilitator should be from the agile development team.

The tangible benefit of this is having a repository of explicit business knowledge about the system and its intended usage. The intangible benefit is a better commitment to the use and acceptance of the new IS by the stakeholders.

Recommendation: Involve Different Stakeholder Types

The agile team should involve various stakeholder types in order to consolidate their opinions about the requirements and the future application of the system. The main objective is to involve not only end-users but also occasional users as well as stakeholders that have indirect relation to the system such as high level managers who will benefit from the system in terms of greater work efficiency of their subordinates.

The tangible benefit is the discovery and integration of various views and opinions about requirements thus giving a more complete knowledge about the IS to be built. This makes the iterative and incremental development easier, because less redesign and rework is needed. The intangible benefit is promotion of the system and increased acceptance of the IS by various stakeholder types.

Recommendation: Link Other Models and Designs with the Enterprise Model

In agile projects IS development activities should begin as soon as the team has enough knowledge to identify the overall system architecture and set targets for the first iterations. To do this, the Enterprise Model does not need to be complete. Artefacts, such as models and designs produced as part of the agile IS development process, should be linked with the Enterprise Model. This will allow identifying which aspects of the domain knowledge or which requirements expressed in the model are supported by the current version of the IS. Figure 2 shows how some of agile requirements modelling artefacts can be linked to EKD sub-models.

Only some of possible linkages are represented in Figure 2. Many others are possible as well (see Section 4.1). The tangible benefit of linking the IS design artefacts to the Enterprise Model is the possibility to identify how different features of the system contribute to business goals, business process and requirements. The intangible result is a reduced need for redesign and rework.

Recommendation: Agile EM in Requirements Process

When EM becomes part of an agile development project it must be done in an agile manner, thus we can introduce the term agile EM. Agile EM process

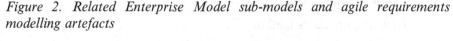

Figure 2. Related Enterprise Model sub-models and agile requirements modelling artefacts

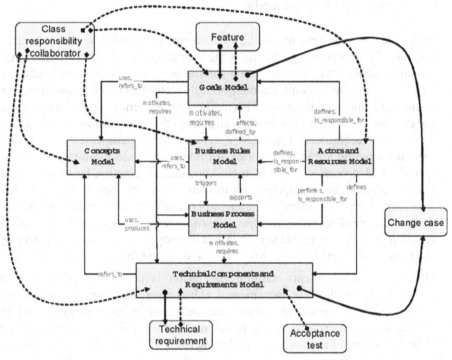

should follow recommendations given in section 4.2. In addition, the process is to be organised to add value to the project. The main purpose of using EM in agile development projects is to provide the development team with high quality requirements in terms of their fit to overall organisation needs. Concerning this:

"…we must constantly remind ourselves that entire requirements discipline within the software lifecycle exists for only one reason – to mitigate the risk that requirements-related issues will prevent a successful project outcome. If there were no such risks, then it would be far more efficient to go straight forward to the code and eliminate the overhead of requirements-related activities. Therefore if your team chooses a requirements method, it must reflect the types of risks inherent in your environment" (Leffingwell, 2002).

Leffingwell (2002) distinguishes between the following three requirements methods that mitigate risks in agile development projects:

- Extreme requirements method
- Agile requirements method
- Robust requirements method

In the extreme requirements method the vision of the system is only verbal and the unit of requirements gathering is the user story, which describes the chunk of functionality that provides value for the user. User stories are written by customers "on site". Using this method little attempt is made to understand or document future requirements. This method recommends that there is always a use case model that, at least loosely, structures the meta-knowledge about user stories. We recommend using EM instead of writing use cases, by reflecting meta-information about user stories in Enterprise Model's sub-models. In this case the EM process consists of meta-knowledge extraction from user stories and its reflection in appropriate sub-models. A tangible benefit of this is more structured meta-knowledge in comparison to use cases and time saving because there is no need to write the use cases for getting a systemic view on the requirements. An intangible benefit is that developers do not have to restructure their knowledge several times according to different modelling formalisms.

Using agile requirements method the vision is no longer verbal and its development method is incremental. Use cases have specifications that elaborate the sequence of events, the pre- and post-conditions, and the exceptions and alternative flows. In this method the vision could be developed at the beginning of requirements gathering using EM. Later the use cases could be attached to the corresponding sub-models of the Enterprise Model.

The tangible benefit of using EM is a shared vision instead of just a vision and a systemic overview of use cases to be implemented. The intangible benefit is a smoother software development process due to a shared vision.

Robust requirements method utilizes all tools of Agile requirements method but on a larger scale and in a more robust manner, including product planning and validation of requirements. Additional modelling techniques such as activity diagrams, message sequence diagrams are also used. In this case EM can be applied iteratively until the consensus among all stakeholders is achieved concerning the vision, concepts and requirements to be addressed. Enterprise Model elements may be linked to the requirements artefacts amalgamated in requirement management tools if there is a possibility to document the link. Tangible and intangible benefits in this case are the same as using the agile requirements method.

To achieve real agility in EM it is necessary to develop tools that support not only representation of the Enterprise Model, but also provide means for effective linking of Enterprise Model elements and other artefacts of requirements exercise in agile development projects.

Recommendations for Tool Support of Agile Modelling Methods

Agile teams are used to simple and effective tools that allow them to focus on the modelling task at hand. EKD similarly suggests using simple tools such as a large plastic sheet on the wall and colourful post-it notes to develop an enterprise model participatively. The main motivation for using the "plastic wall" is that every stakeholder can contribute to the model at any time. On the contrary, if a computerised modelling tool is used during a modelling seminar, then the stakeholders have to channel their input through a tool operator, which usually slows down the creative process. The option to use a networked synchronous collaboration tool also seems too cumbersome for agile developers as the following citation shows:

"It (i.e. modelling with simple tools) is an efficient way to get an overview, there can be several people, you can jump in and modify the picture for each other. The model becomes dynamic and something you build together. ...there certainly are such (collaboration) tools, but it feels a little strained to say – let's sit down and work via network in this program, so that we all can draw in this textbox at the same time. It becomes complicated to talk to each other simultaneously." – Interviewee i6 in (Jönsson, 2004)

Our recommendation is to redraw into a computerised tool only those models that will be kept "alive" during the development project. Others may just as well be discarded, because their value has been consumed once the developers resolved the issue at hand.

The kind of tools that is chosen for documenting the enterprise model depends on the situation in the project and in the organisations. Simpler projects and smaller teams usually choose drawing tools such as Microsoft Visio, while more complex projects might need a repository support and therefore prefer a CASE tool (e.g. Metis). More about the factors influencing EM tool acquisition and usage in practice is available in (Stirna, 2001).

Future Trends

Term "agility" is most commonly associated with relatively small enterprises and IS development projects that are not too sophisticated in terms of quality and security issues. However, increasing dynamics and turbulence of the external environment requests agile behaviour from every enterprise in terms of development of their products and services (Browning et al., 2006). In complex enterprises it is impossible to rely only on tacit human knowledge as a basic backbone of IS development and change projects. Therefore modelling environments able to capture both – business and technical knowledge – are emerging as a means for managing organisational knowledge. These environments differ in what they put as a central element in their modelling effort. Two most popular approaches are agent-oriented and process-oriented ones. Agent-oriented approaches focus on enterprise ontologies (Wongthongtham et al., 2006). Process-oriented approaches suggest treating processes as systems (Browning at al., 2004) and utilising service-oriented architectures (Aoyama, 2006) and business process management systems (Thellken, 2006).

Another way of handling knowledge relevant for organisational and IS development is use of Enterprise Architectures (Schekkerman, 2006). Those architectures aim to represent organisational knowledge that gives answers to questions such as why, what, who (by whom), how, when, where, and with what regarding different issues of enterprise starting with its strategy and ending with technical components of different systems including IS.

All the abovementioned approaches utilize quite sophisticated systems of models which usually are stored in and maintained by a CASE tool, i.e. such as Metis. Those models, if properly developed, may be used for the basis of requirements specification or even code generation. Unfortunately full scope of such models are not suitable for human comprehension, therefore other forms of knowledge representation are being searched that help to manage the knowledge. In comparison, EM provides models that are not beyond of human comprehension and therefore may serve as a mediator between human knowledge and sophisticated forms of knowledge representation in CASE repositories. The role of EM is illustrated in Figure 3.

EM provides answers to the majority of questions incorporated in Enterprise Architecture frameworks (Kirikova, 2000a) and does it in explicit form comprehensible by human brain. This knowledge can later be used in agile development projects. It can also be enriched or related to complex knowledge structures for the development of complex product or service development systems. On the other hand, it may serve as a visualisation means for complex models stored in CASE repositories to be managed by groups of enterprise and IS developers. For EM to achieve this role it is necessary to find flexible forms of knowledge storage that provide different types of interfaces to complex CASE tools or to the artefacts of requirements modelling currently used in small and medium scale agile development projects (Ambler, 2006).

Figure 3. EM and the enterprise model as a mediator between tacit and complex explicit knowledge

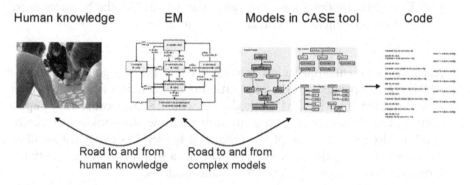

Human knowledge   EM   Models in CASE tool   Code

Road to and from   Road to and from
human knowledge   complex models

In summary, organisational development and the accompanying IS development is becoming increasingly driven by business and enterprise models to achieve agility on an organisational level. This invokes an assumption that enterprise models will be constructed in various degrees of detail and used for various purposes, e.g. for configuring ERP systems and collaboration tools, or for generating information systems. All this requires agile development teams to be capable of acquiring and dealing with the complete picture of the organisational situation and intentions, in order to develop a system that supports true agility of the enterprise.

Concluding Remarks

In this paper we have shown that EM has a potential to be useful in agile development projects. More specifically, the benefits of using EM in agile projects are the following:

- Explicit documentation of dependencies between the real situation in the organisations, the future state of business in which the new IS will be used, and the business decisions made during the IS development process.

- Configuration management on a business level allows more efficient development of business rules which are then incorporated in the IS.

- Using an enterprise model in an agile development project allows to identify and to take into account decisions that affect the borders of the IS.

- Enterprise model explicitly documents the future situation of the organisation and helps to elicit future requirements to the IS.
- Enterprise model allows the agile team to analyse the business impact and consequences of various design alternatives.

Agile development approaches provide a set of general guidelines most of which are independent of the application context. It is efficient to combine agile development with EM methods, i.e. with EKD, because they support participative discovery and integration of multiple stakeholder perspectives and knowledge. Our assumption is that EM is useful not only for small and medium scale agile development projects but also for achieving agility on a large scale and in complex enterprises and projects.

References

Abrahamsson, P., Warsta, J., Siponen, M. T., & Ronkainen, J. (2003). New directions on agile methods: A comparative analysis. In *Proceedings of Conference on Software Engineering.* IEEE Computer Society.

Ambler, S. (2002a). *Agile modeling: Effective practices for extreme programming and the unified process* (1st ed.). John Whiley & Sons Inc.

Ambler, S. (2002b). *Introduction to agile modeling* (White paper). Ronin International.

Ambler, S. (2006). *Agile requirements modelling.* Retrieved September 6, 2006, from http://www.agilemodeling.com/essays/agileRequirements.htm.

Aoyama, M. (2006). *Co-evolutionary service-oriented model of technology transfer in software engineering.* ACM.

Bajec, M., & Krisper, M. (2005). A methodology and tool support for managing business rules in organisations. *Information Systems, 30*(6), 423-443.

Beck, K. (2004). *Extreme programming explained: Embrace change.* Addison-Wesley.

Boehm, B., & Turner, R. (2004). *Balancing agility and discipline. A guide for the perplexed.* Addison-Wesley.

Browning, T. R., Fricke, E., & Negele, H. (2006). Key concepts in modelling product development processes. *Systems Engineering, 9*(2), 104-128.

Bubenko, J. A. Jr., Persson, A., & Stirna, J. (2001). *User guide of the knowledge management approach using enterprise knowledge patterns* (deliverable D3, IST Programme project "Hypermedia and Pattern Based Knowledge Management for Smart Organisations"). Stockholm, Sweden: Department of Computer and Systems Sciences, Royal Institute of Technology, http:// www.dsv.su.se/~js/ekd_user_guide.html.

Bubenko, J. Jr., & Kirikova, M. (2004). Improving the quality of requirements specification by enterprise modelling. In A. G. Nilsson, et al. (Eds.), *Perspectives on business modelling: Understanding and changing organisations.* Springer-Verlag.

Castro, J., Kolp, M., & Mylopoulos, J. (2001). Tropos: A requirements-driven software development methodology. In *Proceedings of the 13th Conference on Advanced Information Systems Engineering, CAiSE 2001, Interlaken, Switzerland.* Springer.

Cockburn, A. (2005). *Crystal clear: A human-powered methodology for small teams.* Addison-Wesley.

Conboy, K., & Fitzgerald, Br. (2004). Toward a conceptual framework of agile methods: A study of agility in different disciplines. In *Proceedings of the 2004 ACM Workshop on Interdisciplinary Software Engineering Research.*

Conboy, K. A. (2006). Framework of method agility in information systems development (PhD thesis, University of Limerick).

Dobson, J., Blyth, A., & Strens, R. (1994). Organisational requirements definition for information technology. In ACM (Ed.), *International Conference on Requirements Engineering 1994.*

F3 Consortium. (1994). *F3 reference manual* (ESPRIT III Project 6612 Deliverable). Stockholm.

Fox, M. S., Chionglo, J. F., & Fadel, F. G. (1993). A common-sense model of the enterprise. In *Proceedings of the 2nd Industrial Engineering Research Conference.* Norcross GA: Institute for Industrial Engineers.

Fraser, J. (Ed.). (1994). *Enterprise state of the art survey* (Part 5. Technologies supporting enterprise modelling, DTI ISIP Project Number 8032). AIAI, The University of Edinburgh. Retrieved August 8, 2004, from http:// agilealliance.org/home.

Jönsson, M. (2004). Agile modeling in Sweden – from practices to principles (MSc thesis, Stockholm University and Royal Institute of Technology, Stockholm, Sweden).

Kirikova, M. (2000a). Explanatory capability of enterprise models. *Data & Knowledge Engineering, 33,* 119-136.

Kirikova, M. (2000b). Potential role of enterprise models in organisational knowledge processing. In E. Kawaguchi, H. Kangassalo, H. Jaakola, & I. A. Hamid (Eds.), *Information modelling and knowledge bases XI.*

Kirikova, M. (2003). Conversion of inventions into requirements for computer based information systems. In *Scientific Proceedings of Riga Technical University, Series: Computer Science, Applied Computer Systems, 4th Thematic Issue.* Riga: Riga Technical University.

Kirikova, M. (2004). Interplay of tacit and explicit knowledge in requirements engineering. In H. Fujita & V. Gruhn (Eds.), *New trends in software methodologies, tools and techniques: Proceedings of the Third SoMet_W04* (pp. 77-86). IOS Press.

Lagerquist, I., Lindmark, M., Stirna, J., & Nyfjord, J. (2006). Adoption of agile development in practice: A qualitative inquiry. In *Industrial proceedings of EuroSPI2006, Joensuu, Finland.*

Leffingwell, D. (2002). *Agile requirements methods.* Rational Software.

Loucopoulos, P., Kavakli, V., Prekas, N., Rolland, C., Grosz, G., & Nurcan, S. (1997). *Using the EKD approach: The modelling component.* Manchester, UK: UMIST.

Nerur, Sr., & Balijepally, VG. (2006). Theoretical reflections on agile development methodologies: The traditional goal of optimisation and control is making way for learning and innovation. *Communications of ACM, 50*(3), 79-83.

Persson, A., & Stirna, J. (2001). An explorative study into the influence of business goals on the practical use of enterprise modelling methods and tools. In G. Harindranath et al. (Eds.), *New perspectives on information systems development: Theory, methods, and practice.* Kluwer.

Persson, A. (2001). Enterprise modelling in practice: Situational factors and their influence on adopting a participative approach (PhD thesis, Stockholm University).

Rittel, H. W. J., & Webber, M. M. (1984). *Planning problems are wicked problems; Developments in design methodology* (N. Cross, Ed.). Chichester: John Wiley & Sons.

Schekkerman, J. (2006). *How to survive in the jungle of enterprise architecture frameworks: Creating or choosing an enterprise architecture framework.* Trafford.

Schwaber, K., & Beedle, M. (2002). *Agile software development with SCRUM.* Prentice Hall.

Stapleton, J. (2003). *DSDM business focused development.* Addison-Wesley.

Stirna, J. (2001). The influence of intentional and situational factors on enterprise modelling tool acquisition in organisations (PhD thesis, Royal Institute of Technology, Stockholm, Sweden).

TEMPORA Consortium. (1994). *TEMPORA users manual.* Swedish Institute for Systems Development.

Thellken, M. (2006). *Business process management systems: Why they are hot and why you should care.* Retrieved December 12, 2006, from http://www.privatehand.com/pdf/transform.pdf.

Theodoulidis, C., Loucopoulos, P., & Wangler, B. (1991). The entity relationship time model and the conceptual rule language. In *Proceedings of the 10th International Conference on Entity Relationship Approach, San Mateo, CA.*

Willars, H. (1988). *Handbok i ABC-metoden* (in Swedish). Plandata Strategi.

Wangler, B. (1993). *Business rule capture in TEMPORA.* Stockholm: SISU.

Wongthongtham, P., Chang, E., & Dillon, T. S. (2006). Ontology-based multi-agent system to multi-site software development. In *Proceedings of the 2004 Workshop on Quantitative Techniques for Software Agile Process, Newport Beach, California.*

Yu, E. S. K., & Mylopoulos, J. (1994). From E-R to "A-R" – Modelling Strategic Actor Relationships for Business Process Reengineering. In *Proceedings of the 13th International Conference on the Entity-Relationship Approach, Manchester, England.*

Zorgios, Y. (Ed.). (1994). *Enterprise state of the art survey* (Part 3. Enterprise modelling methods). AIAI, The University of Edinburgh.

Chapter VIII

Experiences with Modelling Early Requirements

Pericles Loucopoulos, Loughborough University, UK

Abstract

A key challenge in the development of systems is the engagement of domain experts in their articulation, agreement, and validation of requirements. This challenge is particularly pronounced at the early requirements phase when multiple stakeholders from different divisions and often different organisations need to reach agreement about the intended systems. Decisions taken at this stage have a profound effect on the technical and economic feasibility of the project. The S³ approach advocates the use of a modelling process expressed in terms of strategy-service-support dimensions, augmented by appropriate simulation techniques that enable experimentation with different scenarios. The S³ approach has been presented elsewhere. The aim of this paper is to provide insights from a large project in which the author played an active and interventionist part, on the utility of the S³ approach in facilitating stakeholder *engagement in early requirements specification. The action research for this project involved the design of venue operations for the Athens 2004 Olympic Games. Many tens of stakeholders from a wide spectrum of professional expertise participated in the definition of business support systems for 21 competition venues over a period of 3 years. An interesting feature of this project was the use of three different approaches, starting with traditional peer-to-peer knowledge transfer, followed by a typical business process modelling method and finally adopting the S^3 approach and the way of working for the entire design of venue operations. The paper offers insights on all three approaches, insights that reflect on the problem of early requirements in general and on the validation of the effectiveness of the S^3 approach in particular.*

Introduction

There is a high degree of consensus amongst information systems researchers and practitioners that the development of systems is not solely a technical activity but rather organisational factors very often have a profound effect on both the delivered system and the design process. This is particularly acute in today's turbulent business environment where powerful forces such as deregulation, globalisation, mergers, advances in information and telecom-munications technologies, and increasing education of people provide opportunities for organising work in ways that have never before been possible (Malone, Laubacher et al. 2003). Many design situations involve multiple stakeholders from different participating organisations, subcon-tractors, divisions etc who may have a diversity of expertise, come from different organisational cultures and often have competing goals. The success or failure of many projects depends, to a large extent, on understanding the diverse and interacting sets of stakeholder requirements (The-Standish-Group 2003).

Requirements Engineering (RE) as a field of study and practice has traditionally focused on the specification of technical requirements i.e. defining the functional and non-functional properties of target systems (TSE 1977; IEEE-Std.'830' 1984; COMPUTER 1985; Davis, Hsia et al. 1993; Loucopoulos and Karakostas 1995; Nuseibeh and Easterbrook 2000). However, it is increasingly realised that tackling this very important area of requirements is not simply a case of describing what is demanded of the system to be developed but, instead a greater deal of emphasis should be placed on better understanding the complex interrelationships between requirements. This complexity arises due to multiple reasons such as, competing stakeholders' goals, contextual factors, uncertainly about the value of the system to its business and social environment. These are factors that need to be dealt prior to focusing on technical requirements, in the so called *early requirements* phase (Fuxman, Liu et al. 2003; Fuxman 2004; Loucopoulos 2004).

Issues of early requirements include: (a) the customer profiles of a business process, (b) the likely demand for product or service made by each type of customer, (c) the level of desirable service that the business process should strive to achieve, (d) the resources that are required in order to achieve these levels of service and (e) the trade-off between levels of service and requisite resource between all client stakeholders. Only when these issues have been resolved can one then begin to develop specifications of requirements for support systems. The analyst will need to know how the support system interacts with other systems, what kind of levels of service it must achieve, and what is the value of the support system to each class of stakeholder, before engaging into further analysis on functional and non-functional properties of the intended support system.

The *strategy-service-support* (referred to as S^3) has been developed as an approach to tackle these issues (Loucopoulos 2003). This approach is based on the premise that informal (c.f. (Galliers 1993; Leymann and Altenhuber 1994), semi-formal (c.f. (Ould 1995; Kavakli and Loucopoulos 1999) or formal approaches (c.f. (Fuxman, Mylopoulos et al. 2001; Fuxman, Liu et al. 2003) to requirements specification do not fully address the issues relating to early requirements, especially in developing trade-off scenarios that provide insights about the value of the support system to stakeholders.

The S^3 modelling approach advocates a process cycle of *hypothesis formulation*, *testing*, and *re-formulation* until stakeholders have enough confidence about the efficiency of the proposed design. Essentially, one is developing theories, externalised as conceptual models, about the Universe of Discourse and tests these theories for their validity. In terms of the 6 classes of requirements elicitation techniques identified in (Nuseibeh and Easterbrook 2000) (i.e. traditional, group, prototyping, model-driven, cognitive and contextual), the contribution of S^3 is in the *model-driven* and *group* classes. In S^3 models are used to establish the structural aspects of a business process. These models are subsequently subjected to scenario generation in consensus-building stakeholder workshops.

The aim of this paper is *to report on experiences* from a large project on the use of the S^3 approach rather than on the approach itself, in an attempt to demonstrate the value of the approach in establishing a strong framework for early requirements. In addition to describing the use of the S^3 approach, the paper also compares and contrasts this approach to two different approaches that were also used in this application. The paper is organised as follows.

Section 2 gives an explanation of the problem domain. Section 3 introduces the S^3 approach and gives synoptic examples of its use from the problem domain. Section 4 focuses on a discussion on the use of different approaches to early requirements elicitation as experienced by the author in the reported project. Section 5 concludes the paper.

The Problem Domain

All the issues with early requirements, outlined in section 1, were present in a project regarding the design of systems supporting venue operations for the Athens 2004 Olympic Games. The action research on which this paper is based was carried out at the Organising Committee for the Athens 2004 Olympic Games (ATHOC). The project underwent 3 phases during a period of 2 years and involved 175 person months of effort. Initially, elicitation of early requirements was attempted using informal stakeholder facilitation. This was followed by the use of a traditional business process modelling approach which in turn gave way to the S^3 approach that eventually became the main vehicle for eliciting early requirements for 21 applications.

In preparing towards the staging of the Games, ATHOC planed, coordinated and designed for systems most of which were delivered by external contractors. The problem domain is one of *process integration* the characteristics of which may be summarised as follows:

- There are many different *co-operating agents* (systems, ATHOC functional areas, sub-contractors, personnel and procedures). For example, the distribution of results involves the co-ordination of systems concerned with timing, information structuring, information communication, reprographics, and physical distribution.

- Different stakeholders have *distinct goals* and expectations of systems. For example, transportation is solely concerned with safe and timely arrival and departure of spectators whereas catering is concerned with meeting demand during the operation of a venue.

- Although different stakeholders have their own distinct concerns, from a total venue perspective all these need to be considered *holistically*. For example, the demand on catering is influenced by the behaviour of spectators in terms of their arrival and departure, their attendance of sports events etc.

The effect of these characteristics is the transformation that every Games Organising Committee needs to undertake. An Organising Committee is established a few years prior to the staging of the Games. Functional areas such as transportation, security, logistics, marketing etc. are established approximately 5-6 years prior to the staging of the Games, in order to organise and develop the necessary human, information and physical resources for the Games. Whilst at the outset the structure of an Organising Committee is hierarchical and *function-oriented*, this needs to gradually get transformed, as the Games approach, to a venue-based *process orientation* in order to shift emphasis away from internal organisational efficiency towards *venue operation* efficiency.

The term 'venue operations' concerns the systems, actors and procedures that will be implemented in a venue (be it a competition venue or a support venue) within spatial and temporal constraints, for different types of service e.g. security control, crowd management, catering etc. The design of systems supporting venue operations needs to address both their functional requirements (the resources and procedures for their management) and their non-functional requirements (the quality of service provision).

A central issue is the interaction and coordination of domain experts from 27 different functional areas in order to design systems that interact properly and are fully co-ordinated. For example, transportation needs to be co-ordinated with crowd queuing control which in turn need to co-ordinate with security etc. Typically, the stakeholders involved are experts from the Organising Committee, technical suppliers and subcontractors.

The complexity of venue operations increases as the variability of demands increases according to different 'customer' demands. For example, coordinating the processes concerned with spectator services involves many stakeholders from the 27 functional areas of ATHOC and for large venues there are in excess of 100 factors that influence the behaviour of the system.

The problem is graphically illustrated in Figure 1. In a generalised abstract sense, the problem associated with venue operations can be expressed as follows: "Given the temporal and spatial distribution of demand generated by the needs of the various customer groups to participate in a variety of sessions (temporal dimension of demand), that take place at various venues (spatial dimension of demand) provide the necessary system infrastructure in order to achieve a desirable level of service". During each Games' day up to 14 different customer groups participate in different sessions, that take place at any of the 36 different venues. Functional areas, up to 27 of them, need to design the systems and provide for the resource that will satisfy some expected demand for each session at each venue during each day of the Games.

Figure 1. Abstract view of problem domain

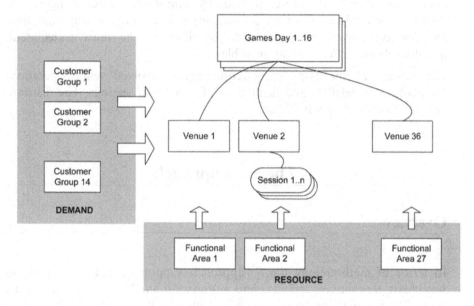

Co-development of business processes and support systems for this problem led to a number of complex decision making activities during early requirements. The following are few examples of frequently faced, typical questions:

- What are the appropriate types and level of resources that will be needed by each functional area for each venue?

- What are the interrelationships and interdependencies of the various functional areas in providing the required services to the various customer groups?

- What is the trade-off between the desired service level and the resource allocation / requirements for each activity involved in a process?

- What is the optimal operational smoothing / resource levelling for the overall process pertaining to a given customer group?

Ultimately, ATHOC had to specify the physical infrastructure (e.g. building works, public transportation etc), support systems (e.g. security systems, reporting systems, catering systems, ATMs etc) and procedures (e.g. protocols for dissemination of results, crowd control etc) in such a way so as to satisfy both the *individual* requirements of each functional area and the *systemic* requirements that arise from the process-oriented view of venue operations. It was therefore, profoundly important to reach agreement between stakeholders from all 27 functional areas on the way that their *interdependent requirements* were to be dealt in the most transparent, quantifiable and effective way possible.

The process of specifying early requirements involved venue operations stakeholders, modellers and facilitators of workshop sessions. The distribution of effort is shown in Figure 2.

The S³ Approach

Overview

In terms of methodology the S³ approach supports a reasoning cycle of *hypothesis formulation*, *testing*, and *re-formulation*. Within this reasoning cycle, S³ deals with strategic, service and support issues.

a.   Strategic issues are organisational and stakeholder goals for improving the organisation's performance.

b.   Service issues are the levels of improvement considered by the organisation.

Figure 2. Effort in specifying early requirements

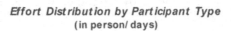

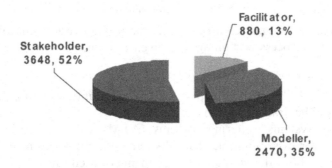

c.   Support issues are the resources policies and actions required to reach the desired service levels.

The S^3 approach is motivated by four 'principles: (a) *Systems thinking* considers independent components that form a unified whole (Richmond 1993; Checkland 1999); for example the business process spectator services involves arrival handling, security checking, crowd management, services etc and the behaviour of each component affects all others, potentially in a profound manner. (b) *Abstract thinking* implies that one moves away from the physical manifestation of processes (Walsham 1994). (c) *Operational thinking* considers the dynamics of a business process and in particular its behaviour over time (Forrester 1999; Sterman 2000). (d) *Solution-first thinking* implies that in attempting to identify requirements one generates a provisional design whose purpose is to highlight potential functionality (Carroll 2002).

On the basis of these four fundamental principles, three types of model are developed: (a) domain ontologies (Aune 1991) that scope the problem space and define the key business objects that participate in a business process; (b) stakeholder goals (Loucopoulos 2000) that determine the high-level intentions of each class of stakeholder; (c) processes (Loucopoulos and Prekas 2003) that fall into the two subcategories of customer-oriented processes and support-oriented processes where the former provides the basis for defining the level of service and the latter the manner in which this will be met.

In terms of processes involved there are essentially two activities: (a) *model building and critiquing* (Andersen, Richardson et al. 1997; Vennix 1999) and (b) *simulation and group deliberation* (Wolstenholme 1995; Fowler 1996). Models are mainly built by analysts with input from domain experts but are critiqued and revised by stakeholders. Analysts also facilitate simulation sessions where model parameters are instantiated by stakeholders. Consensus building stakeholder workshops develop scenarios that facilitate deliberation of alternative future realizations.

An Example from Using the S^3 Approach

A fully described example is beyond the scope of this paper. The purpose of this section is to highlight some of the salient points of S^3 in order to make subsequent discussion of insights more transparent.

In the domain that was briefly introduced in section 2 there were many different *co-operating agents* (e.g. the distribution of results involves the co-ordination of systems concerned with timing, information structuring, information communication, reprographics, and physical distribution). Different stakeholders had *distinct goals* and expectations of systems (e.g. transportation is solely concerned with safe and timely arrival and departure of spectators whereas catering is concerned with meeting demand during the operation of a venue). Domain experts from 27 different functional areas had to arrive to a consensus of the functionality of an entire venue (e.g. transportation needs to be co-ordinated with crowd queuing control which in turn need to co-ordinate with security etc).

Co-development of business processes and support systems for this problem led to a number of complex decision making activities during early requirements. For example, addressing issues such as "what are the appropriate types and level of resources that will be needed by each functional area for each venue?", "what are the interrelationships and interdependencies of the various functional areas in providing the required services to the various customer groups?", "what is the trade-off between the desired service level and the resource allocation / requirements for each activity involved in a process?", "what is the optimal operational smoothing / resource levelling for the overall process pertaining to a given customer group?"

Ultimately, ATHOC had to specify the physical infrastructure (e.g. building works, public transportation etc), support systems (e.g. security systems, reporting systems, catering systems, ATMs etc) and procedures (e.g. protocols for dissemination of results, crowd control etc) in such a way so as to satisfy both the *individual* requirements of each functional area and the *systemic* requirements that arise from the process-oriented view of venue operations. It was therefore, profoundly important to reach agreement between stakeholders from all 27 functional areas on the way that their *interdependent requirements* were to be dealt in the most transparent, quantifiable and effective way possible.

Model Building

In eliciting the goals for the venue operations system, the aim was to understand what determined the successful operation of the system. This involved helping the various stakeholders externalise the (sometimes implicit) goals that they had, capturing these goals, and synthesising that knowledge with information from other sources, such as existing documentation, abstract descriptions of various systems and procedures, and so forth. Stakeholders' goals were thus an initial, high-level expression of system requirements viewed from the perspective of ATHOC, i.e. the *service provider* (as opposed to that of the *user*).

An example of high-level goal was expressed with respect to the overall presence of spectators in a venue. Given that a venue may hold more than one event during a day, at any time there may be spectators arriving at the venue area for one of the upcoming sessions, spectators leaving the venue from one of the past sessions, and spectators participating in a current session. The total number of spectators present has to be somehow controlled for practical reasons such as the availability of resources (e.g. space), but also due to safety concerns. This translates into the goal 'manage the total presence of spectators in the venue area'. This is an abstract goal that needs to be made more specific; to refine it, the stakeholders examined the factors influencing the presence of spectators in the venue and their distribution in the various areas of which it consists.

In order to understand the effects of choices that stakeholders made, it was essential to develop business process models that operationalised the stakeholders' goals. These models could be viewed at both a 'local' level and a 'global' level. Local level process view related to a single customer group, a small area of the venue, and a small part of venue resources and functions (workforce, machinery, consumables). Global level process view corresponded to the dynamic profiling of all venue components, over an extended time frame (e.g. an entire day of the Games), possibly with respect to the needs of more than one customer group.

A distinguishing feature of this type of situation is the large number of different service types that the model must represent, since the behaviour of the venue operations system is affected by each of these service sub-components. As a result, the degree of complexity in the resulting process model rises dramatically.

Process modelling in the S^3 approach is driven by the *strategy* as advocated in stakeholders' goals, by the *service* that one is attempting to offer in meeting this strategy and by the *support* that needs to be deployed in order for the specific level of service to be realised.

Consider the following strategic goal 'Minimise the time that a spectator has to wait in order to get serviced'. The service level will vary according to the spatial location of a particular catering outlet and the temporal demand according to games' schedule. Achieving a service level of less than 5 minutes response will depend in addition on the units and volume of support that is allocated to the particular catering outlet. There are two issues that make the definition of requirements for support systems less than straightforward. Firstly, there is dynamic demand and secondly, this particular service (i.e. catering) is itself dependent on other service units and in turn its behaviour influences other service units. At a basic, local level, the behaviour of each catering outlet is influenced by demand and supply as shown in the model fragment of Figure 3.

The demand is determined in part through the pct of specs per service type variable, which expresses the number of customers expected at each type of service facility per unit of time as a percentage of total spectator presence. Total spectator presence depends on overall spectators' behaviour in the venue area, which interacts with this model fragment through a number of feedback loops (not shown here due to the complexity of the complete model).

The supply is determined by two parameters: the number of Service Points available (e.g. 10 stands selling food), and the specs per channel per minute service rate (e.g. two spectators serviced per service point per minute). According to this representation, spectators arrive at the service facility (going to facilities), queue there for a while if no service point is available (Specs Queue at Facilities), and eventually get serviced (servicing).

Using this model fragment we can elaborate on the way that stakeholder goals were refined through the use of process modelling. We previously mentioned the high-level goal 'Minimise the time that a customer has to wait in order to get serviced'. The realisation of this goal for a given type of service facility, and for a given demand, depends on the availability of supply for that facility. Supply is composed of two independent factors, the number of

Figure 3. Model fragment regarding venue service facilities

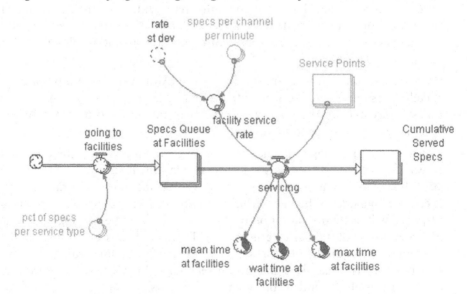

service points and the service rate. Therefore, the initial goal was decomposed into two complementary (i.e. non-competing) goals: 'Maximise the number of service points' and 'maximise the service rate'. These goals are more accurate than the initial one, however they need to be analysed further in order to become quantifiable.

Scenarios

The generation of different scenarios concerning each problem studied, and the simulation of these scenarios with the help of the process models developed, is an essential part of requirements definition in the S^3 approach. Evidence from the use of this approach on a number of industrial-strength applications indicate that scenarios are an indispensable tool for truly understanding the implications of stakeholders in their deliberation of requirements. For example, in the components of the system model that deals with services (ATMs, merchandising, catering, etc), fragment of which is shown in Figure 3, there is a plethora of *stakeholder defined assumptions* regarding demand and supply for each service facility. Each set of parameter instantiation gives rise to a specific behaviour. For example, Figure 4 shows

Figure 4. Simulation results for the 'Merchandising' service

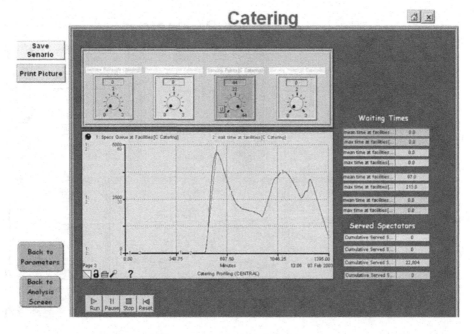

the result of the following choices: (a) all catering outlets are situated in a central area; (b) there are 44 catering outlets in this area.

These two sets of parameters define the way that support may be offered. In addition to these, stakeholders also defined the demand for service as shown in Figure 5. The choices available are: (a) the possible demand for catering set at 15 percent of all spectators and (b) the likely average response of each catering service which is set at 2 minutes per customer.

These 4 sets of parameters dictate the way that *strategy-service-support* interact to give rise to different system behaviours. Although in this example the focus of stakeholders was on catering, the interaction between requirements for catering and requirements for all other components of the system became highly visible. Catering for example, does not exist in isolation. It is influenced by other components and in turn it influences others. Other relevant factors, such as spectators' arrival and departure patterns, were taken into account. The stakeholders involved in scenario generation investigated the range of probable values for each of these parameters, as well as some 'extreme' values that were less probable but worth investigating nonetheless. Each scenario was characterised by the values of *all* independent variables; the number of possible scenarios thus depended on the number of their feasible combinations.

Figure 5. Stakeholder-defined parameters for catering

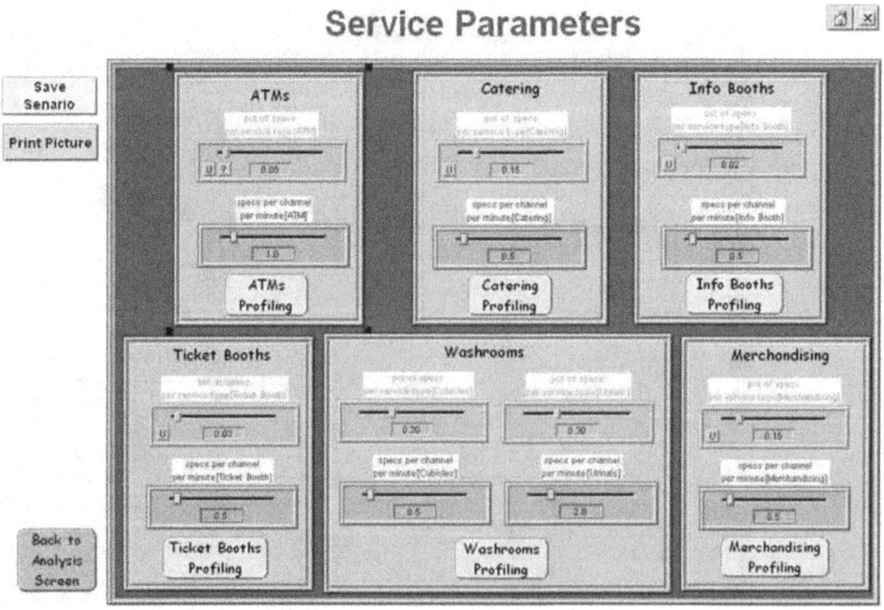

The models were subjected to testing through simulation sessions, in workshops involving stakeholders in groups ranging from 5 to as many as 40. In all workshops the models were presented to project stakeholders together with the corresponding scenarios and simulated runs.

These features enabled stakeholders to reach a consensus about the underlying processes and the implications that each choice would have on overall system behaviour. The first type of result, i.e. results concerning specific components of the system, helped to answer operational questions concerning the rational allocation of resources and the resulting service provision capabilities of the system. The second type of result proved useful for understanding the overall behaviour of a venue, thus answering higher-level, management questions concerning customer presence and distribution, arrival and departure patterns etc.

Reflections on the Application of S^3

Comparison of S^3 with Other Approaches

Prior to the use of the S^3 approach, two other approaches were utilised. First, an informal approach similar to those used in previous Olympic Games was tried out. This approach lasted 8 months and was followed by a more formal method based on a proprietary Business Process Modelling method.

Phase 1 – *the traditional peer-to-peer knowledge transfer through structured stakeholder workshops.* This was the typical approach towards the design of venue operations adopted in previous Olympiads. This approach was adopted early on in the project with the view to developing a 'prototypical design' for a chosen venue. The outcome was voluminous documentation expressed in a textual and tabular manner. This effort consumed substantial resources (2600 person/days) and this was just for one of the 36 venues. Participants in this phase were exclusively stakeholders and consultants from organising committees of previous Olympic Games who acted as facilitators in workshops.

Phase 2 – *the BPM approach based on model inspection and elaboration by stakeholders.* This phase began a little time prior to the end of phase 1 with the aim to reduce development costs and increase quality of designs through the use of conceptual modelling techniques. A *business process modelling* paradigm was chosen together with a CASE tool. The outcome was a set of models that were abstract enough to focus on the customer-oriented processes involved rather than on the physical characteristics of venues. The models were developed by modelling experts and were reviewed by domain stakeholders. However, this approach did not result in clear identification of issues since stakeholders could not visualise the effects of their requirements simply by inspecting static process models.

Phase 3 – *the S³ approach.* Phase 3 involved the adoption of the S³ set of techniques that provided the opportunity to develop both *qualitative and quantitative views* of the potential system. The aim was to encourage the full participation of stakeholders in: (a) overcoming barriers of communication, (b) fully agreeing on the processes involved in servicing different customer groups, (c) understanding the implications that requirements interactions have on the behaviour of different parts as well as on the overall behaviour of the system and (d) reaching agreement on levels of desirable service and the resources that are required to meet these levels. These objectives were achieved through the seamless coupling of model building and scenarios evaluation.

Figure 6 shows the effort expended for the entire project according to the different activities that took place. Although the traditional peer-to-peer approach together with the qualitative approach were tried only a very small number of venues, they nevertheless consumed almost as much as the S³ approach that was eventually adopted for all venues.

Figure 6. The different modelling approaches

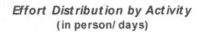

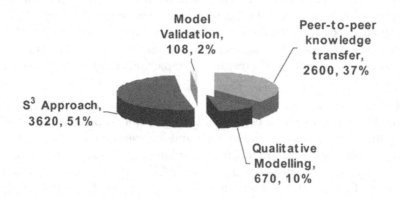

Benefits from the S³ Approach

The absence of a common reference language and the significant variations in experience and background among the participants were the key obstacles during phase 1. The closest substitute for a common reference model was that of architectural plans of venues. This imposed significant constraints on the effectiveness of the workshops, the most constraining of which was exclusive focus on specific operations taking place at specific venues. This fact prevented the participants from fully understanding the implications of service specifications in terms of resource requirements and resulting levels of service. Furthermore, there was no opportunity to generalise the designs resulting in customisation for each venue.

Whilst each group of stakeholders from each functional area at ATHOC seemed to have a general idea of their task in hand, complexity was compounded when faced with the need to develop designs that took into consideration the co-ordination of activities of all functional areas involved in a venue.

These serious shortcomings led ATHOC to the decision to adopt conceptual modelling as the core philosophy of the design tasks. The advantages of conceptual modelling over informal, natural language descriptions are well documented (Bubenko 1979; Loucopoulos 1992; Mylopoulos 1992). The chosen modelling approach during phase 2 was based on the business process modelling paradigm (Scheer 1999). The reason for this choice is to be found in the target of venue operations. All operations in every venue are designed so as to provide the best possible service to a whole set of different customer groups. Such customer groups include athletes, spectators, officials, Olympic family, volunteers, etc. Participation can be quite varied depending on the type of customer group and its particular needs in the different activities during the Games.

The purpose of modelling *customer-driven processes* was threefold. Firstly, the requirements of each customer group had to be formally and system-atically captured. Secondly, the process models gave the context for defining the resources required for each process. Thirdly, on the basis of the identified resources, it was anticipated that stakeholders could articulate, debate and agree the level of service to be offered.

The abstract and conceptual nature of the models provided a 'pluralistic' perspective to the process of venue operations. A venue operation was no longer considered as simply a manifestation of their physical layout. This also provided an opportunity of generalising the concept of venue operations to the extent that the models could be applicable to other venues with similar processing requirements but with different spatial constraints.

Whilst the development of models for venue operations was a catalyst for reaching agreement between stakeholders on the nature of the problem, this agreement did not incorporate an understanding of the *implications* that a particular design choice may have on the *behaviour of the system*.

It became evident during phase 2, that qualitative modelling by itself was not sufficient. Stakeholders experienced difficulties in understanding the dynamics of the system even for the simplest of structures. When the model of, for example, the spectators' processes in the main Olympic Stadium, grew to many tens of process flows (and in excess of 100 control parameters), the model was no longer of value in understanding the system behaviour. Hence, there was a need to engage stakeholders through a process that clearly highlighted all the nuances of the dynamics of the problem and offered them the opportunity to develop different *scenarios* of future designs together with an understanding of the *implications* that each design would have on the system's performance.

This led to the third and *main phase* of the project during which the S^3 techniques were chosen for a seamless way of expressing both the structure of the problem and its dynamics (Loucopoulos, Zografos et al. 2003). Attaching the numerical parameters to the customer process model had a dual advantage: (a) the impact of resource availability on customer service levels was immediately visible, thus aiding the customer-orientation of operations design, and (b) the human, material and other resources identified during functional area process modelling were also represented in the customer behaviour models, serving as the bridging element between the different modelling views. Thus, design ambiguities and the stakeholders' uncertainty on the effect of their design choices were eliminated.

The impact on management practices were evident in the planning process, in evaluating the likely cost of resources and in maintaining a model-based knowledge base of design decisions and solutions.

In terms of financial benefits of the adopted approach, it has been estimated that there were savings of over $69M (Beis, Loucopoulos et al. 2006).

Conclusions

Requirements engineering is considered by many as the most critical of all development activities for socio-technical systems. The sensitive area of early requirements is only recently beginning to be addressed in a methodological sense. Considerable effort is required to bridge the semantic islands that are often formed between different communities of client stakeholders, designers, regulators, etc. Indeed the entire system development process seems to be disadvantaged by lack of techniques to assist with effective communication (Urquhart 2001; Coughlan and Macredie 2002). An in-depth study on industrial practice (Curtis, Krasner et al. 1988) provides evidence that communication is crucial to the entire design process.

In early requirements, when there is a great deal of vagueness and uncertainty about system goals that are often set against a background of social, organizational and political turbulence, the need for a systematic and systemic way of dealing with all co-development aspects seems to be of paramount importance.

The work presented in this paper is an attempt to highlight this need from experiences from a substantial project that involved many stakeholders. These experiences confirm that informal and textual descriptions need to give way to conceptual modelling languages with clear semantics and intuitive syntax so that an application can be defined at an appropriate level of abstraction. This would greatly enhance visualisation of processes that will in turn contribute to a more informed discussion and agreement between stakeholders.

Whilst qualitative-based conceptual modelling approaches seem to be an improvement on purely linguistic-based approaches, they fail to bridge the communication gap between client stakeholders and analysts. The issue of analyst-client relationship has been highlighted by many authors (Kennedy 1994; Bashein and Markus 1997). This type of modelling paradigm that has evolved from work on Databases, Software Engineering or Object-oriented Design, with its analyst orientation, does little to enhance communication.

Empirical evidence from the Athens 2004 Olympics Games project on early requirements concurs with the premise on which the S^3 approach is based namely, that qualitative models need to be enhanced with quantitative capabilities. These capabilities provide opportunities for the generation and evaluation of alternative scenarios with respect to stakeholder choices on their requirements. In the ATHOC application, the S^3 approach proved to encourage group brainstorming through which participants could focus on alternative solutions and to envision potential behaviour of the system prior to its implementation. This way of working supports the way experts work on ill-structured problem settings such as planning and design (Carroll 2002).

Acknowledgment

The examples used in this paper draw from experiences on PLATO, a large project carried out between 2001–2004 on behalf of the Athens 2004 Olympic

Games Organising Committee The author wishes to express his gratitude to his many colleagues, analysts and stakeholders, at the Athens for their contribution to the PLATO project. In particular to Kostas Zografos of the Athens University of Economics and Business, to Nikos Prekas for managing the team of analysts and liaising with stakeholders in the most effective manner and to Dimitris Beis and Gregory Vgontzas for having the insight to adopt new innovative approaches towards the design of venue operations.

References

Andersen, D. F., Richardson, G. P., & Vennix, J. A. M. (1997). *Group Model Building: Adding More Science to the Craft, System Dynamics Review,* *13*(2), 187-201.

Aune, B. (1991). Knowledge of the External World, Routledge, (0415047471), London, New York.

Bashein, B., & Markus, M. I. (1997). A Credibility Equation for IT Specialists, Sloan. *Management Review, 38*(4), 35-44.

Beis, D. A., Loucopoulos, P., & Zografos, K. G. (2006). PLATO Helps Athens Win Gold: Olympic Games Knowledge Modelling for Organizational Change and Resource Management. *Interfaces, 36*(1), 26-42.

Bubenko, J. A., Jr (1979). *On the Role of Understanding Models in Conceptual Schema Design,* In Proc. of the 5th International Conference on Very Large Data Bases (VLDB), Rio de Janeiro, Brazil, Morgan Kaufmann.

Carroll, J. M. (2002). *Scenarios and Design Cognition,* In Proc. of the IEEE Joint International Conference on Requirements Engineering (RE'02), Essen, Germany, 9–13 September 2002, IEEE Computer Society, pp. 3-5.

Checkland, P. B. (1999). Soft Systems Methodology: a 30-year Retrospective, Wiley, (0471986054), Chichester.

COMPUTER (1985). *Special Issue on Requirements Engineering, IEEE Computer.*

Coughlan, J., & Macredie, R. D. (2002). Effective Communication in Requirements Elicitation: A Comparison of Methodologies. *Requirements Engineering, 7*(2), 47-60.

Curtis, B., Krasner, H., & Iscoe, N. (1988). A Field Study of the Software Design Process for Large Systems. *CACM, 31*(11), 1268-1287.

Davis, A., Hsia, P., & Kung, D. (1993). *Status Report on Requirements Engineering, IEEE Software,* (November), pp. 75-79.

Forrester, J. W. (1999). Principles of Systems, Pegasus Communications Inc., (ISBN: 1883823412), Waltham, MA.

Fowler, A. (1996). *Simulations's Evolving Role In Management*, In Proc. of the 1996 International System Dynamics Conference, Cambridge, Massachusetts, System Dynamics Society, pp. 162-165.

Fuxman, A., Liu, L., Pistore, M., et al. (2003). *Specifying and Analysing Early Requirements: Some Experimental Results*, In Proc. of the 11th IEEE International Conference on Requirements Engineering, Monterey Bay, California, USA, September 8–12, 2003, pp. 105-116.

Fuxman, A., Liu, L., Mylopoulos, J., Pistore, M., Roveri, M., & Traverso, P. (2004). Specifying and analysing early requirements in Tropos. *Requirements Engineering Journal, 9*(2), 132-150.

Fuxman, A., Mylopoulos, J., Pistore, M., et al. (2001). *Model Checking Early Requirements Specifications in Tropos*, In Proc. of the 5th IEEE International Symposium on Requirements Engineering, Toronto, Canada, August 27–31, 2001, pp. 174-181.

Galliers, R. D. (1993). Towards a Flexible Information Architecture: Integrating Business Strategies, Information Systems Strategies and Business Process Redesign. *Journal of Information Systems, 3*(3), 199-213.

IEEE-Std.'830' (1984). *IEEE Guide to Software Requirements Specifications*, ANSI/IEEE Std 830-1984, The Institute of Electrical and Electronics Engineers, New York.

Kavakli, V., & Loucopoulos, P. (1999). Goal-Driven Business Process Analysis - Application in Electricity Deregulation. *Information Systems, 24*(3)187-207.

Kennedy, S. (1994). Why Users Hate your Attitude. *Informatics, 2*, 29-32.

Leymann, F., Altenhuber, W. (1994). Managing Business Processes as an Information Resource. *IBM Systems Journal, 33*(2), 326-348.

Loucopoulos, P. (1992). Conceptual Modelling, In P. Loucopoulos and R. Zicari (Eds.), *Conceptual Modelling, Databases and CASE: An Integrated View of Information Systems Development* (pp. 1-26). John Wiley & Sons Inc., New York.

Loucopoulos, P. (2000). From Information Modelling to Enterprise Modelling, In S. Brinkkemper, E. Lindencrona and A. Solvberg (Eds.), *Information Systems Engineering: State of the Art and Research Themes* pp. (67-78). Springer.

Loucopoulos, P. (2003). *The S3 (Strategy-Service-Support) Framework for Business Process Modelling*, In Proc. of the Workshop on Requirements Engineering for Business Process Support (REBPS'03), Klagenfurt/Velden, Austria, June 17, 2003, pp. 378-382.

Loucopoulos, P. (2004). *Engaging Stakeholders in Defining Early Requirements*, In Proc. of the 6th International Conference on Enterprise Information Systems (ICEIS 2004), Porto, Portugal, April 14–17, 2004.

Loucopoulos, P., & Karakostas, V. (1995). System Requirements Engineering, International Series in Software Engineering, McGraw Hill, London.

Loucopoulos, P, & Prekas, N (2003). *A Framework for Requirements Engineering Using System Dynamics*, In Proc. of the 21st International Conference of the System Dynamics Society, New York City, July 20–24, 2003.

Loucopoulos, P., Zografos, K., & Prekas, N. (2003). *Requirements Elicitation for the Design of Venue Operations for the Athens2004 Olympic Games*, In Proc. of the 11th IEEE International Requirements Engineering Conference, Monterey Bay, California, U.S.A., September 8–12, 2003, IEEE Computer Society, pp. 223-232.

Malone, T. W., Laubacher, R., & Morton, M. S. S. (2003). Inventing the Organizations of the 21st Century, MIT Press, Cambridge, Massachusetts.

Mylopoulos, J. (1992). *Conceptual Modelling and Telos*, In P. Loucopoulos and R. Zicari (Eds.), *Conceptual Modelling, Databases and CASE: An Integrated View of Information Systems Development*, John Wiley & Sons Inc., New York:49-68.

Nuseibeh, B., & Easterbrook, S. (2000). *Requirements Engineering : A Roadmap*, In A. Finkelstein (Ed.) *The Future of Software Engineering*, ACM Press.

Nuseibeh, B., & Easterbrook, S. (2000). *Requirements Engineering: A Roadmap*, In Proc. of the 22nd International Conference on on Software Engineering, Limerick, Ireland, June 4–11, 2000, pp. 35-46.

Ould, M. (1995). Business Processes: Modelling and Analysis for Re-engineering and Improvement, John Wiley & Sons, Chichester.

Richmond, B. M. (1993). Systems Thinking: Critical Thinking Skills for the 1990s and beyond. *System Dynamics Review, 9*(2), 113-133.

Scheer, A. W. (1999). ARIS - Business Process Frameworks, Springer, (3-540-64439-3).

Sterman, J. D. (2000). Business Dynamics : Systems Thinking and Modeling for a Complex World, Irwin/McGraw-Hill, (0072311355 (alk. paper)), Boston.

The-Standish-Group (2003). *The CHAOS Chronicles - 2003*, http://www.costx-pert.com/resource_center/chaos_compared.html.

TSE (1977). *Special Issue on Requirements Engineering, IEEE Transactions on Software Engineering.*

Urquhart, C. (2001). Analysts and Clients in Organisational Contexts: A Converstational Perspective. *Strategic Information Systems, 10*(3), 243-262.

Vennix, J. A. M. (1999). Group Model-Building: Tackling Messy Problems. *System Dynamics Review, 15*(4), 379-401.

Walsham, G. (1994). Virtual Organization: An Alternative View, *Information Society, 10*(4), 289-292.

Wolstenholme, E. F. (1995). *Decision Analysis Using Dynamic Simulation*, In Proc. of the System Dynamics '95, Tokyo, International System Dynamics Society, pp. 937-945.

Chapter IX

Determining Requirements for Management Support Systems

Sven A. Carlsson, Lund University, Sweden

Abstract

The nature of managerial work makes the design, development, and implementation of Management Support Systems (MSS) a major challenge. The MSS literature suggests that determining MSS requirements and specification of MSS are the most critical phases in MSS design and development. We present a methodology that can be used as a guide for MSS design, with a primary focus on MSS requirements determination and how requirements can be fulfilled using information and communication technologies (ICT). The methodology builds on Quinn and associates' competing values model (CVM) of organizational effectiveness and current MSS knowledge. The methodology can guide MSS designers in designing MSS that support different managerial roles, i.e. the development of MSS that support managerial cognition and behavior.

Introduction

Management Support Systems (MSS) is a major Information Systems (IS) class. A major problem in MSS design and development is requirements specification. One reason for the problem is that managers perform quite a lot of different roles and activities (Mintzberg, 1973, 1994) and managers' work is not easy to model using traditional modeling techniques, like process modeling. We present a methodology that can be used to guide MSS design, with a primary focus on MSS requirements determination and how requirements can be fulfilled using information and communication technology (ICT). The methodology builds on Quinn and associates' competing values model (CVM) of organizational effectiveness. The presented methodology can guide MSS designers in designing MSS that support different managerial roles, i.e. the development of MSS that support managerial cognition and behavior.

Background

Many types of computer-based IS have been developed to support mangers, including Decision Support Systems (DSS), Executive Information Systems (EIS), and Group Support Systems (GSS) (Davenport and Harris, 2007). MSS usually refer to systems with a broader set of capabilities than, for example, EIS and DSS. An MSS can include electronic communications, modeling capabilities and organizing tools. In this chapter we use the term Management Support Systems to denote ICT-enabled IS that are supposed to support managers.

Studies suggest that a major problem in MSS design and development is requirements specification (Watson et al., 1997). Studies also show that a legitimate need is a key to MSS success (Fitzgerald, 1993; Watson et al., 1997; Hartano et al., 2007). This paper addresses the issues and problems in MSS design in a novel way. In doing so, we build our work on three postulates.

First, MSS is not a particular technology in a restricted sense, but primarily a perspective (vision) on managers and managerial work, the role of information and communication technology (ICT) and ICT-enabled MSS and how to realize this vision in practice. There is room for different perspectives on MSS and obviously also room for different MSS design methodologies. But as noted by Walls et al. (1992) and Hartono et al. (2007) there exists little theoretical work that directly guides MSS design. Our MSS design methodology is based on a well-established theory and model: the competing values model (Quinn et al., 2004).

Second, it is a misconception to think of MSS as systems that just provide managers with information. Part of the misconception lies in the use of the word information. MSS are systems that do more than provide information. MSS are systems that should support managerial cognition and behavior—providing information is only one of several means.

Third, effectiveness is a critical construct in Information Systems (IS) research and practice. Improved effectiveness is often claimed as a desired end for many ICT-enabled IS. Our MSS design methodology is based on the CVM which is underpinned by an effectiveness perspective.

The remainder of the chapter is organized as follows. The next section discusses approaches and methodologies for the design and development of MSS. This is followed by a presentation of the CVM and how it can be an underpinning theory and model for an MSS design methodology. The following section presents our MSS design methodology and how it can be used in MSS design. The final section presents conclusions and recommendations for further research and development.

MSS Design Approaches and Methodologies

There exist a large number of different approaches, methodologies, and methods for the design and development of ICT-based information systems (Avison & Fitzgerald, 1999); Jayaratna (1994) estimates that there are more than 1000 'brand name' methodologies worldwide. Fitzgerald (1993) and Watson et al. (1997) point out that there, for good reasons, are differences between traditional systems development methodologies and MSS development methodologies. After reviewing a number of IS development methodologies, Fitzgerald (2000) suggests that new methodologies are needed and that they can be based on, for example, current management and organizational theories. We present an MSS design methodology based on a current management theory and model.

An issue in the design and development of MSS is related to the relationships between designers, users, and other stakeholders. In general, the writings on IS development recommend that users should be involved in the design process. A problem often encountered in MSS development is that the users (managers) have very limited time for participating in the development process (Fitzgerald, 1993, 1998; Nandhakumar & Jones, 1997; Watson et al., 1997). A way out of this problem is to develop MSS design methodologies that are based on contemporary management models and theories. Such methodologies can support MSS designers in their design work and enhance communication with the users/managers. Before presenting the underpinning theory and model of our MSS design methodology, we review some of the current MSS design and development methodologies.

In a study focusing on the MSS methodologies and methods used by organizations in the US, Watson et al. (1997) found that only two formal methods were used, namely: the critical success factors method (CSF) and the strategic business objectives (SBO) method.

The critical success factors (CSF) methodology can be used to identify managers' information needs (Rockart, 1979). Critical success factors are "...the few key areas of activity in which favorable results are absolutely necessary for a particular manager to reach his goals" (Bullen & Rockart, 1981). The CSF method was extended to include critical decisions and critical assumptions (Henderson et al., 1987). Critical decisions (CD) are the decisions or decision processes that directly affect the success or failure of the CSFs. Critical assumptions (CA) are the assumptions that lead a manager to believe that the CSFs are valid. An MSS should provide information and support related to the CSF, CD, and CA. Lu and Wu (1998) presented the IDEAL method for MSS development. The method builds on CSF and critical success actions (CSA). CSA concern the decisions of actions, i.e. what to do if a particular CSF goes wrong.

Volonino & Watson (1990-91) proposed a strategic business objectives (SBO) methodology. The SBO methodology derives managers' information needs from an organization's objectives and the organization's critical business processes. SBO consists of six steps; the early ones being: identify an organization's strategic business objectives; identify business processes that are critical to the business objectives; prioritize strategic business objectives and critical business objectives; define information needed to support the critical business processes.

Walls et al. proposed a theory for designing vigilant EIS. A vigilant EIS is an information system that helps "...an executive [manager] remain alertly watchful for weak signals and discontinuities in the organizational environment relevant to emerging strategic threats and opportunities."

(Walls et al., 1992). Walls et al. also described an information requirement determination method called the "Critical Attention Tracker."

The above methodologies build in part on management and executive literature. They focus primarily on identifying information needs and especially monitoring information. Although, they can be useful, they have one major limitation. Since they to a large extent focus on information needs they are not complete in generating suggestions for use of ICT for supporting managers. We suggest that focus should be on managerial roles and an MSS design methodoly should address how the managerial roles can be supported by ICT.

The approach we took in developing our MSS design methodology was to review some of the descriptive and prescriptive management literature. The assumption was that the review should point to areas in which ICT can logically aid managers and that it should be possible to develop an MSS design methodology based on the literature. Rockart and De Long (1988) have recommended such an approach. The theory and model we will use build on the work of Robert Quinn and associates. The main reasons for using their work were that:

- They present a comprehensive framework/model of management work and in their work there is a strong link between theory and empirical studies.

- They address the link between how managers perform their managerial roles and performance (effectiveness).

- Their framework/model can be used to understand how ICT can be used to support managers.

The next section presents the competing values model (CVM).

The Competing Values Model and MSS Design

Organizational effectiveness is one of the foundations of management and organization theory, research, and practice (Cameron & Whetten, 1982; Lewin & Minton, 1986). The competing values model (CVM) was, in part, developed to clarify the effectiveness construct (Quinn, 1988; Quinn & Rohrbaugh, 1981, 1983). The CVM perceives organizations as para-doxical (Cameron, 1986; Quinn & Cameron, 1988), and it suggests that to achieve high performance requires an organization and its managers to simultaneously perform paradoxical and contradictory roles and capabilities (Hart & Quinn, 1993). The CVM of organizational effectiveness incorporates three fundamental paradoxes acknowledged in the literature: flexibility and spontaneity vs. stability and predictability (related to organizational structure); internal vs. external (related to organizational focus); and means vs. ends (Quinn, 1988; Quinn & Rohrbaugh, 1983).

Quinn and Rohrbaugh (1983; Rohrbaugh, 1981) found that most measures of effectiveness reflect one of four organizational models: internal process model (IP), rational goal model (RG), open systems model (OS), or human relations model (HR). The four models provide competing views on the meaning of organizational effectiveness. The human relations model is characterized by a focus on internal flexibility to develop employee cohesion and morale. It stresses human resource development, participation, and empowerment. The internal process model is characterized by a focus on internal control and uses information management, information processing, and communication to develop stability and control. The rational goal model is characterized by a focus on external control and relies on planning and goal setting to gain productivity and accomplishment. The open systems model is characterized by a focus on external flexibility and relies on readiness and flexibility to gain growth, resource acquisition, and external support.

The CVM points out the simultaneous opposition in the criteria that organizational members use to judge effectiveness. An organization does not pursue a single set of criteria. Instead an organization pursues competing, or paradoxical, criteria simultaneously. Organizations are more or less good in pursuing the criteria, and, according to the CVM, organizations differ in their effectiveness (Denison et al., 1995).

Quinn (1988, Quinn et al., 2004) translated the construct of effectiveness into managerial roles—two for each of the four organizational models. In the monitor role (IP) a manager collects and distributes information (mainly internal and quantitative information), checks performance using traditional measures, and provides a sense of stability and continuity. In the coordinator role (IP) a manager maintains structure and flow of the systems, schedules, organizes and coordinates activities (logistic issues), solve house keeping issues, and sees that standards, goals and objectives, and rules are met.

In the director role (RG) a manager clarifies expectations, goals and purposes through planning and goal setting, defines problems, establishes goals, generates and evaluates alternatives, generates rules and policies, and evaluates performances. In the producer role (RG) a manager emphasizes performance, motivates members to accomplish stated goals, gives feedback to members, and is engaged in and supports the action phase of decision making.

In the innovator role (OS) a manager interacts with the environment, monitors the external environment (environmental scanning), identifies important trends, is engaged in business and competitive intelligence, develops mental models, convinces others about what is necessary and desirable, facilitates change, and shares "image and mental models." In the broker role (OS) a manager obtains external resources, is engaged in external communication, tries to influence the environment, and maintains the unit's external legitimacy through the development, scanning, and maintenance of a network of external contacts.

In the facilitator role (HR) a manager fosters collective efforts, tries to build cohesion and teamwork—building the "trustful organization", facilitates participation and group problem solving and decision making, pursues "moral" commitment, and is engaged in conflict management. In the mentor role (HR) a manager is engaged in the development of employees by listening and being supportive, is engaged in the development of individual plans, and gives feedback for individual and team development.

After Quinn and Rohrbaughs initial studies, research on CVM has proceeded. This research shows that the CVM has utility as a general framework for organization and management research and practice. The CVM has also been used in the IS field—see, for example, Carlsson and Widmeyer (1994), Sääksjärvi and Talvinen (1996), Järvinen (1997), and Carlsson and Leidner (1998, 2000).

Research suggests that effective managers are capable of balancing and performing contradictory and complex roles (Hart & Banbury, 1994; Hart & Quinn, 1993). Some studies have tried to explain why some managers are considered more successful than others (Quinn, 1988). Research suggests that it is possible to link management behavior to firm performance; for example, Hart and Quinn's (1993) study suggests that managers having the ability to play multiple and competing roles produce better firm performance, especially with respect to organizational growth and innovation (business performance) and organizational (stakeholder) effectiveness. Denison et al. (1995), in a contingency-based study, empirically tested the CVM and the associated roles. They found support for the model and the roles, especially for managers that were considered high performing. Denison et al.'s study led them to define effective leadership as "...the ability to perform the multiple roles and behaviors that circumscribe the requisite variety implied by an organizational or environmental context." (Denison et al., 1995)—the notion of requisite variety is taken from Ashby (1952).

Based on the CVM and Denison et al.'s definition of effective leadership, we define an MSS to be effective to the extent that it is used by a manager in such a way as to support the manager in his different managerial roles, and support managerial cognition and behavior that circumscribe the requisite variety implied by the organizational and environmental context. Our definition of effective MSS is based on a contingency view and postulates: 1) there is no best MSS, and 2) any MSS is not equally effective. The first postulate means that we can not say that a specific MSS, with certain capabilities and characteristics, is the best MSS in all situations. The second postulate means that in a specific situation all MSS are not equally effective. It is possible to differentiate between MSS in terms of their effectiveness.

Hence, the goal of our methodology is to be a guide in MSS design and should lead to the development of MSS which when used will lead to increased effectiveness—according to the definition of an effective MSS.

A New MSS Design Methodology

Before presenting the MSS design methodology a few things about the methodology have to be clarified. Watson et al.'s (1997) study (discussed above) showed that in most cases a number of different "non-formal" methodologies, methods, and techniques were used along with formal methodologies in MSS development; "non-formal" methods include, for example, discussions with support personnel, attending meetings in order to enhance the understanding of what information managers need. This mix of formal and non-formal methodologies, methods, and techniques was also noted by Fitzgerald (1993). Avison and Fitzgerald (1999) and Fitzgerald (2000) point out that the search for the "grand"—and rigid—design methodologies and methods might be over, and the best we can do in some cases is to develop methodologies and methods that can be used as guides and to develop methods suitable for specific types of systems.

Based on the above, our MSS design methodology should primarily be perceived as a methodology for guiding MSS design and in most cases the methodology has to be supplemented with other formal and non-formal methodologies, methods, and techniques.

The MSS Design Methodology

Our CVM-based MSS design methodology is depicted in Fig. 1. The methodology starts with the choice of management situation, scouting and entry phase. It includes how to set up the MSS design project and finding sponsors and champions. The importance of this phase is stressed in the MSS

Figure 1. MSS design methodology

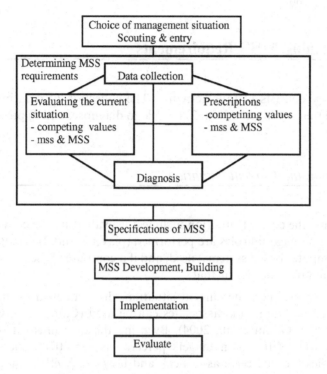

literature and since there exists a good body of knowledge on these issues we will not address the phase here—the reader is commended to consult Watson et al. (1997), Rockart & De Long (1988), Fitzgerald (1993), and Fitzgerald & Murphy (1994) on these issues.

The second phase (determining MSS requirements) consists of data collection, evaluating the current situation, diagnosis, and prescriptions. The third phase includes the technical specification of the MSS, which is followed by the building phase. We, as well as other MSS writers, have found it useful to use prototypes and to develop MSS iteratively. The fifth phase (implementation) includes implementing the MSS, i.e. putting the MSS in the hands of the managers. It also includes education/training and especially for new users a hot-line (in some cases available on a 24 hours basis). The final phase is evaluation, which in most cases brings us back to the second phase. Although, the figure shows a straightforward process, there are in most cases iterations between the different phases.

In the next sections we focus on the second and third phase, since these are the strengths of our methodology and also probably the most critical phases in MSS development (Watson & Frolick, 1993; Watson et al., 1997; Wetherbe, 1991).

Determining MSS Requirements

This phase consists of four activities. The collection of data in order to: 1) evaluate the current situation, 2) be able to diagnose, and 3) prescribe desired changes.

Evaluating the Current Situation

Evaluating the current situation includes: 1) evaluating the competing values and what managerial roles are performed (played), and 2) evaluating the mss (non-computer based systems) used, and if a computer-based system (MSS) is used evaluating the use of that.

In order to evaluate the current situation, different instruments developed and tested by Quinn and associates can be used (Cameron & Quinn, 1998; Quinn, 1988; Quinn et al., 2004). By using the instrument it is possible to evaluate what different managers perceive as the effectiveness constructs, which roles they perceive as critical, and how much effort they are putting into the different roles. In using the MSS design methodology, we have, for example, used the "competing values leadership instrument: self-assessment" (Quinn, 1988). This instrument captures a manager's perception of what roles he is playing and to what degree. We have also used the "competing values leadership instrument: extended version" (Quinn, 1988). This instrument consists of 32 questions (behaviors) and a person completing the instrument has to, on a 7-point scale, respond to how frequently the person performs a specific behavior today and how often the behavior should be performed. The "competing values organizational effectiveness instrument" (Quinn, 1988) has also been used—this instrument measures perceptions of organizational performance. The results can be presented for individual managers or as a summary of individual managers' perceptions.

In part, due to the problem of involving users (managers) in the design process, we have developed a supplementary way to identify the requirements for managerial behavior and cognition. Following the definitions of effective management and effective MSS, requirements for managerial behavior and cognition can be "derived" from an organization's external and organizational context. Carlsson and Leidner (2000) present three contextual characteristics that can be used to identify requirements for managerial behavior and cognition: organizational environment, organizational strategy, and organizational structure. They use the following characteristics: 1) for the external environment: turbulence, competitiveness, and complexity—adapted from Huber et al. (1993), 2) for the strategy: prospectors, defenders, analyzers, and reactors strategy—adapted from Miles and Snow (1978), and 3) for the organizational context: centralization of decision making, standardization of procedures, specialization of functions, and interdependence of organizational units and processes—adapted from Huber et al. (1993). The model presented by Carlsson and Leidner has been used to identify the requirements for managerial variety.

The purpose of evaluating mss and MSS use is to evaluate how mss (non-computer-based systems) and MSS are used by the managers. Using the CVM we can identify four ideal mss/MSS subtypes. For MSS we have named them MSS-IP, MSS-RG, MSS-OS, and MSS-HR (Figure 2). A specific MSS is a combination of the four subtypes and has to larger or smaller extent characteristics of the four subsystems. Here it is crucial get perceived use and usefulness in relation to effectiveness constructs and managerial roles—this can be supplemented by logging actual use of the MSS.

The first subtype (MSS-IP) supports the internal process model and the associated managerial roles; it has an internal and control emphasis. The ends for MSS-IP are stability and control. Most functional and cross-functional quantitative computer-based IS (CBIS) can be used as MSS-IP. Traditional accounting information systems and production systems are good examples of systems used for supporting the IP-model. In most cases the MSS-IP can be built "on top of" transaction-based CBIS (operational systems), for example as a portal on top of an Enterprise Resource Planning (ERP) system (Carlsson & Hedman, 2004). Studies suggest that many MSS are built on top of existing internal CBIS (Watson et al., 1997) and most of these are closely associated with the IP model (Carlsson & Hedman, 2004). From a manager's point of view the performance objective of MSS-IP is to provide user-friendly support for control and monitoring processes.

The second subtype (MSS-RG) has an external and control emphasis. MSS-RG should support a manager in handling semi-structured problems. Examples of MSS-RG capabilities and features are what can be found in "traditional" Decision Support Systems (DSS), i.e. support for goal setting, forecasting, simulations, and sensitivity analyses. Although many DSS have an individual focus, DSS can also be group-oriented (GDSS) and support management teams in strategic planning processes.

The third subtype (MSS-OS) has an external focus and an emphasis on structural flexibility. MSS-OS supports a manager in identifying problems and possibilities by support for environmental scanning, issue tracking, and issue probing. Environmental scanning can be quantitative or qualitative

Figure 2. Competing values model and systems characteristics and capabilities

Human Relations Model	Open Systems Model
Structure	
	Flexibility
Ends: Value of human reosurces	Ends: Resources acquisition, External support
Means: Cohesion, Moral	Means: Flexibilty, Readiness
Systems characteristics and capabilities: Communication & conferences (CSCW & Web 2.0)	Systems characteristics and capabilities: Environmental scanning & filtering (vigilantly) Interorganizational linkages
Internal	*External* **Focus**
Ends: Stability, Control Means: Information management, Communication	Ends: Productivity, Efficiency Means: Planning, Goal setting, Evaluation
Systems characteristics and capabilities: Monitoring & Controlling, Record keeping, Optimizing	Systems characteristics and capabilities: Modelling, Simulation, Forecasting
	Control
Internal Process Model	**Rational Goal Model**

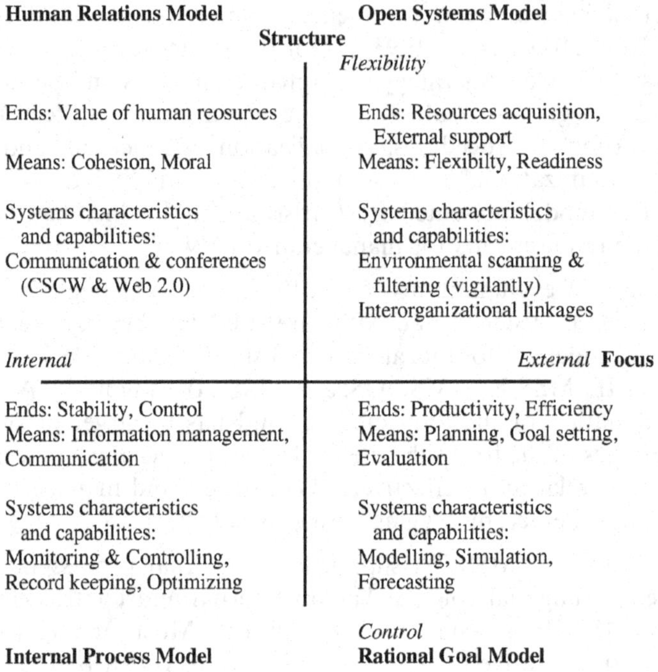

oriented and can include: industry and economic trends, legislative issues, competitor activities, new product and process development, patents, mergers and acquisitions, alliances, national and international events.

The MSS-HR subsystem helps an organization and its managers in the development of the human capital of the organization. Traditionally, MSS-HR capabilities and features of importance have been similar to what can be found in Computer Supported Cooperative Work (CSCW) systems and groupware; for example, ICT, like e-mail, voice mail, and videoconferencing can be used in MSS-HR to overcome distance and time. The rising popularity of user-driven online services, for example, Wikipedia, has drawn attention to a group of technological developments known as Web 2.0 or Enterprise 2.0 (McAfee, 2006; Saveri et al., 2005; Tapscott & Williams, 2006). The technologies include, for example, blogs, Wikis, podcasts, and peer-to-peer networking and are promising to change inter- and intra-organizational collaboration and communication (McAfee & Sjöman, 2006; McKinsey, 2007).

The above has been used in developing in a number of instruments that can be used to evaluate mss and MSS use—the instruments are ideal instruments that have to be adapted to a specific context. The instruments—16-32 questions and 5/7-point scales—are used to have individuals to evaluate how frequently they use mss/MSS for performing specific behaviors (managerial roles) and the person's perceived value of the support (the mss/MSS). We have also in some cases asked the respondents to answer questions about an ideal situation.

Using the instruments and other in-formal methods and techniques it is possible to evaluate the current use of mss and MSS and their perceived usefulness.

Diagnosis and Desired Changes (prescriptions)

A good fit between the current situation and the desired situation (i.e. the managers see no need for a change and the support they receive is good) means that there is no need for a new MSS. But, it is still possible to discuss the design of an MSS, but the primary purpose of the MSS would be to improve the efficiency—the MSS will primarily reinforce and improve the current state (primarily MSS as a personal tool).

If there is a misfit between the current situation and the desired situation or there is a misfit between current support and desired support, then there is a possibility to develop an MSS. In this case the MSS will be used as a means (tool) for focusing organizational attention and learning as well as a means for organizational change (Carlsson, 2002; Carlsson & Leidner, 2000; Vandenbosch, 1999; Watson et al., 1997).

The result of the diagnosis phase will be recommendations concerning how the competing values should be changed and how an MSS should support the different managerial roles in the future. The result will be used in the next phase.

MSS Specification

The output of phase two is desired changes. In the "Specification of MSS" phase these will be transformed into MSS specification; that is, taking the requirements and specify MSS characteristics and capabilities. This will later on lead to the development of an MSS and hopefully when the managers use it will lead to that the desired changes are fulfilled.

We now discuss how MSS can support the different managerial roles by looking at MSS capabilities and MSS information content. Although we propose how MSS can support different managerial roles it is not an MSS's capabilities and information characteristics that will determine the system's effectiveness, but how the capabilities are actually used by managers in their different roles. It should also be noted that new ICT that can be used for MSS will constantly hit the market and technologies will continue to change and evolve rapidly. (See Power's DSS-page at URL http://dssresources.com for reviews of the changing technological context of DSS and MSS.)

To discuss the usefulness of ICT for MSS we use an ICT typology. There are several different ways to classify ICT (George, 1991-92; George et al., 1992). Here we adapt the classification presented by George et al. (1992). They describe seven different ICT. There are no clear boarders between the different types of technologies and a specific MSS has features from more than one type of ICT.

The first type is communication technologies, which is ICT used to foster and support team, organization, and inter-organizational communication. The second type is coordination technologies, which is used to coordinate resources, projects, people, and facilities; for example to ensure that there is a synchronization of tasks and activities both horizontally and vertically. The third type is filtering technologies which are used to filter and summarize information. The fourth type is decision making technologies and techniques. This type is used to improve the effectiveness and efficiency of decision making processes. The fifth type is monitoring technologies, which is used to monitor the status of organizational activities and processes, industry trends, etc. The sixth type is data/knowledge representation technologies, which is used to represent and store data, text, images, animations, sound, and video. The seventh type is processing and presentation technologies which are ICT used to process data and present information. Figure 3 suggests the extent to which each of the seven ICT can be useful in building the different MSS subsystems.

For MSS-IP the key capabilities are: 1) monitoring the status of organizational activities and processes, 2) filtering and summarizing critical information, and 3) support for coordination of resources, projects, people, and facilities.

Monitoring support can be provided by using "standard" MSS software to build MSS for status access and exception reporting and enhanced with structured or free wheeling drill down capabilities. MSS can also include the use of data warehouses, multidimensional databases, and OLAP (On Line Analytical Processing) which, for example, can give a manager the ability to slice and dice a multidimensional database (datacube). The Web browser is becoming an almost universal interface. The browser can be used to integrate an MSS with the organization's intranets. An increasing number of MSS software packages are developed to be Web-ready. This means that OLAP on

Figure 3. ICT technologies for the four MSS subsystems

MSS subsystem Model: Building components / MSS Type:	Internal process MSS-IP	Rational Goal MSS-RG	Open Systems MSS-OS	Human Relations MSS-HR
Communication	**	**	**	***
Coordination	***	**	*	***
Filtering	***	**	***	*
Decision making	**	***	*	**
Monitoring	***	**	***	**
Data/knowledge representation	**	***	**	*
Processing & presentation	**	***	**	**

Key requirement: ***
Somewhat useful: **
Little use: *

data from a data warehouse or a multidimensional database can be directly accessed via the organization's intranet or through a portal (Carlsson & Hedman, 2004). In general, these changed and new capabilities make it possible to use traditional internal control systems more actively and in an ad hoc manner.

Filtering support can be provided by using technologies for filtering and summarizing information from internal information sources. If an organization uses a data warehouse or data marts filtering can be done in the "extract, transfer, load" process and in the "analysis and presentation" process. In order to enhance this, software agents and push technology can be used.

Coordination support, for example, to ensure that there is a synchronization of tasks and activities both horizontally and vertically, can be provided by project management tools, electronic calendars, and workflow management systems. It is possible to use information generated in a workflow management systems to assess the workflow.

Managers in organizations living in increasingly turbulent environment are likely to increase their use of internal real-time information (Bourgeois & Eisenhardt, 1988; Carlsson & El Sawy, 2007; Eisenhardt & Bourgeois, 1990). Traditional MSS are often based on financial data, but many organizations are rethinking their performance measures (Eccles, 1991). There is a shift from treating financial figures as the foundation for performance measurement to treating them as one among a broader set of measures (Kaplan & Norton, 1996). Performance measures related to quality, customers, learning and growing, and even intellectual capital are increasingly used by companies. Balanced Scorecard (BSC) software has been launched by a number of companies and BSC will probably be a standard feature of MSS software and ERP systems. ERP systems can in part fulfill new information requirements. Alternatively, ERP systems make it possible to in a simple way pipeline data from the enterprise system to, for example, a data warehouse that are used by an MSS (Although it from a technical perspective might be simple to pipeline the data, designing an adequate data infrastructure for a data warehouse is far from a simple task (Koh & Watson, 1998).) In many cases this trend requires an organization's top-managers to become more actively involved in information ecology (Cooper & Kaplan, 1998; Davenport & Prusak, 1997). A growing area for presenting relevant information to managers is the use of performance dashboards (Eckerson, 2006) often linked to organizational business performance management (BPM).

For the MSS-RG three capabilities are keys: 1) support for improving the effectiveness and efficiency of decision making processes, 2) data/knowledge representation, and 3) processing and presenting numerical data, text, images, animation, sound, and video. Capabilities found in traditional DSS and GDSS (Group DSS) can be used for generating and evaluating more alternatives, do simulations and quantitative analyses. Many of a manager's decisions are single shot decisions where, for example, decision analysis tools can be used to get consistent decisions. Decision making technologies could also be used to support team meetings. GDSS, if properly supported by group process techniques (Eden & Ackermann, 1998), can be useful as MSS (Watson et al., 1997). GDSS can have tools for: electronic brainstorming, idea organization, voting, stakeholder identification and analyses (Nunamaker et al., 1991). For a recent treatment of how firms can use business analytics, including decision support and business intelligence, to compete, see Davenport and Harris (2007).

For the MSS-OS two capabilities are keys: 1) filtering and, 2) monitoring. Filtering techniques can be used to facilitate electronic communication applying artificial intelligence techniques to sort, distribute, prioritize, and automatically respond to electronic messages (Sprague & Watson, 1996). There is also monitoring and filtering techniques to be used for environmental scanning. These techniques include, for example, the use of intelligent agents and push technology for scanning the internet. Increasingly we can expect that Web 2.0 technologies will be used in MSS-OS, for example, having CEOs and other top-managers use blogs.

For the MSS-HR two capabilities are keys: 1) communication for fostering and supporting individuals and teams, and 2) coordination. Coordination technologies, like project management tools and calendars, can be used to manage and organize the execution of decisions and processes. A major purpose of MSS-HR is to help a manager communicate information that will motivate and allow organizational members to be creative within defined limits of freedom (Simons, 1995). Communication technologies can be used to communicate: 1) basic values, purposes, and direction for organizational members, and 2) codes of business conduct and operational guidelines. For these purposes ICT like e-mail, videoconferencing, electronic documents, and multimedia can be useful. Although the media richness theory (Daft & Lengel, 1986) suggests that a technology like e-mail is a lean medium (compared to face-to-face), but research suggests that lean media can be used in rich ways if an organization encourages and supports rich use (Markus, 1994).

The output of this phase will be a specification of what should be built.

Some Remarks and Some Tips

The MSS design methodology has been developed using a current management and executive theory and model and current MSS knowledge. It has in varying degrees been used in real applications, in management programs, and it has been used in quasi-experimental lab studies. Over the years the method has been enhanced.

We have in the design process used MSS exemplars. Exemplars are descriptions of how different types of MSS can be used to support different managerial roles. The focus in the exemplars is on use and impacts of use and less on technical aspects. The use of exemplars seems to be useful.

We have used Decision Explorer (from Banxia) and GroupSystems (from Ventana) in the second phase. Decision Explorer has been used to identify and present "misfits" and to present and discuss remedies. GroupSystems has been used in lab studies to work through the first three phases, with an emphasis on the second and third phase. Both ways to use computer-based support seem to enhance the process and they both seem to be worthwhile to further explore.

Research suggests that there are changes in the criteria of effectiveness over an organizational life cycle (Quinn & Cameron, 1983). Another emphasis change can be found with regard to management level (Quinn, 1988). Implications of these findings are that the importance and criticality of effectiveness criteria and managerial roles will vary over time as well as between managerial levels. This knowledge can (and should) be used when design an MSS.

Conclusion, Discussion, and Further Research

Although, we see a change in what can be model using traditional modeling approaches (primarily process modeling)—for example, Seidel et al. (2006) show how a creative process in the screen business can be modeled—the nature of managerial work (Mintzberg, 1973, 1994) makes it impossible to use traditional modeling approaches. The MSS design methodology has been presented as a new guide for MSS design and development. The content of the method builds on Quinn and associates' competing values model and current MSS knowledge. The process of the method builds on prescriptions found in most MSS writings, for example, regarding the relationship between the MSS designers and the users (managers), the importance of having sponsors and champions, the iterative process, and the use of prototypes and exemplars.

Future research on the MSS design methodology will include the development of better instruments and better support for the second and third phase (this includes the development of computer-based support). Future research will also include empirical studies addressing the relationship between MSS use and support for managerial cognition and behavior and how this is linked to individual and organizational performance. The result can improve our ability to design MSS and prescribe how MSS can be used to improve individual and organizational effectiveness.

References

Ashby, W. R. (1952). *Design for a Brain*. New York: Wiley.

Avison, D., & Fitzgerald, G. (1999). Information systems development. In W. L. Currie and B. Galliers (Eds.), *Rethinking management information systems* (pp. 250-278). Oxford: Oxford University Press.

Bourgeois, L. J., & Eisenhardt, K. M. (1988). Strategic decision processes in high velocity environments: four cases in the microcomputer industry. *Management Science, 34*, 816-835.

Bullen, C. B., & Rockart, J. F. (1981). A primer on critical success factors. CISR Working Paper #69, Center for Information Systems Research, Sloan School of Management, Massachusetts Institute of Technology, Cambridge, MA.

Cameron, K. S (1986). Effectiveness as paradox: consensus and conflict in conceptions of organizational effectiveness. *Management Science, 32*, 539-553.

Cameron, K. S., & Quinn, R. E. (1998). *Diagnosing and changing organizational culture*. Reading, MA: Addison-Wesley Longman.

Cameron, K. S., & Whetten, D. A. (Eds.) (1982). *Organizational effectiveness: a comparison of multiple models*. San Diego, CA: Academic Press.

Carlsson, S. A. (2002). Designing DSS based on an attention-based view of the firm. In F. Adam, P. Brézillon, P. Humphreys & J.-C. Pomerol (Eds.), *Decision making and decision support in the internet age* (pp. 635-646). Cork, Ireland: Oak Tree Press.

Carlsson, S. A., & El Sawy, O. A. (2007). Managing the five tensions of IT-enabled decision support in turbulent and high velocity environments. In F. Burstein and Clyde W. Holsapple (Eds.), *Handbook on decision support systems* (forthcoming). Heidelberg: Springer-Verlag.

Carlsson, S. A., & Hedman, J. (2004). From ERP systems to enterprise portals. In F. Adam and D. Sammon (Eds.), *The enterprise resource planning decade: Lessons learned and issues for the future* (pp. 263-287). Hershey, PA: Idea Publishing.

Carlsson, S. A., & Leidner, D. E. (1998). Appraising executive support systems: a competing values based approach. In *Proceedings of the 5th European Conference on the Evaluation of Information Technology* (pp. 11-24). Reading, UK.

Carlsson, S. A., & Leidner, D. E. (2000). Impacts of ESS use on managerial behavior and cognition. Working paper, Informatics, Lund University.

Carlsson, S. A., & Widmeyer, G. R. (1994). Conceptualization of executive support systems: a competing values approach. *Journal of Decision Support, 3*, 339-358.

Cooper, R., & Kaplan, R. S. (1998). The promise—and peril—of integrated cost systems. *Harvard Business Review, 76*(4), 109-119.

Daft, R. L., & Lengel, R. H. (1986). Organizational information requirements, media richness, and structural design. *Management Science, 32*, 554-571.

Davenport, T. H., & Harris, J. G. (2007). *Competing on analytics*. Boston, MA: Harvard Business School Press.

Davenport, T. H., & Prusak, L. (1997). *Information ecology*. Oxford: Oxford University Press.

Denison, D. R., Hooijberg, R., & Quinn, R. E. (1995). Paradox and performance: toward a theory of behavioral complexity in managerial leadership. *Organization Science, 6*, 524-540.

Eccles, R. G. (1991). The performance measurement manifesto. *Harvard Business Review, 69*(1), 131-137.

Eckerson, W. W. (2006). *Performance dashboards: Measuring, monitoring, and managing your business*. Hoboken, NJ: Wiley.

Eden, C., & Ackermann, F. (1998). *Making strategy: The journey of strategic management*. London: Sage.

Eisenhardt, K. M., & Bourgeois, L. J. (1990). Charting strategic decisions in the microcomputer industry: profile of an industry star. In Von Glinow and Mohrman (Eds.), *Managing complexity in high technology organizations* (pp. 74-89). New York: Oxford University Press.

Fitzgerald, B. (1998). Executive information systems without executives. In D. Avison and D. Edgar-Nevill (Eds.), *Matching technology with organizational needs* (pp. 298-310). UK: McGraw-Hill.

Fitzgerald, B. (2000). Systems development methodologies: the problem of tenses. *Information Technology & People, 13*(3), 174-185.

Fitzgerald, G. (1993). Approaches to the development of executive information systems and the contrast with traditional systems development. In D. Avison, J. E. Kendall, & J. I. DeGross (Eds.), *Human, organizational, and social dimensions of information systems development* (pp. 339-351). Amsterdam: North-Holland.

Fitzgerald, B., & Murphy, C. (1994). Executive information systems: separating fact from fallacy. *Journal of Information Technology, 9*, 288-296.

George, J. F. (1991-92). The conceptualization and development of organizational decision support systems. *Journal of Management Information Systems, 8*(3), 109-125.

George, J. F., Nunamaker, J. F., & Valacich, J. S. (1992). ODSS: information technology for organizational change. *Decision Support Systems, 8*, 307-315.

Hart, S., & Banbury, C. (1994). How strategy-making processes can make a difference. *Strategic Management Journal, 15*(4), 251-269.

Hart, S. L., & Quinn, R. E. (1993). Roles executives play: CEOs, behavioral complexity, and firm performance. *Human Relations, 46*, 543-574.

Hartano, E., Santhanam, R., & Holsapple, C. W. (2007). Factors that contribute to management support systems success: An analysis of field studies. *Decision Support Systems, 43*, 256-268.

Henderson, J. C., Rockart, J. F., & Sifonis, J. G. (1987). Integrating management support systems into strategic information systems planning. *Journal of Management Information Systems, 4*(1), 5-24.

Huber, G. P., Sutcliffe, K. M., Miller, C. C., & Glick, W. H. (1993). Understanding and predicting organizational change. In G. P. Huber & W. H. Glick (Eds.), *Organizational change and redesign* (pp. 215-265). New York: Oxford University Press.

Jayaratna, N. (1994). *Understanding and evaluating methodologies*. London: McGraw-Hill.

Järvinen, P. (1997). On cultures and information technology applications in organizations. In J. Berlcur & D. Whitehouse (Eds.), *An ethical global information society* (pp. 203-214). London: Chapman & Hall.

Kaplan, R. S., & Norton, D. P. (1996). *The balanced scorecard*. Boston, MA: Harvard Business School Press.

Koh, C. E., & Watson, H. J. (1998). Data management in executive information systems. *Information & Management, 33*(6), 301-312.

Lewin, A. Y., & Minton, J. W. (1986). Determining organizational effectiveness: another look, and an agenda for research. *Management Science, 32,* 514-538.

Lu, H.-P., & Wu, C.-F. (1998). The IDEAL method for guiding MSS development. *Information Systems Management, 15*(5), 56-65.

Markus, M. L. (1994). Electronic mail as the medium of managerial choice. *Organization Science, 5,* 502-527.

McAfee, A. P. (2006). Enterprise 2.0: The dawn of emergent collaboration. *MIT Sloan Management Review,* Spring, 21-28.

McAfee, A. P., & Sjöman, A. (2006). Wikis at Dresdner Kleinwort Wasserstein. Harvard Business School Case 9-606-074, Boston, MA: Harvard Business School Publishing.

McKinsey (2007). How businesses are using web 2.0: A McKinsey global survey. *The McKinsley Quarterly.*

Miles, R. E., & Snow, C. C. (1978). *Organizational strategy, structure, and process.* New York: McGraw-Hill.

Mintzberg, H. (1973). *The nature of managerial work.* New York: Harper & Row.

Mintzberg, H. (1994). Rounding out the manager's job. *Sloan Management Review, 36*(1), 11-26.

Nandhakumar, J., & Jones, M. (1997). Designing in the dark: the changing user-developer relationship in information systems development. *Proceedings of the Eighteenth International Conference on Information Systems* (pp. 75–87). Atlanta, GA.

Nunamaker, J. F., Dennis, A. R., Valacich, J. S., Vogel, D. R., & George, J. F. (1991). Electronic meeting systems to support group work. *Communications of the ACM, 34*(7), 40-61.

Quinn, R. E. (1988). *Beyond rational management: Mastering the paradoxes and competing demands of high performance.* San Francisco, CA: Jossey-Bass.

Quinn, R. E., & Cameron, K. S. (1983). Organizational life cycles and shifting criteria and effectiveness. *Management Science, 9*(1), 33-51.

Quinn, R. E., & Cameron, K. S. (Eds.) (1988). *Paradox and transformation: Toward a theory of change in organization and management.* Cambridge, UK: Ballinger.

Quinn, R. E., & Rohrbaugh, J. (1981). A competing values approach to organizational effectiveness. *Public Productivity Review, 2,* 122-140.

Quinn, R. E., & Rohrbaugh, J. (1983). A spatial model of effectiveness criteria: towards a competing values approach to organizational analysis. *Management Science, 29,* 363-377.

Quinn, R. E., Faerman, S. R., Thompson, M. P., & McGrath, M. R. (2004). *Becoming a master manager.* Third ed., New York: John Wiley & Sons.

Rockart, J. F. (1979). Chief executives define their own data needs. *Harvard Business Review, 57*(2), 81-93.

Rockart, J. F., & De Long, D. W. (1988). Executive support systems: The emergence of top management computer use. Homewood, IL: Dow Jones-Irwin.

Rohrbaugh, J. (1981). Operationalizing the competing values approach. *Public Productivity Review, 2*, 141-159.

Saveri, A., Rheingold, H., & Vian, K. (2005). *Technologies of cooperation.* Palo Alto, CA: Institute for the Future.

Seidel, S., Rosemann, M., ter Hofstede, A., & Bradford, L. (2006). Developing a business process reference model for the screen business – A design science research case study. *Proceedings of the 17th Australasian Conference on Information Systems,* Adelaide.

Simons, R. (1995). *Levers of control.* Boston, MA: Harvard Business School Press.

Sprague, R. H., & Watson, H. J. (1996). *Decision Support for Management.* Upper Saddle River, NJ: Prentice-Hall.

Sääksjärvi, M. M. T., & Talvinen, J. M. (1996). Evaluation of organizational effectiveness of marketing information systems—the critical role of respondents. *Proceedings of the 4th European Conference on Information Systems* (pp. 435-450).

Tapscott, D., & Williams, A. D. (2006). *Wikinomics: How mass collaboration changes everything.* New York: Portfolio.

Vandenbosch, B. (1999). An empirical analysis of the association between the use of executive support systems and perceived organizational competiveness. *Accounting, Organizations and Society, 24*, 77-92.

Volonino, L., & Watson, H. J. (1990-91). The strategic business objectives method for guiding executive information systems development. *Journal of Management Information Systems, 7*(3), 27-39.

Walls, J. G., Widmeyer, G. R., & El Sawy, O. A. (1992). Building an information system design theory for vigilant EIS. *Information Systems Research, 3*(1), 36-59.

Watson, H. J., & Frolick, M. (1993). Determining information requirements for an EIS. *MIS Quarterly, 17*(3), 255-269.

Watson, H. J., Houdeshel, G., & Rainer, R. K. (1997). *Building executive information systems and other decision support applications.* New York: Wiley.

Wetherbe, J. C. (1991). Executive information requirements: Getting it right. *MIS Quarterly, 15*(1), 51-65.

Chapter X

Towards a Holistic Approach to Validating Conceptual Models

Jörg Becker, European Research Center for Information Systems (ERCIS), Germany

Björn Niehaves, European Research Center for Information Systems (ERCIS), Germany

Daniel Pfeiffer, European Research Center for Information Systems (ERCIS), Germany

Abstract

The chapter sketches a holistic approach to semantically validating conceptual models. The quality and thus the validation of conceptual models are of high economic importance. However, only little empirical work has focused on their evaluation so far. This raises the question whether a holistic approach to determining the quality of conceptual models is available yet. In order to describe the current state of research and to expose the so far neglected research fields we develop a two dimensional framework. With the help of this framework we can identify a notable shortcoming on conceptual model evaluation. We can show that there is actually no approach that covers all aspects of the framework. Hence, we describe a procedure model that integrates different evaluation techniques. This procedure model provides a starting point to further elaborate on a holistic evaluation approach.

Introduction

Since mid of the 70's, conceptual models have been employed to facilitate and systematize the process of information systems engineering (Boman, Bubenko, Johannesson, & Wangler, 1997). A remarkable number of modeling languages and methods have been proposed aiming at a more efficient and effective software development (Mylopoulos, 1998; Söderström, Andersson, Johannesson, Perjons, & Wangler, 2002; Yair Wand, Monarchi, Parsons, & Woo, 1995). In the beginning of the 90's, accompanied by new findings in management science, the positive experiences with conceptual models were transferred from information systems engineering to organizational design. This established conceptual models as a widely-used mean for eliciting costumer requirements and documenting the project progress of a software system as well as for describing the business processes and corporate structures in an organization (Shanks, Tansley, & Weber, 2003).

The quality of conceptual models has gained an immense impact on other IT artifacts (Hevner, March, Park, & Ram, 2004; March & Smith, 1995). Software systems are often based on requirement specifications in form of conceptual models. The adequacy of these specifications with regard to the represented application domain determines the acceptability and usability of software systems (Lauesen & Vinter, 2000). An incorrect description of the application domain will lead to problems in the implemented software system and to delays in the project progress. Likewise, the success of a reorganization project is influenced by the adequacy of the underlying organizational models. A problem analysis based on faulty models can lead to wrong and in the end very cost intensive decisions. By this means, the quality of conceptual models has reached a high economic importance.

The scientific and practical significance of conceptual models obliges to engage in the evaluation of these artifacts. During the last years numerous research efforts have been undertaken in order to develop criteria catalogs to evaluate the quality of conceptual models. Nonetheless, only little empirical work has focused on their evaluation (Hevner, March, Park, & Ram, 2004; Söderström, Andersson, Johannesson, Perjons, & Wangler, 2002; Yair Wand & Weber, 2002). This motivates the search for a holistic evaluation approach that covers all phases of conceptual modeling from the creation of the models to their use. Hence, we want to address the following research questions in the course of this paper:

- What are possible elements of a holistic approach to evaluating IT artifacts?

- How can these components intertwine to form a holistic approach on the validation of conceptual models?

The paper is structured as follows: In the next section we describe related work in order to develop a framework sketching possible elements of a holistic approach on the evaluation of IT artifacts. Here, we will describe the three components of this approach in detail. Hence, we will develop a holistic approach on model validation which is presented in the section III. The paper concludes with a short summary of the results achieved and an outlook to future research (section IV).

The *research method* chosen for this aim is that of conceptual research. We will hence provide logical arguments, rather then empirical ones. In the move of our argumentation we will though (where applicable) also refer to empirical research result. Furthermore, we will present additional evidence by giving examples from IS research practice.

Components of a Holistic Approach to Model Validation

The evaluation of IT artifacts has been an active research field for the last 20 years. During that time, manifold approaches to assessing the quality of artifacts have been proposed. Here, several catalogs of IT artifacts have been suggested by IS literature (Brinkkemper, Saeki, & Harmsen, 1999; Hevner, March, Park, & Ram, 2004; Yair Wand & Weber, 2002). Following March & Smith (1995), IT artifacts can be described as constructs, methods, models, or instantiations (see Table 1) while a typical information systems development process features these artifacts the presented order.

Table 1. Artifact dimension of the framework to evaluate IT artifacts

A1	Constructs	Constructs provide the language concepts in which the problem is described and the solution is communicated.
A2	Methods	Methods explicate the processes of how to solve a problem and offer guidance how to search the solution space.
A3	Models	Models utilize the constructs to represent an application domain and express the problem and solution space.
A4	Instantiations	Instantiations constitute the realization of constructs, models and methods in a working system.

A literature review of IT artifacts and IT artifact evaluation shows, that there are three major dimensions which span the evaluation of IT artifacts. They comprise, first, the structure of an artifact, second, the given evaluation criteria, and third, the evaluation approach in terms of a procedure (see Table 2).

The artifact dimension and the evaluation dimension can be consolidated in a conceptual framework. This framework with its two dimensions and examples of corresponding research results is shown in Table 3. To the structure of the artifact belong for example language based meta models for constructs (A1 / E1), intended application domains and conditions of applicability for methods (A2 / E1) or the documents which describe the development process of the software for instantiations (A4 / E1). Evaluation criteria catalogs exist for constructs (A1 / E2), methods (A2 / E2) and instantiations (A4 / E2). Evaluation criteria for software do for instance not only refer to the implementation itself. They rather also incorporate the requirements specificiation or the software documentation. Thus, the evaluation criteria establish a link to the structure of the artifact. An evaluation approach for constructs is for example the ontological analysis

Table 2. Evaluation dimension of IT artifacts

E1	Structure of the artifact	The structure of the artifact is determined by its configurational characteristics (elements, relations etc.) which are necessary for evaluation. Based on this structure, the required information about the artifact can be deduced. The structure represents the information space spanned by the artifact. The evaluation criteria are connected to this information space as they can refer to it.
E2	Evaluation criteria	The relevant aspects of the assessment are stipulated by the evaluation criteria. These criteria pin down the dimensions of the information space which are relevant for determining the utility of the artifact. These criteria can differ on the purpose of the evaluation.
E3	Evaluation approach	The procedure how to practically test an artifact is described by the evaluation approach. It defines all roles concerned with the assessment and the way of handling the evaluation. The result is a decision whether or not the artifact meets the evaluation criteria based on the available information.

Table 3. Framework to evaluate IT artifacts (and exemplary references)

	Structure of the artifact (E1)	Evaluation criteria (E2)	Evaluation approaches (E3)
Constructs (A1)	• language based meta model (Guizzardi, Pires, & Sinderen, 2002)	• construct deficit • construct overload • construct redundancy • construct excess (Y. Wand & Weber, 1990)	• ontological analysis (Rosemann, Green, & Indulska, 2004; Y. Wand & Weber, 1990)
Methods (A2)	• process based meta model • intended applications • conditions of applicability • products and results of the application • reference to constructs (Brinkkemper, Saeki and Harmsen 1999)	• appropriateness • completeness • consistency (Greiffenberg, 2003)	• laboratory research • field inquiries • surveys • case studies • action research • practice descriptions • interpretative research (Wynekoop & Russo, 1997)
Models (A3) Instantiations (A4)	• Subsection II.A • executable implementation in a programming language • reference to a design model • reference to a requirement specification • reference to the documentation • reference to quality management documents • reference to configuration management documents • reference to project management documents (Sommerville, 2001)	• Subsection II.B • functionality • usability • reliability • performance • supportability (Grady & Caswell, 1987)	• Subsection II.C • code inspection • testing • code analysis • verification (Fairley, 1985)

(A1 / E3), methods are evaluated by empirical research methods and for instantiations (A2 / E3) and software engineering community provides methods for quality assessment (A4 / E3). At this point, our literature review provided valuable research contributions on construct (A1), method (A2), and instantiation (A4) evaluation. Regarding the research question, we seek to analyze the elements of conceptual model evaluation (A3) in more detail: model structure (Subsection II.A), model evaluation criteria (Subsection II.B), and model evaluation approaches (Subsection II.C).

Structure of a Conceptual Model

A *conceptual model* is a representation of an application domain expressed in a semi-formal, mostly graphical language with the purpose of facilitating information systems development and organizational design (Evermann & Wand, 2001; Schütte & Rotthowe, 1998). Pfeiffer and Niehaves (2005) have deduced a structure of conceptual models by employing ideas from structuralism as theoretical foundation. With more than 700 publications, structuralism is a well established and broadly applied approach in philosophy of science to describing theories (for a detailed bibliography see Diederich, Ibara, & Mormann, 1994). Structuralism uses a specific frame of concepts to model the inner structure of science. Thereby, it considers science as a huge und complex conceptual network consisting of interdependent theories. Structuralism uses the formal language of elementary set theory as description mechanism. For covering the pragmatic aspects of science, it applies informal ways of representation as well (Balzer, Moulines, & Sneed, 1987).

Taking a *structuralist stance*, conceptual models are, in comparison to theories, less general in nature. The domain they represent is often restricted to a sole company or department. They do not cover the phenomena of a whole scientific field or parts of it as many empirical theories do. Nonetheless, also conceptual models require a certain inner structure to provide all information about the artifact necessary for its evaluation. Contrary to theories, conceptual models are not described in terms of mathematical axioms but in a semi-formal, graphical way. Their semantics results, on the one hand, from the given graphical arrangement of the model elements and their connections among each other. Pfeiffer and Niehaves (2005) call this the *model element structure*. On the other hand, the proposition of the conceptual model is influenced by the meaning of the modeling constructs and the application domain terms which are applied in the model. This second factor is denoted as *terminological structure*. The model element structure and the terminological structure both characterize *model statements*. First, the element structure of a conceptual model contains its actual proposition about the application domain. Thus, the element structure is comparable to the fundamental law of a theory. The element structure uses the terminological structure in order to express the content of a model. The particular arrangement of the model elements and their mutual relations expressed via modeling language constructs and application domain terms represent the empirical claim of the model. By this means, the element structure can describe a certain dynamic or static pattern of the application domain. Second, the terminological structure of a model is closely related to the framing conditions of a theory. Both of them provide the vocabulary to make assertions about the world possible. The terminological structure of a model can contain references to other conceptual models, including language based meta-models or domain ontologies, which define the applied terms and constructs.

We have already described, that a not unessential part of the semantics of a conceptual model descends from a reference to the *language of the application domain* and the *constructs of a modeling language* respectively. If such a reference is missing, the terms in the models are only restrained in their meaning by their connections among each other. Thus, if a conceptual model is not associated with other models, the meaning and existence of its terms originate in the model itself. The correctness of a certain model element is then dependent on the correctness of other model elements and not on its plausibility in terms of an application domain language. In this case, the determination of the meaning of a model element requires an assumption about the correctness of the model element structure. Since conceptual models only cover certain aspects of finite parts of the world they are not able to sufficiently restrict the meaning of all of the constructs and terms they apply. Therefore, isolated models offer a wide range of possible interpretations and provoke misunderstanding. The meaning of the terms has to be reconstructed from the connections among the model elements.

In order to facilitate an effective evaluation of conceptual models, it is crucial that a corresponding approach does not already presuppose the trueness of the model and the existence of its concepts. Hence, conceptual models have to exhibit *inter-model links* in the style of theories to provide an empirical basis which is independent from an assumption about the correctness of the model. The inter-model links establish a mapping between the model elements and its syntactic and semantic meta-languages. The syntactic meta-language can be represented as a language based meta-model which also forms a conceptual model. The semantic meta-language is given by the application domain language and can be described for example in terms of a technical term model (Rosemann, 2003) or a domain ontology (Mena, Kashyap, Sheth, & Illarramendi, 1998). Beside technical term models, also domain ontologies can be considered as conceptual models (Schütte & Zelewski, 2002). However, conversely, only a few conceptual models can be considered an ontology. Conceptual models often do not represent a shared view but the perspective of just a single person or a small group.

Suppose an application domain, as described in Figure 1, where customers can place orders for certain products. An experienced data modeler will represent the "order" in this domain with the two concepts "order header" and "order item". A domain representative who is not well trained in data modeling will hardly be able to understand this distinction. From the model

Figure 1. Entity Relationship Model (ERM) of an application domain

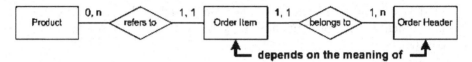

he only gains the insight that an "order header" contains multiple "order items". However his domain experience tells him, that an order is a coherent form. Without any inter-model links the concepts "order header" and "order item" originate in the model itself. Therefore the correctness of the model element "order header" depends on the correctness of the "order item" and vice versa. The domain representative is not able to confirm that the model is an adequate description of the application domain. Until he gains the information that an "order header" contains the master data of an order form and each "order item" stands for a line on the order form he can not come to a decision about the correctness of the model.

Assume that in another case the term "shower" occurs in a data model. This could indicate that model represents the domain of a sanitary equipment company as well as a meteorological institution. Again, without any additional information the correctness of this model could only be evaluated depending on the correctness of the terms and constructs connected with "shower". Theories specify their indented applications to restrain the phenomena which are covered by them. Likewise, conceptual models must state which application domain they want to represent. Their so called *intended application domain* makes sure that an evaluation takes place in the environment the conceptual model aims to describe.

The model core comprises models statements and inter-model links. A conceptual model consists out of the model core and the intended application domain. Figure 2 summarizes the proposed structure of conceptual models in the notation of the Unified Modeling Language (UML) (Object Management Group, 2003).

The conceptual model with its model core, intended application domain and inter-model link form the *conceptual level (L2)*. The conceptual level of a conceptual model contains all constitutive elements that frame its content. The model statement with the model element structure, the terminological structure, the terminological structure of modeling language constructs and the terminological structure of application domain terms belong to the *statement level (L1)*. The elements of this level are used to make propositions about the world within a conceptual model. The statement level comprises the content of the model.

Figure 2. Structure of a conceptual model

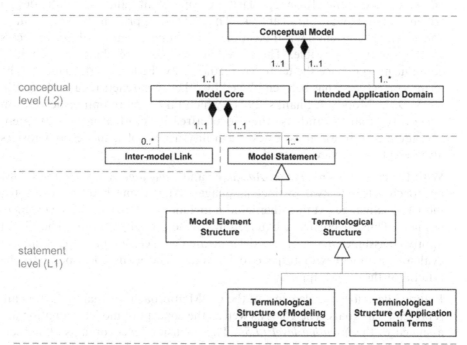

Evaluation Criteria

Several research efforts investigated into criteria catalogues determining model quality (Kesh, 1995; Levitin & Redman, 1995; Lindland, Sindre, & Sølvberg, 1994; D. L. Moody & Shanks, 1994). Here, many different, but often contextually overlapping approaches were presented. All those approaches have in common that their theoretical basis lays in the project experience of the authors. Criteria catalogs are theoretically founded by normative writings and single case studies that confirmed the suitability of the quality factors.

We will focus in our considerations on the Guidelines of Modeling (GoM) (Schütte & Rotthowe, 1998). There are other criteria catalogs with a similar purpose (e.g., Kesh, 1995; Levitin & Redman, 1995; Lindland, Sindre, & Sølvberg, 1994; D. Moody, 1998). We have choosen the GoM because it is a comprehensive approach with a well-elaborated documentation. For the purpose of this section it is sufficient to present one of the approaches and to understand its concepts.

The GoM comprises six quality factors: construction adequacy, language adequacy, economic efficiency, clarity, comparability and systematic design which are explained in Table 4. The GOM approach is based on a constructivist epistemological position which implies that no objective access to the reality is possible. Therefore, in the scope of the approach it is consequent to replace the term "correctness" by the term "adequancy". The term "correctness" has been employed by other researchers (March & Smith, 1995; D. L. Moody & Shanks, 1994), which take a more optimistic view on access to reality and is therefore already contextually occupied. "Adaquancy", however, stresses the utility aspect of a model and fosters an intersubjective view on truth.

With the criteria *Construction Adequacy* and *Language Adequacy* the GOM approach refers to two distinct languages. At the one hand it covers the modeling language. At the other hand it includes the language of the problem domain. Thus, it creates a connection to the model structure. The GOM approach assumes that every model is created with certain propose. A subject evaluates a model with respect to its goals. The goals correspond to the criteria of the GOM approach.

Figure 3 describes the elements of the GOM approach. Its quality factors are represented as goals. The goals as well as the concept of model evaluation are assigned to the *intention level (L5)*. The intension level contains all aspects that are connected with objectives and beliefs. The conceptual model and its modeling purpose belong to the *conceptual level (L2)*. The purpose of the model can be subsumed under the concept of intended application domain which already exists at the conceptual level. The problem domain with its subjects resides at the *subject and community level (L4)*. The subject and community level establishes the connection between a single modeler and his / her corresponding social group or language community. The language is located at the *language level (L3)*. The languages level is concerned with aspects such as modeling language constructs or domain concepts.

Table 4. Quality factors of the GOM approach

Construction Adequacy	Assesses the appropriateness of the model construction with regard to the represented phenomena and problems.
Language Adequacy	Analyses the syntactic compliance of the model with its modeling language.
Economic Efficiency	Defines the level of detail of modeling with respect to the scarcity of resources.
Clarity	Deals with the comprehensibility and explicitness of a model system.
Comparability	Aims at the systematic comparability of models regarding correspondence and similarity.
Systematic Design	Evaluates the inter-model consistency of the concepts in different views (static, dynamic) of a model.

Figure 3. Elements of the GOM approach

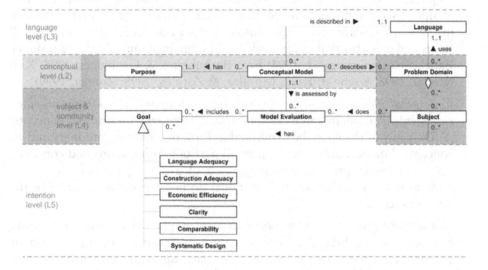

Evaluation Approaches

One approach to evaluate conceptual models is the ontological analysis. An ontology is "a shared and common understanding of a domain that can be communicated between people [...]" (Decker, Erdmann, Fensel, & Studer, 1999). They are "a shared understanding of some domain of interest" (Uschold & Gruninger, 1996). They can be divided into top-level, task, domain, and application ontologies.

Top-level ontologies have frequently and successfully been applied for evaluation. They have been used as theoretical foundation in order to evaluate conceptual modeling grammars (constructs, A1) and modeling methods (A2). Bunge has developed a top-level ontology (Bunge, 1977, 1979) which inspired Wand & Weber to create a framework for evaluating conceptual modeling techniques (Y. Wand & Weber, 1990). Here, Wand & Weber use the term "conceptual modeling grammar", reflecting that only the language aspect (constructs; A1) of a conceptual modeling method is assessed rather than the method as a whole (Yair Wand & Weber, 2002, p. 364). However, an analysis on basis of a top-level ontology cannot assess the content of a conceptual model. It rather focuses on the terminological structure of the modeling language constructs.

Domain ontologies can be used as an instrument to refer to and explicate domain languages. Due to comprehending them as a communication instrument, domain ontologies can be used in order to describe domain languages. Both domain language and domain ontology would possibly comprise such terms as "information system", "user", or "power user", for instance. In general, a domain ontology does not necessarily comprise all terms and concepts that are provided by a domain language (cp. for instance Fadel, Fox, & Gruninger, 1994; Fox, Barbuceanu, & Gruninger, 1998; Kim & Kim, 1998; Uschold, King, Moralee, & Zorgios, 1998; Zuniga, 1999).

Conceptual model statements can be evaluated against the domain ontology statements. A domain language comprises a large set of terms and concepts: A) Only few of them can be explicated in form of a domain ontology and B) conceptual models only refer to a small part of existing terms and concepts. Thus, the terms and concepts being part of a domain ontology or being referred in a particular conceptual model do not necessarily have to be the same (congruent).

Not accepting an ontology as normative or complete, ontological evaluation can only be the first step for evaluating conceptual models. In case of conceptual model evaluation, we advocate applying primarily domain ontologies which do not necessarily comprise all terms and concepts in a domain or that are provided by a domain language (cp. for instance Fadel, Fox, & Gruninger, 1994; Fox, Barbuceanu, & Gruninger, 1998; Kim & Kim, 1998; Uschold, King, Moralee, & Zorgios, 1998; Zuniga, 1999). Thus, one can not make a clear evaluation statement, in case identifying 'ontological deficiencies' such as described above. For instance: What if the conceptual model just intends to focus on certain aspects regarding as relevant and not addressing all concepts being part of the domain ontology? What if one provides certain statements with the help of a conceptual model which just are not part of a domain language or domain ontology? This could include statements on instance level, such as "All 'power users' of the 'information system XYZ' have 'computer experience of more than 10 years'", possibly being part of a conceptual model but not of a domain ontology. In that case, ontologies can only be used in order to evaluate certain terms or constructs used in the conceptual model, for instance if the 'power user' uses an 'information system'. Finally, evaluating statements and other terms and concepts is thus not possible.

Linguistic interpretivism explains as a second theoretical foundation a subjectivist epistemological position by the language a subject applies while striving for knowledge. Kamlah and Lorenzen (1984) established the so called 'school of methodical constructivism', also understood as linguistic interpretivism. Underlying to this approach is an interpretivist position (Lee, 1991; Probert, 2001; Walsham, 1995; Weber, 2004): a) It assumes that there independently exists a 'real world' beyond the realms of human imagination and thinking processes (Weber, 2004). And b) it assumes that the subject striving for knowledge (for instance a researcher) has, as a subject, great impact on the epistemological process of gaining knowledge (Weber, 2004). Interpretivist schools furthermore address the question; in what manner the subject has such influence. Linguistic interpretivism would answer that by the language a subject applies for gaining knowledge of the real world, the knowledge is influenced (Kamlah & Lorenzen, 1984).

Linguistic interpretivism aims at a semantic foundation of languages to make them comprehensible to its addressees. Its objective is the incremental and complete reconstruction of languages. With the aid of colloquial language and practical exercises linguistic interpretivism (re)introduces words and fixes their meaning. Therefore, this approach provides the theoretical basis for analyzing terminological systems, such as domain languages which are used within conceptual models and conceptual model statements. The (re)construction of terms and concepts is carried out in three steps (Kamlah & Lorenzen, 1984):

1. *Exemplary introduction:* In the context of the exemplary introduction in the first step a term is liked to an extra-linguistic activity.

2. *Stating the predicate rules:* For the further consolidation of the correct usage of technical terms from the perspective of a language community, predicate rules are defined next. A predicate rule denotes a regulation which defines the relations between the technical term and other terms.

3. *Explicit definition:* In the third step the meaning of the words is defined explicitly. A definition is conceived as an explanation of a term by means of other already known terms.

Thus, a new term or concept is introduced by *explicit agreement* with respect to its usage and meaning (Kamlah & Lorenzen, 1984). This agreement leads to a relation of concept and term and is shared by a language community as the *knowledge* of using this term (Kamlah & Lorenzen, 1984). Since language as a system of signs is shared by a *language community* as *common knowledge* semantics *and* pragmatics are directly linked to each other.

The verification of conceptual model statements is based on the procedure of interpersonal verification (Kamlah & Lorenzen, 1984). It becomes apparent that consensus on meaning and sense within a group can only be achieved by exchanging speech artifacts. Here, language communities are required to guarantee common understanding of terms and statements. One or more members (subjects) form a language community while a subject can also belong to more than one language community. When evaluating conceptual models and conceptual model statements, formalized linguistic statements part of a particular conceptual model are logically decomposed (deduction). This is done until they are accessible as elemental statements for purposes of interpersonal verification. This takes place by means of a group of subjects who obtain a consensus (or a dissent) on the truth of a certain statement. The main instruments are observation, experiments, interviewing and the interpretation of texts (Kamlah & Lorenzen, 1984).

Figure 4 describes the structure of a language community based evaluation of conceptual model statements. Subject, language community and interpersonal verification result belong to the *subject & community level (L4)*. From the epistemological position of linguistic interpretivism is straight forward to assume that a problem domain is covered by a language community. The language level comprises the domain and the modeling language. Since ontologies are considered as conceptual models both artifacts belong to the conceptual level. The statements [ont], [cm] and [ipv] belong to the *statement level (L1)*.

The process of interpersonal verification can be an extension of ontological evaluation of conceptual models. We have seen that domain ontologies can be a valuable instrument for evaluating conceptual models, if they are accepted as normative and complete. Since domain ontologies often do not fulfill these criteria, there is a need for evaluation procedures that can close this gap. In the move of interpersonal verification terms, concepts and statements of a conceptual model can be evaluated that are not fully covered by a domain-

Figure 4. Elements of a language community based evaluation of models

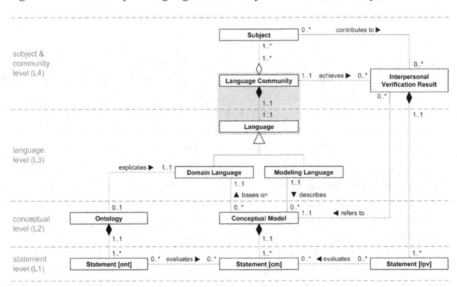

language-based ontology. Here, a domain-language-based ontology can function as a supportive instrument, in case it is partly covering conceptual model statements.

Towards a Holistic Approach to Semantic Validation of Conceptual Models

In the previous section of this chapter, three components of a holistic approach on the validation of conceptual models were presented. The relevant structure of each approach has been compiled in form an UML model (cf. Figure 2-4). To the elements of each UML model a description level has been assigned. Table 5 recapitulates the description levels as they have been defined in section II.

Table 6 contains all description levels (L1-L5) as well as all the corresponding model elements of each evaluation dimension which have been assigned to them (E1-E3). As not every dimension makes a contribution to each level, some cells are marked with "not addressed".

The "structure of the artifact" dimension defines at the *statement level* (L1/E1) the detailed internal assembly of a model statement. The evaluation approach uses the statement (cm) as an input (L1/E3). At the *conceptual level* the inner structure of a conceptual model is declared (L2/E1). The inter-model links establish a connection to the language level and the intended application domain describes the scope and the purpose of modeling. The "evaluation criteria" dimension takes the conceptual model and its purpose as an input (L2/E2). The concept of ontology is additionally introduced by the "evaluation approach" in order to verify the conceptual model (L2/E3). The *language level* is explicitly described by the "evaluation approach" (L3/E3). The language is referenced by the "evaluation criteria" (L3/E2). The

Table 5. Summary of the description levels

L1	Statement Level	The elements of this level are used to make propositions about the world. It comprises the content of an artifact.
L2	Conceptual Level	The conceptual level contains all constitutive elements that frame the content of the model.
L3	Language Level	This level is concerned with modeling language constructs or domain concepts.
L4	Subject & Community Level	Establishes the connection between a single modeler and his / her corresponding social group or language community.
L5	Intention Level	Contains all aspects that are connected with objectives and beliefs.

Table 6. Description levels of a holistic approach

	Structure of the artifact (E1)	Evaluation criteria (E2)	Evaluation approaches (E3)
Statement Level (L1)	• Model Statement • Model Element Structure • Terminological Structure • Terminological Structure of Modeling Language Constructs • Terminological Structure of Application Domain Terms	• Not addressed.	• Statement (ont) • Statement (cm) • Statement (ipv)
Conceptual Level (L2)	• Conceptual Model • Intended Application Domain • Model Core • Inter-model Link	• Conceptual Model • Purpose	• Conceptual Model • Ontology
Language Level (L3)	• Not addressed.	Language	Language Domain Language Modeling Language
Subject & Community Level (L4)	• Not addressed.	Problem Domain Subject	Language Community Subject Interpersonal Verification Result
Intention Level (L5)	• Not addressed.	Goal Model Evaluation	Not addressed.

subject & community level with its elements language community, subject and interpersonal verification result is specified by the "evaluation approach" (L4/E3). The subject is also addressed by the evaluation criteria (L4/E2). Arguing from the epistemological position of Linguistic Interpretivism the problem domain can be considered as a part of the world with its own language community. The goal and the model evaluation at the *intention level* are only explicated by the "evaluation criteria" (L5/E2).

Table 6 shows that no single dimension can cover all levels of description. However, a holistic approach on the evaluation of conceptual models must address all five levels to have the same functional coverage as current approaches have. Therefore, a holistic approach must comprise all three evaluation dimensions. Between the dimensions many interfaces as for example language, statement, conceptual model or subject could be identified.

The three evaluation dimensions render it helpful to also divide the model evaluation process into three phases. The three phases *model construction*, *evaluation planning* and *model validation* are described in Figure 5 including the resulting artifacts of each process step. During the model construction the structural properties of the conceptual model are specified. This phase corresponds to the dimension "structure of the artifact". The evaluation planning phase is concerned with the selection of an appropriate criteria catalog and an evaluation method regarding the particular properties of the conceptual model. Accordingly, this phase is associated with the dimension "evaluation criteria". During the model evaluation the criteria catalog is applied and the model is validated within a language community. Therefore, this phase is closely linked to the dimension "evaluation approaches".

Model Construction

During the construction of a conceptual model, its evaluation must be anticipated. The model must be augmented with all information necessary for

Figure 5. Process of model validation

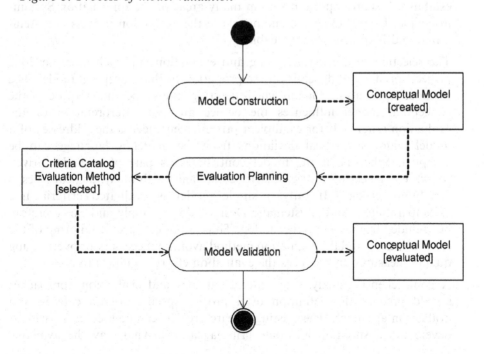

the validation of the artifact. If the model does not provide all required facts it is not comprehensible for the reviewers and therefore not appropriate to support the information systems analysis and design process. The description of the intended application domain, the explication of the domain language, and the specification of the modeling language provide the interface between the construction of the conceptual model and its evaluation. The intended application domain characterizes the scope and the purpose of modeling and defines where the model is applicable. An explication of the domain language facilitates the equal comprehension of the technical terms used in the model. A reference to a modeling language enables the interpretability of the graphical symbols and syntactical components including their spatial arrangement.

Evaluation Planning

The phase of evaluation planning takes as an input a conceptual model with a defined intended application domain as well as a link to a domain and a modeling language. The evaluation of conceptual models is a complex activity that requires planning. A preliminary planning process has established as an important step in many areas of the Information Systems discipline. By including a planning phase the evaluation process is systematized and becomes more traceable.

The selection of a criteria catalog and evaluation approach must be done project specific and depends on the properties of the conceptual model. The intended application domain which describes the scope and purpose of the conceptual model influences the choice and the interpretation of the evaluation criteria. If for example a process reengineer is the addressee of a model minor syntactical deviations from the modeling language can be accepted. Whereas, if the model contributes as part of a model driven software engineering project a strict compliance with all syntactical rules is absolutely crucial. If only a single model is evaluated criteria like "Comparability" and "Systematic Design" do not apply and can therefore be excluded from the criteria catalog. Thus, a project specific tailoring of the criteria catalog and the evaluation method avoids unnecessary or overlapping quality measures and reduces the evaluation efforts significantly.

A comprehensive analysis of criteria catalogs and evaluation approaches should precede the definition of a project specific criteria catalog and evaluation approach. The existing research results can be used as a basis for developing a situation adequate criteria catalog. That way the available knowledge about model evaluation is included and applied in the current evaluation process. By the reuse of existing criteria catalogs and evaluation approaches the completeness and expressiveness of the evaluation result can be increased.

Model Validation

A project specific criteria catalog, in connection with an evaluation method, serves as an input artifact for the phase model validation. A syntactical validation of the conceptual model can be conducted based on the referenced language. Modeling languages can be described in terms of meta models. Meta models define the grammar of a modeling language in a semi-formal way. Therefore, they can be used to automatically validate the syntactical properties of a conceptual model. Also the systematic design of conceptual models can be checked based on the meta model of the language.

An (incomplete) semantic validation of the conceptual model can be achieved by using a domain ontology. This ontological evaluation of the model can be automated. Unfortunately this process cannot achieve a conclusive decision about the semantic correctness of the model. Discrepancies between the model and the domain ontology do not necessarily mean a defect in the conceptual model. The level of granularity and the coverage of the domain elements between model and domain ontology can differ. An additional element in the conceptual model could for example indicate that the domain ontology is not complete. However, it could also point out an incorrectly represented domain object. Therefore, a conclusive decision about the quality of a conceptual model can only be reached by a manual analysis.

The final decision about the compliance with a goal or an evaluation criterion can only be achieved by a language community. Only the language community as the owner of the language is able to determine whether a certain term is consistent with the shared definition of a language concept. Conflicts which arise from an ontological evaluation of the conceptual model have to be discussed by members of the language community and solved by a consensus within the group. Such a debate about a common understanding of a term is crucial for domain languages. However, it is also suggestive whenever the modeling language is not well-known or only partially formalized. Since it is not feasible to formalize the intended application domain of the model its economic efficiency can in general only be determined in a manual, consensus oriented discussion process.

Summary and Outlook

The high economic importance that the validation of conceptual models has reached today marked the starting point of this paper. We found evidence that there exists a shortcoming of research on evaluation of conceptual models. Therefore, we sketched a holistic evaluation framework. The frameworks seeks o provide a broader perspective on how to approach the conceptual model evaluation task. The dimensions structure of the artifact, evaluation criteria and evaluation approach turned out to be sufficient to describe the model evaluation process. Thus, we have then explained these three evaluation dimensions in terms of their existing research results and theoretical foundations. We could identify interfaces between the dimensions and found them compatible. This motivated our attempt to formulate a holistic approach on the validation of conceptual models which covers all three dimensions. We presented this holistic approach by means of a process model. Possible future research might apply the presented holistic evaluation approach in terms of case studies and practical examples. Hereby, insight might be achieved in how far new model evaluation approaches can complement the set of methods presented.

References

Balzer, W., Moulines, C. U., & Sneed, J. D. (1987). *An Architectonic for Science - The Structuralist Program.* Dordrecht et al.: D. Reidel Publishing Company.

Boman, M., Bubenko, J. A. J., Johannesson, P., & Wangler, B. (1997). *Conceptual modelling.* Upper Saddle River, NJ, , USAPrentice-Hall.

Brinkkemper, S., Saeki, M., & Harmsen, F. (1999). Meta-modelling based assembly techniques for Situational Method Engineering. *Information Systems, 24*(3), 209-228.

Bunge, M. (1977). Ontology I: The Furniture of the World (Vol. Band 3). Dordrecht: D. Reidel Publishing Company.

Bunge, M. (1979). Ontology II: A World of Systems (Vol. Band 4). Dordrecht: D. Reidel Publishing Company.

Decker, S., Erdmann, M., Fensel, D., & Studer, R. (1999). Ontobroker: Ontology Based Access to Distributed and Semi-Structured Information. In R. Meersman (Ed.), Semantic Issues in Multimedia Systems. Proceedings of International Conference on Data Semantics DS-8 (pp. 351-369). Boston: Kluwer Academic Publisher.

Diederich, W., Ibara, A., & Mormann, T. (1994). Bibliography of Structuralism II. Erkenntnis, 41, p. 403-418.

Evermann, J., & Wand, Y. (2001). Towards Ontologically Based Semantics for UML Constructs. Paper presented at the 20th International Conference on Conceptual Modeling (ER 2001), Yokohama, Japan.

Fadel, F. G., Fox, M. S., & Gruninger, M. (1994). A Generic Enterprise Resource Ontology. Paper presented at the 3rd Workshop on Enabling Technologies: Infrastructure for Collaborative Enterprises, Morgantown/ WV, USA.

Fairley, R. E. (1985). Software Engineering Concepts. New York et al.: McGraw-Hill Book Company.

Fox, M. S., Barbuceanu, M., & Gruninger, M., & Lin, J. (1998). An Organization Ontology for Enterprise Modelling. In M. Prietula, K. Carley & L. Gasser (Eds.), Simulating Organizations: Computa-tional Models of Institutions and Groups (pp. 131-152). Menlo Park/ CA, USA: AAAI/MIT Press.

Grady, R. B., & Caswell, D. L. (1987). Software Metrics: Enabling a Company-Wide Program. Englewood Cliffs: Prentice Hall.

Greiffenberg, S. (2003). Methods as theories in Information Systems, in German. Paper presented at the 6th International Conference Wirtschaftsinformatik (WI 2003), Dresden.

Guizzardi, G., Pires, L. F., & Sinderen, M. J. V. (2002). On the role of Domain Ontologies in the design of Domain-Specific Visual Modeling Languages. Paper presented at the 2nd Workshop on Domain-Specific Visual Languages, 17th ACM Conference on Object-Oriented Programming, Systems, Languages and Applications (OOPSLA 2002), Seattle.

Hevner, A. R., March, S. T., Park, J., & Ram, S. (2004). Design Science in Information Systems Research. *MIS Quarterly, 28*(1), 75-105.

Kamlah, W., & Lorenzen, P. (1984). Logical Propaedeutic. Pre-School of Reasonable Discourse. Lanham, MD: University Press of America.

Kesh, S. (1995). Evaluating the quality of entity relationship models. *Information and Software Technology, 37*(12), 681-689.

Kim, K.-H., & Kim, Y.-G. (1998). Process reverse engineering for BPR: A form-based approach. *Information & Management, 33*(4), 187-200.

Lauesen, S., & Vinter, O. (2000). Preventing Requirement Defects. Paper presented at the Sixth International Workshop on Requirements Engineering: Foundations of Software Quality (REFSQ 2000), Stockholm

Lee, A. (1991). Integrating positivist and interpretivist approaches to organizational research. *Organization Science, 2*, 342-365.

Levitin, A., & Redman, T. (1995). Quality dimensions of a conceptual view. *Information Processing & Management, 31*(1), 81-88.

Lindland, O. I., Sindre, G., & Sølvberg, A. (1994). Understanding quality in conceptual modeling. *IEEE Software, 11*(2), 42-49.

March, S. T., & Smith, G. F. (1995). Design and natural science research on information technology. *Decision Support Systems, 15*(4), 251-266.

Mena, E., Kashyap, V., Sheth, A., & Illarramendi, A. (1998). Domain Specific Ontologies for Semantic Information Brokering on the Global Information Infrastructure. Paper presented at the First International Conference on Formal Ontologies in Information Systems, Trento, Italy.

Moody, D. (1998). Metrics for Evaluating the Quality of Entity Relationship Models. In T. Ling, S. Ram & M. Lee (Eds.), Lecture Notes in Computer Science (1507 ed., pp.211-225): Springer.

Moody, D. L., & Shanks, G. G. (1994). What Makes a Good Data Model? Evaluating the Quality of Entity Relationship Models. Paper presented at the 13th International Conference on the Entity Relationship Approach (ER 1994), Manchester, United Kingdom.

Mylopoulos, J. (1998). Information modeling in the time of the revolution. *Information Systems, 23*(3-4), 127-155.

Object Management Group. (2003). Unified Modeling Language Specification Version 1.5.Retrieved 2003/11/01, from http://www.omg.org/cgi-bin/doc?formal/03-03-01.pdf

Pfeiffer, D., & Niehaves, B. (2005). Evaluation of Conceptual Models - A Structuralist Approach. Paper presented at the 13th European Conference on Information Systems (ECIS 2005), Regensburg, Germany.

Probert, S. K. (2001). Contemporary Epistemology and IS Methodology: An Interpretive Framework. Paper presented at the 7th Americas Conference on Information Systems (AMCIS 2001), Boston/MA, U.S.A.

Rosemann, M. (2003). Preparation of Process Modeling. In J. Becker, M. Kugeler & M. Rosemann (Eds.), Process Management - A Guide for the Design of Business Processes (pp.41-78). Berlin et al.: Springer.

Rosemann, M., Green, P., & Indulska, M. (2004). Towards an Enhanced Methodology for Ontological Analyses. Paper presented at the 16th International Conference on Advanced Information Systems Engineering (CAiSE 2004), Riga, Latvia.

Schütte, R., & Rotthowe, T. (1998). The Guidelines of Modeling - An Approach to Enhance the Quality in Information Models. Paper presented at the 17th International Conference on Conceptual Modeling (ER 1998), Singapore.

Schütte, R., & Zelewski, S. (2002). Epistemological Problems in Working with Ontologies. Paper presented at the 6th World Multiconference on Systemics, Cybernetics and Informatics (SCI 2002), Orlando, USA.

Shanks, G., Tansley, E., & Weber, R. (2003). Using ontology to validate conceptual models. *Communications of the ACM, 46*(10), 85-89.

Söderström, E., Andersson, B., Johannesson, P., Perjons, E., & Wangler, B. (2002). Towards a Framework for Comparing Process Modelling Languages. Paper presented at the 14th International Conference on

Advanced Information Systems Engineering (CAiSE2002), Toronto, Canada.

Sommerville, I. (2001). Software Engineering (Vol. 6. Ed.). Harlow et al.: Addison-Wesley.

Uschold, M., & Gruninger, M. (1996). Ontologies: principles, methods, and applications. *The Knowledge Engineering Review, 11*(2), 93-155.

Uschold, M., King, M., Moralee, S., & Zorgios, Y. (1998). The Enterprise Ontology. *The Knowledge Engineering Review, 13*(1), 31-89.

Walsham, G. (1995). Interpretive Case Studies in IS Research: Nature and Method. *European Journal of Information Systems, 4*, 74-81.

Wand, Y., Monarchi, D. E., Parsons, J., & Woo, C. C. (1995). Theoretical foundations for conceptual modelling in information systems development. *Decision Support Systems, 15*(4), 285-304.

Wand, Y., & Weber, R. (1990). An Ontological Model of an Information System. *IEEE Transactions on Software Engineering, 16*(11), 1282-1292.

Wand, Y., & Weber, R. (2002). Research Commentary: Information Systems and Conceptual Modeling - A Research Agenda. *Information Systems Research, 13*(4), 363-376.

Weber, R. (2004). The Rhetoric of Positivism Versus Interpretivism. MIS Quarterly, 28(1), iii-xii.

Wynekoop, J. L., & Russo, N. L. (1997). Studying system development methodologies: an examination of research methods. *Information Systems Journal, 7*(1), 47-65.

Zuniga, G. (1999). An Ontology of Economic Objects. *The American Journal of Economics and Sociology, 58*(3), 299-312.

Chapter XI

New Software Methodologies and Techniques for Business Models with Evolutionary Aspects

Hamido Fujita, Iwate Prefectural University, Japan

Abstract

This chapter outlines a number of issues on enterprise design architectures suitable for applications that need flexibility and change in their design. Better understanding of user requirements is needed to reflect the best performance of the system towards its users. Verifying the requirements elicited for best system performance is an essential task for enterprise systems design. The requirements elicited should reflect the user intention, as he/she has demanded. This chapter presents some of the international Lyee project' results led by Fujita (Fujita 2001) and is structured into two parts: one part reflects the collaborative intention outcome and the other part is related to legacy software outcome. The 1st part shows the impact of correct requirements on enterprise design architectures; it also enlists some of the results achieved by our project. The 2nd part shows the impact of Legacy software using new techniques extracted from an intention-oriented tool, namely Lyee builder. This second part also contributes in showing new techniques for handling legacy software, an issue that is important for handling essential problems related to old generation software, which is our current interest. We have succeeded to build a software diagnosis tool based on the Lyee framework, which is currently used in business practices to diagnose programs written in imperative languages.

User Intention and Requirement Correctness

As more organizations turn their attention to enterprise content management, information architects find themselves working with increasingly diverse teams. Planning content management for an enterprise often requires senior management, enterprise architects, record managers, librarians, and web professionals to work together for the first time. Each field brings its own perspective, processes, motivations, and lingo. Miscommunication is a major project risk, potentially leading parties to drop out and pursue their own solution. Information architects must assume the role of leader, strategist, or facilitator in this situation. The scale of such integration means that demands to keep it robust and consistent is largely needed, especially in the current flattening rather than globalized stage of world blooming economy.

Intention and user requirements need to reflect on each other in an efficient way. In the past five years we have worked, together with many researchers, on a joint project to bring about a new state of the art in business enterprise architectures that can be able to generate and integrate systems that fillfull user demands (Fujita, 2001) efficiently and productively. We have expolred a method named Lyee for software development (Negoro, 2001), on which we have made measurable extendable improvements in not only its ability to increase throughput, but more importantly in the quality of its operability as a business development tool.

Information systems become more and more complex over time; our environment and needs are depending on different aspects of related encounter changes. There is a need to focus on the importance of efficient requirements elicitation procedures to achieve the best practice to collect and assess environment changes, during the development stage of information systems. The main contribution is to see how requirement sensitivity has a crucial impact on the life cycle of the product, how user cognitive behavior impacts system performance, the impact of end-user requirement engineering on the validity of the product, and the legacy of the information system on the long run for best cost performance of system operability. Also, we recognize the security aspects or policies impact on the system stability as essential issues on system non-fragility, robustness, and tolerability. These important issues have been examined in this chapter, which also outlines part of the results achieved by Lyee International Project supported by Japanese software industry (Fujita, 2001).

An effective requirements engineering process can lead to improved productivity, quality, and better risk management. All have been supported by empirical studies that have been examined and overviewed in Lyee International Project (Fujita, 2001).

The Lyee way of thinking adopts a philosophical reasoning aspect view on human intention and how this can be collected into a representation through a form expressed in a set of written or spoken sentences in a syntactical representation that can be reflected on a certain conceptual thinking or way of thinking. This form of what is called an open representation (Negoro, 2006), represents one aspect of our thinking on certain problems, using domain-oriented knowledge (cultural, experience or other type of knowledge). These thoughts of reasoning on the way of thinking are important in the creation of our thoughts on a new software methodology that could transform (i.e., convert) our requirements into a form of representation, in a similar way that we transform our thoughts (i.e., needs) into a form of sentences in a specific language.

Negoro (2001, 2002) has contributed in this study with our support, on building up a relationship between axiomatic rules and requirements on a computer program. He builds a universal model related to transforming a hypothetical model based on axioms and rules into a set of vectors and formulas reflecting that existence (i.e., way of thinking). It is like transforming an intention in one's mind into related forms of sentences and expressions reflecting that way of thinking, or what is called user requirement or user intention.

The axiomatic software presented in such a framework is different from axiomatic design methodology (Suh, 2005), which systematically would analyze the transformation of customer needs into functional requirements, design parameters, and process variables.

Most developers think of a software system as the code and components that are the end results of the software development process. As code is written, developers gradually ignore the initial stages of development, specifications and the design of the system, the documentation, the component specifications, and the test cases. This narrow view of software is one of the primary causes of many problems associated with software and its development (Duraes, 2006).

The problem of checking consistency between different program artifacts has been worked on since the early stages of computer science. Attempts at verifying that a program corresponds to its specifications were first made by Hoare (Hoare, 1985) and others. Their methods typically suffered from the necessity to manage program invariants; a difficult task for all programs. Theorem proving (Chechik, 2001) and Temporal logic (Arai, 2006), allows for checking a property that is implied by the program. This approach, although it requires considerable skill and time investment, is useful if not essential in ensuring correctness of software in terms of given consistent requirement representation.

The investigations done in our mentioned project were collected efforts from researchers categorized in research units (Fujita, 2001). There were different assigned units doing joint research on a new state of the art in software science and technologies, under my supervision. There were 14 units from Europe, 3 from Canada, 2 from Australia, 2 from USA, one from Russia, 3 from Japan, one from China and one from Sharjah (UAE). All these units have specific research agreements to do joint research under specific well-formed contracted themes. They were selected according to pre-discussions on different stages, with each unit members, on well-formed research directions in software systems and related IT technologies. The outline of each unit and its outcome may be found at the URL link mentioned in (Fujita, 2001) reference. The reader may refer to the details of each unit outcome. The outcome and results are presented in a joint prototypic tool and academic scientific research papers, as well as special issues journals published by the Elsevier International journal (Fujita, 2003b; Johannesson, 2004; Gruhn, 2006; Fujita, 2007a). One example is new techniques on requirements engineering and meta modeling by Paris unit (France) led by professor Colette Roland. Another example is the Karlstad (Sweden) unit on new techniques for Enterprise modeling and components led by R. Gustas. In this chapter I will devote the discussion on the work outcome that we have done jointly, with the Stockholm unit and Laval (Canada) unit, respectively.

I have selected these two units for this chapter because of their successful achievement that fits the theme of this book and for best performance outcome in the discovery of the suitable state of the art in solving their work contribution efficiently and appropriately.

In regard to the Stockholm unit; that compromised of Stockholm University and the Royal Institute of Technology, and University of Skövde, the basic objective was to bridge the gap between customer intention and stated requirements and verify it. Therefore, we have done a joint research on:

- A formal requirements language
- Verification techniques and supporting technology
- Validation techniques and supporting technology

Figure 1 shows the outline of such research.

An effective requirements engineering (RE) process can lead to improved productivity, quality and risk management, which has been supported by empirical studies (Duraes, 2006).

Figure 1. The outline of the research

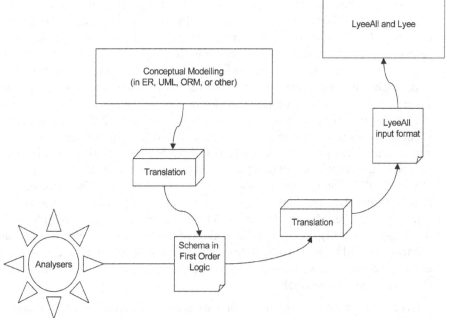

However, we think that RE alone is not the silver bullet solution to improve quality, rather we think providing good Software methodologies can play a big role in creating a better general solution model (Rolland, 2002), (Fujita, 2002). The Lyee methodology has been invented (Negoro, 2000, 2001a, 2001b, 2003) for this purpose.

There are no standards or general rules that we can use to transform our thoughts or intentions to other forms because our needs or requirements can be interpreted in different representations. These representations are relative in its differences depending on stakeholder knowledge on problems in mind. Also, self-consciousness on these requirements is relative in regard to different points of view.

The aim of the Lyee methodology is to bridge the gap between the intention of the stakeholders and the software product to be developed by means of an orderly and tool supported way of working based on the principles of what is called a scenario function programming concept (Fujita, 2003b). However, since there are usually several stakeholders and there is no single intention, every single stakeholder may have his/her own thoughts. Quite often, the intentions are also in conflict with each other. I would like through the approach presented here to overcome such inconsistencies and to reconcile different stakeholder intentions.

The work presented in this paper complements work done by Ekenberg and Johannesson in (Ekenberg, 2002, 2003) in that it provides the input (2) to the mapping (3) in Figure 2.

The collective intentional model (1) is comprised of (Wangler, 2002, 2003)

- A means-ends (goal) model
- A concepts model, i.e. a model of the 'things' dealt with in the enterprise
- A process model

These models would then form the basis for constructing the UML classes and state diagrams that make up the conceptual model (2) (Figure 2), which in turn serves as the input to the mapping (3) (Figure 3) to first order logic. For details of this mapping, the reader may refer to (Ekenberg, 2002).

Goal-driven software requirements capturing builds on the notion of software requirements being developed from the goals of various business stakeholders (Bubenko, 1993). The Lyee software (Negoro, 2000) methodology is based on a similar notion, in that it captures the intention or goal of the customer and from that builds the related software in question. However, capturing and describing this intention is not an easy matter, since the

Figure 2. The process of transforming the collective intention to Lyee style software

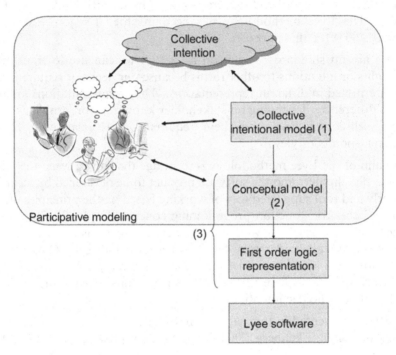

customer may not be completely aware of its needs. Furthermore, the customer's wishes are sometimes in conflict with each other in that some may not be easy and perhaps not even possible to implement at the same time.

Wangler in (Wangler, 2002) has described issues on how intention can exist in many forms in an organization.

1.   Every enterprise has a *mission*, often but not always explicitly expressed in a mission statement.

2.   The enterprise states (should state) *goals* vis-à-vis that mission. The goals form a hierarchy (a directed, non-cyclic graph) of objectives on different levels of abstraction. The lower level, more specific, and goals constitute the realization (i.e., implementation) of the higher-level goals. We sometimes refer to those, more specific, objectives as *business rules*. Low-level goals may also be considered as *tasks* to be carried out in order to achieve higher-level goals.

3.   Goals may be conflicting, i.e. what is stated by one goal may not be possible to realize at the same time as some other goal.

4. *Strategies* and *policies* are formed to define the way in which goals are to be accomplished, and should be formulated such that conflicting goals are to some extent relaxed. The strategies and policies may be considered as more specific, and at the low level of the goal hierarchy.

5. The mission statement, goal structure, strategy, and policies together form the *enterprise intention*.

6. An organizational structure is formed such that organizational units on different levels are made responsible for various goals and tasks.

7. Organizational units comprise sets of individual actors. Actors are usually human but may be artifacts such as computerized information systems. The requirements for such systems are derived from the objectives the organizational unit has or set to achieve.

8. The union of the consciousnesses of each human actor may be said to constitute the organizational (unit) *collective consciousness*.

9. The intention of individual actors vis-à-vis the organization should reflect the intention of the enterprise.

10. Intentions of individual human actors may be conflicting. A *common (collective) intention* may be formulated in consensus-creating activities such as enterprise modeling (e.g. goals, concepts and process modeling).

Figure 3. The process of transforming the collective intention to Lyee software

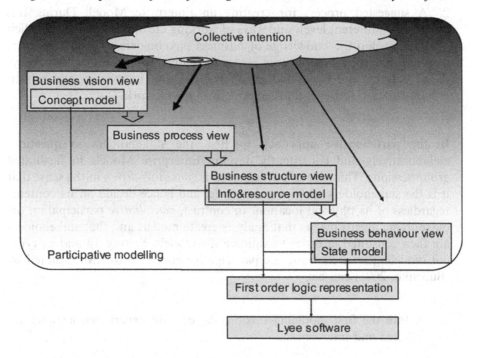

In such an approach (Wangler, 2002), the collective intention is developed among a group of stakeholders focusing on the task of creating a common and agreed upon set of models. These models can later be used as the basis for developing Lyee software. This approach complements work by Ekenberg and Johannesson (Ekenberg, 2002, 2003) in that it provides the class and state-chart models needed as input to the mapping to first-order logic as referenced on Figure 3. The first-order logic description allows for powerful verification and validation (Ekenberg, 2003), and can later be transformed and fed into the LyeeAll Case Tool (LyeeAll is a trademark of case tool built by Catena http://lyee.catena.co.jp/en/index.html).

The collective intention, hence, incorporates both the enterprise intention and the intentions of the involved actors. Enterprise Modeling (EM) is commonly used in the early stages of software development (Bubenko, 1999). In particular, software development practitioners claim that EM is effective for gathering business needs and high-level requirements (Persson, 2001), i.e. for specifying the intentions of the stakeholders of the system.

Any method for EM has two main components:

1. A meta-model, which defines the modeling constructs, syntax, semantics, and graphical notation used to create an Enterprise Model. This is the modeling language.

2. A suggested process for creating an Enterprise Model. During this process, different levels and ways of working are applied in order to elicit and develop the knowledge of business stakeholders or domain experts on different business sectors across the globe. Typical examples of ways of working are facilitated group sessions and interviews, and related information retrieval that support this type of work.

In the participative approach to EM, the stakeholders in question, collaboratively and consistently develop Enterprise Models in facilitated group sessions. This type of participation is *consensus-driven* in the sense that it is the stakeholders who own the model and hence decide on its contents regardless of its physical location. In contrast, *consultative* participation (or outsourcing agent) means that analysts create models and that stakeholders are then consulted in order to validate the models. Setting up and carrying out modeling sessions using the participative approach to EM as stated by (Bubenko, 2001) can be:

1. Before the first modeling session, the domain experts/participants are selected and interviewed.

2. The modeling session is then prepared. It is critical that this preparation is thorough. Objectives are defined and a schedule for the session is prepared.

3. The modeling session is carried out following the prepared schedule. During the session the facilitator is a crucial actor as manager of the group communication process and as keeper of the method knowledge.

4. After the modeling session, the models are documented by using some computer tool and a walk-through session is carried out with the participants in order to validate the models.

5. Based on the documented models, new modeling sessions are prepared and carried out until the problem at hand has been sufficiently analyzed.

Wangler (2002, 2003) argued that the participative approach is a useful way to discover the collective intention and it may provide the necessary input models to the mapping to first order logic studied by Ekenberg and Johannesson (Ekenberg, 2003). This systematic approach could lead to the below models:

•   Information models in the form of class diagrams defining the structure on issues or aspects that we want to maintain information on it.

•   State models in the form of state-chart diagrams defining the states and state-changes that instances of classes of the above models experience during their lifetime.

These models would then be used as input to the transformation to first order logic, for validation or maintainability purposes.

It is evident that the participative approach of (Bubenko, 1999) that is referenced here, is in fact a good way to alleviate the obstacles introduced by the fact that different stakeholders may have differing views on information systems requirements. Empirically, this can enhance the outsourcing style on business enterprises. Such flattening style on business is necessary to promote the recognition of looking into business based globalization scales in different perspectives. The flattening concept has been introduced by Friedman (Friedman, 2006) in his book "The World is Flat". Globalizing style business models, scope of thinking, would have an impact on robustness and consistency on different views and levels of system integration among different infrastructure layers of business models, especially those depending on partial vulnerable solutions as part of the systems integration process. The ten forces that flattened the world business in reality, as mentioned by

Friedman, are: the workflow software, uploading, outsourcing, off shoring (User involvement in system service participation), supply-chaining, in sourcing, in-forming (knowledge discovery by searching, like Google search engine).

As we can see in the actual business world that the demand on intelligent services providers through online supply chains based on outsourcing of large-scale business enterprises, may demand innovative and evolving invariants in terms of enhancement, effectiveness and other quality aspects on business software. As been mentioned by Friedman, due to outsourcing based on new innovative technology, the flattening of business model could make the world transit from large scale business models to small scale ones and this is due to fast networking, intelligent system providers, offshoring and other factors. Having intelligent legacy systems and tolerable information systems would play an essential role in world flattening. World flattening would be interpreted as best performance on economy and business benefits based on the ten forces mentioned above. The emphasis is on the reconfiguration management, system maintainability software application, and embedded system robustness. Legacy systems and automatic program conversion in practice is still the essential player in downsizing mainframe software system infrastructure to a smaller scale. In the following section, I am outlining the new state of the art in this technology, as part of the research collaboration I have done with Laval University, Quebec, Canada.

Automatic Program Conversion and Legacy Systems

Project management and the business enterprise world demand change and maintenance. This should be low cost and easy to be done. Also it should have the capability to be bug free as far as possible. Producing easily and quickly software with high quality is the basic concern of the software development research field. Over the last years, various methodologies and techniques have been elaborated and proposed to improve one or many aspects related to the software development life cycle. However, despite the great effort in this research field, the production of clearly understood and modifiable systems is still an ambitious goal and far from reached. Negoro (2001, 2003) has presented a new methodology, called Lyee (governementaL methodologY for softwarE providencE).

This proposed methodology is intended to deal efficiently with a wide range of software problems related to different fields, and it allows the development of software by simply defining its requirements (Fujita, 2001). More precisely, a developer has only to provide words (Arai, 2003), calculation formulae, calculation conditions, (preconditions) and layout of screens and printouts, and then leave in the hands of the computer all subsequent troublesome programming processes (e.g., control logic aspects). In spite of its recentness, the results of the use of Lyee has shown its good potential. Nevertheless, since both the semantics of Lyee generated software together with the process of automatic generation of software from requirements are described using informal language, difficulties and confusions may arise when trying to understand and study this methodology.

For that reason, we (Mejri, 2003, Fujita, 2004) proposed, a formalization of the process of automatic generation of software together with the semantics of Lyee generated software using process algebra formalization. This formalization led to the definition of Lyee-Calculus, a formal process algebra that easily and naturally supports and implements the basic concepts of the Lyee methodology. In principle, a Lyee generated software is basically made of small components (called vectors in Lyee terminology), where each one of them has an atomic goal, that collaborate together by interaction in order to produce the desired results (global goal). On the other hand, it is commonly known that a process algebra naturally supports concurrency and communication (Fenton, 1993).

Moreover, we have proposed, in (Fujita, 2003a; Mejri, 2004; Mbarki, 2004), an implementation of the constructs of Lyee in the Java language in order to concretely show the efficiency of this calculus and its suitability for the Lyee methodology. In other words, this Java implementation of the Lyee-Calculus provided a means of bridging the gap between Lyee requirement specifications and their implementations, and in turns paves the way to Legacy system through the Lyee framework (Takeda & Fujita, 2004; Negoro, 2006).

This part provides such formalization, using Lyee-Calculus (Mejri, 2003) of the Lyee methodology. This new version takes into consideration some details needed to write real programs. Moreover, we present a new software development environment, LyeeBuilder (Fujita, 2003b) that allows to automatically generate applications from specifications using a GUI. This software allows an end-user to generate his/her software without programming skills.

Below, we briefly present the syntax and the semantics of the Lyee-calculus. Then accordingly, I demonstrate the new formalization of the Lyee methodology using this calculus. Moreover, I outline the implementation in Java of the constructs required by the Lyee-Calculus. Also, I present a new software development environment, named LyeeBuilder that allows to automatically generate applications from specifications using a GUI.

Lyee-Calculus

In this section, I give the syntax and the semantics of Lyee-calculus that I have specially defined to formalize the the Lyee methodology (Mejri, 2003; Fujita, 2004).

Syntax

Lyee-calculus programs are systems composed of independent and parallel processes that communicate using a handshake technique over named channels.

The syntax of processes is presented in Table 1.

The intuitive meaning of each syntactic construction is as follows:

- *Sequence*: [K]·P, where K is a set of actions, is a process that has to perform all the actions in K and then behaves as the process P. The order in which the actions in K have to be executed is not important. Notice that for the sake of simplicity we write $[\kappa_1,.........,\kappa_n]$ instead of $[\{\kappa_1,.........,\kappa_n\}]$. A process can send a value v through a channel ι by

Table 1. Syntax of process Algebra

P, Q ::=	(Processes)
| [K].P	(Sequence)
| P | Q	(Parallel composition)
| P + Q	(Choice)
| P ▷ Q	(Guarded choice)
| P/L |	(Restriction)
$A(\vec{X}) \overset{def}{=} P$	(Definition)
| nil	(nil process)
K, K₁, K₂ ::=	(Set of actions)
| {κ}	(Single action)
| K1 ∪ K2	(Set union)
L, L1, L2 ::=	(Set of channels)
|φ	(Empty set)
| {ι}	(Single channel)
| L1∪ L2	(Set union)
κ ::=	(Action)
| ι!e	(Send)
| ι?e	(Receive)
| τ	(Silent action)
ι, j	(Channel)
e	(Arithmetic expression)

doing the action $[\iota!e]$ v corresponds to the valuation of e). Similarly, a process can receive a value from a channel by doing the action $[\iota?e]$ $[\kappa_1,........,\kappa_n]$. A process can also perform a silent action τ.

- *Parallel composition*: P | Q behaves as processes P and Q running in parallel. Each one of them may interact with the other on channels known to both of them, or with the outside word (environment or the end-user) independently from the other. When two processes synchronize on the same channel, the whole process will perform an action τ and behaves as the remaining process.

- *Choice*: P + Q behaves as P or as Q. The choice is deterministically (made by the environment) if both P and Q do not begin with a silent action, otherwise the choice is not deterministically.

- *Guarded choice*: P $\rhd$ Q is the process that behaves as P until process Q is activated. Whenever the latter is activated, the former is stopped and cleared from memory.

- *Restriction*: P/L is the process that behaves as P except that it can communicate with the environment using channels given in L only.

- Definition: $A(\vec{X}) \stackrel{def}{=} P$ is a defining equation where A is a process identifier, $\vec{X}$ are variables (parameters), and P may recursively involve A.

- *nil process*: nil is the process that cannot perform any action.

Operational Semantics

Hereafter, I give the formal operational semantics of the Lyee-calculus. This semantics is defined by the interaction relation $\xrightarrow{\kappa}$, where P $\xrightarrow{\kappa}$ Q means that there is a reaction amongst the sub processes of P such that the whole can execute the atomic action κ and becomes Q. The relation $\xrightarrow{\kappa}$ is the least relation that satisfies the rules given by Table 2.

Notice that:

1. $\mapsto$ is a relation that simplify processes by eliminating the nil process as follows: $P| \ nil \mapsto P, \ nil+P \mapsto P, \ nil \rhd P \mapsto P, \ nil/L \mapsto nil, \ nil\|P \mapsto P, \ P+nill \mapsto P, \ |P \rhd nill \mapsto P$

2. We denote by [[e]] the set of values containing the result of the evaluation of the expression e. If e is a variable, it evaluation will be its domain (int, real, etc.). For the sake of simplicity, we consider that all variables belong to the real number set.

Table 2. Operational semantics of Lyee-Calculus

$$(R^l_+)\frac{P \xrightarrow{\kappa} P'}{P+Q \xrightarrow{\kappa} P'} \quad (R^r_+)\frac{Q \xrightarrow{\kappa} Q'}{P+Q \xrightarrow{\kappa} Q'}$$

$$(R_!)\frac{v \in \|e\|}{[\iota!e].P \xrightarrow{\iota!v} P} \quad (R_?)\frac{v \in \|e\|}{[\iota?e].P \xrightarrow{\iota?v} P[v/e]}$$

$$(R_\rightarrow)\frac{P \xrightarrow{\kappa} Q' \; Q' \mapsto Q}{P \xrightarrow{\kappa} Q} \quad (R_\tau)\frac{v \in \|e\|}{[\tau].P \xrightarrow{\tau} P}$$

$$(R_{[]})\frac{[K_1].P \xrightarrow{\kappa} P'}{[K_1 \cup K_2].P \xrightarrow{\kappa} [K_2]P'}K_2 \neq \phi$$

$$(R^l_\triangleright)\frac{P \xrightarrow{\kappa} P'}{P \triangleright Q \xrightarrow{\kappa} P' \triangleright Q} \quad (R^r_\triangleright)\frac{Q \xrightarrow{\kappa} Q'}{P \triangleright Q \xrightarrow{\kappa} Q'}S$$

$$(R^r_\triangleright)\frac{P \xrightarrow{\iota?v} P' \; Q \xrightarrow{\iota!v} Q'}{P \triangleright Q \xrightarrow{\tau} Q'}$$

$$(R^l_|)\frac{P \xrightarrow{\kappa} P'}{P|Q \xrightarrow{\kappa} P'|Q} \quad (R^r_|)\frac{Q \xrightarrow{\kappa} Q'}{P|Q \xrightarrow{\kappa} P|Q'}$$

$$(R^\tau_|)\frac{P \xrightarrow{\iota?v} P' \; Q \xrightarrow{\iota!v} Q'}{P|Q \xrightarrow{\tau} P'|Q'}$$

$$(R_=)\frac{P\left[\vec{Y}/\vec{X}\right] \xrightarrow{\kappa} P'}{A(\vec{Y}) \xrightarrow{\kappa} P'}A(\vec{X})=P \quad (R_/)\frac{P \xrightarrow{\kappa} P'}{P/L \xrightarrow{\kappa} P'/L}\kappa_| \in L$$

3. κ_1 is the name of the channel. Used by the action κ, i.e., $\tau_| = \phi$, $(\iota!e)_| = (\iota?e)_| = \{\iota\}$

Example

In this section, we show how to model a cell of memory as a process that interacts with its environment through its communication channels. As shown by Figure 4, we consider that the cell has two ports (channels) of communication, in and out. The basic task of this cell is to infinitely wait for

Figure 4. Cell formalized as a process

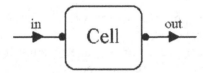

a value on channel in and to make it available on channel out. The same value may be output as much as necessary until a new value is input.

We write the process cell $C^x(v)$, meaning that the memory cell x holds the value v, as follows:

$$C^x(v) \overset{def}{=} [in^x\ ?y].\ C^x(y) + [out^x\ !v].\ C^x(v)$$

By capturing a memory cell as a process, we can add intelligence to it. For instance, we can write a cell that does not allow access to its content until it will be initialized. This smart cell can be defined as follows:

$$Cell(x) \overset{def}{=} [in^x\ ?y].\ C^x(y)$$

Now, giving two processes defined as follows:

$P_1 \overset{def}{=} [in^x\ ?5].nill$, $P_2 \overset{def}{=} [out^x\ ?y].nill$, it is easy to write a program where these two processes communicate through a cell x: $P_1\,|Cell(x)|\,P_2$

Figure 5 shows the interaction between all the involved processes. Here are the different steps of that program execution:

$$P_1\,|Cell(x)|\,P_2 = [int^{ix}\ !5].nil\,|[int^x\ ?y].\ C^x(y)|[out^x\ ?y].nill \overset{\tau}{\longrightarrow} C^x(5)|[out^x\ ?y].nill$$

$$= [int^x\ ?y].\ C^x(y) + [ou5^x\ !y].\ C^x(5)|[out^x\ ?y].nill \overset{\tau}{\longrightarrow} C^x(5)$$

Formalization: Beyond the Lyee Methodology

More details on Lyee calculus operational semantics can be referenced at (Fujita, 2006). Lyee can generate software from simple user requirements. There are successful attempts to formalize Lyee software methodology using Lyee calculus as stated in (Fujita, 2006) and (Fujita, 2004). The implemented

Figure 5. Example of interacting process

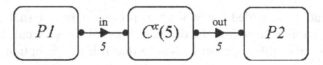

version of the Lyee Calculus within the LyeeBuilder software is slightly different from the one given in (Mejri, 2003). This new version takes into consideration some details needed to write real programs. However, the initial version was given on an abstract level to show the main ideas behind the calculus. It is important to know that this new version can be considerably simplified so that we can obtain more efficient generated programs for legacy systems.

Let Use(e) denotes the set of words used in the expression e. For instance, Use(a*b + 1) = {a, b}. Also, let $F(S)$ be the following function: $F(\phi) = \phi$

$$F(\{x\} \cup A) = \{t_4^x \, ? x\} \cup F(A)$$

Now let's see how to automatically generate software from simple user requirements using the Lyee-calculus. Suppose that the user requirement contains k screens $\{s_1, \ldots s_2\}$. Suppose also that each screen contains a set of statements, where each one of them has the following form: (w, e, c, InOut, type) where w is a word, e its definition, c its condition, InOut to specify if it is input, output, both or neither input nor output (the value i is used for input word, o for output, io for both input and output and empty filed for neither input nor output) and type is its type (the type B is reserved for button).

Lyee Program

The Lyee program $P(s_1, \ldots s_k) = \Psi(s_1, \ldots, s_k) / L(s_1, \ldots, s_k) |) VisualTracer$

Where the set $L(s_1, \ldots, s_k)$ contains all the input and outputs channels and it is defined as follows:

$$L(s_1, \ldots, s_k) = (\cup_{(w,*,*,i/o,*) \in sk} \{d_w\} \cup \{t^{s1}\}$$

This restricts $\Psi(s_1, \ldots, s_k)$ to communicate with the environment only on channels. The meaning of i/o is that this field has to contain the value of i, o or io. We suppose also that s_1 is the first screen that appears when the user runs his/her program.

Furthermore, we added a new kind of process named Visual Tracer which offers the ability to follow the different internal steps executed through the computation of different words. Notice that this part is optional and can be removed.

Control Function

The control function attached to as screen s, is a formalized as follows:

$\Phi(s) = SF(s).\Phi'(s)$ where $\Phi'(s) = ([\iota^s ?true].s.open() + [\iota^s ?false].s.hide()).\Phi'(s)$

This function activates the SF of a screen s ($\Phi(s)$) whenever a true value is received on the corresponding channel ι^s, which formalizes a button or a menu item that a user may use to activate the corresponding screen.

The control function attached to a set of screens is formalized as follows:

$$\Phi(s_1, ..., s_k) = (\left. \right|_{s \in \{s_1, ..., s_k\}} [(\iota^s ?true).\Phi(s) \triangleright [\iota^{s0} ?false].nil$$

This function kills all the processes when it receives a true value on channel ι^{s0}. We suppose that s_0 is the screen that we find when we exit the program (exit screen that does not belong to the screens of the program itself).

Scenario Function

The scenario function, SF(s), attached to the screen s is formalized as follows:

$$SF(s) = W_{04}(s)| W_{03}(s)| W_{02}(s)|$$

Pallet Functions

The three pallets W_{02}, W_{03} and W_{04} of a given screen s are formalized as follows:

$W_{02}(s) =$

$\left. \right|_{(w,*,*,\{i/o\}, \overline{B}) \in s} I_2(w) \left. \right|_{(w,*,*,\{i/o\}, \overline{B}) \in s} L_2(w) \left. \right|_{(w,*,*,*,*) \in s} L_{3e}(w) \left. \right|_{(w,*,*,\{i,i/o\}, \overline{B}) \in s} L_{3_{l_2}}(w)$

$W_{03}(s) = \left. \right|_{(w,*,c,\overline{i},\overline{B}) \in s} L_3(w,c) \left. \right|_{(w,*,c,\overline{i},\overline{B}) \in s} S_4^{L3}(w,c) \left. \right|_{(w,e,c,*,*,B) \in s} R_3(w,c,e)$

$W_{04}(s) = \left. \right|_{(w,*,*,*,*) \in s} S_4(w) \left. \right|_{(w,e,*,\overline{i},\overline{B}) \in s} L_4(w,e) \left. \right|_{(w,*,*,\{o,i/o\}, \overline{B}) \in s} O_4(w) \left. \right|_{(w,*,*,\overline{i},\overline{B}) \in s} L_{3_{O4}}(w)$

where $\bar{B}$ denotes any type except B (complementary of B), where $\bar{i}$ denotes any type except i (complementary of i) and * denotes anything.

Signification Vectors

The signification vectors of a given word x are formalized as follows:

$$L4(x, e) = [j_4^c ? true].[F(Use(e))].L4'(x, e)$$

$$L4'(x, e) = [j_4^c ? true].[j_4^x ! eval].fresh(F(Use(c)), j_4^c).L4'(x, e)$$
$$+ j_4^x ? false].[j_4^x ! \bot].L4(x, e)$$

$$L2(x) = [t_2^x ? z].[j_4^x ! true].L2(x)$$

$$L3(x, c) = fresh(F(Use(c))).[j_4^c ! eval(c)].L3(x, c)$$

$$Var(c) = \phi \Rightarrow L3(x, c) = [j_4^c ! eval(c)].nil$$

$$L3_e(x, c_e) = fresh(F(Use(c_e))).[d_e^x ! eval(c_e)].L3_e(x, c)$$

$$Var(c_e) = \phi \Rightarrow L3_e(x, c_e) = [d_e^x ! eval(c_e)].nil$$

$$L3_{I2}(x, c_{I2}) = [t'^3_{I2} ? x].(ready(Use(c_{I2})).[F(Use(c_{I2}))].[t^3_{I2} ! eval(c_{I2})]$$
$$\neg ready(Use(c_{I2})).[t^3_{I2} ! false]).L3'_{I2}(x, c_{I2})$$

$$L3'_{I2}(x, c_{I2}) = Freash(F(use(c_{I2})).[t^3_{I2} ! eval(c_{I2})].L3'_{I2}(x, c_{I2})$$
$$+ [t'^3_{I2} ? x].[F(Use(c_{I2}))].[t^3_{I2} ! eval(c_{I2})].L3'_{I2}(x, c_{I2})$$

$$L3_{O4}(x, c_{O4}) = fresh(F(Use(c_{O4})) = .[t^4_{O4} ! eval(c_{O4})].L3_{O4}(x, c_{O4})$$

$$Var(c_{O4}) = \phi \Rightarrow L3_{O4}(x, c_{O4}) = [j_{O4}^4 ! eval(c_{O4})].nil$$

- The L4 vector deals with the computation of a given word (variable). Each word in the specification has its own L4 vector.

- The L2 vector transfers the value of an input word to the appropriate memory area. Each input word in the specification has its own L2 vector.

- The L3 vectors deal with the computation of the conditions (condition, whenEnabled, whenInput and whenOutput) associated to a given word (variable). Each word in the specification has its own L3 vectors.

These explanations related to Lyee style of vectors can be referenced in Figure 6 to support the understanding of these relations. The number between brackets represents the sequences in the program example execution. Boxes a and b are screens of an application.

Action Vectors

$$I2(x) = [d_x ?x].[\iota'^3_{I2} !x].([\iota^3_{I2} ?true].[\iota^x_2!x]$$
$$+ [\iota^3_{I2} ?false].Error().[d_x!'''']. [i^{\dot{x}}_2!\perp]).I2(x)$$
$$+ [\iota^3_{I2} ?false].Error().[d_x!'''']. [i^{\dot{x}}_2!\perp]).I2(x)$$
$$O4(x) = [\iota^4_{O4} ?true].[\iota^x_4?x].[d_x!x].O4(x)$$
$$Var(c_{O4}) = \phi \Rightarrow O4(x) = [\iota^x_4 ?true].O4'(x), \text{ where } O4'(x) = fresh([i^{\dot{x}}_4?x]).[d_x!x].O4'(x)$$
$$S4(x) = [j^x_4 ?y].S^x_4(y) | MC^x_4()$$
$$S4^x(y) = [j^x_4 ?z].mc^x_4!true].S^x_4(z) + [i^x_4!y].S^x_4(y)$$
$$MC^x_4() = [mc^x_4 ?true].[l[0]!true,.....,l[n]!true].MC^x_4() + [mc^x_{req}?c].(c :: l).MC^x_4()$$

Figure 6. Synthesis's of the Lyee style program

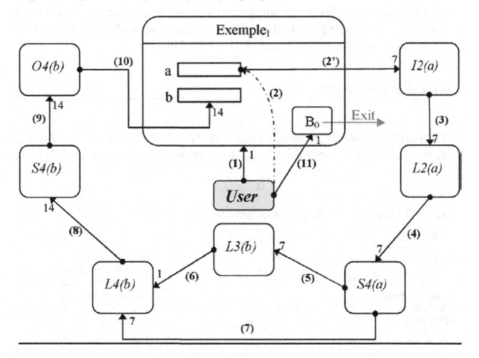

$$R3(b, e, s) = [d_b?clik].[j_4^b!true].(e.f = 'open' \Rightarrow [t^{e.s}!true]$$
$$+ e.f = 'close' \Rightarrow [t^{e.s}!false]).R3(b, e, s)$$

- The I2 vector deals with input from the outside (screen, file networks, etc.) of the program. The input values will be stored in a temporary area and then will be transferred to their final memory area by L2. There is only one I2 vector for all the input words.

- The O4 vector deals with output. Once the computation of a given output word is finished, this vector will output the value of this word in the appropriate place (screen, file, networks, etc.). There is only one O4 vector for all the output words.

- The R3 vector deals with transitions between screens.

The Lyee-Calculus Implementation in Java

A mapping from Lyee-Calculus to Java has been implemented. Our implementation inherits from JCSP (Welch, 2004) since the later provides all the necessary classes to implement concurrent processes constructers. Moreover, a mapping from the Lyee formalization, with Lyee-Calculus, to Java classes has been implemented as shown below.

Lyee-Calculus to Java

The corresponding Java classes and methods of Lyee-Calculus constructs are defined in Table 3. Since there is no direct mapping from [κ].P and P ▷ Q to

Table 3. Mapping from Lyee Calculus to Java code

Description	Lyee-Calculus	Mapping
Sequence	$[\kappa].P$	ArrayChannel class
Parallel	$P \mid Q$	JCSP Parallel class
Choice	$P + Q$	JCSP Alternative class
Guarded choice	$P \triangleright Q$	GuardedProcess class
Restriction	$P \mathbin{/} L$	Identifier scope of Java language
Definition	$A(\vec{X}) \stackrel{def}{=} P$	while (true) { ... }
No action	nil	Empty statement (;)

any construct provided by JCSP, we have defined in (Ktari, 2004; Fujita, 2004) two new classes ArrayChannel and GuardedProcess.

From Lyee Requirement to Java

For each function used to formalize the Lyee oriented program, corresponding a definition class in Java implementation is given. The correspondence between these Java classes and the functions used in the Lyee Formalization are given in Table 4 that shows the mapping from Lyee Formalization to Java code. The code of almost all the classes is very close to the definition of the functions that they implement.

Lyee Builder

Here, a user-friendly GUI builder, called LyeeBuilder, that allows end-user to generate software without programming, is presented. The end-user has just to create a screen to put the desired fields (the definition of words, texts, and button) in each screen and then the code will be automatically generated. When the user inserts an object (button, edit-field, etc.) in a screen, then in the left hand side of the builder, the user can see a list of properties among them those related to the Lyee methodology. The user writes the definition of the word, the calculation condition, etc., (see Figure 7). The connection between two screens can be done via buttons. When the user insert a connection button, he/she would see the name of all his/her created screens and he/she has just to tell what screen has to be visualized when the button is pressed by the end-user.

Table 4. Mapping from Lyee formulization to Java code

Description	Lyee requirement formalization	Mapping
Program	$P(s_1,......,s_k)$	Program class
Control function (1)	$\Psi(s_1,......,s_k)$	Psi class
Control function (2)	$\Phi(s)$	Phi class
Scenario function	$SF(s)$	SF class
Pallet functions	W02, W03, W04	W02, W03 and W04 classes
Action vectors	I2, O4, S4, R3	I2, O4, S4 and R3 classes
Signification Vectors	L4, L3, L2	L4, L3 and L2 classes

Figure 7. LyeeBuilder

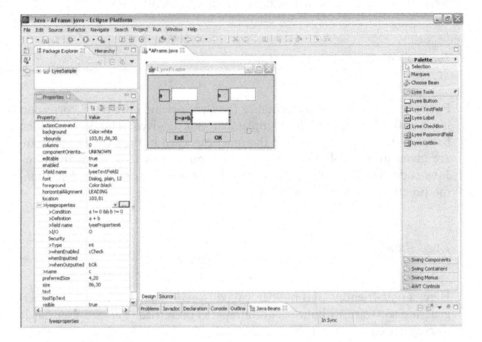

Lyee Properties (Figure 8)

The main fields found in the LyeeProperties area are the following:

- Condition: this is a boolean expression that specifies when the definition of a word is computed.

- Definition: this is an arithmetic or a boolean expression that defines a word.

- I/O: this field specifies whether a word is an input, output or both input and output.

- Security: this field specifies the security level (secret, public) attributed to the word.

- Type: this specifies the type (int, float, string, boolean, button) of the word.

- whenOutput: this is a boolean condition that says when a word could be outputted. An output word can be output only when this condition become true.

Figure 8. Example of word attributes (Lyee properties)

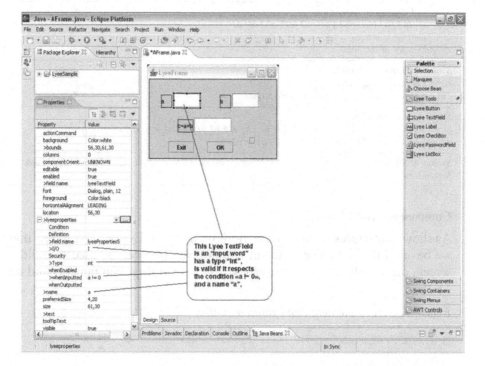

- whenInput: This is also a boolean condition saying when an input word could be accepted. Whenever this condition is false, the input value is rejected.

- whenEnabled: an input area or a button can be available only if a specific condition becomes true. This boolean condition is given by this field.

The new fields whenOutput, whenInput and whenEnabled give more possibilities within software development. For the next version of Lyee-Builder, we want to associate with each kind of action (input, output, compute, etc.) a condition that triggers (activate) it.

Syntax

The language used to give definitions to different fields has the following syntax given in a BNF format by Table 5, see Figure 9.

Table 5. Syntax

Syntax of Arithmetic Expressions:
$a ::= v \mid Id \mid (a) \mid a1 + a2 \mid a1 - a2 \mid a1^* a2 \mid a1/ a2$
Id= Identifier of a word
v= An integer or flat value

Syntax of String Expressions:
$s ::= Constant\ String \mid s1\text{\textasciicircum}s2$
The operator ˆ" allows to concatenate two strings.

Syntax of Boolean Expressions:
$b ::= true \mid false \mid (b) \mid b1 == b2 \mid b1! = b2 \mid b1\ \&\&\ b2\ b1\|b2 \mid s1 == s2 \mid s1! = s2 \mid$
$a1 == a2 \mid a1! = a2 \mid a1 < a2 \mid a1 \leq a2 \mid a1 \geq a2$

Syntax of Screen Actions: ScreenAction ::= ScreenName.open | ScreenName.close | ScreenAction &&
ScreenAction

Components and Properties

As shown on figures in previous sections on a typical LyeeBuilder screen that
we have on the right side different components that can be used to build a
screen, on the left side the (Properties) attached to these components and on

Figure 9. Screen elements and related syntax

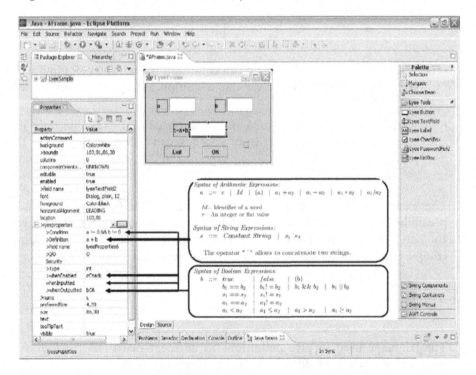

the middle, we have the frame that we want to build. In this section, we present the typical values of the different properties related to the available components (Figure 10).

- LyeeTextField: This kind of component is typically used to input values or to output results. Consequently, the I/O properties could be I, O, or I/O. When it is an input, the whenInput property could be defined to specify a condition that will be used to validate user inputs. When it is an output, the Condition, Definition, and whenOutput fields could be defined. In both cases, the Type field could be used to specify the type of value input or output. By default, the type *int* is considered.

- LyeePasswordField: This kind of component is very close to the previous one except that it is not very convenient to use it as an output (O) or input/output (I/O). Usually, we use it as an input (I).

- Label: This kind of component is typically used to output results. Consequently, the I/O field should be set to O and Condition Definition and whenOutput fields could be defined.

Figure 10. Lyee components

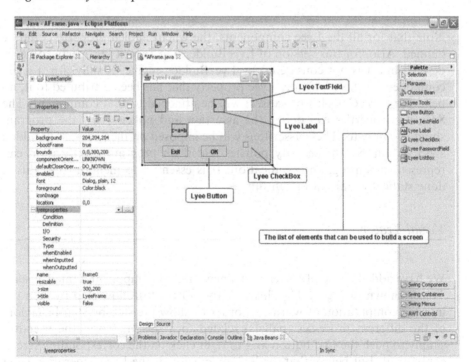

- Button: This kind of component is typically used to activate the computation of some words, to allow the output of other words, and/or to open/close frames (screens). In case we want to open/close frames, this has to be specified in the Definition field of this button. For instance, if the definition of a button B1 is "s0.close", then when this Button is pushed it will close the frame s0 which is the program, i.e. s0.close is equivalent to exit. Now, if the Definition field of the button B1 is "s1.close && s2.open", then when this Button is pushed it will close the frame s1 and open the frame s2. It is important to know that the Type field associated to button has to be set to the value "Button".

- ListBox: This is a special component that is typically used as an I/O word. The input value of such component corresponds to the user-selected items (from the list). The output part corresponds to an expression whose value is added to the component (a new item will be added to the list). Consequently, even if it is typically used as an I/O, the user can use it as an O. Condition and Definition fields could be defined.

- CheckBox: This kind of component is typically used as an input. It is important to know that the I/O field associated to CheckBox has to be set to the value "I". No other fields should be defined.

Note that for all the Lyee components, the whenEnabled property could be defined. Also, for this version of LyeeBuilder, the Security property could be defined but it is not considered by LyeeBuilder engine. Finally, for a given component, if there isn't any Lyee property that has been attributed to it, no behavior (LyeeCalculus processes) will be attached to that component. The Security properties can define the assertion and policies that the program should comply to. These assertions will be imposed on the program as added specification. So the security policies added on program specification can represent new program specification. It is essential to mention that this is done statically and not at run time.

Visual Tracer

We have added to LyeeBuilder tool a new kind of component named Visual-Tracer shown in Figure 11. This new tool offers to follow step by step the internal computation of words. In order to show the step-by-step behaviors of the different processes (pallets) related to a specific word, the user has simply to push the Ctrl button and to right click on the corresponding screen component. But before that, he has to activate, at the Lyee generation code

Figure 11. Lyee Visual Tracer in action

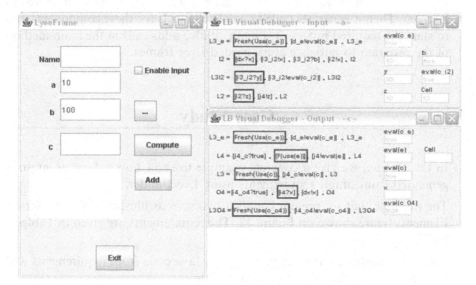

step, the VisualTracer option. This activation is made by adding to the program parameters the following expression: debug n where the constant n corresponds to the idle (specified in ms) that has to be taken into account between each step.

Implementation

To implement the LyeeBuilder, we had decided to build it over the Eclipse Platform, (Eclipse, 2005a) as it is an extensible IDE. Our implementation can be divided into 2 core parts, the visual editor, and the code generator. The editor was built as a plug-in over the Visual Editor Project (VE) (Eclipse, 2005b) which makes easy the creation of visual Java application. The palette was adapted to show Lyee components instead of the usual Java components. These Lyee components are mostly standard Java components to which were added communication channels and the Lyee properties to suit the developer's specifications. VE is also responsible for the generation of the Java code and the displaying of the visual components such as Lyee text fields and buttons. Additional Java code is needed to be generated to have an application corresponding to the specifications made by the developer. The Java Emitter Templates of the Eclipse Modeling Framework (EMF) (Eclipse, 2005c) was used to produce it. When activated, it generates additional code into the Java classes that allow Lyee objects to use the Lyee calculus package. First, it scans the Java source files to get every Lyee components attached to a screen. Then it generates code to create channels for these components and to start the required processes. Finally, it also adds calls in the main method of the program to initialize every needed Lyee frames.

Case Study

In this section, we give a concrete example to show how a Java program is generated from simple requirements using LyeeBuilder.

The example that we present contains two screens illustrated on the Screen Elements figure shown on Figure 12. The requirements are given in Tables 6 and 7.

Figure 13 illustrates show to generate the Java code from requirements and Figure 14 shows the related generated code.

Figure 12. Screen elements

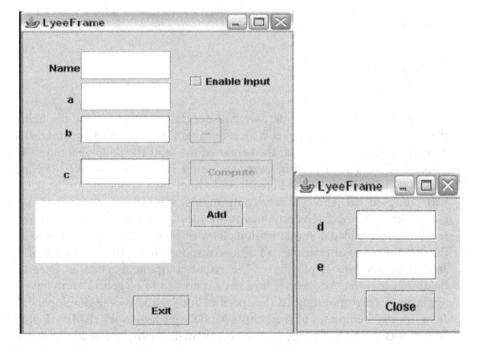

Table 6. Lyee requirement: screen I

	Condition	Definition	Type	I/O	whenInputted	whenOutputted	whenEnabled
name			S	I			cInput
a				I	a != 0		
b		(a*e)-d		O			
c		b*b				bCompute	
list		Name^'' ''^c	S	IO		bAdd	
Selected		list		O			
bNext		frame2.open	B				a != 0
bCompute			B				a!=0 && b!=0
bAdd			B				
bExit		s0.close	B				

The assurance that the generated code reflects the actual requirement is reflected from the confirmation through code running and execution. The conformance on what you see is what you implement. The code is just translating the formulization of Lyee based on Lyee methodology. The generated code is respecting these rules.

Discussion

As has been described we want to improve our implementation and test it on real big systems described in terms of Lyee requirements. We want also to connect this implementation to other user-friendly tools that we have developed in order to automatically generate, from Lyee requirements, reliable and optimized Java codes. More precisely, we plan to plug to LyeeBuilder, the Lyee Analyzer tool which is based on classical static analysis techniques that have been presented in (Fujita, 2006b) to improve many aspects of the Lyee methodology. As a long-term goal, we want to enhance the LyeeBuilder so that it becomes more user-friendly and allows to automatically generate code in different languages (Java, Cobol, etc.) from high level user specifications given in a the meta language. The ultimate goal is to simplify as much as possible the development and especially the maintenance of software. We want also to connect this tool with a legacy translation tool so that we can transform, for example, a Cobol software to

Table 7. Lyee requirement: screen II

	Condition	Definition	Type	I/O	whenInputted	whenOutputted	whenEnabled
d				I			
e				I	d!= 0		
bExit		frame2.close	B				

Figure 13. How to generate Java code from requirement

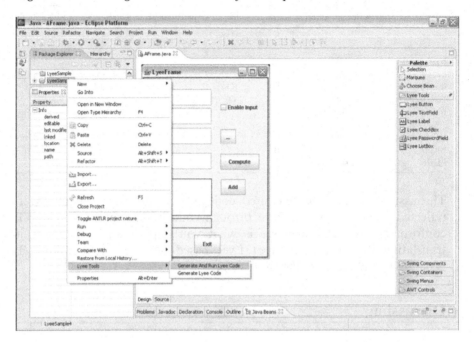

LyeeBuilder specification and update it. Finally, we want to give the LyeeBuilder the possibility of interaction with the different existing tools.

The other important issue is to introduce a formal approach allowing the migration of programs from an imperative language to a declarative one. To that end, we use a simple version of a classical imperative language, denoted by L1 that involves the basic and the important statements such as affectation, conditional instructions, looping, and sequence. The imperative language, denoted by L2, is inspired from the Lyee methodology where software is specified by a set of variable definitions. Contrarily to the Lyee approach however, the definition of a variable may involve some special arithmetic expressions such as looping.

Besides, all the definitions of a given program in L2 are independent form each other's. The semantics attached to each language is denotational where the meaning of a program in a given environment (memory state) is also an environment. We also introduce a formal translation function, denoted by D, allowing the migration of any program in L1 to an equivalent one (with respect to the semantics) in L2 and prove its correctness (Fujita, 2006b, 2007a).

Figure 14. The generated Java code

Future Directions and Other Challenges

Cognitive Analysis Enhancement to Be Integrated with the Requirement Analysis of the Enterprise Model

As this international collaboration has shown through its data analysis, there are many challenges that need more research for advanced system networking. I envisage those listed here are good candidates for potential research funds applications.

An additional issue that emerged from such research studies is to have cognitive human aspects added onto information enterprise design and modelling. However, this aspect was at the beginning among our research interest, but eventually emerged as a necessary issue to have human aspects in software design principles for best systems networking. In (Fujita, 2006c), (Fujita, 2007b) there is an example on analyzing cognitive behavior of users based on different observations and studies. These observations are based on multidisciplinary analysis related to psychological and philosophical analysis views beside the technical analysis. They have proved to be useful to analyse intentional behavior of users at the requirement elicitation phase of any business enterprise. User cognitive analysis based on voice (Kurematu, 2007) and gesture analysis of face has been collectively added to the analysis to specify user intention in addition to the written documentation that was collected from the participation of users by themselves. This experiment (Fujita, 2006c) shows that the cognitive reasoning based on users collected gestures are supportive aids especially for enterprises that deal with applications like medical information systems or highly user oriented applications, like ATM applications.

Such new challenges for research objectives may depend on the interaction between computers (machines) on one side and cognitive analysis of human behavior that could be adapted and treated as machine intelligence for best communication performance on the other side.

Software Maintenance and Security Crises

The well-known software maintenance and security crises have still not been overcome and the proposed remedies are far from resolving the problems. We still have no efficient practical solutions on software maintenance and considered the present ones as only a painting over old programs that need more funds, time, and energy with less anticipated results.

However, despite the tremendous advances in this research field, a lack of simple and potential techniques and tools is today palpable. Developing portable, efficient, reliable, and usable software that requires maintenance with enhanced security is still a challenging issue.

This, we think, is due in one hand to the subtlety and the complexity of the security related problems and in the other hand to the conventional software maintenance experiences that failed or not practically led to best practices. Furthermore, most of software development communities are more interested in developing software faster and faster rather than of the quality and security of the produced code. However, the situation can change with new efficient methodologies, tools and techniques that are able to add qualities to either the existing software or the newly developed one, (Fujita, 2007a). Maintenance free software or bug free software is a new paradigm of challenge in both academia and industry. Software methodologies that can provide such solutions should be investigated for potential utilisation. However, I think without this we may face problems that we have difficulties to tackle, and this is due to the entanglement of application usage involvement in our infrastructures.

The software systems should have user or system oriented security policies that the system may interact through or use for security reasoning enforcement. These security policies include maintenance policies as well as system flexible update and other issues related to system automatic changes. Recently, these issues have been discussed in special issues on Secure Information Systems edited by Fujita (2007a).

The "software quality" is used hereafter in its large meaning and includes, among others, correctness, reliability, efficiency, security, and maintainability.

The topics related to software quality improvement addressed are the following:

- How can we automatically generate software from requirements?
- How can we automatically add new qualities (security or other aspects) to an existing software?
- How can we verify that software is correct with respect to its specification?

We also have succeeded to build a software diagnosis tool based on the Lyee framework (Negoro, 2006), which is now in business practices to diagnose programs in imperative style languages. It is being used in practice for diagnosis in actual business field models.

This tool could detect logical errors in programs. Logical errors are those errors that emerged from a program running in its actual environment. They emerged when the premises or requirement reasoning is not complete. These errors can generate erroneous output or erroneous input to another program and may cause faulting system behavior. They need to be discovered before having the system migrated into actual application. Subject genealogy concept introduced in (Negoro, 2006) could be utilised in this automatic deduction. More work is needed to confirm the correctness of the whole program after a logical error being corrected, also to make the whole deduction be automated without the enrolment of the maintenance engineer.

One practical example on the logical errors in software is: Toyota Prius hybrids cars software crashes. A gas-electric hybrid car was found to have a software bug that causes the car to suddenly stall in some cases, unable to restart. It was a programming error in the smart car's embedded code. http://money.cnn.com/2005/05/16/Autos/prius_computer/. A simple error code is not usually enough to determine *why* the code failed, only *where* it failed. The software problem affects Toyota Prius cars sold in 2005, and causes an affected Prius to either stall or completely shut down when traveling at highway speed.

Other examples on virus infection for impeded systems: A car can get a virus from Bluetooth phone. SC Magazine is reporting: Lexus cars may be vulnerable to viruses that infect them via mobile phones. Landcruiser 100 models LX470 and LS430 have been discovered with infected operating systems. (http://www.windley.com/archives/2005/01/lexus_infection. shtml)

Information Systems Engineering and Flat World Conceptual View

The flat world style concept referenced by Friedman (2006) is concluded from the practices of IT related technologies. It has implications for systems implementation from diverged data analysis to integrated network of processes.

To enhance interpretation of complicated data contents we need to down-scale gaps among different cultural and ethnics slices via process networks and enhance the constructive contact or communication among them, I think issues such as these has a major role in new non-fragile, consistent integration of information engineering. Such integration could create flat world network conceptualization on research practices in order to guarantee that services would be remote, robust, intelligent, and dynamically reconfigurable for the best performance flow of their resources. Such best state of the art research and practices in information engineering of flattened style networking processes turn out to be necessary to research practices.

"Architecture Participation" that involves designing software services allows users to participate in design practices for best integration performance. Tools for uploading and collaboration are needed to integrate participation into the creation of business enterprise models. Also, global optimization is necessary for integrating customers' performance information into the business model to enhance business performance and profit among competitors and business partners. This can be achieved by employing flattened style innovative systems design that can monitor customer preferences and then send data directly to a central planning enterprise model.

This could make us look to the other side (physically or mentally distant objects) on the same dimension, not from a global perspective but as multi disciplinary sectors that can simply exchange thoughts, business, and trade without looking to international barriers or globalized criteria.

Acknowledgment

This chapter is devoted to B. Wangler upon his retirement from Educational and Research institutions as memorial present in this historical occasion on 2007 February, Thank you Benkt for all your hard work achievement and accomplishment.

References

Amon, B., Ekenberg, L., Johannesson, P., Munguanaze, M., & Njabili, U. (2003). From first-order logic to automated word generation for lyee. *International Journal on Knowledge-Based Systems, 16*(7), 413-429.

Arai, O., & Fujita, H. (2003). Mathematical structure model for word based program. *International Journal on Knowledge-Based Systems, 16*(7), 399-411.

Arai, O., & Fujita, H. (2006). Verification of Lyee requirement. In *New Trends in Software Methodologies, Tools and Techniques* (Vol. 147, pp. 340-361). Frontiers in Artificial Intelligence and Applications, Amsterdam: IOS Press.

Bergstra, J. A., & Klop, J. W. (1985). Algebra of communicating processes with abstraction, *Theoretical Computer Science, 37*(1), 77-121.

Berry, G., & Boudol, G. (1990). The chemical abstract machine. In *Proceedings of the 17th ACM SIGPLAN-SIGACT Symposium on Principles of Programming Languages (POPL'90)*. San Francisco, California, United States.

Boudol, G. (1994). Some chemical abstract machines. *Lecture Notes in Computer Science (LNCS), 803*(1994), 92-123.

Bubenko, J. A. Jr., & Wangler, B. (1993). Objectives driven capture of business rules and of information system requirements. *IEEE Systems Man and Cybernetics ('93 Conference),* Le Touquet, France.

Bubenko, J. A. Jr., & Kirikova, M. (1999). Improving the quality of requirements specifications by enterprise modelling. In A. G. Nilsson, C. Tolis, & C. Nellborn (Eds.), *Perspectives on business modelling: Understanding and changing organisations.* Springer-Verlag.

Bubenko, J. A. Jr., Persson, A., & Stirna, J. (2001). User guide of the knowledge management approach using enterprise knowledge patterns. *Hyper Knowledge project deliverable, project no IST-2000-28401.* Stockholm, Sweden: Dept. of Computer and Systems Sciences, Royal Institute of Technology.

Chechik, M., & Ganno, J. (2001). Autmatic anlysis of consistency between requirements and design. *IEEE Trans on SE, 27*(7), 651-672.

Duraes, J., & Madeira, H. S. (2006). Emulation of software faults: A field data study and a practical approach. *IEEE Trans on SE, 32*(11), 849-867.

Eclipes (2005a). *Eclipse foundation*, eclipse.org, http://www.eclipse.org.

Eclipes (2005b). Eclipse Foundation, The Eclipse Visual Editor Project, http://www.eclipse.org/vep/.

Eclipes (2005c). Eclipse Foundation, Eclipse Tools - EMF, SDO, XSD - Home, http://www.eclipse.org/emf/.

Ekenberg, L., Johannesson, P., Amon, B., Munguanaze, M., Njabili, U., Tesha, R. M., & Wangler, B. (2003). Generalised inductive proving of design correctness. In H. Fujita, & P. Johannesson (Eds.), *New trends in software methodologies, tools and techniques,* (Vol. 98)*, Frontiers in artificial intelligence and applications* (pp. 189-199). Amsterdam: IOS Press.

Ekenberg, L., & Johannesson, P. (2004). A framework for determining design correctness. *International Journal on Knowledge-Based Systems, Elsevier 17*(7-9), 249-262.

Fenton, N., & Hill, G. (1993). Systems construction and analysis: Mathematical and logical framework, Published by McGraw-Hill, ISBN 0-07-707431-9, Chapter 8, Algebras.

Frideman (2006). *The world is flat. a brief history of the twenty-first century*, updated and expanded, 2006, ISBN 0-374-29279-5.

Fujita (2001). Lyee Project: http://www.somet.soft.iwate-pu.ac.jp/en/index.html Units outline http://www.somet.soft.iwate-pu.ac.jp/en/unit/sub_unit.html

Fujita, H., & Johannesson, P. (Eds.). (2002). *New trends in software methodologies, tools and techniques* (vol. 84)*, Frontiers in artificial intelligence and applications*. Amsterdam: IOS Press.

Fujita, H., & Johannesson, P. (Eds.). (2003a). *New trends in software methodologies, tools and techniques* (Vol. 98)*, Frontiers in artificial intelligence and applications*. Amsterdam: IOS Press.

Fujita (Ed.) (2003b). Special Issue on: Intention and software process, *International Journal on Knowledge-Based Systems, Elsevier, 16*(7-8), 339-456.

Fujita, H., & Gruhn, V. (Eds.). (2004). *New trends in software methodologies, tools and techniques* (Vol. 111)*, Frontiers in artificial intelligence and applications*. Amsterdam: IOS Press.

Fujita, H., & Mejri, M. (Eds.). (2005). *New trends in software methodologies, tools and techniques* (Vol. 129)*, Frontiers in artificial intelligence and applications*. Amsterdam: IOS Press.

Fujita, H., & Mejri, M. (Eds.). (2006a). *New trends in software methodologies, tools and techniques* (Vol. 147)*, Frontiers in artificial intelligence and applications*. Amsterdam: IOS Press.

Fujita, H., Ktari, B., & Mejri, M. (2006b). Implementing Lyee-calculus in java. *International Journal on Knowledge-Based Systems, Elsevier, 19*(2), 116-129.

Fujita, H., Hakura, J., & Kurematu, M. (2006c). Virtual cognitive model for miyzawa kenji based on speech and facial images recognition. *WSEAS(www.wseas.org) Transactions on Circuits and Systems, 5*(10), 1536-1543.

Fujita, H. (2007a). Special Issue on: Secure Software System. *International Journal on Knowledge-Based Systems, Elsevier, 20*, to appear.

Fujita, H., Hakura, J., & Kurematu, M. (2007b). A recognition based style for miyazawa-kenji virtual model. *WSEAS (www.wseas.org) Transactions on Systems and Control, 2*(3), 289-296.

Gruhn, V., & Fujita, H. (Eds.). (2006). Special issue on: Intelligent software design. *International Journal on Knowledge-Based Systems, Elsevier, 19*(2), 105-106.

Hoare, C. A. R. (1985). *Communicating sequential processes, Prentice Hall international series in computer science.* Prentice Hall.

Johannesson, P., & Fujita, H. (Eds.). (2004) Special issue on: Legacy systems and software change. *International Journal on Knowledge-Based Systems, Elsevier, 17*(7-8), 237-238.

Kurematsu, M., Hakura, J., & Fujita, H. (2007). A framework of a speech communication system with emotion processing. *WSEAS Transactions on Systems and Control, 6*(3), 283-288.

Ktari, B., Mejri, M., & Fujita, H. (2004). From lyee-calculus to java code. In H. Fujita, & V. Gruhn (Eds.), *New trends in software methodologies, tools and techniques* (Vol. 111), *Frontiers in artificial intelligence and applications* (pp. 235-261). Amsterdam: IOS.

Mbraki, M., Mejri, M., & Ktari, B. (2006). Converting an imperative program to a a declarative one. *Journal on Knowledge-Based Systems, Elsevier, 19*(2), 130-140.

Mejri, M., Ktari, B., & Fujita, H. (2003). Lyee-calculus: A formalization of lyee methodology. In H. Fujita, & P. Johannesson (Eds.), *New trends in software methodologies, tools and techniques:* (Vol. 98), *Frontiers in artificial intelligence and applications* (pp. 235-261). Amsterdam: IOS Press.

Mejri, M., Ktari, B., & Erhioui, M. (2002). Static analysis on lyee-oriented software. In H. Fujita, & P. Johannesson (Eds.), *New trends in software methodologies, tools and techniques* (Vol. 84), *Frontiers in artificial intelligence and applications* (pp.375-394). Amsterdam: IOS.

Milner, R. (1980). *A calculus of communicating systems, Lecture Notes in Computer Science 92.* Berlin: Springer-Verlag.

Negoro, F. (2000). Principle of Lyee software, 2000. *IEEE International Conference on Information Society in 21st Century* (IS2000), 121-189.

Negoro, F., & Fujita, H. (2001a). A proposal for intention engineering. *5th East-European Conference Advances in Databases and Information System (ADBIS'2001)*.

Negoro, F. (2001b). Intent operationalisation for source code generation, *Proceedings of SCI 2001*. Orlando, USA.

Negoro, F. (2003). Study on axiomatic rules for building up relationships between requirement and source programs. *International Journal on Knowledge-Based Systems Elsevier, 16*(7), 383-397.

Negoro, F., & Fujita, H. (2006). Theory on software diagnosis for program code validation. In *New trends in software methodologies, tools and techniques* (Vol. 147), *Frontiers in artificial intelligence and applications* (pp. 245-271). Amsterdam: IOS Press.

Nilsson, A. G., Tolis, C., & Nellborn, C. (Eds.) (1999). *Perspectives on business modelling: Understanding and changing organisations*, Springer-Verlag.

Persson, A. (2001a). *Enterprise modelling in practice: Situational factors and their influence on adopting a participative approach*. PhD Thesis, Department of Computer and Systems Sciences, Stockholm University/Royal Institute of Technology, Sweden, ISSN 1101-8526, 2001.

Persson, A, & Stirna, J. (2001b). An explorative study into the influence of business goals on the practical use of enterprise modelling methods and tools. In *Tenth International Conference on Information Systems Development* (ISD2001) Royal Holloway: University of London, 5-7 September 2001.

Rolland, C. (2002). A user centric view of lyee requirement. In H. Fujita, & P. Johannesson (Eds.), *New trends in software methodologies, tools and techniques* (Vol. 84), *Frontiers in artificial intelligence and applications* (pp. 155-169). Amsterdam: IOS Press.

Rolland, C., Souveyet, C., & Ben Aye, M. (2003). Guiding Lyee user requirements capture. *International Journal on Knowledge-Based Systems, Elsevier, 16*(7), 351-359.

Saleem, N. (1996). An empirical test of the contingency approach to user participation in information systems development. *Journal of Management Information Systems, 13*(1), 145-166.

Schuler, D., & Namioka, A. (Eds.). (1993). *Participatory design: Principles and practices*. Lawrence Erlbaum Associates.

Suh (2005). *Complexity: Theory and applications*. Oxford University Press.

Takeda, Y., & Fujita, H. (2004). Legacy System program transformation by Lyee methodology. *International Journal on Knowledge-Based Systems, Elsevier, 17*(7-8), 263-281.

Wangler, B., & Anne Persson (2002). Capturing colllective intentionality in software development. In H. Fujita, & P. Johannesson (Eds.), *New trends in software methodologies, tools and techniques* (Vol. 84), *Frontiers in artificial intelligence and applications* (pp. 262-270). Amsterdam: IOS Press.

Wangler, B., Anne Persson, Johannesson, P., & Ekenberg, L. (2003). Bridging high level enterprise model to implementation oriented models. In H. Fujita & P. Johannesson (Eds.), *New trends in software methodologies, tools and techniques* (Vol. 98), *Frontiers in artificial Intelligence and applications* (pp. 225-232). Amsterdam: IOS Press.

Welch, P. (2004). *Communicating sequential processes for java* (JCSP). http://www.cs.kent.ac.uk/projects/ofa/jcsp/.

Willars, H. et al. (1998). TRIAD *Modelleringshandboken* N 10:1-6 (in Swedish), SISU, Electrum 212, 164 40 Kista, Sweden, 1993.

Woitaszek, M. (2004). *Introduction to occam.* http://www.cs.rit.edu/_msw4585/occam/.

Chapter XII

Refining the Concept
Syndicate Data:
Categories and Characteristics, Definitions, and a View Ahead

Mattias Strand, University of Skövde, Sweden

Abstract

This chapter introduces the concepts of external data and syndicate data. It contributes with a conceptual discussion regarding different categories of syndicate data, as well as definitions and applications thereof. In addition, the chapter also gives a view ahead for syndicate data, with respect to organizational, as well as technological challenges and trends. Thereby, it increases the understanding for syndicate data as a vital component in business intelligence initiatives and explains why external data in general and syndicate data in particular has become prerequisites in modern information systems.

Furthermore, the author hopes that the categorization and view ahead will not only contribute to researchers through the conceptual discussion and the definitions of concepts, but also to practitioners spending resources on data originating from outside the own organization, by increasing the understanding of the concepts and the actors within the industry.

Introduction

The business environment of organizations has changed and nowadays it is commonly agreed that most organizations are competing in an ever-changing marketplace. In order for them to survive and sustain a competitive edge, they must be able to orient themselves in their environment and keep themselves informed of the whereabouts of their, for example, customers, competitors, and suppliers. Otherwise, they may be overwhelmed by the competitive forces constantly influencing them.

In alignment, since it has become increasingly important to monitor the competitive forces influencing an organization, external data have gained more and more attention, and many argue for the benefits thereof (e.g., Alavi & Haley, 1997; Chen & Frolik, 2000; Devlin, 1997; Gray & Watson, 1998; Inmon, 1996; Inmon, 1999; Watson & Haley, 1997).

The following quotations illustrate, on a general level, the perceived benefits of incorporating external data: 1) Oglesby (1999, p. 3) claims that: *"Companies who use external data systems have a strategic advantage over those who don't, and the scope of that advantage is growing as we move deeper into the information age".* 2) Stedman (1998, p. 2) states that *"external data helps us understand our business in the context of the greater world".* 3) Inmon (1996, p. 272) argues that *"the comparison of internal and external data allows management to see the forest for the trees".*

Furthermore, most organizations incorporate their external data from organizations specialized in collecting, compiling, refining, and selling data (Strand, Wangler, & Olsson, 2003; Strand, Wangler, & Lauren, 2004b). Kimball (1996) refers to these specialized and commercial data suppliers as *syndicate data suppliers* (SDSs). Consequently, this specific external data are referred to as *syndicate data*.

Moreover, the research area of syndicate data incorporation is currently expanding and light is being spread on different aspects of such incorporations. Unfortunately, current literature do not contribute in making it explicit that syndicate data for strategic purposes has one set of characteristics, completely different from syndicate data aimed at supporting the operative environment of organizations. Illustrating the differences between the categories is important, since the empirical studies underlying this work show that many organizations also tend to neglect these differences. As a consequence, they encounter problems when ordering, acquiring, integrating, and applying syndicate data.

In addition, definitions of the categories of syndicate data are also included, as well as a view ahead for the whole area of syndicate data incorporation. The view ahead covers topics spanning from detailed technological trends, such as the application of XML for standardizing data packages, to strictly organizational issues, such as changes in the business idea of the SDSs, in which they take a great lot of the responsibility for the data quality and the enrichment of the data they sell/deliver.

The material creating a foundation for this conceptual discussion originates from four interview studies, covering: DW consultants, consumer organizations (two studies), and SDSs. The studies were originally conducted within the scope of a research project aimed at establishing a state of practice description regarding syndicate data incorporation into data warehouses. Still, although the studies were primarily targeted towards the strategic/tactic application of syndicate data, they resulted in an extensive material regarding the concept of syndicate data as such. The total number of interviews are 34, comprising 12 DW consultants, eight banking organizations, five industry-separated organizations (automotive, media, groceries, petroleum, and medical), and nine SDSs. The interviews lasted on an average for 75 minutes and the transcripts ranged from 1370 to 7334 words (4214 words on average). Naturally, published literature has also been thoroughly reviewed, according to the instructions of Webster and Watson (2002).

Background

Literature accounts for two main directions related to the concept external data. Firstly, external data may concern data crossing organizational boundaries, that is, the data are acquired from outside the organization's boundary (e.g., Kimball, 1996). Secondly, external data may also refer to any data stored or maintained outside a particular database of interest, that is, the data are external to the database but internal from an organizational point of view (e.g., Morzy & Wrembel, 2003). Since this work focuses on data which are exchanged between organizations, the direction accounted for by for example Kimball (1996) was adopted. In defining such data, the definition suggested by Devlin (1997, p. 135) was adopted. According to Devlin external data are:

"Business data (and its associated metadata) originating from one business that may be used as part of either the operational or the informational processes of another business."

Furthermore, literature provides several examples of suppliers/sources of external data, besides the SDSs introduced previously. Firstly, there are companies with other core business activities that create huge amounts of data. For these organizations, the selling of data has become one way of letting the large amounts of data cover its own costs (Asbrand, 1998). Asbrand (1998) further exemplifies the idea of data sales with an example from the pharmaceutical industry, in which the National Data Corporation/ Health Information Services (NDC/HIS) in Phoenix, U.S., has opened its 3.5-terabyte DW to any company who wants to access medical data. Customers are, for example, advertising agencies and stock analysts, which use the data in their decision-making processes.

Secondly, the Internet is gaining more and more attention in the literature, due to the enormous amounts of data store on Web pages. For example, Hackathorn (1999) and Felden and Chamoni (2003) suggest *Webfarming* as an application for acquiring external data from the Internet for DW incorporation, by applying intelligent tools that automatically extract data from the Internet, according to predefined search patterns. Furthermore, Cao, Lim, and Ng (2003), Nørvåg (2002), Stolba and List (2004), Walter and Bjorking (2004), Zhu (1999), Zhu, Bornhövd, Sautner, and Buchmann (2000), Zhu, Bornhövd, and Buchmann (2001), and Zhu and Buchmann (2002) describe different applications for acquiring and sharing external data from Web pages. For example, the following applications are introduced: product pricing via competitors Web pages, preparation of marketing campaign based on weather forecasts, and personnel planning based on promoted events advertised on the Internet. Still, the data quality of the data acquired from the Internet is questionable and therefore many organizations hesitate in applying Internet data as a base-line for decision making (Hackathorn, 1999).

Thirdly, external data may also be acquired from business partners (e.g., Alshawi, Saez-Pujol, & Irani, 2003; Chow, Choy, Lee, & Chan, 2005), especially if they are working in supply-chains with integrated systems, such as, for example, EDI. In Alshawi et al. (2003), it is exemplified on how a number of R&D divisions at a pharmaceutical company integrate their business partners' pharmaceutical data into a DW. These business partners include hospitals, contract research organizations, and consultants. The data are then used for conducting research regarding the effects of certain medicines.

Finally, the external data may also be acquired from governmental agencies, county councils or municipalities (Strand et al., 2003; Hafez, 2004). The data mostly refer to private persons, for example, population statistics and demographics (Strand et al., 2003).

Categorizing Syndicate Data

Based on the material originating from the empirical studies, one finds two broad categories of syndicate data, which are acquired and applied in separate manners, but are both contributing as a baseline for decision support.

Firstly, syndicate data may be delivered via different types of online services, meaning that an organization is requesting a certain information element via the SDSs Web-based services (Example 1), hereafter referred to as *online syndicate data*.

Example 1 – Online syndicate data
Image a salesperson at a shop selling cellular phones. To the desk appears a customer who wants to by a new cellular phone. Such a business transaction requires that the customer signs a contract with a service provider for mobile network, with a fixed monthly cost associated. For making sure that the customer is likely to pay the monthly bills from the service provider or to avoid obvious troublemaking customers, the salesperson is required to conduct a check of the customer's creditability. Therefore, the salesperson asks the customer for his or her civic registration number. The number is then sent online to a credit service catered for by a SDS, with a request for information regarding registered payment complaints. Based on the result of such request (absence or existence of registered payment complaints), the customer is allowed or disallowed to buy the cellular phone with the associated mobile service subscription.

This category of syndicate data is not representing the syndicate data application normally associated with tactic or strategic decision-making, although organizations occasionally incorporate singular data units in their decision support systems via online services. Instead, this category of syndicate data is normally related to business functions at an operative level and may be characterized as small and singular information units regarding a particular organization or a private person. The data may concern, for example, a postal address, a registry of delayed payment, an annual income, or the number of children in a household. Thereby, the coverage of the data is very narrow and since it is distributed via the Internet, the data format is more or less standardized. Selecting a supplier for these data is also rather easy, since the data concern singular, standardized data units, which are simple to derive and does not require complex refinements or derivations. In addition, selecting which data to acquire is also easy and straightforward, since it aims at solving a delimited and specific operative decision matter. Furthermore, since the data are needed when a certain situation arise, it is normally acquired on-demand, although the service per se often is based upon a contract with a SDS.

Moreover, the service is frequently applied and with a random intervall. If considering Example1, it is likely that a store selling cellular phones have a lot of customers per day. Thereby, the data acquisition frequency is high. Furthermore, since the data amounts are very small (singular units) the complexity of incorporating such data is low. Instead, it is displayed in the GUI of the user and once the customer transaction is completed, the need for the data is gone. Thereby, it never becomes integrated into an internal system. Finally, the pricing procedure of this king of services is rather straightforward, in that each request via the Web-based service is associated with a fixed cost.

Secondly, syndicate data may also be acquire or purchased in batches, meaning that a SDS, via different data distribution technologies (e.g., FTP-nodes, Web hotels, CD-ROMs, and e-mail attachments) distributes the data to a customers for database integration. This is normally the category of syndicate data associated with tactic and strategic decision-making. These data will hereafter be referred to as *syndicate batch data* (Example 2).

Example 2 – Syndicate batch data
In Company A, the personnel responsible for the billing of their customers are experiencing problems in establishing reasonable credit repayment schedules. Therefore, they decide to address a SDS selling credit ratings (CR) of organizations. Since Company A is having a rather extensive customer stock, it is not considered feasible to state an online request for every customer, i.e. purchasing online syndicate data. Instead, they decided to purchase the data and integrate it into their own data warehouse. To establish a business relation, Company A decides upon a needed data set, establishes a contact and contract with a SDS, and starts to subscribe to the data on a monthly basis. The syndicate batch data is then applied in the following manner. Company A incorporates, from the SDS, a CR value of organizations ranging from 1 to 5, in which 5 indicates a customer with a superior credibility, whereas 1 is a serious warning flag. These values are derived values created in a data refinement process by the SDS. By combing the CR ratings with the internal credit

repayment schedule, standardized to 4 weeks, Company A may automatically recalculate the repayment schedule of each customer. The automatic recalculation updates the credit repayment attribute in the customer master dimension in their DW as follows: CR 1 = 4-4 weeks; CR 2 = 4-3 weeks; CR 3 = 4-2 weeks; CR 4 = 4-1 week; and CR 5 = 4±0 week. Consequently, a customer with a CR 1 is not allowed to pay via an invoice at all. Instead, such a customer must always pay in advance, whereas as customer with a CR 5 still is allowed a repayment schedule of 4 weeks. By applying syndicate batch data for automatic recalculations of the customers' repayment schedules, Company A reduces previous manual workload. In addition, since the data is subscribed to on a monthly basis, the recalculated payment schedules are automatically recalculated by the DW, if the CR of a certain customer changes.

Syndicate batch data are normally complex and comprises large data sets which may involve hundreds of attributes and millions of rows of data. Thereby, it is very broad in its coverage. In addition, although some data formats are standardized and the SDSs are putting a large effort on structuring the data according to XML (extensive markup language) standards, the formats and structures of the data are being objects for costly and time-consuming tailoring (Adelman, 1998; Strand, Wangler, & Niklasson, 2004a; Strand, Wangler, Lundell, & Niklasson, 2006). Furthermore, the identification of possible suppliers varies between straight forward and very difficult. A straightforward selection of a supplier is often due to the fact the suppliers may be in a monopoly situation and is the only SDSs capable of delivering a certain data set. However, selecting the most appropriate supplier for data incorporation may also be very problematic, since several data suppliers often are capable of providing the same data (Strand et al., 2004b). In addition, the SDSs are not only competing with the actual data they sell. Instead, a majority of the suppliers indicated that they naturally compete with data and services offered, but equally much with other, competitive means, like, for example, data availability, degree of data refinement, and the customer support offered (Strand & Lundell, 2005).

Furthermore, the selection of data, once a particular supplier has been selected, may also be hard, since most SDSs deliver differing but overlapping data sets (Strand et al., 2004b; Zhu & Buchman, 2002). In alignment, the suppliers strived towards offering different standardized sets or packages of data, of which the customers must select one or several for incorporation. As a consequence, the consumers sometimes are forced to procure a more expensive and extensive data set, with respect to content, for being able to acquire a specific attribute. However, the suppliers also claimed that they allow a high degree of tailoring of the data, since the customers have such varying demands. To illustrate, Respondent 6 (Interview study towards syndicate data supplier) gave the following statement (translated from

Swedish): "*We try to have standardized solutions, but it has become evident that our customers have very diverging demands, so for being able to compete, flexibility is a key-word. Therefore, we try to build a generic platform that allows flexibility towards each and every customer*".

With respect to the incorporation of syndicate batch data, there are two main approaches existing. The by far most common, and exemplified above, is the *subscription service approach*. The subscription service means that the customers receive data on a regular basis, according to the established contract between the two parties. The second approach for incorporating syndicate batch data is the *on-demand approach*. This approach is generic for the two categories of syndicate data, but for syndicate batch data, it is still acquired for an internal data integration purpose. The strongest argument for incorporating syndicate batch data on-demand is solely based on monetary issues. Customers with no regular needs for refreshing their decision support systems do not want to pay in vain for the data (Strand et al., 2004a). Still, since the subscription service approach is the far most common incorporation interval for syndicate batch data, it is reasonable to characterize the acquisition interval as periodic, although random acquisitions also are conducted. In addition, the acquisition frequency is rather low, since most organizations subscribe on certain data sets periodically, for example, monthly, quarterly, or annually.

Furthermore, the technological, as well as, organizational challenges related to the incorporation of syndicate batch data makes the complexity of such incorporation high. Organizations incorporating such syndicate data into their systems may face a lot of problems, e.g., the costs associated with syndicate batch data (Oglesby, 1999), data integration issues (Adelman, 1998; Damato, 1999), data quality issues (Zhu & Buchmann, 2002), and data trust issues (Zhu & Buchmann, 2002; Strand & Wangler, 2004; Strand et al., 2004b). Altogether, the palette of problems that an organization may encounter when incorporating syndicate batch data into their systems makes these initiatives rather complex, time-consuming, and costly.

Finally, the SDSs' pricing of the syndicate batch data is very difficult and requires to be noticed. In contrast to online syndicate data, which are rather straightforward, syndicate batch data incorporation is a much more complex phenomenon. The sales contracts of syndicate batch data may be negotiated several times with respect to its content, in which the customer may decreases the data amounts as a means for lowering the costs. At the same time, the SDSs have to conduct costly efforts in selecting the appropriate data from their internal sources and compile it according to the customers' demands. If solely applying a pricing procedure based on data amounts, the supplier would have to conduct a lot of knowledge-requiring work in selecting only the appropriate data, but only getting paid for relatively small amounts of delivered data. To exemplify, one of the respondents in the SDS interview study (Respondent 5) gave the following statement (translated from Swedish) to emphasize the pricing dilemma of syndicate batch data: "*Not long ago, we hade a customer that requested a XML-file with every company in Stockholm, that is a joint-stock company and has a profit that exceeds 10 percentage of the turnover. This type of request is common, but we often negotiate the pricing individually for each customer. In this case, we calculated the price of the data set based on the number of data rows. In that price, we also distributed the costs for selecting, sorting, and compiling the data per row. The customer found the price to high and since the price was based on number of rows, she also added a selection on companies with at least 40 employees. Thereby, the number of rows were drastically reduced and consequently, also the price. However, for us it became problematic, since it meant more work for us but less money in compensation. How do you make it obvious for the customers that they are paying for information as well as exformation?*"

To summarize the categorization and characterization of syndicate data, Table 1 was included.

Moreover, since the above categorization makes a distinct division between categories of syndicate data, it is important also to introduce definitions thereof. The definitions introduced below are based upon the general definition of external data given by Devlin (1997), but specialized in accordance to the characteristics given in Table 1. For *online syndicate data*, the following definition is proposed:

"*Singular units of business data (and eventually its associated metadata) frequently and on-demand purchased from a syndicate data supplier and targeted towards the decision making processes of the operative environment of another business.*"

Table 1. Comparing online syndicate data and syndicate batch data

Syndicate data category Characteristic	Online syndicate data	Syndicate batch data
Business level support	Operative	Tactic, strategic
Data amounts	Small, singular data units	Large, complex data sets
Data coverage	Narrow	Broad
Data format	Standardized	Tailored
Supplier identification	Easy	Easy to hard
Data selection	Easy	Easy to hard
Incorporation approach	On-demand	On-demand, subscription
Acquisition interval	Random	Periodic, random
Acquisition frequency	High	Low
Incorporation complexity	Low	High
Pricing	Straightforward	Complex

The definition strongly emphasizes small amounts of data being frequently incorporated on-demand, for supporting operative decision-making. It also indicates that metadata occasionally may be attached, but this is not always the case. Mostly, the metadata only concerns a date from which the singular data unit is valid or when it was last updated.

For *syndicate batch data*, the following definition is proposed:

"Large sets of business data and its associated metadata purchased from a syndicate data supplier, via subscriptions and/or on-demand, and targeted towards the strategic and/or the tactical decision making processes of another business."

In alignment with the characteristics given in Table 1, this definition states the proposed support for strategic decision-making and the existence of subscriptions for batches of data. Furthermore, for syndicate batch data incorporation, metadata are utmost important, since it otherwise becomes more or less impossible to accurately incorporate the data into another business.

A View Ahead

Although online syndicate data and syndicate batch data diverge in their applications, they share some key issues that will be further emphasized in the future. First of all, the results of the empirical studies unanimously indicate that the incorporation of syndicate data will increase. Both the customers and the SDSs anticipated that the syndicate batch data will be the category that increases the most. Besides the fact that online syndicate data currently claims the largest proportion of the market and thereby is difficult to expand further, the two parties indicates the same motive for the anticipated increase of primarily syndicate batch data. The customers put forward an increased need for being able to perform, with assistance of powerful systems, intelligent analyses of prospects and existing customers as the strongest. In alignment, the SDSs motivate the anticipated increase with fact that their customers invest in systems which are becoming more and more capable of handling large amounts of data and visualize reports and results of queries in a more "intelligent" manner. In addition, the SDSs also indicates that for their own success, syndicate batch data will be utmost important, since this category is still somewhat unexplored among first and foremost small and medium sized enterprises (SMEs). Thereby, there have the opportunity of a market that may still expand. Still, at the same time they also indicate that their will be a fierce competition for claiming this market.

Secondly, regardless syndicate data category and its applications, high quality data are always a business cornerstone for the SDSs, or as Respondent 3 (Interview study with SDSs) expressed it: *"Without high quality data, you may equally well go and apply for liquidation, so tough is the competition. High quality data is not a sales argument, it is rather a lifeline"* (Translate from Swedish). In alignment, the results of the empirical studies also illustrate that the customers nowadays has become more data quality sensitive and demand high data quality. Therefore, the data quality verifications conducted by the SDSs will further increase in extent. Currently, the SDSs conduct manual, as well as, automatic data quality verifications. The manual data quality verifications may be to phone private persons and actually asking them for the spelling of their first- and surnames. Still, since this is very time-consuming, and thereby costly, these types of data quality verifications are conducted on a random sample basis. The automatic verifications may be to, for example, compare a city name in an address, towards a list of valid spellings of city names. To illustrate, a city indicated as either Gotenburg or Grothenburg in a customer city attribute is automatically translated into Gothenburg. However, as much of the data that the SDSs compile and refine is acquired from governmental agencies, with loads of manual input, spelling errors are rather common and may be more troublesome to correct than the example included above. As a consequence, the SDSs have started to apply more and more advance linear, as well as non-linear techniques, for verifying the quality of the data they sell. In addition, the results of the empirical studies also indicate that the consumers of syndicate data and even private persons have become more aware of the importance of correct data, and therefore, the SDSs have also notice an increased interaction with their customers, in which they contact are contacted by customers pointing out the existence of errors in the data.

Furthermore, although the incorporation of the two categories of syndicate data differs widely, a contract is always established between the SDS and the customer organizations, in which the cost for the data and permitted applications of the data are strongly regulated. For example, all suppliers strongly regulate that the customer organizations are solely permitted to apply the data in their own business processes. Thereby, they are not allowed to sell the data to other organizations or to share the data with business partners. At the bottom-line, the customers are regulated so that they may not start a competing activity.

In addition, the results of the empirical studies also show that the establishment of stronger business relations, hereafter referred to as constellations, will increase in the future. For online syndicate data, the business relationship takes the shape of an ordinary supplier-consumer constellation between the consumers and the SDSs (Figure 1A). These constellations are normally built upon service level agreements, regulating the availability of the data and support utilities. For syndicate batch data, the business relationships becomes more complex, since such incorporations often are influenced, or even initiated, by consultants. For syndicate batch data, three major constellations have been identified (Figure 1B), that is, a *hardware/software supplier-consumer constellation* between the customers and consultants, a *syndicate batch data supplier-consumer constellation* between the customers and the SDSs, and a *certification constellation* between the SDSs and the consultants.

For syndicate batch data incorporation, the constellations between the customers and any of the other two parties are rather well-known and represent classical supplier-consumer constellations. However, the third constellation, that is, the *certification constellation* between the SDSs and the consultants, is less well-known. Still, both the consultants and the SDSs

Figure 1. A) Online syndicate data incorporation builds upon a binary supplier-consumer constellation between the customers and the SDSs. B) Syndicate batch data incorporation builds upon a three binary constellations between the customers, the SDSs, and the consultants.

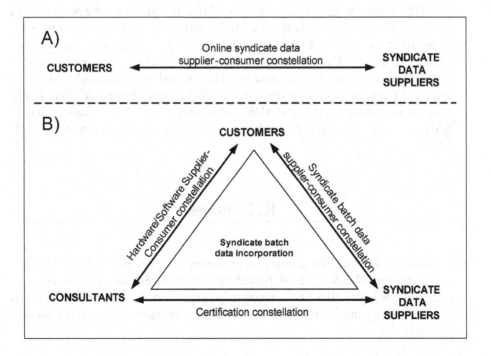

indicated during the interviews that this is something that will become more and more common in the future. The basic idea of the constellation is that a particular SDS and a particular consultant company agree upon certificates regarding data formatting and data structuring. If a customer then procures, for example, a decision support system from the consultant, the selection of SDSs should be certificate-driven. In the long run, the idea is to motivate the certificates to the customers with the incentive of reduced resources for transforming and integrating the syndicate data with internal data, since the data are already formatted and structured according to the requirements of the consultant's solution. However, since these initiatives are new, it is important to investigate if the certificates actually do contribute as intended or if such certificates create other problems not anticipated. Obviously, certificates make it more difficult to replace a SDS with other suppliers adhering to a diverging certificate.

Finally, from a technological perspective, XML is granted a lot of interest by a majority of the SDSs and is considered as the next major trend in syndicate data incorporation. For example, Respondent 5 (Interview study with SDSs) stated that: "*XML in combination with the Internet is, for us that have been writing communication protocols, like a dream come true. It is a complete dream*" (Translated from Swedish). The enormous interest for XML originates in the abilities catered for with respect to data extraction, data formatting, and data integration. Also the customers stated the importance of XML, although they strongly indicated that the SDSs are the beneficiaries of XML. Respondent 3 (Interview study with banking organizations) even stated that: "*They [the SDSs] will most certainly take advantage of the cost reductions that XML may contribute with, but I would be very surprised if that is reflected on the invoice the send us*" (Translated from Swedish). Still, the results of the interview study towards the SDSs also indicate that there is still much work remaining for the SDSs, until they may take full advantage of XML or until they transformed there products or services into a XML format.

References

Adelman, S. (1998). Estimating a data warehouse pilot project? *DM Review*. Retrieved March 21, 2004, from http://www.dmreview.com/editorial.

Alavi, M., & Haley, B. (1997). Knowledge management systems: Implications and opportunities for data warehousing. *Journal of Data Warehousing*, *4*(1), 2-7.

Alshawi, S., Saez-Pujol, I., & Irani, Z. (2003). Data warehousing in decision support for pharmaceutical R&D supply chain. *International Journal of Information Management, 23*(3), 259-268.

Asbrand, D. (1998). Making money from data. *Datamation*. Retrieved June 21, 2000, from http://datamation.earthweb.com.

Cao, Y., Lim, E. P., & Ng, W. K. (2003). Data model for warehousing historical Web information. *Information and Software Technology, 46*(6), 315-334.

Chen, L., & Frolick, M. N. (2000). Web-based data warehousing – Fundamentals, challenges and solutions. *Information Systems Management, 17*(2), 80-86.

Chow, H. K. H., Choy, K. L., Lee, W. B., & Chan, F. T. S. (2005). Design of a knowledge-based logistics strategy system. *Expert Systems with Applications, 29*(2), 272-290.

Damato, G. M. (1999). Strategic information from external sources – A broader picture of business reality for the data warehouse. Retrieved March 20, 2002, from http://www.dwway.com.

Devlin, B. (1997). *Data warehouse: From architecture to implementation*. Harlow: Addison Wesley Longman.

Felden, C., & Chamoni, P. (2003). Webfarming and data warehousing for energy tradefloors. In J. Liu, C. Liu, M. Klusch, N. Zhong, & N. Cercone (Eds.), *Proceedings of the International Conference on Web Intelligence (WI2003)* (pp. 642-645). Los Alamitos, CA: IEEE Computer Society.

Gray, P., & Watson, H. J. (1998). Present and future directions in data warehousing. *The DATA BASE for Advances in Information Systems, 29*(3), 83-90.

Hackathorn, R. D. (1999). *Web farming for the DW – Exploiting business intelligence and knowledge management*. San Francisco: Morgan Kaufmann Publishers.

Hafez, H. A. A. (2004). Web based data warehouse in the Egyptian cabinet information and decision support center. In R. Meredith, G. Shanks, D. Arnott, & S. Carlsson (Eds.), *Proceedings of the 2004 IFIP International Conference on Decision Support Systems (DSS2004): Decision Support in an Uncertain and Complex World* (pp. 402-409). Prato, Italy.

Inmon, W. H. (1996). *Building the data warehouse* (2nd ed.). New York: John Wiley & Sons.

Inmon, W. H. (1999). Integrating internal and external data. *The Bill Inmon.com library LLC*. Retrieved February 9, 2002, from http://www.billinmon.com.

Kimball, R. (1996). *The data warehouse toolkit*. New York: John Wiley & Sons.

Morzy, T., & Wrembel, R. (2003). Modeling a multiversion data warehouse: A formal approach. In O. Camp, J. Filipe, S. Hammoudi, & M. Piattini (Eds.), *Proceedings of the 5th International Conference on Enterprise Information Systems (ICEIS) - Part 1* (pp. 120-127). Setubal: Escola Superior de Tecnologia do Insituto Politécnico de Setubal.

Nørvåg, K. (2002). Temporal XML data warehouses: Challenges and solutions. In *Proceedings of Workshop on Knowledge Foraging for Dynamic Networking of Communities and Economies*, October 29–31, Shiraz, Iran.

Oglesby, W. E. (1999). Using external data sources and warehouses to enhance your direct marketing effort. *DM Review*. Retrieved March 18, 2002, from http://www.dmreview.com.

Stedman, C. (1998). Scaling the warehouse wall. *Computerworld*. Retrieved March 13, 2003, from http://www.computerworld.com.

Stolba, N., & List, B. (2004). Extending the data warehouse with company external data from competitors' websites: A case study in the banking sector. In *Proceedings of Data Warehousing 2004 (DW 2004)*. Germany: Physica Verlag.

Strand, M., & Lundell, B. (2005). Syndicate data incorporation into data warehouses: Contrasting consumer problems with supplier viewpoints. In D. Konstantas, J.-P. Bourrières, M. Léonard, & N. Boudjlida (Eds.), *First International Conference on Interoperability of Enterprise Software and Applications (Interop-ESA'05)* (pp. 421-432). London: Springer-Verlag.

Strand, M., & Wangler, B. (2004). Incorporating external data into data warehouses - Problems identified and contextualized. In P. Svensson, & J. Schubert (Eds.), *Proceedings of the 7th International conference on information fusion (Fusion'04) – Vol. 1* (pp. 288-294). Mountain View, CA: International Society of Information Fusion.

Strand, M., Wangler, B., & Lauren, C.-F. (2004b). Acquiring and integrating external data into data warehouses: Are you familiar with the most common process?. In I. I. Seruca, J. Filipe, S. Hammoudi, & J. Cordeiro (Eds.), *Proceedings of the 6th International Conference on Enterprise Information Systems (ICEIS'2004) – Vol. 1* (pp. 508-513). Porto: INSTICC – Institute for Systems and Technologies of Information, Control and Communication.

Strand, M., Wangler, B., Lundell, B., & Niklasson, M. (2006). Syndicate data incorporation into data warehouses: A categorization and verification of problems. *Fourteenth International Conference on Information Systems Development (ISD'2005)*. Karlstad, Sweden, August 15-17. (Accepted for publication in Kluwer/Plenum Press proceedings).

Strand, M., Wangler, B., & Niklasson, M. (2004a). External data incorporation into data warehouses: An exploratory study of identification and usage practices in banking organizations. In J. Grabis, A. Persson, & J. Stirna (Eds.), *Proceedings of the CAiSE Forum at the 16th International Conference on Advanced Information Systems Engineering* (pp. 103-112). Riga: Riga Technical University.

Strand, M., Wangler, B., & Olsson, M. (2003). Incorporating external data into data warehouses: Characterizing and categorizing suppliers and types of external data. *Proceedings of the Ninth Americas Conference on Information Systems* (pp. 2460-2468). Tampa, Florida, USA. (CD-ROM).

Walter, R., & Bjorking, L. (2004). Aggregating the aggregators – An agnostic approach. *Information Services and Use, 24*(3), 121-130.

Watson, H. J., & Haley, B. J. (1997). Data warehousing: A framework and survey of current practices. *Journal of Data Warehousing, 2*(1), 10-17.

Webster, J., & Watson, R. T. (2002). Analyzing the past to prepare for the future: Writing a literature review. *MIS Quarterly, 26*(2), 13-23.

Zhu, Y. (1999). A framework for warehousing the Web contents. In L. C. K. Hui, & D. L. Lee (Eds.), *Proceedings of the 5th International Computer Science Conference on Internet Applications* (pp. 83-92). Berlin: Springer-Verlag.

Zhu, Y., Bornhövd, C., & Buchmann, A. P. (2001). Data transformation for warehousing Web data. *Proceedings of the 3rd International Workshop on Advanced Issues of E-Commerce and Web-Based Information Systems* (pp. 74-85). Los Alamitos, CA: IEEE Computer Society.

Zhu, Y., Bornhövd, C., Sautner, D., & Buchmann, A. P. (2000). Materializing Web data for OLAP and DSS. *Proceedings of the 1st International Conference on Web-Age Information Management* (pp. 201-214). London: Springer-Verlag.

Zhu, Y., & Buchmann, A. P. (2002). Evaluating and selecting Web sources as external information resources of a data warehouse. In T. W. Ling, U. Dayal, E. Bertino, W. K. Ng, & A. Goh (Eds.), *Proceedings of The Third International Conference on Web Information Systems Engineering* (pp. 149-161). Los Alamitos, CA: IEEE Computer Society.

Chapter XIII

Interconnecting E-Business Model Components

Eva Söderström, University of Skövde, Sweden

Vinay Kumar Mandala, HB Technologies Inc., USA

Abstract

This chapter is about electronic business (e-business) models that have emerged and altered the traditional ways in which to do business. An e-business model is a specialisation of a business model, and is an organisational plan for how to work with the products or services intended to bring profit and revenue, and using ICT and the Internet in doing so. E-business models consist of components. Components constitute a business concept, i.e. an idea that an organisation wants to bring into reality. Our research has focused on the interconnections between e-business model components. The analysis of the e-business model components and their interconnections results in a framework in the form of a model displaying the connections between the clustered components. The purpose of the chapter is to explain an overview of e-business model components and show how value is created and added at each component level.

Introduction

Electronic business (e-business) can be defined as the use of information and communication technologies (ICT) to support business activities (Davis, 2004). It poses significant challenges for organisations as it affects both how organisations relate to external parties (customers, suppliers, partners, competitors and markets) and how they operate internally in for example management activities, processes, and systems (Hayes & Finnegan, 2005). Part of the complexity is that e-business in many cases underlies organisational change, which is displayed in the business models that came with the commercialization of the Internet during the 1990's. These models reflect organisational change, technology sophistication and so on. An e-business model is a specialisation of a business model, and the concept is discussed frequently in literature, for example: Business models on the web (Rappa, 2003), Internet business models (Afuah & Tucci, 2001), B2B and B2C Business models (Alt & Zimmerman, 2001), and business model for electronic markets (Timmers, 1998).

In essence, an e-business model is an organisational plan for how to work with the products or services intended to bring profit and revenue, and using ICT and the Internet in doing so. The concept is often used to describe key aspects of a given business (Hedman & Kalling, 2003; Afuah & Tucci, 2001; Osterwalder & Pigneur, 2002). E-business models consist of components that are related, or interconnected, in terms of a logical flow of value, i.e. the order in which each component is defined and how it affects the value of other components (Pateli & Giaglis, 2004; Morris, Schindehutte, & Allen, 2005). So far, not much research has focused on the interconnections between components. Even so, the topic is important, since e-business model success depends on the fit between components, how each component is defined, and how they affect each other (Hamel, 2000; Morris et al., 2005; Shafer, Smith, & Linder, 2005; Afuah & Tucci, 2001; Osterwalder & Pigneur, 2002). Our work concentrates on interconnections.

Even though there seems to be a relative consensus when it comes to identifying the constituent elements of an e-business model, these elements – components – are given various names and definitions in literature (for our definition, see section 3). Component themselves are an essential aspect in the successful definition of an e-business model (Linder & Cantrell 2000; Osterwalder & Pigneur 2002; Afuah & Tucci, 2001; Hamel, 2000; Timmers, 1998). Limited research has been conducted towards identifying the logical flow of value between components. There are interconnections, as we will term the relationships between the components, for example when one component affects another in terms of cost-effectiveness, and trade-offs and optimization. Finding these interconnections in the right blend is necessary to achieve competitive advantage (Hayes & Finnegan, 2005). Our work concentrates on addressing e-business model components and their interconnections between them.

E-Business Models

The current interest in e-business and e-commerce is a reflection of the increasing importance of informatics to organisational performance both in terms of its internal processes and in terms of its external relations with customers and suppliers (Davis, 2004). The business environment of the new millennium is responsive, dynamic and competitive, and is in a constant state of customer-focused change initiated by innovations in ICT. E-business is the result of combining the broad reach and vast resources of the Internet with information technology systems (Du Plessis & Boon, 2004). Many organisations rely on IT and IS to support their business processes. The differences between industrial age business models and e-business models are business rules and assumptions of how business is done.

Defining E-Business Models

In literature, e-business model definitions delimit the nature and components of a model and determine what a good e-business model constitutes (Morris et al., 2005). We will define an e-business model from a combination of three things:

1. **Architecture** for product or service, description of business actors, roles and relationships, and a method for use of resources to deliver value to customer differentiated from its competitors using the properties of the Internet and ICT (Timmers, 1998; Afuah & Tucci, 2001)

2.   **Core logic** of a firm (Linder & Cantrell, 2000) or a business concept (Hamel, 2000) on which all other elements are constructed

3.   **Choices for value creation** while marketing the value and earning profits and revenue from the value through electronic means, where this value can be products (physical or electronic) or services (Osterwalder & Pigneur, 2002; Shafer et al., 2005; Rappa, 2003)

Why E-Business Models?

E-business models are essential in decision-making activities, in particular in how to change traditional business models to e-readiness. Motivations for studying e-business models vary. Current research is mainly focused on defining e-business models and specifying the key components (Pateli & Giaglis, 2004). A profitable e-business model is a continual challenge (Martinez, 2000), consisting of adopting emerging technologies, dealing with security and trust, change, aligning IS with firm resources, and so on. Finding the key components of an e-business model and fit between these is the key issue to consider for any organisation's success (Afuah & Tucci, 2001). Current work on defining key components in e-business models deals with decomposing these models into atomic elements. Still, work remains in terms of defining the interconnections between components. Before explaining the interconnection we have identified, we first introduce the components concept.

Components

Components are the fundamental constructs of e-business models (Afuah & Tucci, 2001). This section presents an overview of components and their role in e-business models, which is a central aspect in this chapter.

Introduction to Components

Components constitute a business concept, i.e. an idea that an organisation wants to bring into reality. Typically, this consists of a product or service that a firm wants to create and offer to its customers for making revenues (Rappa, 2003). In order to realise such an idea, parts or elements required must be identified. These elements are formulated in an architecture that shows realisation and strategic choice (Osterwalder & Pigneur, 2002). The architecture can be considered as an e-business model.

It should be noted that components often are defined from a software or technology perspective, in which case they are "*a physical and replaceable part of a system that conforms to and provides the realization of set of interfaces*" (Larsen, 2000). This is not our perspective. Instead, e-business model literature views components as pieces of business models, and essential for an organisation in order to create, deliver and earn profit. They are hence activities and important aspects involved in value creation (Afuah & Tucci, 2001; Osterwalder & Pigneur, 2002).

Component Taxonomy

Table 1 outlines various (types of) components given by authors so far in literature. The horizontal rows represent component names, while vertical columns represent the respective authors. The components are then clubbed together in the horizontal rows. The crosses in the table map a component on the x-axis to an author in the y-axis. The row on x-axis with more than one cross mark represent the component addressed with same name corresponding to different authors in y-axis. The table is large, and will take up two full pages.

Key E-Business Model Components

This section outlines e-business model key components, values, possible linkages between them and a framework describing all these key components, with their values and interconnections. Before we do this, we need a set of key components. Table 1 were used to identify interconnections between the components. The components were clustered based on their definitions. Two or more components with the same or agreeing definitions were grouped and given a name. This process was iterated until all components in the table belonged to a cluster. These clusters are the set of key components: mission, target market, value proposition, value chain, capabilities and resources, channel, partner networks, revenue and pricing, customer value, implementation. Each component cluster will be described in the remainder of this section.

Table 1 (a). Taxonomy of components

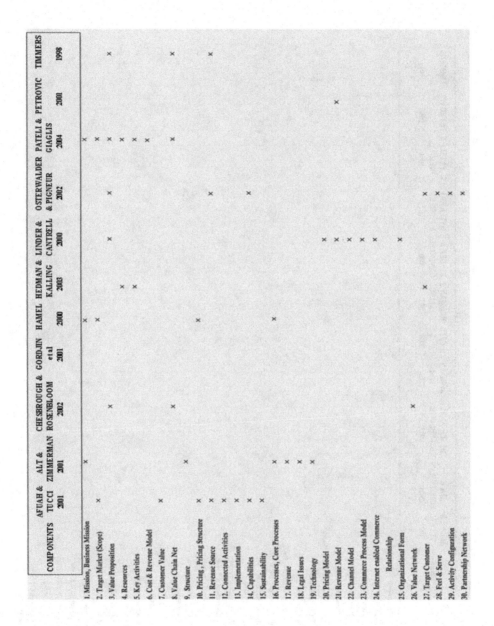

COMPONENTS	AFUAH & TUCCI	ALT & ZIMMERMAN	CHESBROUGH & ROSENBLOOM	GORDIJN et al	HAMEL	HEDMAN & KALLING	LINDER & CANTRELL	OSTERWALDER & PIGNEUR	PATELI & GIAGLIS	PETROVIC	TIMMERS
	2001	2001	2002	2001	2000	2003	2000	2002	2004	2001	1998
1. Mission, Business Mission		×			×				×		
2. Target Market (Scope)	×				×						
3. Value Proposition			×				×	×	×		×
4. Resources									×		
5. Key Activities						×			×		
6. Cost & Revenue Model						×			×		
7. Customer Value	×		×						×		
8. Value Chain Net											×
9. Structure		×			×						
10. Pricing , Pricing Structure	×										
11. Revenue Source	×								×		×
12. Connected Activities	×										
13. Implementation	×										
14. Capabilities	×							×			
15. Sustainability	×										
16. Processes, Core Processes		×			×			×			
17. Revenue		×									
18. Legal Issues		×									
19. Technology		×									
20. Pricing Model							×				
21. Revenue Model							×			×	
22. Channel Model							×				
23. Commerce Process Model							×				
24. Internet enabled Commerce Relationship							×				
25. Organizational Form							×				
26. Value Network			×								
27. Target Customer						×		×			
28. Feel & Serve								×			
29. Activity Configuration								×			
30. Partnership Network								×			

Table 1 (b). Taxonomy of components

COMPONENTS	AFUAH & TUCCI	ALT & ZIMMERMAN	CHESBROUGH & ROSENBLOOM	GORDIJN et al	HAMEL	HEDMAN & KALLING	LINDER & CANTRELL	OSTERWALDER & PIGNEUR	PATELI & GIAGLIS	PETROVIC	TIMMERS
	2001	2001	2002	2001	2000	2003	2000	2002	2004	2001	1998
31. Information								×			
32. Trust & Loyalty								×			
33. Value Model										×	
34. Resource Model										×	
35. Production Model										×	
36. Customer Relationship Model										×	
37. Capital Model										×	
38. Market Model										×	
39. Basis Of Differentiation					×						
40. Core Competencies					×						
41. Strategic Assets					×						
42. Cost Structure			×					×			
43. Fulfillment & Support					×						
44. Information & Insight					×						
45. Relationship Dynamics					×						
46. Profit Structure								×			
47. Suppliers					×	×					×
48. Partners					×						
49. Coalition					×						
50. Resource & Assets								×			
51. Buyers											×
52. Customer Ownership				×							
53. Value Object				×							
54. Price Setting				×							
55. Casuality of Revenue				×							
56. Market Segment				×							
57. Value Activity			×			×					
58. Competitive Strategy			×			×					
60. Offering											

Key E-Business Model Components

This section outlines e-business model key components, values, possible linkages between them and a framework describing all these key components, with their values and interconnections. Before we do this, we need a set of key components. Table 1 were used to identify interconnections between the components. The components were clustered based on their definitions. Two or more components with the same or agreeing definitions were grouped and given a name. This process was iterated until all components in the table belonged to a cluster. These clusters are the set of key components: mission, target market, value proposition, value chain, capabilities and resources, channel, partner networks, revenue and pricing, customer value, implementation. Each component cluster will be described in the remainder of this section.

Mission

The first step in defining an e-business model is to set a "mission" of the firm to capture what the e-business model is designed to accomplish. It encompasses things such as value proposition, strategic intent, purpose, and goals (Hamel, 2000). It must be established how an IS should be used and aligned with resources (Hedman & Kalling, 2003). The central idea is that an information system must 'fit' its organisational context: the organisation, its strategy, its processes and its environment for better performance (Davis, 2004). A firm's mission mainly depends on the understanding of the *business landscape* and its *creative thinking*:

1. *Business Landscape*: Concerns knowledge about the potential market and its behavior, social changes, the impact of government policies, the impact of innovations, ICT and the behaviors of competitors, technological changes, and the possible dynamism of all these make an outline of all of which may impact on decisions made by the mission planners (Pech & Slade, 2004).

2. *Creative Thinking*: Concerns outweighing competitor tactics and is essential to avoid repetitive reactions and to create new wealth (Hamel, 2000). E-business applications like knowledge management foster a culture of innovation and creativity which is a key element in ensuring agility for an e-business (Du Plessis & Boon, 2004).

Target Market

"Target Market" to which customers (demographic or geographic) the value is offered, and the range of products/services that embody this value (Afuah & Tucci, 2000). It captures the essence of where the firm does or does not compete (Osterwalder & Pigneur, 2002). In an e-business environment, organisations need knowledge about its markets, customers, products and services, possibly provided by knowledge management activities. Factors that influence assessing the target market are: *market orientation* and *market segment*:

1. *Market Orientation*: The coordinated behaviour of different organisational functions aimed at seeking and gathering information from consumers, the competition and the environment; disseminating this information throughout the organisation; and designing and implementing a response in accordance with the information obtained, all based on the identification and construction of distinctive organisational capabilities, with a view to satisfying consumers by providing them with higher value (Blesa & Bigneu, 2005).

2. *Market segment*: Includes determining how much of the needs of the segment a firm can profitably serve (Afuah & Tucci, 2001). The Internet has enabled firms to reach any geographical location (Afuah & Tucci, 2001), and can hence create new customer segments (Osterwalder & Pigneur, 2002).

Value Proposition

A value proposition is simply an appraisal of efforts compared to its cost and valuation which can be made in reference to indirect benefits or direct benefits. A value proposition is really the sum of all that goes into an effort (Ott, 2000). How a company attracts its customers or delivers its value can make its E-business model substantially different from that of another firm (Linder & Cantrell, 2000). Value proposition is mainly dependent on *cost element* and *marketing* elements.

1. *Cost element*: The cost element is based on price, effort and risk taken by a firm in developing a product or offering a service (Osterwalder &

Pigneur, 2002). Cost element is one of the aspects where a firm competes in the competitive environment.

2. *Marketing*: Includes exposing a firm's value to customers, and to magnify the value proposition to customer (Timmers, 1998). Marketing the product electronically is faster, cheaper and more efficient than other mechanisms (Bharat, 1999).

Value Chain

The value chain concept was first proposed by Porter as a means of identifying the business actions or stages that transform input to output (Walters, 2004). It consists of strategically important company functions or activities that create both costs and customer value. The concept of the value chain is driven by increasingly sophisticated and prevalent information technologies, particularly the Internet, and changes the market dynamics in allowing new value chains to form with new coalitions, products and services in the market (Chang, 2005). Three things have the power to influence or alter value chains: Linkages, dynamics, and the information process:

1. *Linkages*: a firm's competitive position is affected not only by the set of linkages within the company's own value-chain activities, but also by the value-chain linkages between buyers and suppliers (Nordberg, Campbell, & Verbeke, 2003). Each link is dependent on the other and the strength of the value chain is dependent on the strength of each links (Walters, 2004).

2. *Dynamics*: Traditionally, the value chain has dealt with customer service by understanding each single link in the organisation. In the electronic age, a more dynamic view is needed (Walters, 2004). Customer perceptions change and a constant focus of market dynamics is hence needed (Chang, 2005).

3. *Information process*: Companies adopt the value adding information process in three stages: visibility, mirroring capability, and customer relationships (Rayport and Sviokla, 1999). Visibility concerns an ability to see physical operation more effectively through information; Mirroring capability concerns how firms' substitute virtual activities for physical forms in e.g. identifying core processes; and Customer relationships concerns how firms use IT to establish new customer relationships.

Capabilities and Resources

In literature, the terms "resource", "capability", and "competence" are used interchangeably. They represent the tangible and intangible assets of the firm in developing strategies. Tangible resources include factors containing financial or physical value as measured by the firm's balance sheet. Intangible assets, or strategic assets, include factors that are non-financial or non-physical (or non-financial) in nature and are rarely firm's balance sheet (Hamel, 2000; Afuah & Tucci, 2001; Galbreath, 2005). Capability is broad concept with many elements and attributes. It includes skills of employees and the abilities and expertise of the top management layers (O'Regan & Ghobadian, 2004). Dynamic capabilities are processes that use resources to integrate, reconfigure, gain and release resources matching market change (Eisenhardt & Martin, 2000). Core competencies form the higher level than capabilities and resources. Core competencies are particular processes in firm that play major part in forms existence (Schwaningar & Flaschka, 1995). There are two main reference points against which capabilities can be calibrated to check their potential to become core: the competitive environment and the business mission of the firm which is also relevant for identifying core capabilities (Andreu & Ciborra, 1996). The cross functional teams, human resources, skilled personal teams also contribute a firms capabilities. Human resources are one of the important capabilities of the firm (Schwaningar and Flaschka, 1995).

Channel

"Channel" is the way a firm goes to the market and how it actually reaches its customers (Osterwalder & Pigneur, 2002; Hamel, 2000). There are two categories: direct channel and indirect channel. *Direct channel* involves use of internet and ICT which made new ways of reaching the customer and avoiding geographical barriers, whereas *indirect channel* is the use of intermediaries, retails middlemen (Matear, Gray, & Irving, 2000; Bharat, 1999). Channel support also includes aspects of sales force training, technical assistance, marketing know-how, promotional support, after sales service (Matear et al., 2000). It is essential to have multiple distribution channels to provide multiple ways of marketing, including more customer segments, can focus more on target markets (Bharat, 1999). Consumers on the web are getting smarter in using e-tailers for convenience and comparison-shopping, and the provision of online cost and quality comparisons, customer responses, etc. in company webs can attract customers (Baharat, 1999).

Partner Networks

According to Hamel (2000), *"partners are supply critical components to final products"*. E-business models depend on partners to maximize return on capital. Partnerships help firms to lower costs and strengthen market positions, and can take the form of integrated relations or strategic alliances, service contracting or online platforms (Osterwalder & Pigneur, 2002). E-business provides an electronic internet based platform to allow collaboration through the sharing of data, information and knowledge (Du Plessis & Boon, 2004). Partnering strategies aim at achieving mutual benefits through a coordinated effort. The Internet channel provides firms with superior marketing strategies to market its products and services through partner networks, allow collaboration with employees and its supplier partners through electronic Internet based platforms (Du Plessis & Boon, 2004).

Revenue and Pricing

Revenue and Pricing define the economic structure for a firm. Revenue sources mainly depend on the pricing mechanism, i.e. a firm's ability to identify various sources of revenue implemented through a variety of pricing mechanisms (Morris et al., 2005; Linder & Cantrell, 2000). A revenue model refers to the specific ways in which an E-business model enables revenue generation, describes the logic of what, when, how and why the company receives compensation in return for the products. Rappa (2003) identified a variety of e-business models where each signifies different kinds of revenue models and hence there exists a variety of revenue sources which firms can use.

Pricing determines the profits for the value offered. Firm needs a comprehensive pricing plan in which all the key component areas like price timing, price execution, price control, price setting and price implementation, value added mechanisms are included. The value-added component in pricing is demonstrated in four areas: product availability, form utility, the level of research and development, and quality (Lancioni, 2005).

Customer Value

Customer value is a major area where an e-business model is relevant. Customer value is considered central to competitive advantage and long-term success of business organisations (Khalifa, 2004). The value of customer satisfaction is particularly important in case of services that are intangible.

Value-based/value-focused strategies increase likelihood of success for firms from this perspective. Here, customer value means the factors *trust, loyalty,* and *quality*:

1. *Trust*: Depends on customer's view that the service provider's service meets their expectations. Human aspects (customers) form the core in all virtual organisations that conduct e-business through ICT, networks and knowledge. One of the important element here is trust and confidence, which are intimately linked to consumers' rights, like identification, authentication, privacy, and confidentiality (Mezgar, 2003).

2. *Loyalty*: Loyalty and profits are strongly linked to customer value. Customers are loyal to a company as long as it offers them superior value compared to its competitor (Khalifa, 2004). Changes in the market environment can quickly alter prices and technologies, but close relationships with loyal customers can last a lifetime.

3. *Quality*: Customer relationships depend on how well a product or service measure up to the customer's original quality expectations. Quality is regarded as one of the few means for service differentiation and competitive advantage.

IT capabilities help in raising the level of trust by dealing with security issues. Data mining, use of database for customer activity and data analysis helps in selecting target customers, building relations with customers (Sigala, 2005).

Implementation

Implementation involves organisational *structure*, information *systems*, and *people* in the firms:

1. *Structure*: Organisational structure creates the infrastructure to support the implementation of decisions. Within e-business, the organisational structure is short-lived. Afuah & Tucci (2001) characterise organisational structure as being mainly organic (skilled, technical personal at higher level are present), and mechanistic (designers talk directly with marketing personnel).

2. *Systems*: Systems must be in place for information to flow. Within a firm, various kinds of systems exist, such as the critical information flow systems. Information systems and ICT systems are part of organisational form (Lyons, 2005).

3. *People*: Includes employees, consumers and other actors. It is important for firms to acquiring skilled personnel and to reward employees (Afuah & Tucci, 2001). Stakeholder value advocates a belief that a firm has social responsibilities that go beyond shareholder value creation to encompass other stakeholders such as employees, consumers, and society at large.

Interconnections

So far, we have explained e-business models, and their constituent parts – the components. Using the identified components and their values described in the previous section, we can now identify the interconnections between them. The term "value block" will be used to address both value proposition and value chain. The concept hence includes all the key activities that enable a value creation process. The remainder of this chapter will introduce 11 e-business model component interconnections.

Mission – Target Market

Mission refers to target market for which the value is proposed (Afuah & Tucci, 2001, Osterwalder & Pigneur, 2002; Morris et al., 2005). Through the mission value "business landscape", the ground is set for where a firm wants to launch a product. This requires creative thinking or business concept innovation (Hamel, 2000). When selecting the target market, market orientation is necessary (Blesa & Bigneu, 2005). Through product segments, firms can focus on which segments it can compete with its business concept (Afuah & Tucci, 2001). Market orientation helps in understanding the business environment of the product segment in which a firm wants to compete. It also leads the acquisition of capabilities and resources based on the information obtained (Blesa & Bigneu, 2005; Pech & Slade, 2004).

Mission – Value Block

As explained, "value block" contains both value chain and value proposition. Value propositions are offered to selected product segments, characterized mainly by customer relationships, as these are the heart of business. The cost element determines the efforts behind developing products. Based on the cost element, firms can propose value combinations of high or low cost to target customers (Osterwalder & Pigneur, 2002; Linder & Cantrell, 2000). Framing a firms mission also depend on value chain activities (Pateli & Giaglis, 2004; Afuah & Tucci, 2001; Osterwalder & Pigneur, 2002; Hamel, 2000). The value's associated with a value chain are linkages, dynamic view, visibility, and mirroring capability. All these factors shape a firm's value chain and must be considered in drawing firm's mission (Rayport & Sviokla, 1999).

Mission – Capabilities and Resources

A firm's capabilities and resources component depends on its mission. The business mission is also relevant for identifying core capabilities (Galbreath, 2005; O'Regan & Ghobadian, 2004; Andreu & Ciborra, 1996). The processes, positions and paths within dynamic capabilities help firms to coordinate personnel, suppliers, and decisions based on its processes of technologies, infrastructure, and routines. Environmental changes helps in keeping track of target markets and accordingly acquiring new skills, personnel. Core competencies are the key processes capabilities of firm that are not possessed by its competitors. Effective teams are made based on environmental changes.

Value Block – Capabilities and Resources

Capabilities and resources are crucial to for all types of value chain activities since they shape products/services (Galbreath, 2005; O'Regan & Ghobadian, 2004). The value chain component depends on capabilities and resources in acquiring personnel, skills, and teams. The dynamic capabilities, effective teams, core competencies and environmental changes or market changes through ICT's collectively affect the value proposition. The network of suppliers, buyers and firm coalitions amplify firm's resources and this is called a value network (Hamel, 2000). As explained, capabilities and resources are important in delivering new value propositions evolved from value chain activities.

Value Chain – Partner Networks

Partner networks enable value chain activities within the value block, and also to magnify value propositions to customers (Tapscott, 1999; Hamel,

2000; Jones, Chonko, & Roberts, 2003). The main factor that drives the relation between partner networks and the value chain is mutual benefits (Hamel, 2000). The processes and paths within the value chain help create new partnerships and to switch to multiple alternative with changing market environment.

Value Proposition – Revenue and Pricing

As explained in the target market to value proposition relation, converting value proposition into income requires an understanding of the revenue and pricing mechanisms. Price setting for a product can be decided by obtaining price sensitivity through customer factors and customer relationship management. Dynamic pricing mechanisms are applied based on market share, type of firm, product or service type. New value propositions arrived from virtual value chains can be source of gaining revenues. The pricing and revenue for value propositions offered to target markets depend on kinds of distribution channels (Afuah & Tucci, 2001; Rappa, 2003).

Channel – Value Block

Channel helps a value chain in finding suitable suppliers, and provides faster communication through convenience and comparison factors (Bharat, 1999; Matear, 2000). New distribution channels (e-tails, hybrid channels) have enabled new forms of businesses, and also different types of transition, in delivering new value chains formed from value deconstruction (Timmers, 1998; Bharat, 1999). Raising customer confidence in buying products also helps a firm to propose value to a greater number of customers.

Target Market – Value Proposition

The primary function of an e-business model is to articulate a value proposition which requires preliminary definition of what the product offering will be and in what form the customer may use it. This requires specification of the market segment component, as well as understanding revenue sources, pricing mechanisms (Afuah & Tucci, 2001; Rappa, 2003). It help in transforming value propositions into steady income (Brunn, Jensen, & Skovgard, 2002). The interconnection mainly depends on the customer relationships and cost element through proper orientation of market and selected market segments.

Mission – Customer Value

Customer priorities are essential for setting a firm's mission. Selecting target market, understanding customer needs, and accumulation of processes, skills and activities are based on customer priorities and thereby value creation. This is how firms approach mission to value creation in accordance with customer needs (Dumas & Blodgett, 1999; Farquhar & Langmann, 1999). Trust is important, as well as loyalty.

Value Block – Customer Value

Customer value is a scale by which all other elements of an e-business model will evaluate and align themselves. Value propositions offered online mainly depend on trust, loyalty and quality (Khalifa, 2004; Afuah & Tucci, 2001; Farquhar & Langmann, 1999). One of the major concerns in conducting business online is dealing with security; trust in transactions over the Internet. Ensuring secure transactions, using security technologies, services and measures are essential in raising the level of trust (Mezgar, 2003). Quality of value can be improved through e.g. ICT capabilities, and efficient logistics. Customers will be loyal to a firm as long as it delivers value through safe secure transactions and superior quality.

Mission – Implementation

Implementation mainly depends on organisational structure (Afuah & Tucci, 2001). ICT and IS significantly impact and are formed by the organisation. When setting the mission, a firm must define its structure (centralized, decentralized, outsourcing some of its functions), systems (transaction based systems, information flow systems, ICT systems etc) and people (employees, skilled personnel). Through the business landscape and market orientation, firms can decide what organisational structure is needed for value creation, what systems to include, and what kind of people that are needed for delivering value to these target markets (Pech & Slade, 2004).

Framework

The analysis of the e-business model components and their interconnections has resulted in a framework in the form of a model displaying the connections between the clustered components (see Figure 1). The idea is to show how value is created and added at each component level.

The mission component shows the business strategy, goal and core competences, as well as target markets and capabilities and resources needed. It also describes the organisational structure and how the systems and processes are implemented. These things can be encompassed through the business landscape and creative thinking. Only when these aspects have been properly clarified, other components can be identified and defined. In the Value block, the value chain activities containing all the key processes for constructing value is added at each level. New value propositions can be obtained through virtual value chains. It heavily depends on the core processes and designs, in accordance with market dynamics. Value chains can be stable when all their activities are strongly linked to delivering the value proposition.

Figure 1. Framework for e-business model component interconnections and values

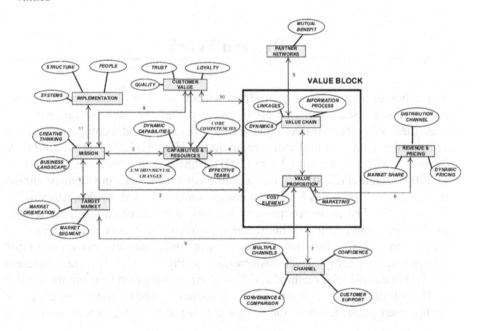

Through customer value, firms gain insights on trust, quality and loyalty factors by which activities are constantly monitored. With changing customer perceptions and environmental changes, organisations try to deliver new value propositions or modify their existing products. Thus, as value propositions change, new pooling of resources, dynamic capabilities, and effective teams are needed. Partner networks help in creating new value propositions, and to market value propositions through partners to enter into new markets. Organisations must effectively market their value propositions to target markets, magnifying the value to customer segments. The value offered will depend on e.g. cost elements in developing the product and marketing costs. There are various distribution channels for delivering value. New value chains and value propositions will be sources of revenues. Successful implementation of systems requires a good organisational structure. Based on firm offerings and missions, as well as impacted by ICT, the structure is selected. Skilled personnel at all levels are collectively responsible for a firm's success.

The framework is useful in viewing critical success factors associated with each e-business model component, as well as dependencies between these components. Interconnections show 'fit', i.e. how each component depends on other component(s), and the order in which each component is defined based on the factors associated with them. It may also help firms to assess their essential components and what IS to adopt based on their type of e-business model.

Related Work

There has been considerable progress within the area of e-business models, even though research in this area started rather recently. So far, we have identified only a few sources considering e-business model components, their relationships and role. Examples include: Hamel (2000), Osterwalder & Pigneur (2002), Afuah and Tucci (2001), Shafer et al. (2005), and Morris et al. (2005). Hamel (2000) provides a framework for describing business model components. It contains four main components, each subdivided into smaller components. The main components are linked by three connections termed as "bridge components". This framework provides a very detailed view of each component, but relationships are only shown between major components, at a high level. Osterwalder & Pigneur (2002) state e-business model issues and relationships and base their ontology on four pillars, similar to Hamel. Each pillar contains other components. The relationships are given within each pillar, i.e. how the elements in a pillar relate, as well as connect the pillars to one another. However, relationships are shown only within and between pillars. Afuah & Tucci (2001) describe that firms will be able to determine which components and linkages that are strong or weak compared to those of their competitors by raising the quality of linkage between components. Still, it is unclear how link quality can be raised, and how component affect one another.

Shafer et al. (2005) used an affinity diagram to show business model components, while also defining a successful business model. The affinity diagram is based on components from 12 business models. The approach is helpful when classifying and clustering components, but does not clarify interconnections between them. Based on similar considerations, Morris et al. (2005) identified six components in e-business models, and propose a three-level framework with six decision areas at each level. They neither discuss interconnections.

Overview of Results

This research has provided an overview of currently available and successful e-business model definitions. We have pointed out an agreed set of components based on literature and the identified taxonomy of components (Table 1), as well as values associated with each component. Interconnections have been shown based on values. The framework presented includes components, values and interconnections. The contributions of our work can be summarised as follows:

1. *Overview of e-business models*: details what an e-business model is, what it constitutes, potential actors, and purpose, based on an extensive literature review.

2. *Framework for e-business model components and their interconnections*: the framework deals with e-business model components, their possible classification and associated values, and interconnections.

In conclusion, e-business model research grows at a fast pace. Many traditional business models have already changed to "e-readiness", and technological sophistication is seen in all processes and areas of e-business models. From our overview, it is clear that definitions vary from revenue sources and profit generation to the strategy perspective and architecture. It is also evident from the comparison between different researchers that e-business model decomposition has varied greatly. Components are made up from values, which raise the quality of interconnections between components. Through the e-business model component framework, components and connections are shown using the value flow. Value is added to product at each level of component and the fit between components in adding this value to product depend on corresponding component values or factors.

References

Afuah, A., & Tucci, C. (2001). *Internet business models and strategies: Text and cases*. New York: McGraw Hill.

Alt, R., & Zimmerman, H. (2001). Introduction to special section-business models. *Electronic Markets, 11*(1), 3-9.

Andreu, R., & Ciborra, C. (1996). Organisational learning and core capabilities development: The role of IT. *The Journal of Strategic Information Systems, 5*(2), 111-127.

Bharat, R. (1999). The internet and the revolution in distribution: A cross-industry examination. *Technology in Society, 21*(3), 287-306.

Blesa, A., & Bigné, E. (2005). The effect of market orientation on dependence and satisfaction of dyadic relationships. *Marketing Intelligence and Planning, 23*(3), 249-265.

Brunn, P., Jensen, M., & Skovgard, J. (2002). e-Marketplaces: Crafting a winning strategy. *European Management Journal, 20*(3), 286-298.

Chang, E. K. (2005). Business use of the Internet, a longitudinal study from a value chain perspective. *Industrial Data and Management Systems, 105*(1), 82-95.

Davis, P. B. (2004). *e-Business*. USA: Palgrave Publications.

Dumas, C., & Blodgett, M. (1999). Articulating values to inform decision making: Lessons from family firms around the world. *International Journal of Value-Based Management, 12*, 209-221.

Eisenhardt, K., & Martin, J. (2000). Dynamic capabilities: what are they? *Strategic Management Journal, 21*(10–11), 1105-1121.

Farquhar, B. J., & Langmann, G. (1998). Consumer needs in global electronic commerce: The role of standards in addressing consumer concerns. *Electronic Markets, 8*(2), 9-12.

Galbreath, J. (2005). Which resources matter the most to firm success? An exploratory study of resource-based theory. *Technovation, 25*(9), 979-987.

Hamel, G. (2000). *Leading the revolution*. Boston, USA: Harvard Business School Press.

Hayes, J., & Finnegan, P. (2005). Assessing the of potential of e-business models: Towards a framework for assessing the decision-makers. *European Journal of Operational Research, 160*, 365-379.

Hedman, J., & Kalling, T. (2003). The business model concept: Theoretical underpinnings and empirical illustrations. *European Journal of Information Systems, 12*, 49-59.

Jones, E., Chonko, L. B., & Roberts, J. A. (2003). Creating a partnership oriented knowledge creation culture in strategic sales alliances: A conceptual framework. *Journal of Business & Industrial Marketing, 18*(4/5), 336-352.

Khalifa, A. S. (2004). Customer value: A review of recent literature and an integrative configuration. *Management Decision, 42*(5), 645-666.

Lancioni, R. A. (2005). A strategic approach to industrial product pricing: The pricing plan. *Industrial Marketing Management, 34*(2), 177-183.

Larsen, G. (2000). Component based enterprise rrameworks. *Communications of the ACM, 43*(10), 25-26.

Linder, J. C., & Cantrell, S. (2000). *Changing business models: Surveying the landscape*, Working Paper, Accenture Institute for Strategic Change.

Lyons, M. H. (2005). Future ICT systems-understanding the business drivers. *BT Technology Journal, 23*(3), 11-23.

Martinez, P. (2000). *Models made "e": What business are you in?* Centers for IBM e-business Innovation.

Matear, S., Gray, B., & Irving, G. (2000). What makes a good export channel relationship? *Asia Pacific Journal of Management, 17*, 539-559.

Mezgár, I. (2003). Role of trust in networked production systems. *Annual Reviews in Control, 27*, 247-254.

Morris, M., Schindehutte, M., & Allen, J. (2005). The entrepreneur's business model: Toward a unified perspective. *Journal of Business Research, 58*, 726-735.

Nordberg, M., Campbell, A., & Verbeke, A. (2003). Using customer relationships to acquire technological innovation: A value-chain analysis of supplier contracts with scientific research institutions. *Journal of Business Research, 56*(9), 711-719.

O'Regan, N., & Ghobadian, A. (2004). The importance of capabilities for strategic direction and performance. *Management Decision, 42*(2), 292-312.

Osterwalder, A., & Pigneur, Y. (2002). An ebusiness model ontology for modeling ebusiness, *15th Bled Electronic Commerce Conference-eReality: Constructing the eEconomy,* Bled, Slovenia, June 17-19.

Ott, J. (2000). Defining a value proposition for information security...The complete picture. *Information Systems Security, 9*(4).

Pateli, A., & Giaglis, M. (2004). A research framework for analyzing ebusiness models. *European Journal of Information Systems, 13*, 302-314.

Pech, R. J., & Slade, B. W. (2004). Manoeuvre theory: Business mission process for high intensity conflict. *Management Decision, 42*(8), 987-1000.

Du Plessis, M., & Boon, J. B. (2004). Knowledge management in ebusiness and customer relationship management: South African case study findings. *International Journal of Information Management, 24,* 73–86.

Rappa, M. (2003). Business models on the Web. *Managing the Digital Enterprise.* Retrieved May 2, 2003, from http://digitalenterprise.org

Rayport, J. F., & Sviokla, J. J. (1999). Creating value in the network economy, In Tapscott Don (Ed.), *Harvard Business Review.* USA.

Schwaninger, M., & Flaschka, M. (1995). Intelligent organizations: Building core competencies through information systems. *Electronic Markets, 16–17,* 6-8.

Shafer, S. M., Smith, J. H., & Linder, J. C. (2005). The power of business models. *Business Horizons, 48,* 199-207.

Sigala, M. (2005). Integrating customer relationship management in hotel operations: Managerial and operational implications. *Hospitality Management, 24,* 391–413.

Tapscott, D. (1999). *The digital economy: Promise and peril in the age of networked intelligence.* USA: McGraw Hill.

Timmers, P. (1998). Business models for electronic markets. *Electronic Markets, 8*(2), 3-8.

Walters, D. (2004). New economy new business models – new approaches. *International Journal of Physical Distribution & Logistics Management, 34*(3-4), 219-229.

Chapter XIV

Experiences from Technology Transfer Initiatives at SISU

Janis Bubenko Jr., Royal Institute of Technology and Stockholm University, Sweden

Eva Lindencrona, VINNOVA (Swedish Governmental Agency for Innovation Systems), Sweden

Abstract

The institute SISU (Swedish Institute for Systems Development) was formed by the Swedish govermnet in 1984 based on the support of more than 20 organisations in business, industry and in the civic sector. SISU operated during 1985 to 2000. In this chapter we reflect on our experiences from this initiative to technology transfer in Sweden in the field of information systems development tools and methods. We are concerned with transfer of knowledge as well as of technical prototypes from academic research to product development, exploitation, and practical use in organisations. We reflect over a number of collaborative projects, national as well as EU-supported, initiated by SISU. We describe, firstly, which were the main "products" of technology transfer, and, secondly, which are the main factors that influence (or hinder) the success of a technology transfer initiative of this kind. The purpose of writing this chapter is to contribute to the experiences of the European Commission of successful technology transfer activities in Europe.

Introduction

Sweden's first university department in information systems was established in 1966. Research on methods and tools for information systems development started almost immediately, primarily by the research groups CADIS and ISAC. Research as well as publication activities of these and other groups during the seventies has been extensively described in the 40th anniversary book, published by the department (Bubenko, Jansson, Koller, Ohlin, & Yngström, 2006). University research in Sweden started to grow during the seventies. Several persons in organisations in business, industry as well as in the public sector showed a considerable interest in this research. In the early eighties the situation had matured so much that a question could be formulated: can knowledge and technology transfer from university research to practical application be somehow facilitated and enhanced?

In this chapter we reflect on our experiences from an initiative to technology transfer in the field of information systems in Sweden. We are concerned with transfer of knowledge as well as of technical prototypes from academic research to product development, exploitation, and practical use in organisations. Our experiences emanate from our work in SISU – the Swedish Institute for Systems Development. SISU was formed in 1984 and existed until the end of 2000. In this chapter we wish to describe, firstly, which are the main "products" of technology transfer, and, secondly, which are the main factors that influence (or hinder) the success of a technology transfer initiative.

Background

SISU was formed in 1984 as a result of an initiative by SYSLAB (the SYStems development LABoratory at the department of computer and systems science,

KTH and Stockholm University). Instrumental in this process was SYSLAB's industrial advisory group.[1] Leading researchers from SYSLAB together with the advisory group contacted a large number of Swedish organisations in order to obtain financial support for forming a research foundation. A considerable support was obtained. A "supporting user and partner organisation" called ISVI[2] (Intressentföreningen för SVensk Informationssystemutveckling) was established with 21 organisations and companies as members. SISU's research plans for the first three years, 1985 – 87, were worked out and documented in a "Framework Program" (ramprogram). All members of ISVI guaranteed to support SISU's research according to the Framework Program.

The Swedish government decided in the autumn of 1984 to establish the operation of the industry research institute SISU starting January 1st, 1985. SISU was initially financed by STU[3] and by ISVI. The 1985 budget of SISU was about 8 MSEK. Thirteen researchers[4] were transferred from SYSLAB to SISU in January 1985. In its "peak era" (1990 – 1993) SISU had about 35 supporting organisations, an annual turnover of about 35 million Swedish crowns, and a staff of about 40 employees. SISU continued its operations until 2000, during the last two years as part of a research company Framkom. The foundation had a concluding passive period 2000 – 2004. SISU's managing directors were Janis Bubenko (1985 – 1992), Thomas Falk (1992 – 1994), Eva Lindencrona (1995 – 1998) and Mikael von Otter (1998 – 2000).

SISU's Mission and Initial Work Areas

The main goal of the SISU institute was to act as a technology transfer engine between academic research and practical application. By this we mean that SISU should take in ideas, knowledge and software prototypes developed in academia and further develop and package them so that their usefulness could be demonstrated in practical situations. It was our hope that this demonstration would stimulate commercial organisations to "take over", or "productify" the knowledge, method or prototype for further development and exploitation. SISU's areas of activity were determined in a "framework program" which was approved by the supporting organisation ISVI. It is natural that this first set of directions of SISU coincided very much with the research areas pursued by SYSLAB.

SISU's main areas of activity during the first years were:

1.   The Information Centre (information dissemination, education),

2.   Management of Information and Data Resources,

3.   Methods and Tools for Problem-oriented Systems Development,

4.   Interactive Systems – Office Information Systems.

The task of the first area was to disseminate information about SISU's research as well as information about other international research activities and results applicable in Sweden. This was essentially a "knowledge transfer" activity. It included seminars and courses. Courses could be open to all or they could be given to particular organisations.

The second area had the goal to exploit one of SYSLAB's strong and internationally well known assets: conceptual modelling as an activity in the information systems development process.

The third area dealt with CASE tool development. SYSLAB had developed an idea to build a graphics oriented "meta-tool", i.e. a tool by which CASE-tools for particular methods could be built. This meta-tool was called RAMATIC. As the members of ISVI were using different methods, this activity was expected to be beneficial to all supporting organisations.

The fourth area dealt with development of a prototype for developing distributed object management systems. The prototype was called OPAL. OPAL should be used for quick implementation of interactive systems, at this time called "office information systems".

Initial Technology Transfer – the First Three Years

The information Centre was perhaps the easiest to instigate. SISU's personnel were active in a comparatively large network of international researchers and centres. Colleagues appreciated visiting SISU and share their knowledge in a number of topic areas, such as office information systems, databases, conceptual modelling, CASE technology, Artificial Intelligence, and Software Engineering. Seminars and courses organised by SISU were well attended. SISU did also organise company-specific education on a number of topics. For instance, SISU was responsible for a 10 week course in modern IT, involving several of the topics mentioned above, for the company ABB in Västerås. This particular course was carried out in close cooperation with DSV, the department of Computer and Systems Science. Additional "products" of the centre was the monthly magazine "SISU Informa" and the report series "SISU Analys".[5] These publications were distributed to all supporting organisations.

The conceptual modelling area generated a number of advisory and consulting activities as well as modelling courses. In the consulting activities SISU personnel and persons from organisations collaborated in practical design and development of systems. This resulted in knowledge transfer in several practical applications. Also a modelling language SIMOL was developed. A considerable number of modelling projects were initiated where SISU personnel took a leading and tutoring role. Modelling was primarily done in the health management sector with the purpose to improve patient information exchange. These projects pointed out the difficulty in transferring modelling knowledge to laymen. On the other hand, this work improved SISU's competence in participatory modelling, to be a few years later used in collaborative national as well as in EU-supported projects. It also acted as a door-opener to join a number of EU-projects. Furthermore, SISU's modelling approach was later picked up by a number of private consultancy companies who adjusted and packaged the research results into commercial method-products.

The idea of creating a CASE "meta-tool" was born in the early eighties. This project was called RAMATIC. It exploited both our modelling knowledge and an earlier academic product – the associative database management system of CS4 (Berild & Nachmens, 1977). The problem was that we underestimated the complexity of the venture to build such a meta-tool. Furthermore, the computer and software technology in the mid eighties was not ready for such an effort. For instance, no windowing techniques existed on the computers. Another problem was that we started building the meta-tool not using object-oriented technology. The technology was not mature enough at this time. An additional difficulty was that we were too optimistic to find potential producers and exploiters of this tool. To make it a robust and user friendly product would require both more advanced computer and software technology and personnel resources in the range of several hundred person-years. Consequently, we did not manage to find an organisation that was willing to take such a risk. On the positive side we can mention that, at the end of the three year period, we could apply the tool to practical cases in some companies, e.g. Volvo Car and Televerket (now Telia). We can also report that RAMATIC later became used in a number of collaborative EU-projects for building experimental CASE-tools for particular methods developed in these projects. In a sense one can say that the CASE tools and SISU's knowledge of building such tools was one of the roots for SISU's early and successful participation in several EU projects. For instance the meta-tool was used in project TEMPORA and in project F3.[6] Some collaboration with the university of Jyväskylä was also initiated regarding meta-tool technology (Rossi et al., 1992).

The fourth activity involved building an extremely complex software system. Significant resources were assigned to developing a prototype for software development in the area of distributed, interactive office information systems. The prototype was designed to make use of recent advances in hardware, software and communications technologies. Ideas implemented in this prototype were novel. It was an object-oriented system architecture that could define, create, and manage active objects in a distributed environment. It demonstrated system properties that can be seen in full operation today, e.g. workflow systems, CSCW-systems, and objects with properties similar to cookies, viruses, and "spy-ware". This kind of objects were discussed by the originators of the object-oriented OPAL system before we even had heard of Personal Computers, Windows, workstations, the World Wide Web and all its peculiarities. At the late eighties, on the other hand, no Swedish organisation could be found, willing to take the economic risk to make a product out of these prototypical ideas. Some ideas of OPAL are described in (Ahlsen, Björnerstedt, & Hulten, 1985)

During this period planning for collaborative projects was initiated. Six working groups, staffed by employees of SISU and of ISVI, used a large part of 1985 to analyse the need for research in systems development among the companies and organisations of ISVI. A number of project proposals were presented to the members of ISVI. It was decided that six of the proposals should eventually be initiated. Later a permanent technical advisory committee of ISVI was formed. The committee, staffed by ISVI experts, would give advice to leading researchers of SISU regarding its research programme.

Another interesting activity that we proposed in 1985 was to use the electronic conferencing system KOM (on DSV's Digital Equipment DEC 20/20 computer) for communication between SISU and its supporting organisations, and among themselves too. This was more than five years ahead of the start of internet. Unfortunately our initiative failed, mainly due to problems with equipment compatibility.

At this stage it is probably reasonable to ask – was SISU's first framework program too optimistic? Should the transfer problems not have been anticipated? The initial framework program, where the above research areas and tasks were described, was accepted by the supporting organisation ISVI without any serious critique. How could this happen? There are at least two reasons. Firstly, we did perhaps not bother ourselves to sufficiently well examine the critical question: can this be done with available time and resources? In our enthusiasm, we did not want to hear anything that might reduce our ambitions. The second is that ISVI-people perhaps did not always understand the complexity of the tasks we were proposing, but they trusted us and they wanted to believe us. We conclude this section, nevertheless, that, even if the prototypes themselves were not turned into products, they served as concrete ideas and tools for knowledge transfer and introduced new ways of thinking and new methods in the ISVI group of companies and organizations.

Succeeding Projects and Transfer Initiatives

After 1988 SISU continued to generate and carry out a large number of national as well as international, collaborative projects where the supporting organisations from ISVI and European enterprises took an active part. Collaborative projects can be seen as one of the most efficient ways of knowledge transfer. It is important to note that the transferring of knowledge is bidirectional. Knowledge created in research projects was introduced in the collaborative projects. Knowledge of practical problems and requirements was observed in the same projects and at the same time new, shared knowledge was created. In the sequel we describe some national as well as some international (within the EU framework) projects.

National Projects

One national project is TRIAD that generated a vast amount of knowledge of business modelling in organisations. This was essentially a follow-up project of area 2 above. The technology to be transferred was not a software product, but rather a particular business modelling method – participatory modelling. The main actors in the project were Statskontoret, Sweden Post, Televerket, and Ericsson. The project was, however, open for additional participants from ISVI. More than 100 persons from ISVI organisations took part in different knowledge generating activities of TRIAD thus supporting and carrying out the transfer of modelling knowledge. The concrete products of <TRIAD were a large number of training seminars in business and information modelling and a vast number of handbooks and guidelines for various aspects of business modelling. TRIAD also produced a by-product: a very easy to use, simple Macintosh based graphical modelling tool called Business Modeller. Regretfully, Business Modeller was not exploited outside the TRIAD project.

The HYBRIS project generated a hypertext-based tool that allows inexperienced computer users to navigate in and retrieve information from large corporate databases at a conceptual level. The information in the databases is represented in a conceptual model, called an information map. By pointing and clicking directly in the information map, users can retrieve

Figure 1. The mangement group of TRIAD: Hans Willars SISU, Teddy Hector, Sweden Post, Ingemar Dahlstrand, Ericsson, Sören Lindh, Statskontoret, Åsa Laestadius, Televerket (now Telia), Stig Berild, SISU, Björn Norén, Televerket, and Bertil Andersson, Televerket (project manager). Ulf Åsen, Sweden Post, Björn Nilsson, Peter Rosengren, and Lars Bergman, SISU are missing in the picture.

information from the databases. Constraints that restrict the information search can be formulated. The graphical query is then translated to SQL (Structured Query Language) and sent to the database. The result of the SQL-query is brought back to the HYBRIS tool where the users have different alternatives for manipulating the result. HYBRIS became practically applied, in particular at Televerket (Swedish Telecom).

Effective IT is the name of a fairly large, two-year, umbrella-project run 1993 – 95. It was initiated by a preliminary study project ordered by Sweden's ministry of industry and business and by NUTEK. The aim of Effective IT was to investigate the possibility to define a national research program for improved and more effective use of IT in Swedish business and industry. Five subprojects were carried out: 1) Improving the quality of systems development, 2) Management of legacy systems, 3) Economy and Management of IT, 4)

Tools for business development and modelling, and 5) Business communication and EDI. Effective IT involved a large number of supporting organisations.

A two-year joint project, The Electronic Newspaper, with partners Dagens Nyheter, Telia, Instititet för Medieteknik, and SISU analysed new possibilities for producing and interacting with a newspaper enabled by advances in computing, communication, and media technology. The project resulted in a prototype newspaper with advanced possibilities for searching of information and for communication between readers.

The project E-society (2004 – 2006) concerned various topics deemed relevant for the society in the future, such as internet services, information noise, privacy, and security. The project was partly financed by SISU and carried out at the Santa Anna IT Research Institute AB.

International Projects

One of the distinguishing initiatives of SISU was its participation in the European strategic programme for research and development in information technologies (ESPRIT). Also non-EU countries, but belonging to the European Economic Area[7] were invited to participate in the ESPRIT 2 programme at their own cost.[8] SISU understood very early the scientific, technological, and the economic importance of joining the ESRPRIT programme. Work on forming of consortia and on preparing project proposals started in 1987.

In 1988 the KIWIS proposal, with SISU as partners, was awarded EU-support for 3,5 years starting Jan. 1st, 1989. The goal of KIWIS was to develop a knowledge-base system to support sophisticated applications requiring complex operations on data and knowledge, possibly located in other systems, i.e. a federated database architecture. KIWIS started an era of SISU where several more EU-projects were awarded. A greater part of SISU personnel became part time engaged in European collaborative project work. During the period from late eighties until the year 2000 SISU participated in more than ten EU-supported projects, These projects pursued a number of advanced topics, such as, temporal-deductive information modelling, multi-media object management, accessing information in heterogeneous corporate databases, advanced techniques in requirements engineering, and several more topic areas.

These EU-projects considerably extended SISU's contacts with European companies as well as with research institutes and university departments. They significantly enlarged SISU's and our supporting organisations' knowledge and experience about systems development principles, approaches, and methods, including supporting tools. Our participation in European activities thus directly helped many of SISU's supporting organisations to prepare themselves for future collaboration in the European union. Last, but not least, these projects gave SISU improved financial means to engage young persons in advanced research activities leading to a higher academic degree as well as to prototypes and ideas about starting up own companies (see below).

Other International Activities

During a couple of years one of SISU's researchers (Stig Berild) was stationed in Silicon Valley as a member of the Swedish Technical Attaches in the US. Stig reported back to SISU's supporting companies valuable observations of the information technological development in the USA. Later Eva Lindencrona was during one year temporarily employed by the European Commission in Brussels. Eva's work in Brussels gave SISU and its

Figure 2. Project review meeting of the EU-project TEMPORA at SISU in ELECTRUM, Kista, 1990. TEMPORA included participants from Greece, UK, Belgium, Norway, and Sweden.

supporters valuable information about how the commission was performing strategic planning of research and development in the IT area as well as information about criteria for evaluation of project proposals.

Conferences

SISU personnel has been active in the Very Large Data Base conference series since its start in 1975. In 1985 SISU (together with DSV) were hosts of the VLDB-85 held in Stockholm (Vassiliou & Pirotte, 1985). A record number of more than 800 delegates attended the conference. Many of them were from industry, business, and the public sector. In 1989 and 1990 SISU took the initiative to arrange the first and second Nordic[9] Conference on Advanced Information Systems Engineering (CAiSE) (Nilsson 1989; Steinholtz et al., 1990). Both conferences were attended by a large number of international delegates making it a considerable achievement for SISU as well as for the Nordic countries. CAiSE has now developed into a very successful annual, international conference event, including large number of workshops, such as EMMSAD and REFSQ. Both VLDB and CAiSE should be seen as effective knowledge dissemination activities. Conferences also served as a means to introduce new technologies to business and public services. An example of this is a seminar organised by SISU in spring 1995 on internet services where Tim Berners-Lee presented the new WWW service. Another example is a series of seminars on "business intelligence" organised by SISU during 1996–97. New technology was demonstrated in the SISU laboratory. An example of that was the "live-board" computer initially developed by Xerox.

Academic Degrees

Already from the start of SISU an agreement was established with the department of Computer and Systems Science (DSV) to cooperate in the area of graduate education. Many SISU employees registered at DSV as PhD candidates. They did not receive any scholarships for their studies, but SISU was in general very concerned to allocate PhD candidates tasks which harmonised with their thesis works. Also their work load was, in critical thesis writing stages, adjusted to make it possible to complete the thesis. Senior staff at SISU gave considerable supervision and help to the PhD candidates regarding technical matters of their theses. PhD degrees have been awarded to more than 10 former employees of SISU.

Spin-off Companies – Knowledge Transferred into Commercial Products and Consulting Work

A number of spin-off companies have been created by people from SISU. Most of them are based on and exploitation of results from SISU's participation in EU projects. "Research is the transformation of money into knowledge and transformation of knowledge into money is innovation". Here are some samples of "Innovations" indirectly created by SISU.

NeoTech AB

In the late eighties – almost two decades after the relational models breakthrough in the database research field – commercial relational database systems were rapidly increasing their market shares. It was decided that the time had come to take relational database design methodology to the business scene in Sweden. In 1987, Christer Hultén and Lars Söderlund founded NeoTech and Stefan Britts joined a year later. NeoTech's expertise covers: 1) Tactical issues concerning business information requirements and the use and refinement of this information, 2) Methodology issues of classification, structuring and description of business information, and 3) Technical issues in database organization and in retrieval and communication of data in networks. NeoTech's clients include several large companies in Sweden.

CNet

CNet was established in 1995 by a research group within SISU (including Matts Ahlsén, Peter Rosengren, Stefan Paulsson, and Ulf Wingstedt) and became a separate company in 1998 to commercialise results from the EU-projects Intuitive and Multimedia Broker. These projects had developed graphic search interfaces for multimedia databases and multimedia services intended for electronic publishing. The separation resulted in a software product, which in 2006 is still an important part of the company's business. It was also an early application of XML technology. The company's core business is their own portfolio of products, together with a solid knowledge in information systems development with Internet technology. During the years, the company has developed a number of products focused on semantic knowledge-techniques.

Projectplace International AB

Projectplace International AB was founded in January, 1998 by Mattias Hällström, Magnus Ingvarsson and Peter Engstedt (prev. Johansson). The company is based on ideas developed within the European research project Coop-www in which the tool BSCW (Basic Support for Cooperative Work) was developed. Projectplace International develops and provides web services for those working in projects together with colleagues, customers and partners. The business concept is to improve efficiency and quality in project-oriented organizations by providing a web service that simplifies planning, implementation and follow-up of projects. The clients are project managers, IT departments and project-intensive organizations in private and public sector. The company has subsidiaries in Norway, Holland, Great Britain and Germany. Language-specific versions of the web service and locally adapted services are offered.

ALKIT Communications AB

ALKIT Communications AB is a small research oriented company bridging the gap between university research and practical applications. Results from the EU-supported project Intercare has been a starting point for this activity. The company was initiated by Lars-Åke Johansson, a former SISU employee, and a number of colleagues. ALKIT co-operates with many universities, e.g. Luleå Tekniska Högskola, KTH, CTH, and Karolinska Institutet, as well as with organisations in the private and in the civic sector, e.g. Volvo Cars, Volvo Aero, SAAB, Sandvik, Stockholms Läns Landsting, Socialstyrelsen, and several more. Areas of expertise are modelling and development of IT strategies, component based design, and synchronous video communication.

Concluding Comments

Traces of SISU' activities can today be found in several places and modern practices of Sweden. Firstly, SISU's leading role and documented experience in business and enterprise modelling has contributed to university education by establishment of new types of educational programs and courses. For instance, courses in participatory business modelling are available at the IT-university in Stockholm as well as in Skövde, and at Riga Technical University (Latvia). Secondly, methods and prototypes developed at SISU were some of the main ingredients in starting up the new spin-off companies (above). Thirdly, people from supporting organisations of SISU, who participated in the many collaborative national or international projects, transferred to their organisations new knowledge which eventually was integrated in the practices and methods of these organisations.

The knowledge transfer initiated by and carried out by SISU is, in retrospect, indeed substantial. Initially, making up our first framework program, we anticipated knowledge transfer to be of two kinds:

1.   Transfer of methods and method knowledge to practical use in organisations by education and training

Figure 3. The figure shows the cover of SISU's annual report to its supporting organisations in 1990/91. One of SISU's main ambitions at this time was to stimulate the participation of Swedish organisations and enterprises in collaborative projects of the Europen Union.

2.   Transfer of prototypes to existing organisations which then would turn
     them into practical products on the market

The first kind of transfer can be considered as successful while the second
kind of transfer largely was less immediately successful.

Transfer of knowledge about conceptual modelling and enterprise modelling
took place in most SISU projects (TRIAD, EU-projects). Many organisations in Sweden as well as abroad do now perform participatory modelling as
part of developing and IT-aligning their organisations. Modelling is also one
of the main services and products of most of the spin-off companies of SISU
(see above). It should, however, also be mentioned that transfer of modelling
knowledge has taken a considerable time. Modelling is something that
requires skills of abstraction as well as skills in facilitating group-work. It is
not the case that many people in business and industry are, initially, skilled in
these abilities. Nevertheless, we can now conclude that SISU's training
activities, conferencing activities, and running of collaborative projects
nationally as well as internationally, has significantly contributed to
awareness of and use of conceptual and enterprise modelling in many
organisations in Europe.

On the other hand, our intention to transfer of prototypes to existing
organisations which then would turn them into practical products on the
market was not immediately successful. Why was it so? We believe in the
following reasons:

- Very few IT people in industry and public service, by that time, had an
  academic degree in IT, and most often did not know what kind of
  results that could be expected from R&D.

- The cost of developing a marketable product is normally extremely high
  (perhaps in the range of several hundred person-years). Large Swedish
  IT-companies were not willing to make such a commitment.

- Making an advanced product also required extremely skilled and
  knowledgeable workers. These were not often at hand.

- Very few people in Sweden really understood and anticipated the value of
  prototypes developed by SISU. They were also unsure about the "practical
  need" of such a product. The "business value" of potential tools to be
  developed based on SISU prototypes were not very clear by that time.

- Productising a complex prototype for a market was a considerable risk.
  People in business also understood that Sweden was a too small market
  in order to productise the prototype. Their knowledge of how to
  approach foreign markets was not well developed at that time.

- One particular problem, that did not make contacts with business and industry simpler, was the case of "rotating people": people in organisations whom SISU had established close relations with were, in several cases, moved to other positions in their organisation. This lead to disrupted contacts with that organisation which took time and resources to restore.

What happened instead of the anticipated knowledge transfer as above, was that groups of SISU's own employees decided to take the risk of developing and making products of ideas and prototypes developed within SISU. Looking at the set of spin-off companies above, this kind of technology transfer was obviously successful. SISU played some role in supporting the formation of these companies. In some cases the company initiators could use large networks of contacts in Sweden developed during their time at SISU. In other cases SISU supported the employees with continued part time work during the formation stage of the companies.

In conclusion, our experience shows that in most cases the best "receiving organisations" in technology transfer situations are companies formed by the same people who developed the technology in the first hand.

A Comment on References – the SISU WEB-site

The main objective of SISU was to disseminate information and knowledge to organisations in Sweden. In order to make this knowledge transfer as efficient as possible, the Swedish language was chosen. Consequently, the primary aim of SISU's workers was not to strive for international publications in journals and conferences. Practically all material (reports, handbooks, etc.) produced were in Swedish. Between 300 and 400 reports were produced. About 250 of them are accessible on-line. This set includes also reports on SISU's research framework programs. The reader is directed to web-site http://www.sisuportal.com/, developed by CNet, where these reports and documents can be examined.

Dedication

This paper is dedicated to our friend Professor Benkt Wangler in connection with his retirement. As a SISU employee for 10 years, Benkt has primarily been responsible for information system development tool and method development at SISU. Benkt has been instrumental in several EU-projects of SISU, such as TEMPORA, Nature, MILORD, LYNX, HOD, and ESPITI, and also in EU-projects of DSV, ORES and HYPERBANK. These projects have resulted in a vast amount of publications by Benkt and colleagues as well as of a large number of Ph.D. works.

References

Ahlsen, M., Björnerstedt, A., & Hulten, C. (1985). OPAL: An object-based system for application developmen. *IEEE Database Engineering Bulletin*, *8*(4), 31-40.

Berild, S., & Nachmens, S. (1977). CS4 a tool for database design by infological simulation. *3rd International Conference on Very Large Data Bases*. Tokyo: IEEE Computer Society.

Bubenko, J. A. Jr., Jansson, C.-G., Kollerbaur, A., Ohlin, T., & Yngström, L. (Eds.) (2006). *ICT for people. 40 years of academic development in Stockholm*, Kista, Sweden: Department of Computer and Systems Sciences at Stockholm University and Royal Institute of Technology.

Nilsson, B. (Ed.) (1989). *The first Nordic Conference on Advanced Information Systems Engineering (CAiSE)*, Kista, Sweden: SISU.

Rossi, M., Gustafsson, M., Smolander, K., Johansson, L.-A., & Lyytinen, K. (1992). Metamodelling editor as a front end tool for a CASE shell. *CAiSE'92*, Manchester, UK: Springer Verlag.

Steinholtz, B., Sølvberg, A. & Bergman, L. (Eds.) (1990). *Second Nordic Conference on Advanced Information Systems Engineering (CAiSE'90)*. Kista, Sweden: Springer Verlag.

Vassiliou, Y. & Pirotte, A. (Eds.) (1985). *11th International Conference on Very Large Data Bases*. Morgan Kaufmann.

Endnotes

[1] Members of the group were Rune Brandinger (chair), Valand Insurance Co., Krister Gustavsson, Statskontoret, Gunnar Holmdahl, ASEA Information Systems, Göran Kling, Volvo-Data, Sten Martin, Swedish Defence, Per-Olov Persson, Riksdataförbundet, Sven-Erik Wallin, Esselte Datacenter, and Kurt Wedin, Vattenfall.

[2]   ISVI memebers in 1984 were: ASEA, DATALOGIC, DBK, ENEA, ERICSSON, FÖRSVARSSTABEN, GÖTABANKEN, IBM, INFOLOGICS, KOMMUNDATA, PROGRAMMATOR, SAAB-SCANIA, SE-BANKEN, SKANDIA, STATSKONSULT, STATSKONTORET, TELEVERKET, VALAND, VATTENFALL, VOLVO-DATA, AND VOLVO-PV.

[3]   STU – Styrelsen för Teknisk Utveckling (The Swedish Board for Technical Development).

[4]   These researchers were Matts Ahlsén, Peder Brandt, Stefan Britts, Janis Bubenko, Roland Dahl, Tord Dahl, Mats-Roger Gustavsson, Christer Hultén, Lars-Åke Johansson, Eva Lindencrona, Stefan Paulsson, Lars Söderlund, and Håkan Torbjär. SISU's first secretary was Marianne Sindler.

[5]   These reports had the ambition to give a popular introduction to complex, technological topics such as "Conceptual Modelling", "Graphical Tools for Systems Development", "ADA Technology", "Office Information Systems", etc.

[6]   A large number of technical working papers on RAMATIC were produced in these projects but they were, regretfully, never published.

[7]   Other countries of EEA at that time were Norway, Finland, Austria, Iceland, and Lichtenstein.

[8]   For Swedish participants of ESPRIT 2 the costs were absorbed by NUTEK, the follow-up organisation of STU.

[9]   The third and subsequent CAiSE conferences were denoted "International".

Chapter XV

On IT-Modelling in a Cross-Competence World

Arne Sølvberg, NTNU - The Norwegian University of Science and Technology, Trondheim, Norway

Abstract

The deep penetration of computers in all realms of society makes technological change the key driver for changing our lives. This will result in a change in approach, from viewing the role of IT as mainly supporting other disciplines, to the integration of IT concepts, tools and theory into modelling theories of the supported disciplines. This chapter discusses some aspects of the relationship between the IT as a modelling discipline, and the modelling disciplines of the domains where IT is applied. IT deals with data and data processes, while application domain models deal with entities of the domain and how they interact. Cross-competence models must deal with both, and with how models of the information technology discipline relate to the various models of the domain disciplines.

Introduction

How fast information technology develops! Performance/price ratios for central ICT components have doubled every 18-24 months for many years. So performance/price ratio may be expected to increase 100-fold over 10 years, and 1000-fold over 15 years. Incremental costs for communication and data storage are approaching zero. In 2012-2015 we should expect that the processing capacity of a large computer is comparable to that of the human brain, and in 2020 that capacity will probably be available on desktop computers.

Computers will be everywhere, in almost every artefact, in the background of almost every organised human activity. The deep penetration of computers in all realms of society makes technological change the key driver for changing our lives. This will result in a change in approach, from viewing the role of IT as mainly supporting the other disciplines, to the integration of IT concepts, tools and theory into modelling theories of the supported disciplines.

Because information technology provides component solutions to almost every other discipline we experience increasing fragmentation pressures on the discipline of IT itself. Every domain where IT is used seems to contain seeds for creating their own kind of discipline where IT is integrated with the domain specific knowledge. We often see labelling like, e.g., medical informatics, organisational informatics, and industrial informatics. And we sometimes see that common IT knowledge is reinvented in new application settings.

Over the years there has been an ongoing fight between IT and those who apply IT. The argument has been that those who apply IT are at the centre, that it is much simpler to learn the IT which is necessary for someone in the application field, than it is for an IT professional to learn the application field. The counter argument has been that the problems of the different application fields are similar as seen from the IT perspective. The similarities are much stronger than the differences. So it is easier for an IT person to learn the application field than the opposite! This disagreement has to a large extent formed the curricula at different education institutes, depending on the balance of the political power between the appliers and the technology providers.

This fight should come to an end. The systems that we try to build and maintain are too complex to be manageable unless integration among the various knowledge components is achieved.

This essay discusses some aspects of the relationship between the IT as a modelling discipline, and the modelling disciplines of the domains where IT is applied.

Cross-Competence Activities: Computers and Applications

Computer science is probably one of the few disciplines that can not render useful results unless being related to another discipline. ICT – Information and Communication Technology – subsumes computer science. ICT also to some extent subsumes some of the applications of computers, when the computer part is large compared to the applications. The following lines out a model for thinking about cross-competence ICT systems design.

The figure below divides the application world in four areas, Infosam2020 (2004), those of the:

- material world
- biological world
- cognitive man's world
- organised man's world

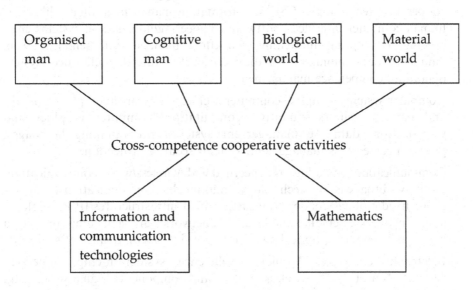

Application areas for ICT

Core technologies

This 4-divided world is seen from the perspective of information technology. The purpose is to build computer based artefacts. These intelligent artefacts are intended to relate to an environment of the 4-divided world. The enabling technologies are:

- ICT
- Mathematics

ICT is the major core enabling technology. Mathematics is necessary for building a modelling based design methodology.

Core Technologies, the Knowledge Platform

ICT is the core technology, together with applied mathematics. ICT is a broad technology area. It is rather loosely defined. Broadly speaking we understand ICT to encompass the knowledge areas of information systems technology, computer systems, communication technology and electronics.

Information systems technology may be characterised by the words cooperation technologies/CSCW, information management/digital libraries, human-computer interfaces, software engineering/information systems engineering, conceptual modelling, workflow management, semantic web, databases, data mining/information retrieval, artificial intelligence, system operation, competence management.

Computer systems comprise computer architectures, supercomputers, micro- and nano-computers, quantum computation, computer graphics and visualization, database management systems, programming languages, program correctness management, systems security protection.

Communication technology is concerned with wireless/wired communication, mobility, broadcasting technology, multimedia communications, convergence fixed/mobile/broadcast/unicast, unified infrastructures/IP technology, ad hoc networks, personal and local area networks, ambient computing, ultra high speed networks, optical switching, user interfaces, quality of service.

Electronics comprises Ambient intelligence, system-on-chip, embedded systems, "smart dust", wireless systems and components, signal processing, VLSI, nanotechnology, optics/photonics, quantum communication, spintronics, mechatronics, functional materials, navigation, remote sensing, sensor/transducer technology, audio/video technology.

Particular ICT relevant areas of applied mathematics are cryptography, coding theory, computation science/numerics, signal processing/wavelets, statistics.

Together these comprise the core technology knowledge platform.

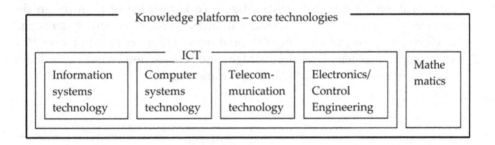

Application Areas – the Multidisciplinary Knowledge Platforms

Cross-competence cooperative activities relate the core technologies to the ICT application areas of the material world, the biological world, and the worlds of organised and creative humans. The four worlds may be loosely described as follows:

- The material world comprises sound and sight, energy, heating, lighting, energy sources and distribution, new materials, transport, travel, vehicles, roads, housing, smart houses, buildings, cities, clothing.

- The biological world is associated with demography, life support, sustaining health/healthiness, medical diagnosis and treatment, old age, food, food safety, nutrition, cosmetics, exercise/fitness, gene therapy, plants, animals, and so on.

- The cognitive man's world is associated with communication, entertainment, education/training edutainment/infotainment, art, games, man at work, man at leisure, mobility, fashion, lifestyle, experiences, meaningfulness, personalized services to relieve/simplify/sort/save time.

- The organised man's world is associated with companies, government, social (support) systems, schools, universities, hospitals, banking, commerce, sustainable systems, service provisioning, politics, democ-racy, voting, organization of leisure, safety and security, law and order, sustainability, reliability, vulnerability, environmental issues.

All of these have associated artefacts and devices of different kinds. Each broad application area consists of a number of niches, and each niche is associated with a body of cross-competence knowledge of its own. So the knowledge platform that is necessary in order to build modern systems and artefacts in the world of computers and information, consists of core ICT knowledge, mathematical knowledge and cross-competence knowledge which is relevant to the individual application niche.

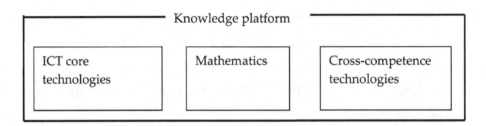

Cross-competence knowledge comprises the knowledge of a chosen domain with the knowledge of how to apply ICT in that domain. Cross-competence technologies are associated with engineering, with the design and installation of systems. Engineering is in itself a cross-competence activity. Examples of cross-competence technologies are sustainable electricity production, energy (systems) optimization, intelligent energy distribution, electricity storage systems, bionics, gene technology, medical equipment/systems.

ICT-Based Systems are Artifacts that Interact with Their Environments

Every successful systems building activity results in an artifact that connects to external entities in its environment. An artifact is a technical device created by people. The environment is material nature, biological nature, people, organizations, and/or systems of other artifacts. ICT based artifacts are usually expected to display some kind of "intelligent" behavior, due to its nature as a programmed and programmable device. Hence, we shall call them intelligent artifacts.

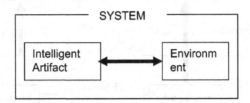

The (intelligent) connections between the artefact and the environment are of three major kinds. The artefact may observe the state of the environment, it may intervene and change the state of the environment, and it may interact with other artefacts or humans in the environment. An artefact may also be (naturally) physical or biological connected to entities in its environment.

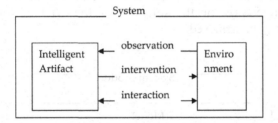

Examples of (intelligent) connections are video photographing (observation) of people moving in a shopping mall, feeding a display, and possibly feed an on-the-fly analyser of the pictures in order to detect unusual behaviour. Another example is modifying the electricity supply to a stove in order to have a temperature profile of the cooking process that will result in a crust on the pork (intervention). Still another example is to have the laptop request whether the laptop-user would prefer to have the computer shut down immediately, or to bother to activate the electricity supply, due to low battery level (interaction).

To be able to display true intelligent behaviour the intelligent artefact must have access to a model of the artefact itself, its environment and to a model of the interplay between the artefact and the environment. The artefact must be able to refer to a model which is a mapping of the system (of the artefact in its environment), and the model must map on a level of detail that is suitable to a predetermined level of intelligent behaviour.

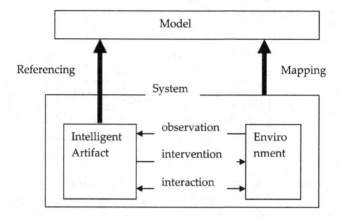

The system and the model together form a system product. The model is necessary in order to comprehend the system and its behaviour. For example, an artefact without documentation is not a complete product. The model is dual purpose: it provides an explanation of the system for the users, and it provides a reference for the software of the artefact, so that intelligent behaviour may be achieved.

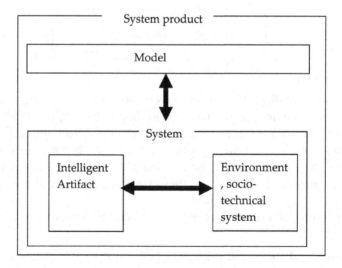

It is evident from this presentation that a model of a system product must be a mapping of the system, which is an integration of the artefact and its environment. So the appropriate knowledge platform must comprise ICT core technologies, mathematics and cross-competence technologies. Without mathematics one has fairly little hope of dealing with models in an intelligent way, without ICT knowledge one has little hope of building useful intelligent artefacts, and without cross-competence knowledge one has little hope of dealing with the integration of ICT in the chosen domain.

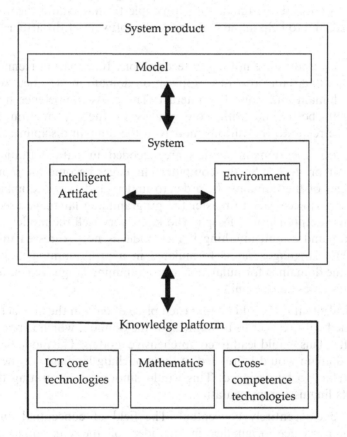

As the penetration of computers in almost every domain of human activity continues, new modelling approaches will emerge that integrate ICT and the domains where ICT is applied. This important development will occur at the intersection of ICT and other disciplines. Conceptual and technological tools developed within ICT are already seen to influence the modelling in other sciences that investigate complex systems, most notably in biology and chemistry, and in engineering sciences.

Aspects of Modelling in the Cross-Competence World

Information Systems Engineering has always been concerned with modelling in a cross-competence world. An artefact to be made has always been seen to relate to its environment. A basic belief has been that unless this relationship is explored and described properly, chances are slim that the designed artefact will function properly. The modelling languages have been designed with two purposes in mind: to help people to understand the system to be designed, and to help in the building of the software of the artefacts and their data.

The two purposes are not easily reconcilable. Information technology deals with data and data processes. Application domain models deal with entities of the domain and how they interact. The cross-competence models must deal with both, and with how models of the information technology discipline relate to the various models of the domain disciplines.

In practice the domain models are encoded in data definitions and in computer programs. So the computer languages become the representation languages of the domains. In order to understand how a domain model is realized it is necessary to master the programming language used. But that prevents comprehension. People who know very well the model of a domain may not understand anything if the model is not expressed in a familiar modelling language, but is formulated in a programming language. And unless the domain is formulated in a programming language neither software nor data bases can be built.

The ideal situation would be that each piece of data in the artefact to be built is defined with respect to the entities of the domain, which is represented by this data. This would lead to comprehensive models. The modelling language of the domain would be related to the modelling language of the IT-part of the artefact to be designed. This would amount to separating the concept from its linguistic representation.

Knowledge is entirely conceptual. The field of conceptual modelling in computer science originates in the idea of the conceptual schema in databases. This idea merged with ideas for information systems development methodologies, e.g., requirements engineering, process modelling. Research in the conceptual modelling area is mostly reported in proceedings of the CAiSE conference series and in the Entity-Relationship conferences. Early work is reported in EU-projects, e.g., the TEMPORA project (1989-1994). This project concerned itself with temporal issues, how to build conceptual models that captured historical data, and lent themselves to temporal reasoning (see e.g., Theodoulikis et al., 1991).

Comprehension requires mutual understanding. In order to achieve mutual understanding between two actors it is necessary to share both syntax and semantics of the interchanged data. Syntax issues are solved if there is a willingness to do so, e.g., emerging EDI-formats and XML-dialects. The deep and unsolved issues are with the semantic issues. The actors have to share a model of what the data are about. Semantic interoperability is about how to achieve such mutual understanding. To solve the problem of semantic interoperability is, in general, not achievable. The current state-of-the-art applies rather simple conceptual models. They are mostly either on the level of thesauri models or they apply well-known knowledge modelling techniques from artificial intelligence. The research question in conceptual modelling is how well we may achieve mutual understanding by, e.g., analysis of concept structures, and the practical question is whether this is enough to be useful.

A core issue is the characterization of knowledge in such a way that it can be stored in the web and effectively and efficiently retrieved by those who search for this knowledge. Knowledge providers and the knowledge consumers rarely communicate directly. In other realms of intellectual life we resort to modelling when knowledge is intended to be communicated to others and to be subjected to examination independently of the knowledge provider. Knowledge modelling thus becomes a core issue also in the creation of the semantic web.

References

Infosam2020 (2004). From http://www.ime.ntnu.no/infosam2020/oldpage/ Conference/proceedings.html#1.

Theodoulikis, C., Loucopoulos, P., & Wangler, B. (1991). A conceptual modelling formalism for temporal database applications. *Information Systems, 16*(4), 401-416.

Author Biographies

Jörg Becker is full Professor for Information Systems and Information Management, Director of the European Research Center for Information Systems (ERCIS), and Head of the Department of Information Systems at the University of Muenster. He holds Master and a PhD degree of Business Administration from University of Saarland, Germany. Jörg's research areas contain information management, management information systems, conceptual modeling, philosophy of science, eGovernment, and process management. He is editor-in-chief of the Journal for Information Systems and e-Business Management (ISeB) and editor of various journals. As part of his academic work, he is personal advisor to CIOs of well-known companies.

Janis A. Bubenko Jr (Ph.D, Docent, Dr. Ing. h.c., ACM Fellow) is professor emeritus in Information Systems at the Royal Institute of Technology and Stockholm University. He is the founder of the Swedish Institute for Systems Development, SISU, and was its managing director during 1985–92. Bubenko is the author/co-author of seven textbooks in the areas of Information Systems and the author/co-author of more than 150 research reports and published articles. Current research includes Nordic History of Computing, Requirements Engineering and Enterprise Modelling methods.

Sven A. Carlsson (sven.carlsson@ics.lu.se) is Professor of Informatics at School of Economics and Management, Lund University. His current research interests include: the use of IS to support management processes, knowledge management, enterprise systems, technochange, design and redesign of e-business processes in electronic value chains and networks in turbulent and high-velocity environments. He has a keen interest in the use of critical realism in IS research. He has held visiting positions at universities in

Europe, Australia, USA, and Singapore. He is a regional editor for *Knowledge Management Research and Practice*. He has published more than 100 peer-reviewed journal articles, book chapters, and conference papers and his work has appeared in journals like *JMIS*, *Decision Sciences*, and *Information & Management*.

Prof. Hamido Fujita is a professor at the faculty of software and information science, in Iwate Prefectural University, Japan, where he is directing the Intelligent software laboratory. He is also the general chair and founder of the SOMET conference series. http://www.somet.soft.iwate-pu.ac.jp/en/conference/index.html. He was the leader of the Lyee international research project in which he managed worldwide research collaboration team members within Europe and other parts of the world. He was a visiting Professor at University of Paris, Sorbonne, visiting professor at Stockholm University, visiting professor at University of Technology, Sydney, and other universities in Canada and the United States. He has published many journal papers and books on legacy systems and software evolutions.

Remigijus Gustas is a professor at the department of Information Systems, Karlstad University, Sweden. He is a doctor (1986) and docent (1991) in information systems. Remigijus Gustas was granted a habilitated doctor degree (1999) in the area of information system engineering. His main teaching subjects are 'System Analysis and design', 'Object-Oriented Modelling', 'Database Systems' and 'Enterprise Modelling'. Remigijus Gustas is a leader of the research group on enterprise system architecture design. He has been involved in a number of industrial and EU financed IT projects. Remigijus Gustas is the author of one monograph and more than 60 research publications. His research interests lie in the area of Conceptual Modelling, Information system analysis and design, Semantic and Pragmatic aspects of Enterprise Modelling, Service-Oriented Models.

Prima Gustiené is a doctoral student and lecturer at the department of Information Systems, Karlstad University. She holds a higher education diploma in Information systems from Karlstad University and another diploma from Vilnius Teachers Training Institute. In 2001 Prima Gustiené began to work as a teaching assistant at the Department of Information Systems, Karlstad University. She is involved in Object-Oriented System design and System Development courses. Her research areas are Semantic and Pragmatic aspects of communication, Enterprise and Service-Oriented Modelling, Graphical Representations of business processes. Prima Gustiené participated in the research project on Models and Methods of Electronic Commerce and in the international research project on new software technologies that sponsored by the Japanese industry.

Prasad M. Jayaweera received his BSc Honors Degree in Computer Science Special from University of Colombo, Sri Lanka in 1995. Jayaweera completed his Doctor of Philosophy degree in 2004 at the Royal Institute of Technology, Stockholm, Sweden. In 2004, he was promoted to a Senior Lecturer in Computer Science at the University of Ruhuna and he is also serving as a Visiting Lecturer in Computer Science and eCommerce for University of Moratuwa, University of Sri Jayewardenapura and Sri Lanka Institute of Information Technology. Jayaweera has contributed to several industry-collaborations/research projects and has published his research work at national and international forums on Business Process Modeling, Process Patterns, and Electronic Commerce Systems Designing.

Paul Johannesson received his BSc in Mathematics, and his PhD in Computer Science from Stockholm University in 1983 and 1993, respectively. He holds a position as professor at the Royal Institute of Technology, where he works in the area of information systems. Johannesson has published more than 100 papers on federated information systems, translation between data models, languages for conceptual modelling, schema integration, the use of linguistic instruments in information systems, process integration, e-commerce systems design, and analysis patterns in systems design. He has been the project leader of and participated in several national projects on information integration, the use of IT in teaching information systems design, process modelling and integration, and IT in health care.

Marite Kirikova has received Dr.sc.ing degree in Information and Information Systems from Riga Technical University, Latvia, in 1993. She is an associated professor at Riga Technical University, author of more than fifty scientific publications on information systems and knowledge management, did field research in knowledge management and e-learning at Boise State University, USA, and field research in enterprise modelling and requirements engineering at Stockholm University and Royal Institute of Technology, Sweden. Her research interests concern engineering of educational process, knowledge management, information systems development, requirements engineering, enterprise modelling, business process analysis and change management.

John Krogstie has a PhD (1995) and a MSc (1991) in Information Systems, both from the Norwegian University of Science and Technology (NTNU). He is Professor in Information, Systems at IDI, NTNU, Trondheim, Norway. He is also a senior advisor at SINTEF. He was employed as a manager in Accenture 1991–2000. John Krogstie is the Norwegian Representative for IFIP TC8 and vice-chair of IFIP WG 8.1 on information systems design and evaluation, where he is the initiator and leader of the task group for Mobile Information Systems. He is general chair of CAiSE'07 the conference. and has published around 80 refereed papers in journals, books and archival proceedings since 1991.

Dr. Eva Lindencrona is Director at VINNOVA (Swedish Agency for Innovation systems) in the Office of the Director General. She gained her Ph.D. in Informatics in 1979 at Chalmers Technical University. She has been research manager at Stockholm University and the Swedish Research Institute for Information Technology and was until 1998 MD of the Swedish Institute for Systems Development (SISU). She had previously worked in industry as a systems developer and a consultant. Dr. Lindencrona has been active in international standardisation and has been the international chair of an ISO subcommittee on data exchange. Dr. Lindencrona has served as expert and evaluator for a number of EU R&D programmes as well as for R&D programmes in Sweden, Norway and Germany.

Pericles Loucopoulos is professor of Information Systems in the Business School, Loughborough University, United Kingdom and adjunct professor at the University of Manchester. He is the co-editor-in-chief of the *Journal of Requirements Engineering*, associate editor for *Information Systems* and serves on the editorial boards of the *Information Systems Journal,* the *Journal of Computer Research, Business Process Management Journal, International Journal of Computer Science & Applications*, the *International Journal of Computing and ICT research*, among others. He has served as General Chair and Programme Chair of six international conferences and has been a member of over 150 Programme Committees of international conferences. He has published over 150 papers in academic journals and conference proceedings on the engineering of information, and the tools, methods and processes used to design, develop and deploy information systems in order to meet organisational goals.

Peter McBrien After graduating in 1986 with a BA in Computer Science from Cambridge University, and a period working for Racal and ICL, Peter McBrien joined the Department of Computing at Imperial College London as an RA in 1989, working on the Tempora Esprit Project. He obtained his

PhD from Imperial College London in 1992, under the supervision of Chris Hankin. In 1994, he joined Department of Computing at King's College London as a lecturer, and returned to the Department of Computing at Imperial College London in August 1999. He is currently a senior lecturer in the department, and his research areas focus on data integration and data modelling.

Vinay Kumar Mandala is a Java Consultant at the company HB Technologies Inc., Florida, USA. He completed his MSc at the University of Skövde. His masters thesis concerned e-business models and their components. Vinay Kumar Mandala was born in India, but moved to Sweden to earn his masters degree in Computer Science and primarily in Information Systems. His research interests include enterprise modelling and the management of models through standards.

Björn Niehaves conducted his PhD studies in Germany, Switzerland and Sweden in the field of epistemology and design science research. He studied business administration, political science and philosophy and received a Master degree in Business Administration (Dipl.-Kfm.) and Master of Arts in Political Science and Philosophy (MA). His main research interests are in the field of conceptual modeling, design science research, epistemology, eGovernment, process management, and IT consulting. Björn is member of the AIS Special Interest Group eGovernment (SIGEGOV), AIS Special Interest Group Philosophy (SIGPHILOSOPHY) and IFIP Working Group 8.5 Information Systems in Public Administrations.

Anne Persson is Senior Lecturer at the University of Skövde, Sweden. She has received a degree of Doctor of Philosophy in Computer and Systems Sciences from Stockholm University, Sweden (2001). Persson's research interests include enterprise modelling methods and tools, requirements engineering as well as knowledge management and organizational patterns. Persson is an author or co-author of some 50 research reports and publications and has participated in three EU financed research projects. She has co-developed the EKP—Enterprise Knowledge Patterns and the EKD—Enterprise Knowledge Development approaches.

Daniel Pfeiffer works as a Ph.D. student at the European Research Center for Information Systems (ERCIS). He holds a Master degree (Dipl.-Wirt.-Inf.) in Information Systems from Dresden University of Technology (TUD), Germany. He was awarded with the Lohrmann medal as best graduate of TUD in 2004. In 2003 he worked as visiting assistant in research at Yale University, Department of Computer Science. In 2002 he received a scholarship from the German National Academic Foundation. Daniel's main research interests are in the area of conceptual modeling and method engineering.

Colette Rolland is currently Professor of Computer Science in the department of Mathematics and Informatics at the University of PARIS-1 Panthéon Sorbonne where she has worked since 1979. She leads a Master degree in 'Information & knowledge Systems' and a PhD curriculum in 'Information & decision systems' jointly with CNAM and ESSEC. Her research interests lie in the areas of information modeling, databases, temporal data modeling, object-oriented analysis and design, requirements engineering and specially change engineering, method engineering, CASE and CAME tools, change management and enterprise knowledge development. She has supervised 84 PhD theses and has an extensive experience in leading research projects and conducting co-operative projects with the industry.

Janis Stirna is an assistant professor at Jönköping University, Sweden. He has received a degree of Doctor of Philosophy in Computer and Systems Sciences from the Royal Institute of Technology, Stockholm, Sweden (2001). Stirna's research interests include enterprise modelling methods and tools, organisational patterns, agile development approaches, as well as knowledge management and transfer of best practices. Stirna is an author or co-author of some 40 research reports and publications and has participated in nine EU financed R&D projects. He has co-developed the EKP — Enterprise Knowledge Patterns and the EKD — Enterprise Knowledge Development approaches. Stirna also has fifteen years of experience in practical system development and consulting in several European countries.

Ph.D. Mattias Strand is an assistant professor at the University of Skövde, Sweden. Strand's research is focused on organizational and technical aspects of decision support systems, knowledge management, and business intelligence. His doctoral thesis focused on external data incorporation into data warehouses and contributed with a state-of-practice description, as well as guidelines aimed at supporting organizations incorporation of external and syndicate data into data warehouse. Strand currently holds a position as Deputy Head at the School of Humanities and Informatics, University of Skövde.

Arne Sølvberg is Professor of Computer Science at The Norwegian University of Science and Technology, Trondheim, Norway, since 1974. He received a siv.ing. (M.Sc.) degree in Applied Physics in 1963, and a dr.ing. (Ph.D.) degree in Computer Science in 1971, both from The Norwegian Institute of Technology. He is Dean of NTNU's Faculty of Information Technology, Mathematics and Electrical Engineering since 2002. His main fields of competence are information systems design methodology, database design, information modelling, information systems engineering environments, and model driven design. He has been active in international organizations for research cooperation. He was Norwegian national representative to IFIP General Assembly in 1979–82. He has been chairman of IFIP WG8.1 for Information Systems Design in 1982–88. He was a trustee in the VLDB Endowment until 1994. He was a co-founder of the CAiSE conference series.

Dr. Eva Söderström holds a PhD in Computer and System Science from the University of Stockholm/Royal Institute of Technology. Her research focus is on standardization, primarily for in electronic business as well as for interoperability purposes. Other relevant areas are IT strategy management in small and medium-sized businesses. She is currently employed as an assistant professor at the University of Skövde, and also manages the Centre for Teaching and Learning in Higher Education. Dr Söderström has over 60 publications, primarily in international fora. She teaches at both a BSc and MSc level, and is a member of several industry-focused projects, both in Sweden and in Europe.

Dr. Hans Weigand has studied Computer Science and Mathematics at the Free University in Amsterdam. His Ph.D thesis was about the application of linguistic theory in knowledge engineering. In 1989 he moved to Tilburg and worked as senior-researcher in the ESPRIT II project SPRITE (database support for technical documentation). Since 1991 he is Lecturer at the Faculty of Economics of Tilburg University and participated in the LIKE project sponsored by the Netherlands Organization for Scientific Research (NWO). He has participated in several external projects, including two recent ESPRIT projects, TREVI (news filtering) and MEMO (electronic commerce). He has been co-organizing two international workshops on the Language/Action Perspective (LAP) and is one of the initiators of the SPECIE platform for Electronic Commerce.

Index

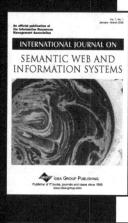